The Open Society as an Enemy

A critique of how free societies turned against themselves

J. McKenzie Alexander

 Press

Published by
LSE Press
10 Portugal Street
London
WC2A 2HD
press.lse.ac.uk

Text © J. McKenzie Alexander, 2024

Images © listed individually in source captions

First published 2024

Cover design by Glen Wilkins

Print and digital versions typeset by T&T Productions Ltd, London.

ISBN (Paperback): 978-1-911712-26-8
ISBN (PDF): 978-1-911712-27-5
ISBN (EPUB): 978-1-911712-28-2
ISBN (Mobi): 978-1-911712-29-9

DOI: https://doi.org/10.31389/lsepress.ose

This work is licensed under the Creative Commons Attribution-NonCommercial 4.0 International (CC BY-NC 4.0) License (unless stated otherwise within the content of the work). To view a copy of this license, visit https://creativecommons.org/licenses/by-nc/4.0/ or send a letter to Creative Commons, 444 Castro Street, Suite 900, Mountain View, California, 94041, USA. This license allows for copying and distributing the work, providing author attribution is clearly stated and that you are not using the material for commercial purposes.

Third-party images featured in this book are not covered by the book's Creative Commons license. Details of the copyright ownership are given in the individual image source information.

The full text of this book has been peer-reviewed to ensure high academic standards. For our full publishing ethics policies, see https://press.lse.ac.uk

Suggested citation: Alexander, J. McKenzie, *The Open Society as an Enemy: A critique of how free societies turned against themselves*, London: LSE Press, https://doi.org/10.31389/lsepress.ose License: CC BY-NC 4.0

To read the free, open access version of this book online, visit https://doi.org/10.31389/lsepress.ose or scan this QR code with your mobile device:

For Julia
aliquid quo maius nihil cogitari potest

Contents

List of figures   vii
Acknowledgements   ix
Preface   xi

Introduction   1

Part I: Don't come around here no more   25
The cosmopolitan conception of the Open Society

1. Consider the wall   27
2. You should have picked different parents   33
3. The room where it happens   37
4. Go your own way   45
5. It's the economy, stupid   55
6. Nowhere, man   69
7. Concluding remarks   79

Part II: The panopticon of the soul   101
The transparent conception of the Open Society

8. The book of life   103
9. Unwanted inferences   107
10. Lifting the veil   115
11. Letting it all hang out   125
12. Don't you forget about me   131
13. Returning to the past   137
14. We'll be watching you   147
15. Concluding remarks   153

Part III: Safe spaces   173
The Enlightenment conception of the Open Society
16. Generation Wuss?   175
17. Trigger warnings   177
18. Safe spaces   183
19. No-platforming   195
20. Concluding remarks   207

Part IV: Modern tribes   223
The communitarian conception of the Open Society
21. Joshua's question   225
22. On polarisation   229
23. Social identity, in-group bias, and norms   241
24. The psychology of modern tribes   251
25. Authenticity and the WINOs   257
26. Intersectionality   267
27. Epistemic closure and extreme groups   273
28. The collision of horizons   281
29. Concluding remarks   287

We can work it out   301

Index   346

List of figures

1	The first inkblot from Rorschach's test	11
3.1	A classification of countries according to their regime type, as of 2017	38
5.1	Efficiency gain from complete elimination of international barriers (% of world GDP)	56
5.2	Efficiency gain from partial elimination of barriers to labour mobility	57
5.3	The unemployment rate in the US, from 1950 to 2000	60
5.4	Comparison of the long-term effects of immigration on wages for native and immigrant workers	62
10.1	The decline in the cost of sequencing an individual human genome	120
13.1	Two illustrations of the Easterlin paradox	141
13.2	Natural log of income versus percentiles for 2010 US	143
14.1	Bentham's Panopticon	148
22.1	Comparisons between three different societies as an intuition pump for a measure of polarisation	230
22.2	Ideological polarisation within both houses of the US Congress, 1879–2013	233
22.3	Ideological grouping of UK political parties before the 2015 and 2017 general elections	234
22.4	Regional outcomes for the two UK referendums on whether to remain part of the EC (1975) or the EU (2016)	235
22.5	Change in real income between 1988 and 2008 at various percentiles of global income distribution	236
22.6	Time-series plots of polarisation by predicted internet use	238
23.1	The multiple layers of personal identity	242
23.2	Adding group structure introduces a number of new pathways along which conflict might emerge	247

23.3	A **2** × **2** categorisation of stereotypes	248
26.1	The fracturing of tribes along the lines of intersectional identities	269
29.1	A slightly rugged fitness landscape	308

Acknowledgements

Few books are written in isolation, and this book offers no exception to that generalisation. Over many years, I have had the good fortune to discuss many of the ideas in the following pages with many people. Their comments have informed the subsequent discussion in numerous ways. In these polarised times, given that some of the claims I argue for will undoubtedly be viewed by some as controversial, I don't want to inconvenience any of my discussants by suggesting they might have agreed with or endorsed any particular argument. You all know who you are, and I am grateful for your help along the way.

An author is lucky if they receive sound guidance from a good editor. In writing this book, I have had the good fortune to be guided by several excellent editors. I would like to thank Prof. Patrick Dunleavy, the Chair of LSE Press, to whom this manuscript was submitted. He spotted potential in what I was trying to do, which was no mean feat given that I manage to break many conventions of the traditional academic monograph while also avoiding the format of mainstream popular philosophy. When Prof. Dame Sarah Worthington took over as Chair of LSE Press in 2024, her support and encouragement was invaluable as I worked to transform the manuscript into a less ungainly beast, reigning in some of the rhetorical excess. As Managing Editor, Alice Park was given the herculean task of turning my Americanese into something resembling British English. I am very grateful for her help and advice along the way. Every single page of this book has greatly benefited from the counsel of these three people, and the book would have been significantly worse without it. Orlando Morley proofread and fact-checked several key chapters, enhancing the accuracy and quality of the book. I am very grateful for his assistance. Finally, I would like to thank Ellie Potts, as Communications Coordinator, for her phenomenal work on communications and publicity.

Most importantly, I would like to thank my parents, Trisha and Jack, and my partner, Julia, for their unwavering support and encouragement over the years. This book would not have seen the light of day if it were not for them. Thank you all so much for everything.

How to cite this book part:

Alexander, J. McKenzie (2024) *The Open Society as an Enemy: A critique of how free societies turned against themselves*, London: LSE Press, pp. ix–23. https://doi.org/10.31389/lsepress.ose.a. License: CC BY-NC 4.0

Preface

To borrow a phrase from Tolkien, this tale grew in the telling. It started life back in 2013 as a public lecture involving material that eventually found its way into Part II, and was released as a podcast entitled "The Open Society as an Enemy" on the now-defunct iTunes U.[1] At the time, the plan was to concentrate primarily on issues concerning social media, the transparent nature of modern life, and the erosion of privacy in the age of the internet. As is often the case, life got in the way of making further progress after the public lecture was delivered, and the project was shelved with the intention of getting back to it one day.

Days turned into years, but the ideas kept percolating in the background. It was only during a research sabbatical in 2017–18 that I was able to brush off my notes and revive the project. By then, its scope had expanded to include other areas, motivated by concerns over populist swings in Western governments that led to the election of Donald Trump in the 2016 US Presidential election and the UK's vote to leave the European Union, but with a belief that those movements were manifestations of a deeper phenomenon. In the meantime, more had happened, which meant that much of what had been written needed to be rewritten. All of this led to more scribble, scribble, scribble towards another damned thick, square book. A little more than half of the book was written during that sabbatical, but life intervened again, and the project returned to the shelf as I took on an administrative role in the fall of 2018. I had hoped to make some progress on the project while in that post, but then COVID-19 appeared, and the world turned on its ear yet again. The first full draft was finally completed in October 2022.

One problem with writing a book about the *zeitgeist* is that if you take too much *zeit*, the *geist* changes. One constant worry during the writing of this book was that the phenomenon with which I was concerned would self-correct, and I would wind up with little more than an extended note about what one person was worried about during the first quarter of the 21st century. The only good thing I can say about the extended period of social upheaval of the past few years is that the main argument and analysis of the book remains, I believe, as salient and relevant as ever.

I was trained as an analytic philosopher, but this is not a work of analytic philosophy. Its scope is too broad and its intertwined themes are too varied to conform to the normal conventions of that tradition. In my more cynical moments, I say that analytic philosophy is where important problems go to crawl inside their own navel and die.[2] When faced with a problem, all too often, the first instinct of an analytic philosopher is to take out their conceptual cleaver and chop, chop, chop the problem down to its clearest, most precise, and least interesting formulation. However, real life is messy and tangled and complicated, and frequently the analysis of a messy, tangled philosophical problem stripped of all complexity offers little guidance on what to say about the original.

If this is not a work of analytic philosophy, then what is it? It is, most assuredly, not an attempt to build a grand philosophical theory in the spirit of 19th-century system builders. It is not an attempt to provide the definitive answer to a single problem or even a set of problems. It is, one might say, an attempt to provide a philosophically sensitive, empirically informed analysis of a social problem that spans multiple disciplines and affects people from all walks of life, casting a general malaise upon contemporary society. It is an attempt to weave a tapestry from a great many threads, providing a picture, from one perspective, of what has come to pass and why. It is, to adopt a phrase, a work of *synthetic* philosophy. It offers analysis and aims at rigour, but its primary ambition is to articulate a problem where the whole is greater than the sum of its parts and cannot be solved if we only concentrate on solving each part in isolation.

There are many shortcomings in the analysis provided. The most obvious is that each of the four main parts addresses themes that could easily be the subject of a self-contained book.[3] Trying to draw attention to the many *interconnections* between these themes and how they mutually shape our present understanding of the Open Society requires, of necessity, not only brevity but omission. A second shortcoming is that this book largely concentrates on trends that have played out in the US and the UK. This is because the book draws upon my own experience as an American expatriate who has lived in the UK for the past twenty-plus years. And perhaps a third shortcoming is that, with a topic such as this, additional examples that illustrate the phenomenon I am concerned with appear more rapidly than it is possible to address. The Tristram Shandy paradox has never felt so real as when writing this book.

No book will persuade every reader of every point. I hope that most readers will agree with some of what I say, and that some readers will agree with most of what I say. This book has been written over such a long period of time that I am no longer sure that *I* still agree with everything that I say. But maybe that's how it should be. To adapt a phrase from Groove Armada, "If everybody thought the same, we'd get tired of talking with each other." That holds for our past and future selves as well.

Introduction

It is difficult to recall the optimism that existed in the West at the end of the 1980s. Although the Tiananmen Square protests ended on 4 June 1989, with the Chinese military brutally crushing the popular uprising, that event was followed by the fall of the Berlin Wall on 9 November and, only a few years later, by the collapse of the Soviet Union on 26 December 1991. For those alive at the time, it was not just a profound change in the global order but the decisive end to the ideological conflict underlying the Cold War. To some, it seemed we were experiencing the "end of history", even if it took several more years for Francis Fukuyama's book of that name to appear. The optimism even found its way into the electronic music of the time. The Jesus Jones song, "Right Here, Right Now", released shortly after the Wall fell, captured the *zeitgeist* perfectly:

> Right here, right now
> there is no other place I want to be
> Right here, right now
> watching the world wake up from history

That this optimism no longer exists is clear. This book offers an analysis of why that is, and attempts to correct a broad conceptual shift that may have been partly responsible.

Each generation experiences an event X that burns itself into the collective consciousness. That event provides a focal point in future conversations, enabling people to ask *where were you when X happened?* For my generation, the aptly named Generation X, our X was the fall of the Berlin Wall. For my parents, members of the Baby Boomer generation, their X was the assassination of John F. Kennedy. For the Millennials, X was the terror attacks of 9/11 and the collapse of the Twin Towers. For Generation Z, which came of age during the early 2000s, I suspect their X is less of a singular event than the overwhelming awareness of climate change, political intransigence, and the need for urgent action. Maybe, for them, X will refer to the answer to the question, *when did you realise something had to be done?*

For all these values of X, the fall of the Berlin Wall is unique. In what way? The fall of the Wall and the opening up of East Berlin were positive events, one that inspired hope and symbolised transformative change on an international scale not previously thought possible. It is a curious coincidence that the Berlin Wall fell during the formative years of a generation that would be known for being cynical and disinterested – the first generation predicted to earn less than their parents – and the generation to whom the term "slacker" was liberally applied. Nevertheless, when news channels showed footage of ordinary people taking sledgehammers to the Wall, the one thought on everyone's mind was that, whatever happened before, the future was going to be very different.

There is a Yiddish proverb that says, "If you want to make God laugh, tell him your plans". History's unfolding has a way of confounding expectations. Liberal democracy is under threat from the rise of populists and authoritarians. The popular movements collectively known as the "Arab Spring" did not result in greater freedoms and the blossoming of democracy in the countries where they happened, with the possible exception of Tunisia. The tragedy of the Syrian civil war continues. War is on the verge of breaking out in the Middle East. Public debate in America has become coarse and toxic. Racism and xenophobia have become more prevalent. Many people have grave doubts about the value of international institutions such as the United Nations or free-trade economic agreements. The United Kingdom decided to leave the European Union in part due to concerns over immigration and a rejection of the four freedoms of the European Union. Russia has engaged in shadowy exercises of power, challenging the values and credibility of Western institutions. It also invaded Ukraine. And China's emergence as the pre-eminent superpower is nearly complete as it prepares to take centre stage as the largest national economy on the planet.[1] Taken together, the post-World War II order is unravelling before our eyes.

Some suggest that this collapse is due to the fact that people have had quite enough of the economic upheaval caused by globalisation. In the US, concerns over the economy have been interwoven with concerns about illegal immigration. Trump's pledge to build a wall along the southern US border tapped into people's fears about Hispanic migrants flooding their communities and taking their jobs. In the UK, the concern was with *legal* immigration, for membership in the European Union required that the UK respect the free movement of people. And, while the UK did benefit from free movement, people were understandably worried about the need to protect, as Gordon Brown put it, "British jobs for British workers". In both the US and the UK, fears over immigration or demographic change led a number of people to believe that their way of life was being threatened by the resulting societal shifts.[2] In Hillary Clinton's book, *What Happened*, she quoted a Republican voter who said Democrats "wanted to take away his guns and make him attend a gay wedding". In the UK's referendum on whether to leave the EU, the division of votes into pro-Brexit and pro-Remain was complicated by the fact that two million British expatriates living abroad were excluded (BBC News 2016), and that the vote was divided sharply along generational lines. But there is more at play here than just people's concerns over economics, immigration, or political disagreement between demographic groups.

To see that those issues are only part of the story, it is important to note that a number of recent political upheavals were facilitated by effective (dis)information campaigns on social media. We are still learning the full effect of Cambridge Analytica, the secretive political consulting firm that closed in 2018 after the news broke about its influence over elections around the world, but we know one thing for certain: political campaign managers from the past could only have dreamed of creating the kind of targeted advertisements that are now possible. Such advertising has an insidious side to it – social media, not subject to traditional regulations covering election advertising, effectively weaponises people's personal information, allowing them to be manipulated by advertisements tailored to their psychological profiles.

Coexisting with all of the above is the increased polarisation of society, which is both a cause and effect of some of the phenomena mentioned above. Our group identities have become increasingly dominant, often with unfortunate consequences. Online, group identity can override a person's qualifications, with arguments discredited on the grounds of who the author is rather than what they say. Knowledge is increasingly politicised, and increasingly moralised. More remarkably, it has been shown that communication across group boundaries can actually *increase* polarisation. When a person's group membership is seen as core to their identity, information undermining beliefs relevant to that identity can prompt the person to double down and, paradoxically, raise their degree of belief.

All of these factors, at all levels of society, help fuel popular resentment, transforming our current age into what Pankaj Mishra has called an "age of anger". People from all walks of life feel as if they are facing existential threats. What do people do during times of existential threats? They try to protect themselves. How do they protect themselves? By rejecting what they see as the source of the threat and turning towards leaders who acknowledge their fears and offer solutions that are typically easily articulated with clear scapegoats. Perhaps it is not surprising that so many voted for Trump in 2016; after all, he declared "I am your voice. I alone can fix it. I will restore law and order". Similarly, perhaps it is not surprising that so many in the UK voted for Brexit; after years of grinding austerity, who wouldn't want to give the system a good kick? When faced with complex problems admitting no easy solution, simple political slogans promising to "take back control" or "make America great again" provide comfort.

The Open Society and Its Enemies

What, if anything, does all the above have to do with the Open Society, the topic of this book? I believe the above events reveal an important conceptual shift, and a revaluation of values, related to the core principles of Western democracy. It is for this reason that I began by contrasting the sense of optimism unleashed by the collapse of the Wall with the current climate of anxiety and fear and the rise of populism, pivoting towards authoritarianism. In order to appreciate the exact nature of this conceptual shift and revaluation of values, we first need to step back in time to 1945, when the philosopher Karl Popper published his influential critique of totalitarianism, *The Open Society and Its Enemies*.

Karl Popper was an unusual figure to have written a sweeping historical critique on the intellectual origins of totalitarianism. At the time, Popper was known as a philosopher of science, not a political philosopher, and best known for his theory of *falsificationism*, a view about what distinguishes scientific theories from other, nonscientific, systems of belief. Essentially, falsificationism states that the distinguishing feature of scientific theories is that they entail specific claims which can be tested empirically. If the claim is found to hold, the theory is *corroborated* since the empirical finding is consistent with it. We cannot conclude, though, that the theory is true because we have only checked one claim out of the infinitely many the theory entails. But what we can conclude, if the claim is found not to hold, is that we have *falsified* the theory. We have found a prediction that is incorrect.[3] Theories that have this property are said to be *falsifiable*, and falsifiability, according to Popper, is the distinguishing feature of scientific theories. Falsifiability suggested a principled way to distinguish astronomy from astrology and evolution from intelligent design. This idea of what distinguishes scientific theories from other types of belief has become embedded in popular culture and is known to people who have never otherwise heard of Karl Popper.

Popper's move into social and political philosophy was facilitated by three things. First, he was a polymath with a wide range of scientific, philosophical, and political interests – in addition to an unwavering confidence in his own abilities.[4] Second, in his youth, Popper's political interests led him to study the writings of Marx, eventually joining an organisation he describes in his autobiography (Popper 1992, p. 32) as "the association of socialist pupils of secondary schools". However, Popper became disenchanted with Marxism after a number of his associates were shot by the police on 15 June 1919 in a street protest in Vienna.[5] He also had growing reservations about Marx's theory of historical materialism, ultimately concluding that the view was unscientific. (Popper discusses this at length in his book, *The Poverty of Historicism*.) Third, the rise of Nazism in Germany and the looming threat of the annexation of Popper's native Austria made him fear for his safety; all of Popper's grandparents were Jewish. Popper emigrated to New Zealand in 1937, taking a job as a lecturer at Canterbury University College in Christchurch. It was there that Popper wrote *The Open Society and Its Enemies*, which he later described as his "war effort".

What, exactly, is meant by the expression "the Open Society"? For Popper, the Open Society was a society in which individuals had the freedom to choose the kind of life they wanted to live and how they wanted to live it. The Open Society was *open* in the sense that the future possibilities for a person were not ruled out simply by virtue of their social position and social practices that kept each person in their place. In writing about the Open Society, Popper frequently contrasts it with the "organic or biological theory of the state". According to that theory, "a closed society resembles a herd or a tribe in being a semi-organic unity whose members are held together by semi-biological ties – kinship, living together, sharing common efforts, common dangers, common joys and common distresses" (Popper 1945a, p. 186). How does a closed society resemble an *organic* unity? For Popper, the core idea was that an organic unity has an overarching commonality of purpose for each of the component parts (namely, keeping the organism alive) combined with the fixed, static nature of each part's role in achieving that purpose.

A closed society is one where each person has their assigned place. Medieval societies, with clear class differences between the serfs, nobility, and royalty, where this order was decreed by God in the divine right of kings, provide one example. In a closed society, people are denied both the opportunities and freedom to develop and shape their lives according to their values and desires. In contrast, an Open Society is one "in which individuals are confronted with personal decisions" (Popper 1945a, p. 186) – decisions that involve substantive choices about one's life trajectory and the kind of person one wants to be. That openness, freedom, and *indeterminacy* of the future, which allows people to write their life stories, is at the heart of Popper's conception of the Open Society.

Popper thought that a primary threat to the Open Society, perhaps even the greatest threat, derived from faulty epistemology. In particular, Popper believed that closed societies relied upon people's failure to embrace an attitude he called "critical rationalism". In a critical rationalist mindset, people interrogate their beliefs and the reasons why they hold them, always challenging their beliefs and asking if they have good reasons for what they believe. A natural parallel with Popper's theory of falsificationism can be seen: if we find that we don't have good reasons for what we believe, we should either suspend judgement or revise our beliefs. This isn't quite the same thing as falsificationism, for not all of our beliefs can be empirically tested in the same way as scientific theories. Moral theories, for example, don't make descriptive claims about the world that can be empirically tested. Instead, moral theories make normative claims about how one should act or how one should evaluate outcomes. Nevertheless, critical rationalism still applies to moral theories, for we can ask why we hold the moral beliefs we do. This is one way moral progress is made.

According to Popper, knowledge became politicised in closed societies. For instance, Nazi Germany's theories of racial superiority had no basis in fact, but reams of pseudo-scientific material were produced to support those views for political reasons. In the Soviet Union, Trofim Lysenko advocated a number of utterly misguided agricultural theories that were amenable to Soviet ideology; these theories rejected Mendelian genetics and the theory of evolution by natural selection as Western propaganda. ("Survival of the fittest" was seen by some communists as free market economics written into biology.) Biologists who dissented from Lysenko's views were sent to prison camps or executed. As a result of Lysenko's influence, agricultural yields actually declined in the Soviet Union until Lysenkoism was abolished after the death of Stalin.[6] China not only suffered from Lysenko's influence, having imported his theories as part of good communist ideology, but created its own disaster in the Great Leap Forward where Mao's ideologically influenced economic theories destroyed the economy and led to the death of over 30 million Chinese people due to famine.[7]

It's been a long time since the reign of Lysenkoism in the Soviet Union, but Popper's concern about the dangers of politicised knowledge is as relevant as ever. Today, the politicisation of knowledge occurs more subtly. Instead of being couched in explicitly ideological terms, it is often masked by spurious evidential concerns and the cultivation of fear, uncertainty, and doubt.[8] We see this in both the US and the UK. The denial of climate change, despite its well-established status within the scientific community, is one egregious illustration of the politicisation of knowledge. In the US, alongside climate change denial, we find efforts to overturn Obamacare, despite it being a reasonable attempt to patch the dysfunctional US healthcare sector given the socioeconomic and political constraints that impede reform.

In the UK, the politicisation of knowledge is illustrated by the following anecdote. During the run-up to the EU referendum, Michael Gove dismissed predictions about the economic damage that leaving the EU would cause by saying, "people in this country have had enough of experts" (see Mance 2016). Experts don't always get it right, and so the frustration expressed by Gove is understandable. The vast majority of economists around the world received a great deal of criticism for failing to predict the financial crisis of 2008. Yet, if you are not going to consider expert advice, what will you base your judgement on instead? When it comes to complex issues with potentially harmful long-term consequences, Michael Gove's remarks are nothing less than shocking. Given his attitude towards experts, perhaps we should not be surprised that as Secretary of State for Education he approved opening three schools advocating creationism (Vasagar 2012).

Concerns about the politicisation of knowledge continue to be well-founded, and there is reason to believe critical rationalism has come under attack throughout the West, just as when Popper was writing. The main difference between Popper's time and our own is that, whereas Popper was concerned with the subversion of knowledge by totalitarian governments, in the contemporary period we are now seeing the subversion of knowledge by populist governments of all ideological stripes. But there is, I believe, more at play here than just the politicisation of knowledge. The Open Society, in a variety of senses different from those that concerned Popper, has come under attack in recent years, for reasons other than the politicisation of knowledge. To see this, we need to reflect on the concept of the Open Society and the multiple senses that it possesses. And this requires understanding the peculiar kind of concept it is.

Rorschach concepts

Popper's conception of the Open Society centred around personal freedom and the absence of rigid class structures. This sense of the Open Society was key to how the West framed the conflict between the competing political ideologies that lay at the heart of the Cold War. Yet there are a number of other ideas suggested by the term "Open Society" that goes beyond Popper's conception, although they are certainly related to it. Take freedom of movement, or informational transparency, or the value of diverse societies, for example. How can a single concept play such an important coordinating role in society while remaining so nebulous?

I suggest that the concept of the Open Society serves as a coordinating device for social and political discussions. In a highly influential paper, Taylor (1971) identified two different kinds of meaning something can have, and examined how those different kinds of meaning influence people's behaviour. The first type of meaning was *intersubjective* meaning, which just referred to a meaning shared across society. Typical examples of intersubjective meanings are those attached to words in ordinary language, such as "table" and "chair", "to run", "to laugh", and so on. However, intersubjective meanings also go beyond linguistic meaning. Holding up your hand with the palm facing outwards is nearly universally understood to mean *stop*; a beckoning gesture means *come here*. Other behaviours display more cultural variation: nodding one's head means *yes* in most Western countries but *no* in Bulgaria. The intersubjective meanings of society make communication possible and facilitate collective action. Intersubjective meanings are necessary for *individuals* to operate as a *group*.

However, intersubjective meanings, on their own, are not enough to transform a *group* into a *community*. Creating a community requires something above and beyond that which enables people to coordinate, because people can coordinate their activities without there being anything that binds them together. This is the function of Taylor's second kind of meaning, which he called *common* meaning. The phrase *common meaning* might suggest something prosaic or done frequently, but Taylor drew on the sense of *common* as something *belonging to the whole community*. Common meanings are special in that they provide the foundation of our social existence. Taylor explains the idea as:

> Common meanings are the basis of community. Intersubjective meaning gives a people a common language to talk about social reality and a common understanding of certain norms, but only with common meanings does this common reference world contain significant common actions, celebrations and feelings. These

are objects in the world that everybody shares. This is what makes
community. (Taylor 1971, p. 30)

It is natural to think that common meanings, because they are the basis of
a community and are shared by the community, are those things that the
community has reached a consensus on. However, this isn't quite right.

Taylor immediately challenges that understanding with the following clarificatory remarks (emphasis added):

> We cannot really understand this phenomenon [of how common
> meanings create community] through the usual definition of consensus as convergence of opinion and value. For what is meant
> here is something more than convergence. Convergence is what
> happens when our values are shared. But what is required for
> common meanings is that this shared value be part of the common world, that this sharing be shared. But we could also say that
> common meanings are quite other than consensus, *for they can
> subsist with a high degree of cleavage*; this is what happens when a
> common meaning comes to be lived and understood differently
> by different groups in a society. (Taylor 1971, pp. 30–31)

The fact that Taylor says that common meanings can subsist "with a high degree of cleavage" is no accident. The verb *to cleave* is, curiously, one of those words that is its own antonym. If you consult the Oxford English Dictionary (OED), the first sense of *cleave*, meaning "to part or divide by a cutting blow; to split", derives from the Old English *cléofan*. As an example, the OED cites a usage from the King James Bible in 1611: "Abraham [...] claue the word for the burnt offering" (Genesis 22:3). The second sense, meaning "to stick fast or adhere" derives from the Old English *clifan*. Here, the OED provides an example from the Coverdale Bible of 1535: "their tonges cleued to the rofe of their mouthes" (Job, 29:10). These two different words in Old English converged over time in their pronunciation and spelling to the single word we now have, with two utterly opposing senses.

To say that common meanings provide a basis for community while being able to subsist with a high degree of cleavage is to say that common meanings have the ability to unify and divide *at the same time*. This is a well-known phenomenon. Fierce debates can erupt between individuals who appear otherwise to be in broad agreement. The ambiguities of common meanings, and their role in creating a shared perception of a community can be leveraged by masterful politicians to suggest agreement where little, in fact, exists.

To illustrate this, recall Donald Trump's campaign slogan "Make America Great Again". Many commentators were struck by the fact that he was running for president with a slogan acknowledging American decline. Trump's gloomy call sharply contrasted with that of Franklin Delano Roosevelt who, in the midst of the Great Depression, ran on "Happy Days Are Here Again" (1932), "Remember Hoover!" (1936), and "Better a Third Termer than a Third Rater" (1940). A less-noted feature is that the slogan "Make America Great Again" is largely devoid of content. Make America great, in what way, and how? The genius of Trump's slogan is that each individual who endorsed "Make America Great Again" could cheer in support, yet have a different understanding from everybody else as to what exactly it meant.

However, one might also argue that the slogan was not entirely devoid of content because American history provided some common ideals on which to build, such as the preservation of individual liberty. But note that appealing to these ideals doesn't solve the problem so much as push it back a stage, for the notions of *individual liberty* and *personal freedom* are also common meanings with the power to cleave. "Make America Great Again" could mean any of the following, in any rank ordering: from rolling back the forces of globalisation, to restoring coal mining, to bringing back manufacturing, to providing greater environmental protections (think of the residents of Flint who couldn't drink the municipal water), to reducing the influence of special interests in Washington, to achieving greater economic growth, to reducing illegal immigration, to reducing crime, to fixing crumbling American infrastructure, to increasing individual incomes, to creating more jobs, to reducing taxes, to reducing American debt, to increasing the strength of the armed forces, to reducing or eliminating multiculturalism, to working to eliminate racism, to protecting social security, to restoring traditional family values, to restoring white nationalism, and so on. A crowd could, in principle, endorse the *statement* "Make America Great Again" without there being a single unambiguous *policy* or *plan* or *goal* commanding a majority.

Something very similar happened in Britain with the referendum on leaving the EU. Consider the following passages from Theresa May's Brexit speech on 17 January 2017 (emphasis added):

> *The result of the referendum* was not a decision to turn inward and retreat from the world.[...]
>
> Business isn't calling to reverse *the result*, but planning to make a success of it. The House of Commons has voted overwhelmingly for us *to get on with it*. And the overwhelming majority of people – however they voted – *want us to get on with it too*.

What was it about the referendum outcome that enabled Theresa May to speak with confidence about *the result of the referendum*? What was the "it" that Theresa May claimed people wanted the government to *"get on with it"* in such a hurry?

For completeness, here is the complete text that was put before the British people in the referendum: "Should the United Kingdom remain a member of the European Union or leave the European Union?"

That's it. As Green (2017) noted in his article in the *Financial Times*:

> The proposition is that the UK remains or leaves the EU. There is nothing on when this should happen, or how it should happen, whether by Article 50 or other means (such as a new treaty). There is nothing, at least explicitly, on whether Britain should remain part of the EU single market or customs union (both are possible without being members of the EU) [...] And there is nothing on what type of relationship, if any, the EU and UK should have after Brexit.

This matters, because what Green has pointed out is that the question put before the voters was *fundamentally ambiguous*. The referendum asked an abstract question about whether an outcome, capable of being realised in multiple ways, *should* be realised, leaving the actual specifics of the implementation open to each voter's interpretation. This makes any talk of *the result of the referendum*, which the government needed to *get on with it*, a bit suspect.

Let me introduce a term of art for those concepts whose common meaning in a society is heavily dependent on the subjective understanding of the individual. Let us call them *Rorschach* concepts. This name is derived from the famous psychological test designed by Hermann Rorschach in his 1921 book, *Psychodiagnostik*. The test consists of presenting ten inkblots, following a certain procedure, to a subject, who is invited to comment on what they see in each image. (Figure 1 reproduces the first inkblot from Rorschach's inkblot test.) An important part of the diagnosis lies in observing *how* the subject examines and responds to the inkblots, in addition to what they say. Given the abstract nature of the blots, it is clear that much of the response elicited lies in the mind of the subject and is projected onto the blot.

There's an old joke about the Rorschach test. It goes as follows:

> A patient goes to see a psychologist, complaining of an inability to concentrate. The psychologist shows the patient the first inkblot.
> "That's two people having sex," the patient says.
> The psychologist reveals the second inkblot.
> "That's two people having sex in a park."
> The psychologist then shows the third inkblot.
> "That's two people having sex on a beach."
> "You seem rather obsessed with sex," the psychologist remarks.
> "What, me?" The patient says. "You're the one with all the dirty pictures!"

The reason this joke works is that there is no fact of the matter about what the Rorschach inkblots mean. What a person *sees* is just what the person *projects*. Each person's projection is constrained only by the shape of the

Figure 1: The first inkblot from Rorschach's test

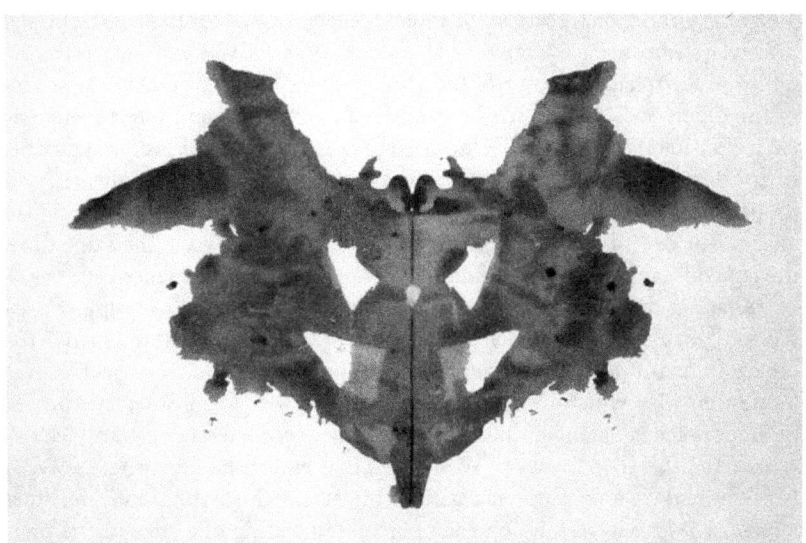

Source: Hermann Rorschach (1921), public domain.

inkblot, which is the same for everyone. Rorschach concepts are similar. In speaking of *making America great again*, that concept was nothing more than an empty vessel waiting to be filled by the hopes and dreams of the listeners. Yet each person's understanding was not completely unconstrained, for the concept of American greatness appears in many of the common meanings forming the foundation of American society. A similar phenomenon happened in the Brexit campaign. "Leave the EU" provided a nearly blank slate on which voters could project their favoured vision for a post-EU Britain. The idea of what it meant to "take back control" had few constraints on its interpretation.

Rorschach concepts, despite their ambiguity and subjectivity, often feature in the common meanings Taylor talked about. One mechanism by which common meanings cleave society is through individuals projecting onto concepts their own subjective understandings, where imperfect overlap can yield solidarity or sow discord, depending on which aspects are made salient. With Rorschach concepts, the danger is not only that people can talk past each other, but that illusions of agreement can be cultivated while masking deep divisions.

The Open Society as a Rorschach concept

Understanding the Open Society is philosophically challenging because the Open Society is a Rorschach concept. Given this, our task is two-fold. The first task is analytic: we must make clear what we talk about when we talk about the Open Society. In what follows, I make no claim to provide an exhaustive analysis as the concept of the Open Society is far too rich. What I will do is look at a number of aspects of the Open Society, grouped into four families of interrelated ideas. Each family can be thought of as one way to project meaning onto the Rorschach concept of the Open Society. Each of these four senses of the Open Society will first be examined in isolation and interrogated, as critical rationalism requires. Once that is done, the second task is synthetic: to consider how the four senses of the Open Society are interconnected and mutually reinforcing. The synthetic task requires understanding how trying to advance or curtail one sense of the Open Society can have, at the same time, the concomitant effect of curtailing or advancing a different sense.

What are these four senses of the Open Society that will occupy our attention? In Part I, I consider a *cosmopolitan* conception of the Open Society centred around states, citizenship, and the free movement of people. It is a question with which we must engage because the global order, predicated on nation-states having exclusive sovereignty over its territory – an idea derived from the 1648 Treaty of Westphalia that ended the Thirty Year's War – is predicated on a fundamental natural injustice. This natural injustice, that a *birthright lottery* bestows on each person citizenship of a state not of their choosing, creates a world rife with structural inequality. It creates an environment ripe for conflict between the *haves* and the *have-nots*, especially when the roles could so easily have been reversed if people had simply been born to different parents.

In Part II, I consider the *transparent* conception of the Open Society, centred around the availability of information and the diminished privacy of the modern world. Here, I argue that the Open Society is Janus-faced. Transparency of process and freedom of information are important virtues for public institutions and are necessary conditions for democracies to flourish. But what about informational transparency concerning individuals? We are in the middle of a vast, unsupervised worldwide experiment regarding the collection and analysis of information about persons. Companies harvest individual data at a level inconceivable only a few decades ago. Is radical transparency, an instrumental good for controlling the potential excesses and abuses of power by powerful institutions, equally good when applied to individuals? I argue that perhaps the greatest shortcoming of the dystopian novel, *1984*, is that Orwell was insufficiently paranoid.

In Part III, I consider the *Enlightenment* conception of the Open Society, centred around the free exchange of ideas. In this sense, an Open Society is one in which its citizens entertain and critically discuss ideas. It is not necessarily liberal; it is about embracing a general intellectual attitude of curiosity and the cultivation of tolerance. A liberal can be dogmatic and intolerant, and a conservative can be *laissez-faire* regarding the beliefs and behaviours of others. A conservative society, in the sense defended by Edmund Burke, could certainly open to the free exchange of ideas: it would just adopt a sceptical attitude towards social reform, requiring that change be evidence-based and grounded in experience.⁹ But what are we to make of claims by some that the free exchange of ideas can not only constitute *harm*, but harms from which people should be protected? Issues of trigger warnings, safe spaces, and no-platforming of speakers have played a heated role in Western culture wars. I argue for a nuanced understanding of the issues at play and try to dial down the temperature of this heated debate.

In Part IV, I examine the *communitarian* conception of the Open Society, centred around polarisation, tribalism, and intergroup conflict. This sense of the Open Society is loosely related to the original conception of the Open Society introduced by the French philosopher Henri Bergson 13 years prior to Popper's book. In his book, *The Two Sources of Morality and Religion*, Bergson characterises a closed society as one "whose members hold together, caring nothing for the rest of humanity, on the alert for attack or defence, bound, in fact, to a perpetual readiness for battle" (Bergson 1935, p. 229). An Open Society rejects this mentality and embraces a broad, diverse community. This matters because our social identities infuse each of our lives, yet when social identities are made salient, conflicts readily emerge from psychological dispositions such as ingroup biases and the fundamental attribution error.¹⁰ How do we resolve this core tension between valuing our social identities and their ability to generate conflict?

These four different senses of the Open Society – cosmopolitan, transparent, Enlightenment, and communitarian – form the analytic core of the book. They are not the only way to theorise the Open Society, but they are mine. Some senses overlap with Popper's Open Society, some overlap with Bergson's Open Society, and others are very different. Consequently, the vision of an Open Society I offer expands on that articulated by both Popper and Bergson.

One may well ask why am I modifying the concept of the Open Society in the way proposed? In particular, one might ask why not stick with the Popperian concept, since that is the one with the greatest historical legacy? Or, for those not too concerned with history, why not engage with the concept of Open Society as developed by Gaus (2021)? The latter question is easy: my concerns and aims are very different from Gaus's. Although it is true that societies are complex systems, they are not always best understood via complex systems theory. As for the former question, there are two reasons.

The first reason is that Popper's concept of the Open Society is more narrow than mine. His primary concern was to defend democratic societies against attack from several fronts. One front involved authoritarian or totalitarian worldviews (hence his concern with Plato and Marx) that sought to replace democracies from the *outside*. Another front involved various personal attitudes, such as intolerance, that undermine the viability of democracies from the *inside*. The solution to both, for Popper, involves cultivating a critical rationalist attitude; in so doing, we will recognise our fallible nature (thereby undermining a willingness to endorse Plato's authoritarian regime with the wise philosopher-kings at the apex) and see the errors of historicism (thereby neutralising threats from Nazism or Marxism). But my concept of the Open Society defends *value pluralism*, and does not accord pride of place to democracy, necessarily.

The second reason is that Popper's defence, as noted above, places critical rationalism and scientific method at its core. In Volume 2 of *The Open Society and Its Enemies*, he describes critical rationalism as the attitude based on "argument and experience" and the view that "I may be wrong and you may be right, and by an effort we may get nearer to the truth". This attitude is "closely akin to the scientific attitude". While I believe in the importance and power of science, Popper's claim that "we may get nearer to the truth" gives me pause. Truth about the *natural* world, or logic and mathematics, I can get behind; but truth about the *social* world is trickier. In a diverse world with competing value systems, moral codes, religious doctrines, and conceptions of rational action, *whose* truth is Popper referring to?

In contrast, my concept of the Open Society has an existentialist foundation. It is grounded in respect for individual freedom, the right to self-determination, freedom of association, and a consistency principle. I will argue in Part I that from this minimal core we can derive a concept of the Open Society compatible with value pluralism and, as John Stuart Mill put it, a diverse range of "experiments in living". The attitude of critical rationalism will presumably feature in some of those experiments, but not necessarily all. If people freely choose, on an informed basis, to reject a life based on a scientific attitude, who am I to judge?

The Open Society as an enemy

When we reflect on the four different senses of the Open Society I've described, we discover that a curious *inversion of values* has occurred. In many parts of the Western world, a movement has emerged that perceives each aspect of the Open Society as a threat rather than something to be celebrated. The free movement of people is rejected, the free exchange of ideas is seen as disturbing, and the value of diverse communities is called into question as polarisation divides us. Informational transparency, rather than serving to hold the powerful to account, instead opens up the lives of ordinary citizens for monitoring and manipulating, and transforms our identities into commodities to be sold. This inversion of values explains the title of the book. It also explains the titles of each of the four main parts, for those titles express the sentiment rejecting that aspect of the Open Society. The title of Part I, "Don't come around here no more", expresses the rejection of the cosmopolitan conception of the Open Society. Part II's title, "The panopticon of the soul", refers to a world in which social media has made the inner lives of each person knowable to all, subverting the transparent conception of the Open Society. The title of Part III, "Safe spaces", describes how some try to shield themselves from ideas challenging their core beliefs, rejecting the Enlightenment conception of the Open

Society. Part IV's title, "Modern tribes", characterises how increased polarisation partitions diverse communities into groups according to certain defining characteristics, retreating from the communitarian conception of the Open Society.

The value-inversion of the Open Society is a profoundly important change, and one that has occurred largely without us being aware it was happening. During the Cold War, the values underlying the Open Society were core values of the West, and promoting the Open Society with all of its associated liberties was a key difference between Western democracies and those countries under authoritarian control. Today, the Open Society is seen by many as no longer an all-things-considered good. Some doubt its value altogether. This is unfortunate because, if Popper was right and the Open Society gave people the freedom to choose the kind of life they want to live and the chance to live it, think about the consequences of critiquing the Open Society. Critics of the Open Society, under the guise of populism, portray it as an enemy, and in so doing serve the interests of authoritarians and powerful organisations. If, as Baudelaire wrote in 1869 that "the devil's finest trick is to persuade you that he does not exist", an equally impressive trick is to invert the meaning of the Open Society such that populist leaders, acting with a democratic mandate, can enact policies restricting individual freedoms and opportunities.

Although I believe that the Open Society is, at present, seen as an enemy by some, I also believe this is a grave mistake. A central aim of this book is to rehabilitate the concept of the Open Society. What I hope to achieve, at least partly, is to establish how many of those aspects of the Open Society that are seen as a threat are overblown. This defence of the Open Society is sometimes challenging, because the perceived threats of, for example, the free movement of people has a firm grip on some people's worldview. But, I argue, when we step back and take into account moral and economic considerations, the free movement of people deserves to be endorsed, although admittedly with important qualifiers. (Anyone who claims I am arguing for open borders has not read the book.) In other cases, the defence of the Open Society is easier because the perceived threats result from an incorrect realisation of the ideal. This is the case, I argue, for the transparent conception of the Open Society, where the current state of society has made the lives of ordinary people transparent instead of increasing the transparency of organisations and institutions. These are just a fraction of the issues that are discussed in the course of this book.

There are two further reasons to revisit the defence of the Open Society. The first is that I believe one focal point of Popper's critique of authoritarianism and totalitarianism is no longer relevant. At the time Popper was writing, authoritarianism and totalitarianism were frequently underpinned by historicist beliefs: that history unfolds according to general laws. While Marxists, Leninists, Maoists, and Nazis frequently did perceive the world in this way, contemporary authoritarians and totalitarians often do not bother to justify themselves with historicist narratives. Instead, we find that they pursue power through other means that do not need general laws of history. People appeal to ideas of restoring national glory, the rectification of historical injustices, or raw economic self-interest, but those narratives do not need historical laws. This is explored in Part I.

The second reason is that Popper's focus on the *politicisation* of knowledge, while important, is incomplete. Today we also find the Open Society under threat from the *moralisation* of knowledge. The free exchange of ideas is threatened, in some quarters, by those who wish to suppress debate and enquiry out of concern that what we might call "ideational harm" will be done. Certain ideas are not even entertained as possibilities by some groups simply because they conflict with their social identity, leading to those ideas being rejected prior to the consideration of evidence or other reasons for belief. This is explored in Parts III and IV.

And that is why the concept of the Open Society needs to be revisited again – Popper's defence, despite its brilliance and influence, needs a reboot. We need to engage with contemporary objections to the Open Society, showing why they are misguided, on moral, political or pragmatic grounds, in ways relevant for our time. Only someone with Popper's knowledge of and respect for the history of philosophy could think that, in order to show what was wrong with Nazi totalitarianism, it was necessary to begin with Heraclitus.

The final point I argue is that undoing the value-inversion of the Open Society requires another break with Popper's thought. Given his rejection of historicism, it is no surprise that Popper rejected grand attempts to solve social problems. His preferred method was "piecemeal social engineering" (Popper 1945a, p. 18) that concentrated on isolated, local problems. However, rehabilitating the Open Society requires more than piecemeal social engineering, as this is no mere local problem. The rehabilitation requires a philosophical enquiry into the very kind of society we want to create. It requires answering questions such as: what freedoms do we wish to protect, and what freedoms are we willing to give up in order to make other forms of social organisation possible? These questions cannot be solved in a piecemeal fashion, for they involve global comparisons and trade-offs along dimensions not obviously comparable. Yet decisions must be made because a policy choice in one area has implications for others, and it is by no means obvious that we can achieve the maximal good for all senses of the Open Society at the same time. I elaborate on this topic in the final chapter, though these questions remain in the background throughout the book, particularly in Part II.

Rejecting piecemeal social engineering means adopting a broader perspective on society, reflecting carefully on the kind of world we want to create. Part of the reason the Open Society has become an enemy, I believe, is that we have trusted local solutions proposed by piecemeal social engineering without thinking about what negative externalities might be generated when those solutions, each individually having good reasons behind them, are combined. As a result, we now stand at a tipping point in human history where we are confronted with the existential dangers of moving forward without paying sufficient attention to where we are going.

In some ways, I argue the Open Society can be an enemy, but often not for the reasons we might initially imagine. Once we have rehabilitated our understanding of the Open Society, we can begin to see which aspects are worth preserving and which need to be curtailed in order to support human freedoms, preserve personal autonomy, and create lives worth living in societies worth living in. Given the scale of that task, it goes without saying that this book does not, and could not, provide the last word on any of its subjects. What it does provide is a view, a theory, and a warning.

Notes

Preface

[1] If you know it exists and go searching for it by name, you can find a recording buried in the archives of the LSE's Public Event Podcasts. It's not quite the digital analogue of being on display in a cellar, in the bottom of a locked filing cabinet stuck in a disused lavatory with a sign on the door saying "Beware of the Leopard", but it's close.

[2] The original draft of this work featured a more crude (and accurate) expression, here, but a trusted editor persuaded me to substitute a more family-friendly expression in its place.

[3] For Part I, see Blau and Mackie (2017); Borjas (2016); Kondoh (2017); Nowrasteh and Powell (2021) and Watson and Thompson (2021). For Part II, see Brin (1998) and Solove (2008, 2011). For Part III, see Baer (2019), Ben-Porath (2017), Lukianoff and Haidt (2018), Downs (2005). For Part IV, see Haidt (2012). This list is not exhaustive, of course.

Introduction

[1] Although some are beginning to question whether this will, in fact, happen. The upcoming demographic decline in China, caused by decades of its one-child policy, may prevent it from surpassing the US (see Cox 2022; Sharma 2022).

[2] In the US, for example, various census projections predict that the white portion of the population will become a numerical minority around 2045. Since ethnic minorities tend to vote Democrat rather than Republican, some Republicans view this as an existential threat.

[3] Falsificationism relies on the inference rule known as *modus tollens*: from (i) if T, then P, and (ii) not-P, it follows that not-T. Here, let T be a theory, and P some particular proposition implied by the theory T, which we will interpret as a *prediction*. If we conduct an experiment to see whether the prediction P is true, and we find it isn't, then – following the scheme of *modus tollens* – from not-P, it follows that not-T. That is, we have shown the theory T is false. However, trying to turn this kernel of an idea into a workable scientific methodology proves to be extremely complicated. For example, theory T will normally be composed of a number of logically independent propositions T_1, $T_2,...,T_n$, where T is really the *conjunction* of all of these propositions. That is, T is logically equivalent to T_1 and T_2 and ... and T_n. Therefore, when we find that T is false, we have only established that at *least one* of the T_i is false. How do we know which one? And how do we know that what sounds like a grand discovery — *we have shown that T is false!* — isn't just a really minor failing ("we have found that T_1 is wrong because we put a decimal point in the wrong place"), and adjusting that fixes the problem. At the end of the day, no

one has shown how to turn the kernel of the idea behind falsificationism into a viable scientific methodology. Nonetheless, as noted, it retains its grip on the popular understanding of how science works.

[4] One of my favourite examples is the following anecdote from a former colleague of mine at the LSE. Apparently, Noam Chomsky was invited to give a seminar at the LSE on the topic of the evolution of language not long after his book *Syntactic Structures* had established him as a highly influential and revolutionary thinker in linguistics and the philosophy of language. Chomsky began his lecture and had only been speaking for a few minutes when Popper interrupted him, taking the rest of the hour to lecture Chomsky about his (Popper's) theory about the evolution of language, much to Chomsky's astonishment.

[5] The precise details of this event are obscure, as Popper only vaguely alludes to them in his autobiography. He writes:

> In Vienna, shooting broke out during a demonstration by unarmed young socialists who, instigated by the communists, tried to help some communists to escape who were under arrest in the central police station in Vienna. Several young socialist and communist workers were killed. I was horrified and shocked by the brutality of the police, but also by myself. For I felt that as a Marxist I bore part of the responsibility for the tragedy — at least in principle. Marxist theory demands that the class struggle be intensified, in order to speed up the coming of socialism. Its thesis is that although the revolution may claim some victims, capitalism is claiming more victims than the whole socialist revolution.
> (Popper 1992, pp. 32–33)

It is clear that the event profoundly unsettled Popper. The best reconstruction of the events that I know of is provided by Artigas (1998, pp. 204–05), and it is this version that I reference here.

[6] See Lewontin and Levins (1976) for a detailed discussion of the ideological roots of Lysenkoism and its consequences.

[7] Dikötter (2010) provides an excellent account of this tragic period of Chinese history.

[8] In their excellent book, *Merchants of Doubt*, Naomi Oreskes and Erik Conway chronicle the way this was done in the tobacco and the fossil fuel industries. There is growing concern that something similar is being done by the food industry regarding the role of sugar.

[9] As Burke wrote, on the nature of political reform:

> I must see with my own eyes [...] touch with my own hands not only the fixed but the momentary circumstances, before I could venture to suggest any political project whatsoever [...] I must see the means of correcting the plan [...] I must see the things; I must see the men. (Burke 1996, p. 326).

[10] The fundamental attribution error is a cognitive bias, first identified by Ross (1977). It states that people, when characterising the behaviour of others, underemphasise environmental factors and overemphasise dispositional or character-based factors. For example, when someone describes another person's behaviour of which they disapprove, they are much more likely to describe it as resulting from character flaws than being situationally influenced.

References

Artigas, Mariano. (1998). "The Ethical Roots of Karl Popper's Epistemology." *Acta Philosophica* (2):197–233.
https://doi.org/10.17421/1121_2179_1998_07_02_Artigas
Baer, Ulrich. (2019). *What Snowflakes Get Right: Free Speech, Truth, and Equality on Campus*. Oxford University Press.
https://doi.org/10.1093/oso/9780190054199.001.0001
BBC News. (24 May 2016). "Expats lose Supreme Court bid for EU referendum vote."
https://www.bbc.co.uk/news/uk-36370522
Ben-Porath, Sigal R. (2017). *Free Speech on Campus*. University of Pennsylvania Press.
Bergson, Henri. (1935). *The Two Sources of Morality and Religion*. Macmillan and Co., Limited. Translated by R. Ashley Audra and Cloudesley Brereton, with the assistance of W. Horsfall Carter.
Blau, Francine D. and Christopher Mackie (eds.). (2017). *The Economic and Fiscal Consequences of Immigration*. The National Academies of Sciences, Engineering, Medicine.
https://doi.org/10.17226/23550
Borjas, George J. (2016). *We Wanted Workers: Unraveling the Immigration Narrative*. New York: W. W. Norton & Company.
Brin, David. (1998). *The Transparent Society*. Perseus Books.
Burke, Edmund. (1996). *The Writings and Speeches of Edmund Burke (Volume III: Party, Parliament and the American War–1794)*. Oxford: Clarendon Press.
https://doi.org/10.1093/actrade/9780198224143.book.1
Cox, Simon. (18 November 2022). "Will China's economy every overtake America's in size?" *The Economist: A World Ahead*.
https://www.economist.com/the-world-ahead/2022/11/18/will-chinas-economy-ever-overtake-americas-in-size
Dikötter, Frank. (2010). *Mao's Great Famine: The History of China's Most Devastating Catastrophe, 1958–62*. Bloomsbury Publishing.
Downs, Donald Alexander. (2005). *Restoring Free Speech and Liberty on Campus*. Cambridge University Press.
https://doi.org/10.1017/CBO9780511509780
Gaus, Gerald. (2021). *The Open Society and Its Complexities*. Oxford University Press.
https://doi.org/10.1093/oso/9780190648978.001.0001
Green, David Allen. (3 August 2017). "The tale of the Brexit referendum question." *Financial Times*.
https://www.ft.com/content/b56b2b36-1835-37c6-8152-b175cf077ae8
Haidt, Jonathan. (2012). *The Righteous Mind: Why Good People are Divided by Politics and Religion*. New York: Pantheon Books.

Kondoh, Kenji. (2017). *The Economics of International Immigration: Environment, Unemployment, the Wage Gap, and Economic Welfare.* Springer.
Lewontin, Richard and Richard Levins. (1976). "The Problem of Lysenkoism." In Rose, Hilary and Steven Rose (eds.), *The Radicalisation of Science: Ideology of/in the Natural Sciences*, chapter 2, 32–64. The Macmillan Press Limited.
https://doi.org/10.1007/978-1-349-86145-3_2
Lukianoff, Greg and Jonathan Haidt. (2018). *The Coddling of the American Mind: How Good Intentions and Bad Ideas are Setting Up a Generation for Failure.* Penguin Press.
Mance, Henry. (3 June 2016). "Britain has had enough of experts, says Gove." *Financial Times.*
https://www.ft.com/content/3be49734-29cb-11e6-83e4-abc22d5d108c
Mishra, Pankaj. (2017). *Age of Anger: A History of the Present.* Penguin Books, Ltd.
Nowrasteh, Alex and Benjamin Powell. (2021). *Wretched Refuse? The Political Economy of Immigration and Institutions.* Cambridge University Press.
https://doi.org/10.1017/9781108776899
Oreskes, Naomi and Erik M. Conway. (2011). *Merchants of Doubt: How a Handful of Scientists Obscured the Truth on Issues from Tobacco Smoke to Global Warming.* Bloomsbury Publishing.
Popper, Karl. (1992). *Unended Quest: An Intellectual Autobiography.* Routledge. First published as "Autobiography by Karl Popper" in *The Philosophy of Karl Popper* in *The Library of Living Philosophers*, ed. Paul Arthur Schlipp, Open Court Publishing, 1974.
Popper, Karl R. (1945a). *The Open Society and Its Enemies: Volume One — The Spell of Plato.* Routledge & Kegan Paul.
Popper, Karl R. (1945b). *The Open Society and Its Enemies: Volume Two — Hegel and Marx.* Routledge & Kegan Paul.
Rorschach, Hermann. (1921). *Psychodiagnostik: Methodik und Ergebnisse eines warhrnehmungsdiagnostischen Experiments (Deutenlassen von Zufallsformen).* E. Bircher.
Ross, Lee. (1977). "The intuitive psychologist and his shortcomings: Distortions in the attribution process." *Advances in experimental social psychology* 10:173–220.
https://doi.org/10.1016/S0065-2601(08)60357-3
Sharma, Ruchir. (24 October 2022). "China's economy will not overtake the US until 2060, if ever." *Financial Times.*
https://www.ft.com/content/cff42bc4-f9e3-4f51-985a-86518934afbe
Solove, Daniel J. (2008). *Understanding Privacy.* Harvard University Press.
Solove, Daniel J. (2011). *Nothing to Hide: The False Tradeoff between Privacy and Security.* Yale University Press.
Taylor, Charles. (September 1971). "Interpretation and the Sciences of Man." *The Review of Metaphysics* 25 (1):3–51.

Vasagar, Jeevan. (17 July 2012). "Creationist groups win Michael Gove's approval to open free schools." *The Guardian*. https://www.theguardian.com/education/2012/jul/17/creationist-groups-approval-free-schools

Watson, Tara and Kalee Thompson. (2021). *The Border Within: The Economics of Immigration in an Age of Fear*. The University of Chicago Press. https://doi.org/10.7208/chicago/9780226270364.001.0001

PART I
Don't come around here no more
The cosmopolitan conception of the Open Society

1. Consider the wall

In 221 BCE – the final year of the Chinese Zhou dynasty – King Zheng of Qin defeated the armed forces of Qi, which was the last remaining independent state out of seven. This victory ended a war of domination that lasted more than 250 years, and led to the collapse of the Zhou dynasty and the establishment of the Qin dynasty in its place. Zheng became its first emperor. As the first emperor of the first dynasty of what would become Imperial China, Zheng's place in history was assured. In the West, Zheng's legacy would become known through an enduring piece of defensive architecture.

During the Warring States era, before Zheng became emperor, many groups had built extensive protective defences, mostly consisting of earthen walls, on their territorial perimeters. Despite Zheng's success in consolidating his empire from within – he implemented numerous political and economic reforms to promote stability – his empire was repeatedly threatened by outsiders. In particular, a confederation of nomadic tribes from the region now known as Mongolia routinely attacked the kingdom. Unable to defeat the tribes outright, Zheng opted for an alternative method of defence. Noting all the numerous unconnected walls leftover from the Warring States period, Zheng ordered hundreds of thousands of labourers to link them together. Over the next 1,800 years, this structure would be extended, expanded, and rebuilt and eventually came to be known as the Great Wall of China.

Walls, material and immaterial, have featured with increased prominence in the public consciousness. Example one: in June 2015, Donald Trump kicked off his presidential run with a now-famous policy announcement. He said: "I will build a great wall. I will build a great, great wall on our southern border, and I will make Mexico pay for that wall." Why a wall? Trump's argument was pragmatic: "Walls work." Trying to make good on his pledge to build the Great Wall of America turned out to be one of the most contested battles Trump fought during his time in office. "Build the wall!" became a popular crowd chant during his massive stadium events. As progress on his wall failed to materialise,[1] Trump adopted a tough, "zero tolerance" approach to illegal immigration, separating the children of illegal immigrants from their parents. After much humanitarian outcry, the policy was eventually stopped, but not

How to cite this book part:

Alexander, J. McKenzie (2024) *The Open Society as an Enemy: A critique of how free societies turned against themselves*, London: LSE Press, pp. 25–100. https://doi.org/10.31389/lsepress.ose.b. License: CC BY-NC 4.0

before thousands of children had been separated from their parents. Remarkably, there seemed to have been no clear policy in place to reunite parents with their children (Kopan 2018). In the absence of a physical barrier to keep immigrants out, it seems the Trump administration decided to try its hand at creating an immaterial, psychological barrier. The Trump administration was, I suspect, betting that the threat of being separated from one's children indefinitely would provide a deterrent sufficient to stop parents and children from attempting to enter the US illegally.

Example two: in 2016, the UK voted to leave the European Union (EU), effectively voting to create a new, immaterial wall between the UK and the EU – one made of laws and regulations. Leaving the EU, with its free movement of people and goods, would require – despite all the promises of politicians to the contrary – erecting new barriers to travel and trade that hadn't existed previously. Although the vote to leave took many people by surprise at the time, the benefit of hindsight allows us to now see that the vote to leave should have surprised no one. The UK's vote to leave the EU was a product of grievances that had been building for years and that, as we will discuss in Part II, had most efficiently been exploited by political actors using insights extracted from social media.

Although fewer than half of the eligible voters voted to leave the EU, the leave vote constituted 51.9% of the turnout. Since the referendum outcome was determined by a simple majority on a binary choice – rather than, say, requiring a two-thirds supermajority to be decisive – the matter was considered settled. And so 17,410,742 people – less than one-quarter of the population – determined the future course for a country of 65.6 million, including 13.9 million children incapable of voting.[2] Those children now face a life with fewer opportunities than before.[3]

These two examples from the US and the UK are drawn from my own experience as a dual citizen of these countries, but evidence regarding the growth in anti-immigrant attitudes in other Western countries exists. The trends wax and wane over time, as one might expect. Semyonov *et al.* (2006, p. 426) found a "substantial rise in anti-foreigner sentiment" in twelve Western countries between 1988 and 2000.[4] All these countries witnessed an increase in such attitudes between 1988 and 1994, with some experiencing a levelling off afterwards. Some even observed a slight decline, but the overall sentiment was still noted to be higher than at the start of the study. A later study by Dennison and Geddes (2018, p. 111), using data from Eurobarometer, reported a curious finding: in the "vast majority" of the 28 EU member states, anti-immigrant attitudes decreased from 2014 to 2018 even though political support for anti-immigration parties increased.[5]

What, if anything, unites these examples? I suggest that each of them illustrates decisions and actions taken by those who conceive of one conception of the Open Society as an enemy. The nature of the perceived threat varies across the examples and, as I will argue, even though not all of the perceived threats are equally valid, they share enough of a common core to warrant bringing them together for purposes of analysis. The particular conception of the Open Society here is a *cosmopolitan* conception. As a school of thought, cosmopolitanism admits of so many varieties that it is difficult to identify what they have in common beyond "the nebulous core [...] that all human beings, regardless of their political affiliation, are (or can and should be) citizens in a single community" (Kleingeld and Brown 2019). But that nebulous core provides enough of a guide for us to get started, and we will make more precise the specific cosmopolitan conception of the Open Society with which I am interested as we go along.

Let's begin by unpacking the nebulous core. Kleingeld and Brown provide a nice taxonomy of possible cosmopolitan views based on how one understands the "single community" of which all humans are citizens. Some philosophers take the single cosmopolitan community to be determined by our *moral* obligations to others. Moral cosmopolitanism then admits a number of different views depending on how one understands the nature of our moral obligations to others.[6] Others advocate for a form of *political* cosmopolitanism wherein the single community to which people belong derives from the bonds of some political union. Here, too, we find a variety of possibilities, ranging from modest forms featuring a combination of nation states and supranational organisations to more extreme forms that advocate the eradication of separate nations in order to form a single "world state".[7]

Other forms of cosmopolitanism exist. The two that will occupy most of our attention in this part of the book are *economic* and *cultural* cosmopolitanism. Varieties of economic cosmopolitanism trace back to the emergence of international trade from the age of exploration and have been defended by economists such as Mill, Ricardo, Hayek, and Friedman. As a view, economic cosmopolitanism has considerable conceptual overlap with economic globalisation, and for that reason has come under criticism from a number of different directions, with few defenders outside of economics.[8] Concerns over cultural cosmopolitanism underlie much of the discussion in the West regarding multiculturalism, both for and against, from both sides of the political spectrum. From the right, worries about cultural erosion and the loss of local communities prompt pushback against cultural cosmopolitanism. From the left, worries about cultural appropriation and, so to speak, the loss of control over the "intellectual property" of ethnic identities also prompt pushback against cultural cosmopolitanism.

Now recall the two examples discussed earlier. The anti-immigration sentiment behind President Trump's ambition to build the Great Wall of America and the UK's decision to detach itself from the EU can be seen as a rejection of political cosmopolitanism. In both cases, this rejection of political cosmopolitanism was, in part, fuelled by concerns deriving from both economic and cultural cosmopolitanism, wrapped in the rhetoric of populism. In the US, Trump encapsulated these concerns in a pithy quote shortly after Ford announced that it was planning to move its small car production to Mexico:

"It used to be, cars were made in Flint and you couldn't drink the water in Mexico. Now, the cars are made in Mexico and you cannot drink the water in Flint. That's not good." (see Hains 2016). In the UK, the EU had for years been represented by tabloids as an out-of-touch, bureaucratic organisation forcing its economic regulation onto a reluctant population. The myths circulated about the EU were fascinating in both their specificity and their absence of grounding in fact, such as the claim that EU regulations on the sale of cabbage were 26,911 words in length.[9] Concerns in the UK about legal migration arising from the free movement of people within the EU also dominated headlines, in addition to speculation about the possible consequences for British society if Turkey were to join the EU (Erlanger 2016).

The cosmopolitan conception of the Open Society matters because it provides an alternative vision to the world in which we live, where the spatially delineated nation state remains the primary, most fundamental unit of political organisation. National identities and expressions of national interests influence and thwart attempts to coordinate action on a global scale on topics as diverse as international trade, international tax and finance law, nuclear nonproliferation, climate change, and the global response to COVID-19. National identity is so central to our conception of what it means to be *human* that Article 15 of the UN's Universal Declaration of Human Rights states that everyone has the *right* to a nationality.[10] Possession of nationality is granted protection in the same document that lists the right to life, liberty, and security (Article 3); freedom from enslavement (Article 4); protection from cruel and inhuman punishment (Article 5); the right to marry and found a family (Article 16); freedom of thought, conscience, and religion (Article 18); freedom of opinion and expression (Article 19); and the right to participate in the cultural life of the community (Article 27).

But there is an important difference between the rights enumerated above and the right to a nationality. Consider, for example, the right to life, liberty, and security (Article 3) or protection from cruel and inhuman punishment (Article 5). Both of these rights are inextricably linked to our existence as embodied creatures. Article 3 concerns our capacity to exercise agency and free will, while Article 5 concerns our capacity to feel pleasure and pain. In both cases, the legally protected human rights derive from moral protections associated with those capabilities. Other rights appearing in the Declaration arguably have a similar origin. The right to marry and found a family (Article 16) and the right to participate in the cultural life of a community (Article 27) make sense as objects of moral concern given biological facts inherited from our evolutionary origins, such as how we raise children and our pro-social dispositions as a species. To put the point somewhat starkly: if we reproduced like oysters,[11] would there be a need for a protected right to form a family? And if we were solitary creatures like the polar bear or moose, the right to participate in the cultural life of a community would probably not be important enough to warrant protection. Instead, perhaps, we would have the right to be *spared* having to participate in the life of a community. Some people feel that way as it is. As Sartre wrote at the end of his play *No Exit*, hell is other people.

In contrast, the right to a nationality derives from a contingent fact of human existence that is predicated upon a particular, historical solution to the problems of social coordination and organisation. The right to a nationality is thus more akin to the right to be presumed innocent until proven guilty in a public trial (Article 11); the right of individuals to own property (Article 17); or the right to work and free choice of employment (Article 23). As such, we must recognise that this apparently unalterable form of political organisation – this foundation of social reality – is a contingent social construct that exists for a variety of historical, cultural, and functional reasons. The contingent construct of the nation state yields, in many cases, a number of benefits, but at the same time it creates many negative externalities. With all of the global challenges we face – especially, the existential threat posed by climate change – we must ask whether the concept of a nation state – given its geographically defined nature, its division of people into (mostly) non-overlapping groups, and its forcing people to live according to the outcome of a natural lottery they had no part in designing – requires adjustment. If, as I argue, the answer is *yes*, this shows the value of the cosmopolitan concept of the Open Society.

2. You should have picked different parents

Let us begin with the question of how people receive citizenship in the first place.[1] There are two primary ways in which nationality is conferred upon individuals. The first is *jus soli*, Latin for "right of the soil". This refers to those states that confer nationality to those individuals born in their territory. *Jus soli* can be applied with or without restrictions. Unrestricted *jus soli* grants citizenship to any person born in the territory of a state regardless of the status of his or her parents. Restricted *jus soli*, as the name suggests, requires that one or both parents satisfy certain conditions in order for the child to acquire citizenship.

In the US, unrestricted *jus soli* was introduced by the Fourteenth Amendment in 1868, three years after the end of the American Civil War. This amendment included a citizenship clause specifying that, "All persons born or naturalized in the United States, and subject to the jurisdiction thereof, are citizens of the United States and of the State wherein they reside." Prior to the Civil War, the children of slaves were not citizens, and the Fourteenth Amendment played an important role in abolishing slavery by ensuring that all people born in the US at least had equal legal status as citizens. Although the text has generally been seen as supporting a form of unrestricted birthright citizenship that grants nationality without restrictions – admittedly leading to a small cottage industry of "birth tourism" where pregnant women travel to the US for the specific purpose of giving birth[2] – the requirement that persons born in the US must be "subject to the jurisdiction thereof" has been interpreted as placing a few limited restrictions. Since foreign diplomats have diplomatic immunity, they are not subject to the jurisdiction of the US and, so, their children are not eligible for citizenship.

Unrestricted *jus soli* exists in a number of countries, but the trend has been to move towards applying restrictions. It's no longer enough, for many countries, to simply be within their territorial borders when your personal contribution to the next generation emerges. For example, New Zealand – which had mostly unrestricted birthright citizenship until 31 December 2005[3] – now grants citizenship only if at least one parent is a citizen, or permanent resident of New Zealand, or if required to prevent the child from being stateless. The latter type of restriction is fairly common.

The second way in which nationality is acquired is *jus sanguinis*, Latin for "right of blood". According to this principle, what matters is not *where* the person was born but what their parents' nationality is. The UK grants citizenship to any child born abroad to British parents (known as "citizenship by descent"), *provided that* the parents did not themselves obtain their British citizenship by descent. This stops the chain of citizenship by descent from going beyond one generation in cases where there are no naturally obvious ties to Britain. Since there is no inconsistency between *jus soli* and *jus sanguinis*, countries can implement a combination of both schemes. The US has a number of conditions under which a child born abroad will be granted US citizenship. The relevant government website (US Department of State 2024) provides a taxonomy of most of the cases you can imagine occurring, ranging from a child born to parents who are US citizens (and married) to a child born "out-of-wedlock" to a mother who isn't a US citizen and a father who is.

The relevant moral point is that both *jus soli* and *jus sanguinis* bestow nationality to a child based on conditions surrounding their birth. Since different nationalities confer massive differences in life opportunities, and the nationality one acquires at birth is derived from the nationality of one's parents – a matter obviously beyond one's control – we have here one source of great natural injustice, an injustice that derives solely from the natural lottery that assigns properties to individuals at the time of their birth.[4] Consider the simple matter of life expectancy. In 2023, the CIA World Factbook (US Central Intelligence Agency 2024) identified Monaco – the tiny European microstate on the French Mediterranean coast – as the country with the highest life expectancy at 89.6 years; the country with the lowest life expectancy was Afghanistan – a landlocked country straddling Central and South Asia – at 54.1 years. That a person can face the misfortune of having their life expectancy cut nearly in half simply due to an unlucky outcome in the natural lottery is a moral outrage. And then there are all the other differences, also deriving from this natural lottery, in people's ability to exercise their rights as enumerated in the UN's Universal Declaration: protection from cruel and inhuman punishment; freedom of thought, conscience, and religion; freedom of opinion and expression, and so on.

It is important to identify the right target for our moral outrage. It is not simply *that* people have such fundamentally different opportunity sets which is troubling, although this fact is surely sufficient reason to be troubled. The real objection is that the *background conditions* that give rise to these different opportunity sets are so widely accepted as a natural fact of life, without asking why things are the way they are.

In writing about social constructivism, Ian Hacking identified the following criterion for when people begin to call attention to some aspect X of society as socially constructed: "In the present state of affairs, X is taken for granted; X appears to be inevitable" (Hacking 1999, p. 12). Let X = citizenship acquired via birthright, and you have the present state of affairs. As Shachar writes in her book *The Birthright Lottery* (emphasis added):

> To the extent that citizenship is a valuable resource, it is currently secured on the basis of a morally arbitrary set of criteria. Birthright membership principles that sanction such distribution

deserve the same critical analysis appropriate to any other social institution that stands in the way of the equal realization of opportunities. Such analysis is, though, conspicuous for its absence. *The almost casual acceptance of ascription as a basis for assigning political membership is so prevalent that we tend to simply take it for granted.* (Shachar 2009, p. 4)

In other words, the real problem with the injustices created by the natural lottery that assigns citizenship to persons based on accidents of birth is that there is no good theoretical justification for doing so.

Injustices deriving from differential outcomes in the natural lottery are nothing new. If we ignore, for simplicity of argument, the fact that most human attributes are generally the product of both nature and nurture and concentrate on the *potential* people have at birth,[5] even then we find that life is replete with such inequalities. Some people are born with the potential to be smarter than others (when raised in the right environment, not subject to bad luck, and so on), some are born with the potential to be taller or healthier or faster or more attractive or more sociable, and so on. These differences, even apparently minor and insignificant ones, can make a material difference in a person's life. Scholz and Sicinski (2015) found a statistically significant correlation between the perceived attractiveness of men and their earnings. Similar connections have been found to hold between a person's height and their earnings (Case and Paxson 2008; Judge and Cable 2004). And people – even women – with deeper voices are generally perceived to be more authoritative (Anderson and Klofstad 2012).

Although we cannot do anything about innate differences in the potential people have at birth, it is generally recognised that, to the extent it is feasible, a just society will try to create an environment where differences in potential, resulting from factors beyond a person's control, are minimised. In part, this is because there is an intuition that such innate differences in potential are *unfair*[6] in that people did not do anything to deserve the potential they have. In cases where policy is an effective lever for mitigating such differences, appropriate rules and procedures can be put in place to help provide a "level playing field" for all. The playing field is never made completely level, but some of the most egregious injustices can be partially ameliorated. Taxes redistribute income from richer areas to poorer areas, helping fund services in those areas beyond what could be paid for by the immediate community. Those differences in services provide for alternative environments, which make a material difference in people's potential. Educational institutions have made great – albeit still incomplete – strides in helping people realise their potential and even in changing the way in which people think about differences in potential.[7] In cases where policy cannot really provide methods of ameliorating outcomes from innate differences (i.e., of how tall someone is) or in cases where we think that certain innate differences should not be a factor in determining one's life prospects (i.e., how deep someone's voice is or how attractive they are considered to be), we introduce rules and procedures to try to prevent those differences from mattering. Inequalities deriving from the natural lottery are not eliminated, but we make the effort to design policies such that the variance in outcomes resulting from those inequalities is less than it would be in the absence of these policies.

These attitudes sit uneasily with the growth of populist nationalism that we see taking place in many countries and the subsequent efforts to reduce immigration and tighten enforcement at the border. What the above discussion about potential intends to show is that we are willing to go through considerable effort and expense to try to *design out* the undesirable consequences of the things *that we had no hand in creating* – such as inequalities in a person's potential deriving from their genetic endowment. Yet, at the same time, the movement to tighten borders and restrict immigration is a concentrated effort to *design in* the undesirable consequences of *something that we humans explicitly created*, namely, national identities attached to individuals at birth and a rigid system of immigration that enforces the relative advantages or disadvantages that creates. The current system of citizenship, which randomly rewards or denies opportunities to persons, aiding or thwarting their life ambitions, effectively punishes a person for not having the foresight to pick different parents. Addressing this fundamental injustice is one key point in favour of the cosmopolitan conception of the Open Society.

3. The room where it happens

The simple injustice generated by the birthright lottery masks another injustice, which is equally important, albeit operating indirectly. It concerns the ability of people to participate in the decision-making processes that determine the policies endorsed and actions taken by their country. In most democratic countries, the right to vote is restricted to citizens, but there is a surprising amount of variation in practice when it comes to the details. As an illustration of the kinds of variation in practice, consider the EU. The 1992 Maastricht Treaty granted all EU citizens the ability to vote in *local* elections, wherever they happened to live in the EU. In light of this, some EU states decided to go further and extend the right to vote in local elections to any foreign resident satisfying certain conditions. In 1996, Estonia granted foreign citizens over the age of 18 (as well as stateless persons) the right to vote, but not run for office, in local elections if they had lived in the country for at least five years (Heinsalu *et al.* 2016, p. 89). Belgium adopted a similar policy in 2004. Some EU countries are a little more lenient: as of 2024, Denmark lets non-EU foreigners vote if they have been resident for four years; Finland requires them to have been resident only for two. Other European countries are less open: as of 2024, France, Germany, and Italy do not allow non-EU foreigners to vote at all.

When it comes to national elections, very few countries allow non-citizens to vote. One notable exception is Uruguay, but it grants foreign nationals the right to vote only after a 15-year residency period. The most inclusive is New Zealand, which passed a law in 1975 allowing all permanent residents to vote in all elections, regardless of their citizenship status.[1] The right to hold office, though, even in New Zealand, is still reserved to citizens. This occasionally catches people by surprise. In 2002, Kelly Chal was included as a candidate on the party list of the United Future Party. New Zealand uses a mixed-member proportional representation system, and she was expected to join Parliament under this system. When it was realised that she did not have New Zealand citizenship, she was removed from the party list.

Of course, not all countries are democracies, as Figure 3.1 shows. But even in those countries that are not democracies, the very possibility of being in the room where it happens still generally depends on being a citizen of that country. There's no democracy at all in North Korea – the Supreme People's Assembly has no power and simply waves through laws written by the Workers' Party of Korea (WPK) (British Broadcasting Corporation 2019) – but the very

Figure 3.1: A classification of countries according to their regime type, as of 2017

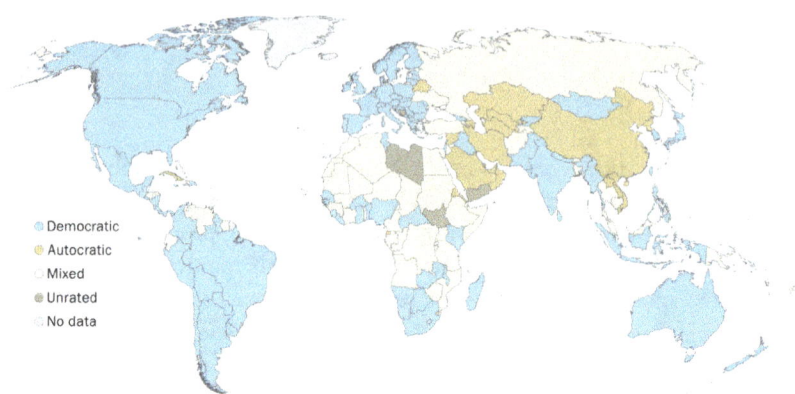

Source: from Desilver (2019). Created using data from the Systemic Peace Polity IV Project. Copyright Pew Research Center, Washington, D.C.
Notes: countries identified as "mixed" have governments featuring elements of both democratic and autocratic regimes. Countries identified as "unrated" have either collapsed, been occupied, or were in the middle of regime change.

possibility of being an advanced member of the WPK, or of being a highly-ranked member of the army, and, therefore, being amongst the elite who do have some influence, requires being a citizen. This point holds more generally. Newson and Trebbi (2018) analysed the patronage networks of the ruling elites in autocratic societies and found interesting differences between sub-Saharan Africa, China, and North Korea. In sub-Saharan Africa, the patronages "are proportionately allocated to different ethnic groups according to the share of that ethnic group in the country population at large". In contrast, the patronages in China tend to be allocated according to certain biographical traits, such as belonging to prominent families, holding military rank, being affiliated with the Communist Youth League of China, and so on. The secrecy of North Korea makes it even more impenetrable than China, but analysing co-appearances of elites in official photographs of state events allows Newson and Trebbi to show the importance of personal ties while, at the same time, uncovering elements of factionalism. But, in all cases, however the ruling elites are selected, they are generally citizens.

The fact that citizenship is – although generally, not exclusively – a necessary precondition for participating in the political decision-making of a country, democratic or not, matters for the following reason: political decisions taken by a country often have consequences that spill across borders, affecting people who are not citizens and who, therefore, played no part in the making of those decisions. Climate change provides perhaps the most salient illustration of this point. As all of us are affected by the climate, all of us have a vested interest in preventing climate change.[2] Policy decisions taken by large, polluting countries such as the US and China have far-reaching consequences for people who do not live in either country, affecting citizens of small countries such as Tuvalu far more than the actual climate policy decisions taken by their home country (Roy 2019). Other issues that illustrate this point are local policies regarding antibiotic use in medicine (Sifri *et al.* 2019) and agriculture (Moyer 2016), which contribute to the rise of antibiotic-resistant bacteria, and the production and use of so-called "forever chemicals", which contaminate groundwater and collect in the human body (Feldscher 2022). Many other examples exist.

The intuition appealed to in the above discussion – that individuals ought to have a say in those decisions that affect them – is known in democratic theory as the "All-Affected principle". It is one of several principles proposed as a solution to what is known as the *boundary problem*: when we talk about "we, the people" coming together to make collective decisions, what determines how that group is constituted? Which principle determines who counts as a legitimate member of that group? The true nature of the challenge is fully appreciated once we realise that, "[t]he question itself generates a general paradox of founding for democracy in that any act of legitimate democratic constitution of 'the people' or 'demos' would itself already require a legitimately constituted 'people' or 'demos' to engage in that act" (Owen 2012, p. 130). Some have expressed scepticism about the possible solutions to the paradox. Whelan (1983) claims that "brief reflection suffices to show that the boundary problem is one matter of collective decision that cannot be decided democratically".

In *practice*, the boundary problem has typically been decided by contingent matters of fact. Historically, as societies have evolved from small bands of people to larger tribes, to settlements and so on, the answer to the question "who decides" was determined by things such as spatial proximity, kinship ties, or force.[3] In *principle*, what we would like to have is an independent reason sufficient to command assent from those lying on both sides of the boundary. If each individual independently and freely agreed to their proposed state of being inside or outside the group, a spontaneous solution to the boundary problem would emerge – one not requiring a prior democratic procedure.

The All-Affected principle attempts to solve the boundary problem by proposing a moral principle about who has the right to participate. Owen (2012, p. 131) formulates it as follows: "All whose interests are actually affected by a decision should be able to participate as equals in the democratic decision-making process." The relative simplicity of the principle hides a number of important philosophical subtleties that impact both its feasibility and plausibility. Let us work through these before turning to the matter of how the All-Affected principle might be justified.

The most important question is *what does it mean to be affected*? One proposal is the following: a person is affected by a decision if that person is changed by the decision. What does it mean for a person to be changed? One well-known criterion of change, due to Geach (1969, p. 71), says that a person x has changed if there is some predicate P such that "$P(x)$ at time t_1" is true and "$P(x)$ at time t_2" is false for some time $t_2 > t_1$. If the local authorities take a decision to purchase your home via eminent domain, with immediate effect, in order to demolish it and build a freeway bypass, the predicate 'My home is at such-and-such address' is true prior to that decision being taken and false afterwards. In this case, the criterion delivers the right result: you have been changed by the decision, so you were affected by the decision, and so, according to the All-Affected principle, you should have been able to participate in the decision-making process.

Geach called his criterion of change the *Cambridge criterion* because the concept of change it identified featured quite prominently in the work of the great Cambridge philosophers Bertrand Russell and John McTaggart. But two problems arise if we interpret the phrase "actually affected" in the All-Affected principle as a Cambridge change. The first is that it is virtually impossible to use the All-Affected principle to *exclude* people because Cambridge changes are so permissive in what they count as a change. The second is that the definition of a Cambridge change is relative to a language and hence is limited to what can be expressed in that language.

To see why Cambridge changes don't allow individuals to be excluded by the All-Affected principle, let's step back and consider, from the point of view of metaphysics, what it means to say that two entities A and B are different. A good place to start is Leibniz's principle of the Identity of Indiscernibles: if A and B are different, then there must be some property that is not shared by both A and B.[4] If a person is changed at some time t, then there must be some property acquired or lost by that person at t. In Geach's definition, the property gained or lost is the one referred to by the predicate P.[5]

There are two kinds of properties individuals can have: *intrinsic* properties and *relational* properties. An intrinsic property of an object is one which the object has independent of context. For people, typical examples of intrinsic properties include *mass* and *height*.[6] It's important to not think of intrinsic properties as somehow being essential to a person because the intrinsic properties of an object can change. One reason so many people go on a diet after the holiday season is that their mass – an intrinsic property – has increased. People's height tends to change as they get older, as they slowly shrink in stature. Intrinsic properties are context-independent *at the particular moment in time we are considering*: if you were teleported to the Moon, Mars, or Venus, your mass and height wouldn't change at the particular instant you arrived.

In contrast, a relational property is a property an object has according to some relation which holds between another one or more objects. Examples of relational properties, for people, are "is a child of", which holds between the person and both of their parents, and "is a friend of", which holds between the person and each one of their friends. There's also no upper limit on the number of objects a relational property can apply to. The relational property "is collinear with" holds between an object and *two* other items: the two items determining the line on which the object falls. More complex relational properties can easily be constructed. On a very permissive theory of properties, "is in the same universe as" is a relational property which holds between all existing things.

The problem Cambridge changes create for the All-Affected principle is that any change that affects a single person propagates via the relational properties to give rise to further changes that affect many (arguably, *all*) other people. Here's how. Suppose that, as above, the local authorities invoke eminent domain to compulsorily purchase your home in order to demolish it and build a new freeway. This creates a change that affects you. Because you have changed – you are now homeless – you are not, strictly speaking, the *same* person you were before: you now have a different property, namely, the property of being homeless. Now consider the relational property "is a friend of" which holds between you and each of your friends.[7] Each of your friends is now friends with a slightly different person – the recently made homeless you – and this means that one of the relational properties held by each of your friends now connects them to a slightly different person. This induces a change in each of your friends. And because each of your friends is now slightly different than they were before, it induces a further change in everyone else *they* are connected to by a relational property. And this process continues, seemingly without end. A change to a single person thus affects everyone else, and so the All-Affected principle doesn't *exclude* anyone from any decision.

Before we consider solutions to this first problem, let us briefly mention the second problem: that Cambridge changes are language-dependent. The criterion for a Cambridge change requires identifying some predicate P such that the truth value of P applied to a person changes over time. But what if our language doesn't have a suitable predicate? Not all decisions which have consequences have consequences which can be described by a predicate in our language, at least the way it is at the moment. In some cases, we might be able to appeal to a vague predicate like "is uncomfortable" to capture decisions which make a person feel unsettled or that something is wrong, without being able to identify precisely why. But it is a very real possibility that some decisions which affect people, who therefore ought to be involved in the making of those decisions, do so in ways which escape the expressive capabilities of our language. This is very much one of the main themes in the literature on epistemic injustice (see Fricker 2006, 2007).

One might respond that Geach's notion of a Cambridge change is the wrong theory of change to use for determining who is affected by a decision in order to apply the All-Affected principle. More precisely, the objection is that changes that propagate through relational properties, thereby creating indirect changes to third parties, are insufficient on their own to identify the kind of "affect" that the All-Affected principle should target. The spirit of this objection is, I believe, largely correct, but a complicating feature is that sometimes indirectly affected persons *are* relevant for inclusion under the All-Affected principle. Suppose a town made a decision to compulsorily purchase and demolish 5km^2 of housing in order to build a park. The impact of rendering so many people homeless would clearly have knock-on effects that propagate throughout the wider community, precisely through the variety of social relations that generate the rippling outward effect of a Cambridge change. Many people made homeless would seek to move in with friends or family. People unable to move in with friends or family would compete for increasingly scarce rental accommodation, given the unexpected increase in demand, and some would find themselves unable to afford housing, thereby having to leave the community where they had an established life. All of the people affected by these indirect effects are, it seems, rightly included under the All-Affected principle. The main difference is that the discussion in the above example was framed in terms of the causal consequences that flow from a Cambridge change rather than the Cambridge change itself. But it's not clear whether that is a distinction that makes much of a difference.

Instead of rejecting Geach's theory of change outright, I suggest that two revisions need to be made in order to make it suitable for use in the All-Affected principle. The first is that we need to restrict the set of predicates used to identify a change. In Geach's theory, *any* predicate applied to a person that changes its truth value over time counts as a change. This is clearly too broad as we have seen. Yet how is the set of predicates that matter determined? This matter cannot be settled *a priori* from a philosopher's armchair, as it is itself a matter for democratic deliberation. Every democratic community needs to decide for itself what counts as an "interest actually affected by a decision".[8] And this presents an interesting complication regarding how the All-Affected principle solves the boundary problem. Suppose that people individually assent to the All-Affected principle, in the abstract, to form a political union. Those people are, in general, agreeing to form a political union *without knowing in advance* whether – in any particular case that may matter to them in the future – that the community will decide that they are able to participate in the making of the decision.[9] For this reason, agreeing to enter into a political union involves elements of both trust and faith. Each person P is saying that they *trust* other individuals to act appropriately in future deliberations and not exclude them from relevant discussions when P believes it to be in their interest. And each person P is, to some extent, taking it on *faith* that the set of predicates to which the All-Affected principle will be applied in the future will adequately represent the cares and concerns that P will have at that point in time.

If the set of predicates used to determine what counts as a change is subject to community revision, this also gives a way of addressing the second concern mentioned above: that Cambridge changes are language dependent. Language changes over time based on the use and expressive needs of a community. As new predicates are introduced, and old predicates revised, new types of change become identifiable through the new expressive capabilities of language.[10] As an illustration, consider the concept of a *microaggression*, first introduced by

Pierce (1970). Although subtle acts signalling negative or hostile attitudes towards minority groups have existed as long as the ability of humans to discriminate, until the term was coined there was no single concept that concisely captured the phenomenon experienced multiple times a day by so many people. Expanding the expressive capacity of language by adding a new term like "microaggression" allows people to not only better characterise their experiences but it enables political coordination and action.

The second revision that needs to be made in order to render the idea of a Cambridge change suitable for application in the All-Affected principle is that a choice has to be made regarding how far along the chain of Cambridge changes we will go before we draw a line and say that the person affected is too remote from the original change to warrant inclusion in the decision-making process. Note that this is not the same thing as saying that the *material effect* on the person is too small to warrant inclusion, although it will often be the case that remoteness correlates with limited materiality. As above, though, what counts as being "too remote" for inclusion cannot be determined *a priori* but will also need to be decided by the community itself, as attitudes towards remoteness can shift over time.

What is the point of this extended discussion regarding the boundary problem and the All-Affected principle? It is to make clear the full extent to which there is a second natural injustice potentially resulting from the circumstances of an individual's birth over which they had no control. If we generally agree that a person ought to have a say in those decisions that affect them, then the capability of a person to do so is largely a function of the political system of the country into which they are born. This is, of course, obviously true when we are contrasting authoritarian with democratic societies. But what the discussion of Cambridge changes and the All-Affected principle serves to highlight is that *even in* democratic societies, the very possibility of having a say in those decisions that affect a person depends on pre-existing community standards regarding which predicates are recognised as triggering a change for the individual – thereby causing the person to count as *affected* – and bringing them into the decision-making fold. These pre-existing community standards may align with what a person counts as important, but they may not. And so, if we think that a person ought to have a say in those decisions that affect them, and that this ability should be limited as little as possible by natural injustices deriving from a person's birth, it is natural to embrace a cosmopolitan conception of the Open Society. In particular, imagine a world in which there is much greater potential for people to move freely between states, or to create new states, combined with international institutions having more power to curtail the ability of states to act in ways that impose negative externalities on others. Although such a political cosmopolitanism wouldn't correct for every inequality resulting from the natural injustices experienced by self-determining agents unable to choose their parents or country, it would at least go some way to partially mitigate them.

In the next chapter, I discuss in greater detail this cosmopolitan conception of the Open Society and provide an argument for why we should endorse that particular form of cosmopolitanism. After doing so, I will turn to address the two main practical criticisms raised by people against this conception of the Open Society: the economic consequences of allowing much greater freedom of movement of people than we do at present and its socio-cultural consequences on local communities.

4. Go your own way

If at this point you feel the pull of the All-Affected principle as both a solution to the boundary problem and a legitimating principle for the formation of political communities, you might start to worry about how it would work in practice. In particular, consider the problem discussed in the previous chapter: how are we to determine whether a person affected by a decision should be included in the decision-making process? Previously, I said that this was a matter for the community to decide. Let's think through the implications of this solution more carefully, beginning with an objection to the All-Affected principle from Robert Nozick.

In *Anarchy, State, and Utopia*, Nozick provides the following argument to show that there are certain real limits of the All-Affected principle:

> If four men propose marriage to a woman, her decision about whom, if any of them, to marry importantly affects each of the lives of those four persons, her own life, and the lives of any other persons wishing to marry one of these four men, and so on. Would anyone propose, even limiting the group to include only the primary parties, that all five persons vote to decide whom she shall marry? She has a right to decide what to do, and there is no right the other four have to a say in the decisions which importantly affect their lives that is being ignored here. (Nozick 1974, p. 269)

This objection strikes many as eminently sensible: *of course*, the woman has the exclusive right to decide, and the men have no right to have a say in the matter. Yet much of the force of this thought experiment derives from certain background assumptions such as individualism, respect for personal autonomy in key life decisions, and an understanding of marriage largely according to Western values. If we consider cultures where arranged marriages are the norm, where suitability considerations play a larger role, and where the relationship is viewed not as merely a bond between two *people* but, rather, between two *families*, the force behind the intuition begins to fade. In different cultural settings, where the practice of marriage has roots in different social and moral norms, the set of people affected by the decision who have a right to have a say in the decision, may well vary. It might seem strange to Western audiences that other people beyond the bride and the groom could or should have a say in the marriage decision, but there is ample precedent for such practices throughout history. Marriage between nobility in medieval Europe often involved political calculations extending beyond the preferences of the bride and groom.

The point of this observation is that who counts as a relevant party affected by a decision, and who thereby has a right to have a say in the making of that decision, depends in part upon the moral beliefs held by that society. It also depends on social norms and other cultural practices regarding how decisions are made. If two societies vary in their moral and social norms, then that can yield differences in how they interpret the All-Affected principle in cases that, on the surface, appear quite similar.

Taking moral pluralism seriously poses a problem for political cosmopolitan theories because how can there be a "single community" to which all people are citizens, if, at the same time, different cultures, states, societies, or communities[1] can occupy substantially different moral spheres, with potentially substantive disagreement regarding the rights and obligations their members have? For this reason, it is more common for political cosmopolitan theories to be derived from a conceptually prior *moral* cosmopolitanism. For example, according to Kant's moral philosophy, moral principles are derived from the requirements of rationality alone; all rational individuals, human or otherwise, are thus subject to the same moral requirements. Given this, all humans belong to the same moral community, creating a moral cosmopolitanism that provides the foundation for the political cosmopolitanism he later developed in *Toward Perpetual Peace*. Similarly, some forms of utilitarianism, which treat "utility" as a measurable quantity of individual well-being according to some objective set of criteria,[2] can also yield a single moral community, whereby all are tasked with helping create the "greatest good for the greatest number". Such a moral cosmopolitanism also lends itself towards providing a foundation for some form of political cosmopolitanism. But neither of these two routes is readily available in a world containing a plurality of incompatible moral beliefs.[3]

Obtaining a political cosmopolitanism that allows for moral pluralism requires a different foundation. Let's begin from an existentialist perspective on the grounds that existentialism more accurately characterises the fundamental human condition and the historically and socially contingent grounding of value, meaning, and morality. One classical formulation of existentialism, according to Sartre, takes as its core principle the idea that "existence precedes essence". That short phrase expresses the idea that as human beings born into the world, our existence as physical, embodied creatures is prior to the formation and establishment, through acts of individual choice, of those goals and values that are seen by us as constituting us as individuals. Webber (2018, p. 14) elaborates further on this point, writing: "In its canonical form, the claim that existence precedes essence is the view that an individual's behaviour is to be explained through the set of projects that they have pursed and that have become sedimented." The term "sedimented" refers to an important concept in existentialist thought but before explaining what it is, let us see why it is necessary to introduce this concept in the first place.

Individual freedom – and, in particular, freedom of choice – plays a central role in existentialist thought. But it is important to understand what exactly is being claimed when it is said that existence precedes essence and what it means for a person to create their essence through free acts of choice. For one thing, it is not to say that human nature is infinitely flexible and that all aspects of who we are, are determined by choice. Such a claim would run counter to experience. To take one example, for most people, the types of people they are sexually attracted to isn't *chosen* but *experienced*. One may choose whether or not to act on any particular instance of attraction but claiming that the attraction itself is chosen doesn't correctly describe our inner mental lives. Here's another example: all people have certain skills or activities they are naturally better at, or prefer doing, than others. There is a real sense in which possessing these skills and preferences is essential to who we are, in that we obviously wouldn't be the same person if we had different abilities or preferences (recall our earlier discussion of the Identity of Indiscernibles), but that isn't the sense of "essence" that Sartre and others had in mind.

In Sartre's original sense, a person's 'essence' is teleological in nature, related closely to an idea that Aristotle referred to as "*to ti ên einai*" in the *Metaphysics*. The phrase "*to ti ên einai*" is difficult to translate into English, as we have no exact analogue, but we can approach the basic meaning through its literal translation: "the what it was to be". To get a grip on this obscure turn of phrase, first note that "to be" should be understood in the temporally extended sense, referring to the *process* of living, wherein that process involves the pursuit of certain projects. Next, let us imagine that we are, at some point, reflecting on an earlier extended temporal process of such a kind. It is perfectly coherent to ask *what it was*, in a general sense, to involve oneself in the pursuit of those particular projects: what was the totality of values, beliefs, understandings, and meanings bound up in the activity? How did all of one's cognitive architecture, so to speak, fit together as one pursued, or failed to pursue, those projects? For Sartre, a person's essence is this totality as determined by their projects: the *what it was to be*.

Early statements of existentialism, such as Sartre's *Being and Nothingness*, were criticised for endorsing a conception of individual freedom too radical to be plausible. Consider the discussion above on what it means to say that existence precedes essence. A person's essence is determined by the projects they pursue. What determines whether a person continues to pursue the projects that they have in the past? Simply, the choice of the person to do so:

> Sartre's version of the view that existence precedes essence was that an individual's outlook, the reasons for action that they encounter and respond to in the world, depend on the values at the heart of their projects, which have no weight or inertia of their

own but are sustained only by the agent's continuing tacit or explicit endorsement of them [...] if an agent chooses to abandon a project, then that project will offer no resistance to the agent overcoming it. (Webber 2018, pp. 4–5)

The radical freedom of Sartre's early existentialism, the idea that the only thing standing between the endorsement or rejection of any particular project is the choice of the individual, is incredibly liberating. That radical freedom suggests great possibility regarding people's ability to create and reshape their essence as they wished. But this form of existentialism had one crucial flaw: it was incompatible with the phenomenology of commitment. More generally, it misrepresented the complex interplay between individuals, their society, and the challenges that presented for the exercise of individual freedom.

The problem lurking within Sartre's early existentialist writings quickly became apparent to Simone de Beauvoir, an author and philosopher who was one the founding members of the existentialist movement in post-war France. Beauvoir is best known for her book *The Second Sex* – the influential text often credited with initiating second-wave feminism and which contained the famous phrase, "One is not born, but rather becomes, a woman." In addition, she wrote a number of philosophical novels and the long essay "The Ethics of Ambiguity", later published as a book, among many other works. Although now recognised as a significant philosopher with an important intellectual legacy spanning multiple fields, during her lifetime, Beauvoir never attained the same degree of public acclaim as Sartre and her peers. This is unfortunate, for Beauvoir's development of existentialist theory is superior to Sartre's in many respects; so much so that Sartre's later existentialist writings, such as *Saint Genet*, explicitly adopt Beauvoir's formulation, implicitly rejecting his early framing (see Webber 2018, p. 125).

The problem of commitment, for Sartre, is as follows: if all that stands between my pursuit of a project and my abandonment of it is a *choice*, with the project itself having no grip on my attitudes, then it is hard to see how that means I am *committed* to that project, in the way we normally speak. For example, if I have been committed to my activist work on, say, preventing climate change for the past decade, should I be able to simply wake up one morning and walk away to take a job with Exxon?[4] It seems that an important part of being *committed* to a project is that it is, in fact, psychologically difficult to abandon it, even if one has good reason to do so. Reasons, on their own, can be insufficient to cause an agent to act. How many of us, when discussing an unsatisfactory relationship or a dysfunctional friendship or a work environment that has become politically unpleasant, have said, "Yes, I *know* I should walk away, *but*...". That paralysis of reason is the phenomenology of commitment in action.

Sartre is not unaware of this problem, but his diagnosis and analysis are unsatisfactory. Sartre notes that our projects are often interconnected in complex ways such that if I make changes to one project, I will often need to make changes to other projects as well. If I value those projects (i.e., continue to endorse them), then the knock-on effects of abandoning one project might give me pause. Consider the example of planning a complex holiday itinerary. If I have booked flights to several destinations, arranged accommodation, contacted friends to arrange visits, made restaurant reservations, and so on, then abandoning one leg of the trip (think, project) is not inconsequential. I have other plans (read, projects) that depend on it in non-trivial ways. Abandoning that leg of the trip means that I have to make new arrangements and invest effort to establish a new coherent set of travel plans. It is this kind of consequence that Sartre (2003, p. 454) has in mind when he writes: "I could have done otherwise. Agreed. But at what price?"[5] Yet it is easy to see that attempting to capture commitment via knock-on effects of interconnections between projects simply cannot work. Why? Suppose I simply abandon *enough* projects so that most, if not all, of the knock-on effects are circumscribed within the set of projects mutually abandoned and thereby simultaneously jettisoned. Consider how, in 1895, artist Paul Gauguin walked away from his life in Paris to take up residence in Tahiti, leaving his wife, five children, friends, and family behind. If I simply abandon *every* project of mine, there is no Sartrean price to pay at all. But the very possibility of doing so is the antithesis of commitment.

And so we arrive at the concept of *sedimentation*. The idea of sedimentation is originally due to Maurice Merleau-Ponty, who developed it as part of his theory of freedom and as a critique of Sartre's views in *Being and Nothingness*. Beauvoir's insight was that Merleau-Ponty's concept of sedimentation could be modified and incorporated into existentialist philosophy to accommodate the problems faced by Sartre's view regarding commitment.[6] The essential idea behind sedimentation, for Beauvoir, is this: the consequences of my pursuing a project are not merely external, in the sense of changing the world, or internal, in the sense of affecting other projects of mine. Pursuing a project over an extended period of time changes *me* as well: the values involved are held more intensely, and the beliefs are assigned greater weight.[7] The term "sedimentation" is a metaphor, but an apt one, for the repeated pursuit of a project that causes it to be increasingly influential in how my life flows around it, just like how the depositing of sediment in a river shapes the current.

Sedimentation thus explains the phenomenology of commitment in a way that Sartre's original understanding of projects cannot. If I have pursued a project over many years, the reason I cannot readily abandon it through a simple act of choice is that the values and beliefs have become sedimented over time, closing off certain possibilities at the present moment. However – and the importance of this cannot be understated – sedimentation is still, for Beauvoir, compatible with the metaphysical freedom envisioned by existentialism in the "existence precedes essence" slogan. How so? The sedimentation of projects only closes off possibilities *at the moment*: it does not *restrict* the space of possibility in the sense of what is ultimately achievable by a person. If a possibility is closed off by sedimentation, effort is required to undo the sedimentation before that possibility can be realised. If your feet have become mired in clay, you are not less metaphysically free than someone whose feet are not so encumbered, nor is the set of places you can go restricted in any way which threatens to upset that freedom: you just need to dig yourself out before you can move.

Let us put all these ideas together to see how we arrive at a political cosmopolitanism that allows for moral pluralism. The identity of individuals is shaped by the society in which they are born and raised in the sense that many individual beliefs and values are initially acquired through a process of socialisation rather than rational deliberation. This sedimentation of beliefs and values, acquired from the society and the context in which we are raised, in a sense, constitutes another version of the natural lottery of birth with which this chapter has been so concerned. However, under Beauvoir's version of existentialism, this sedimentation is still compatible with individuals being free to critique and reshape their character and values through acts of choice and exercise of the will.[8] The extent of sedimentation will determine how much effort is required, but Beauvoir's point is that it remains *possible*. Given this, and in accordance with the fundamental value placed upon individual freedom, it follows that we should respect the autonomy of the individual to choose the life they want to live.

One aspect of choosing one's life involves choosing with whom one wishes to associate. Although all persons are born into a community and a society, that community and society are not initially chosen by the person. As people mature, individuals can engage with, or distance themselves from, their inherited community. This exercise of one's freedom to associate can be correlated with endorsing or rejecting the sedimented values and beliefs acquired through socialisation, but it need not be. The point remains: respect for individual freedom entails respect for freedom of association, which requires that we allow for the migration of people across social groups, as they choose in accordance with pursuit of their life projects, to the greatest extent possible. The phrase "to the greatest extent possible" masks a myriad of practical complexities, but the most important balance to be struck involves a compromise between people's freedom to associate and form self-governing communities – that can create exclusionary rules regarding who may join – and a *consistency principle*, which states that people, as members of a community, should not act in ways that thwart the core freedoms that allowed that community to be formed in the first place. The consistency principle is not entailed by respect for individual freedom or freedom of association but, rather, is a requirement of conceptual coherency on the grounds that one should not use one's freedom to deny the same to others. Together, the respect for individual freedom, the respect for freedom of association, and the consistency principle comprise the *minimal core* required for the version of cosmopolitanism I endorse.

Note that the prohibitions required by the consistency principle are community specific: they apply to members *of* a community, with specific reference to the core freedoms that allowed *that* community to be formed in the first place. It is easy to see how the consistency principle is compatible with free communities having highly permissive practices. However, properly understood, this principle also allows for the formation of communities with highly restrictive social practices for its members, so long as those members freely accept and endorse those restrictive practices as one of their life projects. There is no inconsistency, on existentialist grounds, with a person choosing the life of a convent, monastery, or an ascetic order. What the consistency principle prohibits is two things. First, it prohibits the denial of a community member's ability to exercise their freedom to go their own way and choose an alternative life outside of that community. Second, it prohibits the community from acting to thwart the relevant freedoms of others, including those outside the community, which were necessary for the community itself to form. This second prohibition is important, for it yields a minimal form of the All-Affected principle that cuts across community boundaries.

The requirements of the consistency principle resonate with Popper's solution to the *paradox of tolerance*. In the endnotes to the first volume of *The Open Society and Its Enemies*, Popper observes that the tolerance of the Open Society could be its undoing, enabling an enemy within to flourish. In particular, "if we extend unlimited tolerance even to those who are intolerant, if we are not prepared to defend a tolerant society against the onslaught of the intolerant, then the tolerant will be destroyed, and tolerance with them" (Popper 1945, p. 226). The solution, then, is that "We should therefore claim, in the name of tolerance, the right not to tolerate the intolerant" (Popper 1945, p. 226). The Open Society allows people to form communities through freedom of association, developing their own Millian experiment in living, *provided that* they extend that same tolerance towards others. The moment a group attempts to curtail the freedom of others, they commit a violation worthy of sanction.

When the Open Society defends tolerance by sanctioning the intolerant, it must acknowledge the full range of options available. Sometimes modest sanctions will suffice, such as engaging in constructive dialogue with the offenders to show how and why their actions violate the consistency principle and persuading them of its value. But other violations will require the exercise of force.[9] Some may wonder if there is not an inconsistency here: does not my conception of the Open Society allow for people to form communities built around a commitment to pacificism and non-violence? Yes, my conception of the Open Society allows people to form communities built around such values; however, it is an undeniable fact that such communities are vulnerable to the intolerant. The Open Society, functioning as a protective umbrella for a range of experiments in living, must be grounded in pragmatism and *realpolitik*. Here, the Open Society follows Rousseau, "taking men as they are and laws as they might be".

Thus we arrive at a form of political cosmopolitanism, wherein all individuals have the freedom to choose which groups or communities they associate with and develop particular values, traditions, and social practices as they see fit. But the political cosmopolitanism it yields is very different from the one of Anacharsis Cloots: instead of a single world state, we arrive at a world containing an array of communities linked by political and economic ties, sometimes partially overlapping, sometimes hierarchically contained. But it is not a world entirely free of global governance, for the consistency principle imposes a requirement to ensure that negative externalities created by one group, community, or state do not unduly impinge upon the freedom of others. And it is not a world that requires *only* minimal oversight, for communities are free to adopt additional rules that go above and beyond the minimal requirement.

A political cosmopolitanism that allows people to move freely between groups, communities, or states is a laboratory in which multiple experiments in living are run in parallel. Each political unit can adopt its preferred solution to the local challenges it faces. Different social practices will have differential rates of success from which all can learn if information is shared.[10] When the free movement of people is allowed, political cosmopolitanism becomes a cultural evolutionary process with *group selection* operating at the aggregate level. When people can vote with their feet, ineffective and oppressive forms of social organisation will struggle to remain viable in the long run. Remember that the Berlin Wall was built to prevent people from escaping East Berlin to West Berlin.

This political cosmopolitanism is compatible with moral pluralism, at least according to some metaethical theories. In a previous work (see Alexander 2007), I argued that morality was best understood as a *social technology* for solving the interdependent decision problems which arise from people's social existence. An *interdependent decision problem* is one where the outcome depends on the choices and actions taken by multiple individuals. In such problems, conflict often exists because people have different and incompatible preferences, and each person is seeking to bring about the outcome they would most like to see realised as individuals. According to this conception of morality, moral systems provide rules for minimising conflict (e.g., guidance on how one should act towards others) as well as guidance regarding preference formation (e.g., what it is that one should want). When this system is followed, it serves to minimise conflict and maximise individual preference satisfaction within that society. From this, the possibility of moral pluralism follows almost immediately: variation in environment, culture, and history will yield different sets of interdependent decision problems that need to be solved by societies. It is natural that different sets of interdependent decision problems will likely admit different solutions, and these different solutions will give rise to different moral systems.

Some might find that unsettling, but I suggest that such a political cosmopolitanism would result in a net improvement in the world in which we currently find ourselves. For the different moral systems – each one a society's own expression of their collective project – would exist within a protected global space whereby individuals could, if they so chose, exercise their freedom to associate with an alternative community that aligned better with their own life's projects. In contrast, the world in which we live is designed to thwart people's freedom to construct meaningful lives, unless they find themselves dealt a lucky hand in the birthright lottery.

Let us now step back and reflect on our central question: what are we to make of the cosmopolitan conception of the Open Society? Over the last three chapters, I have argued that there are a number of points in its favour. The cosmopolitan conception of the Open Society provides a way to address the natural injustices arising from the birthright lottery. If we assume that some variant of existentialism correctly captures the fundamental human condition – I have endorsed Beauvoir's formulation – then, as we have seen, political cosmopolitanism flows naturally from the need to respect individual freedom. Most importantly, this form of political cosmopolitanism does not require that one accept any particular moral theory but only that the fundamental metaphysical freedom of individuals ought to be respected.

It is time now to turn to two of the most pressing objections to the cosmopolitan conception of the Open Society: that it is economically infeasible and that a world of open borders would undermine the socio-cultural distinctiveness of local communities. I address each of these questions in the following chapters.

5. It's the economy, stupid

One argument against the cosmopolitan conception of the Open Society – and its implication that borders between nation states need to be treated as highly porous, thus allowing the ready flow of people between states – is that the economic consequences of doing so would be disastrous. We have already seen how populist politicians, ranging from Donald Trump in the US to the Brexiteers in the UK, have suggested how a great influx of immigrants pouring into the country would result in them stealing "our" jobs, with a concomitant increase in crime and a drain on the welfare state, to boot. In the UK, even Gordon Brown – an economically astute politician, who was no great opponent of the globalised economy – played with the trope, advocating "British jobs for British workers" (Summers 2009).

Ultimately, this is an empirical question: if we were to reduce barriers to immigration substantially, or even eliminate them completely, what would the economic consequences be? Since no global experiment of that kind has been conducted, the next best way to answer the question is to try to get a grip on the issue through the use of economic models. In an influential paper, Clemens (2011) looked at a number of estimates on how world GDP would be influenced by (a) eliminating all policy barriers to trade, (b) eliminating all barriers to capital flows, and (c) eliminating all barriers to the flow of labour. Figure 5.1 reproduces a table from Clemens's paper, which lists the respective findings. The point to note, Clemens stresses, is that "the gains from eliminating migration barriers dwarf – by an order of a magnitude or two – the gains from eliminating other types of barriers" (Clemens 2011, p. 84). The numbers border on being unbelievable: the lowest estimate is that world GDP would increase by "only" 67%, with the largest estimate being an increase of 147.3%. As world GDP in 2020 was estimated to be $85.2 trillion,[1] the estimated gains resulting from eliminating immigration restrictions completely range between *$57.1 trillion and $125.5 trillion per year.*

If the potential gains from eliminating migration restrictions completely are eye-wateringly large, the potential gains from partially eliminating migration restrictions are also pretty impressive. Figure 5.2 lists some estimates of the efficiency gains resulting from the partial removal of barriers to immigration. The smallest estimated gain is given by Walmsley and Winters (2005), who calculate a gain of 0.6% to the world GDP from a net emigration rate of 0.8%. However, with world GDP at $85.2 trillion in 2020 (The World Bank 2024),

Figure 5.1: Efficiency gain from complete elimination of international barriers (% of world GDP)

All policy barriers to merchandise trade
1.8   Goldin, Knudsen, and van der Mensbrugghe (1993)
4.1   Dessus, Fukasaku, and Safadi (1999)[a]
0.9   Anderson, Francois, Hertel, Hoekman, and Martin (2000)
1.2   World Bank (2001)
2.8   World Bank (2001)[a]
0.7   Anderson and Martin (2005)
0.3   Hertel and Keeney (2006, table 2.9)

All barriers to capital flows
1.7   Gourinchas and Jeanne (2006)[b]
0.1   Caselli and Feyrer (2007)

All barriers to labor mobility
147.3   Hamilton and Whalley (1984, table 4, row 2)[c]
96.5   Moses and Letnes (2004, table 5, row 4)[c]
67   Iregui (2005, table 10.3)[c,d]
122   Klein and Ventura (2007, table 3)[e]

[a] These studies assume a positive effect of trade on productivity; the other trade studies assume no effect.
[b] Change in consumption rather than GDP.
[c] Assumes two factors of production, immobile capital, and no differences in total factor productivity. Estimates from Hamilton and Whalley and from Moses and Letnes cited here assume no differences in inherent productivity of migrants and nonmigrants. Some much smaller estimates in Moses and Letnes assume that poor-country emigrants at the destination are $1/5$ as productive as nonmigrants at the destination, which (as the authors note in their footnote 12) is certainly extremely conservative.
[d] Computable general equilibrium (CGE) model.
[e] Assumes three factors of production and international differences in total factor productivity in a dynamic growth model.

Source: Clemens (2011), Table 1. Copyright American Economic Association; reproduced with permission of the Journal of Economic Perspectives.

this small 0.6% increase amounts to $511.2 billion. How significant is $511.2 billion? According to the 2020 figures, this gain was larger than the individual GDP of all but the 23 largest countries. According to this data set, Belgium's GDP in 2020 was $526 billion, ranking it 23rd, with Thailand ranking 24th with a GDP of $500 billion. Even a modest increase in global migration would be equivalent to boosting the world economy by adding a whole new economically developed country.

Figure 5.2: Efficiency gain from partial elimination of barriers to labour mobility

	Removal of barriers	Net emigration rate (% origin-region population)	Efficiency gain (% world GDP)
Moses and Letnes (2004, 2005)	Complete	73.6	96.5
	Partial	29.3	54.8
	Partial	10.3	22.0
Iregui (2005)	Complete	53	67
	Partial	24	31
Klein and Ventura (2007)	Complete	>99	122
	Partial	14.8	20
	Partial	7.3	10
Walmsley and Winters (2005)	Partial	0.8	0.6
	Partial	1.6	1.2
van der Mensbrugghe and Roland-Holst (2009)	Partial	0.8	0.9
	Partial	2.0	2.3

Notes: The Moses and Letnes figures on emigration rates from are from Moses and Letnes (2005) table 9.3; figures on efficiency gains are from Moses and Letnes (2004) table 9, scaled to assume equal inherent labor productivity across countries (for example, 10 percent elimination of wage gap gives $774 billion gain in table 9, multiplied by the ratio 96.5/9.6 in table 5 to equalize inherent labor productivity, and divided by world GDP gives 22 percent). Iregui (2005) figures are from tables 10.3, 10.6, 10.8, and 10.9. Klein and Ventura (2007) figures are from tables 2 and 7 (emigration rates calculated from population allocations given 80 percent initial population allocation to poor region). Walmsley and Winters (2005) figures from tables 4 and 11, assuming 80 percent of world population starts out in (net) migrant-sending countries. Van der Mensbrugghe and Roland-Holst (2009) figures come from tables 6 and 7, and likewise assume 80 percent of world population starts out in (net) migrant-sending countries. World GDP in 2001 is taken to be $32 trillion, doubling (in 2001 dollars) to $64 trillion by 2025.

Source: Clemens (2011), Table 2. Copyright American Economic Association; reproduced with permission of the Journal of Economic Perspectives.

The initial estimates of the potential economic gains from greatly opening up immigration are pretty impressive: there was a reason that Clemens included, as a subtitle to his paper, the rhetorical question "Trillion-dollar bills on the sidewalk?" But one might worry about the models' underlying assumptions, which have not been mentioned. For example, three of the papers cited by Clemens assume that capital is not mobile, while two others assume it is mobile. We know, for a fact, that capital is mobile, but which model provides the more accurate estimate? (It's not always the case that including more accurate assumptions in a model yields more accurate predictions.) In addition, considerable variation exists across all the different models regarding assumptions about the nature of the production function as well as in the overall productivity of labour. There is also a question about how sensitive the results are to *when* migration is assumed to occur and when the benefits are measured. In a later study, Desmet *et al.* (2018, p. 908) find that "complete liberalization yields output gains of 126% [of world GDP] and welfare gains of 306 percent". This aligns quite well with the upper end of the estimates found in Clemens' review, but the Desmet *et al.* paper assumes that all of the increase in migration happens in the first year of opening up borders, in addition to tracking effects 600 years into the future. Given that economists struggle to predict recessions *next year*, we might take these figures with a grain of salt.

It is perfectly reasonable to be concerned about how the results of an economic model depend on its assumptions, but the fact that we have *multiple* models, all in rough qualitative agreement, is potentially a virtue. This view is known in the philosophy of science as *robustness analysis* and the intuition behind it is as follows. The one thing we can be sure about models – economic or otherwise – is that all models make simplifying assumptions and all models are literally false. Yet if we have a collection of models, where each model in the collection makes *different* simplifying assumptions but, nevertheless, *each* model in the collection yields a qualitatively similar result, then that should give us increased reason to believe that something in the neighbourhood of those results may actually be true. Why? The argument is that such convergence shows that the result does not depend on any *particular* set of simplifying assumptions. Each model smooths out real-world complexities in different ways, but no matter how the smoothing out is implemented, a similar result still appears.[2] This idea was neatly encapsulated by Levins (1966, p. 423) in the slogan: "our truth is the intersection of independent lies." In the case of increased migration, the multiple independent lies all intersect at a common point: significant economic growth.

To drive the point home, Clemens provides a quick back-of-the-envelope Fermi estimate[3] to show that, to a first approximation, the order of magnitude of the projected benefits is not implausible. Suppose that the world is divided into two regions, one "rich" and one "poor", where one billion people live in the rich region and six billion live in the poor region. In addition, suppose that, on average, people in the rich region earn $30,000 a year and people in the poor region earn $5,000 a year. Suppose that migrants from the poor region have lower productivity than natives from the rich region (perhaps due to differences in education, etc.) such that when someone moves from the poor region to the rich region, they only gain 60% of the difference in income ($25,000 × 0.6 = $15,000). Furthermore, suppose that as migration continues over time, the net benefit received by migrants decreases further due to supply and demand to only half of the initial benefit, or $7,500. If half of the people in the poor region move, then the net gain is three billion times $7,500, or *$22.5 trillion*. That quick estimate is below the other estimates in Figure 5.1 but not by much. It is only two-and-a-half times less than the lower estimate of $56.7 trillion and five-and-a-half times less than the upper estimate of $124.8 trillion. As Fermi estimates go, that's well within the order of magnitude of accuracy one typically expects.

Given that, let us assume for the sake of argument that the overall economic gains, to destination countries, of greatly opening up migration are both substantial and positive. At this point, opponents of open borders often turn to other arguments to try and establish that, the positive economic gains notwithstanding, the negative externalities created by greatly increasing migration are sufficiently significant to warrant a much smaller increase, if any at all. These arguments typically appeal to *distributional* concerns about *who* benefits from the predicted economic gains, both in the source country as well as in the destination country. Let us consider some of these arguments in turn, drawing upon the excellent analysis found in Chapter 2 of Nowrasteh and Powell (2021), who survey the relevant literature.

One argument concerns the possibility of a "brain drain" in the source countries from which migrants depart. If highly skilled individuals leave low-productivity countries to take more lucrative jobs in high-productivity countries, then won't it be the case that the source countries – which already were disadvantaged due to their lower productivity – will suffer further because the remaining workforce will consist of those individuals whose skills were not strong enough to enable them to take jobs elsewhere?[4] That is a reasonable concern, but there are two mitigating factors. First, the emigration of highly skilled workers increases the value of those same skills in the local economy, potentially incentivising people to acquire skills who might not otherwise have done so. Furthermore, the very *possibility* of emigration can motivate people to acquire skills up to the level required to emigrate. If they later choose to not do so (e.g., for family reasons), those skills remain in the local economy. The overall effect may be to minimise the net effect of brain drain. Second, people who emigrate often send money back to friends or family members in the source country in the form of remittances.

> For the sending countries, the welfare impact on the staying natives depends on a tradeoff. [...] these source countries would ceteris paribus be better off without emigration because a larger labor force implies greater variety in production and consumption. However, absent emigration, there would be no remittances. For countries such as El Salvador or the Philippines, where remittances account for more than 10% of GDP, the latter effect dominates and the average native stayer is about 10% better off under the current levels of migration. (di Giovanni *et al.* 2015, pp. 170–1)

That said, it's important to recognise that not all countries with high levels of emigration are better off. Shortly after describing the net positive effect on El Salvador and the Philippines, di Giovanni *et al.* state that Mexico, Trinidad and Tobago, and Turkey would be 1%–5% better off if no emigration occurred. The important point is that, given the sizeable gains that can be achieved from

Figure 5.3: The unemployment rate in the US, from 1950 to 2000

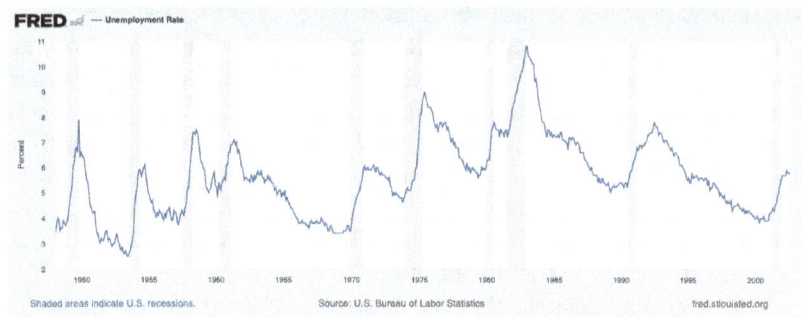

Source: US Bureau of Labor Statistics (2024), retrieved from FRED®
Graphs ©Federal Reserve Bank of St. Louis. 2024. All rights reserved.
Courtesy of Federal Reserve Bank of St. Louis.

increasing migration worldwide, the overall negative net consequences for some (not all) countries lie well within a range capable of being resolved via redistributive policies rather than stopping migration entirely.

Turning attention to negative externalities created in the destination countries, additional common arguments against migration are as follows. First, there is a common perception that immigrants "steal" the jobs of native workers, increasing unemployment. Second, for those native workers who manage to retain a job, it is thought that immigrants push down the wages of native workers. Third, immigrants take valuable limited resources away from native residents, such as places in schools, and increase demand for services, such as the police, the fire department, and healthcare. Let us consider each of these arguments in turn.

The idea that immigrants steal the jobs of native workers, thereby increasing the rate of unemployment in the destination country, is a form of what is known as the "lump of labour" fallacy. The term originates in an article entitled "Why Working-Men Dislike Piece-Work", published by David F. Schloss in 1891. According to the fallacy, there is a fixed amount of labour required by a society – the "lump" – so any allocation of labour that gives one worker more work, necessarily takes work away from at least one other person. This mistaken understanding of the economy is what, in the 1950s, drove fears about mass unemployment due to the introduction of automation in factories and, more recently, has contributed to questionable economic policies being introduced by governments.[5]

The reason the lump of labour fallacy is a fallacy is that it fails to recognise that the economy is a dynamic entity. The amount of labour required can increase when the economy grows and can decrease when the economy shrinks as in times of a recession. In their discussion of the fallacy, Nowrasteh and Powell (2021) note that, according to the fallacy, *any* introduction of new workers into the economy – not just immigrant labour – would have the same effect. They then point out that historical data from the US economy shows the exact opposite: in 1950, the US had 60 million workers. By 2018, the US had over 160 million workers due to an increase in the number of women in the workforce[6] and the massive growth in population caused by the post-war baby boom. The unemployment rate in September 1950 was 4.4%, and the unemployment rate in September 2000 was 3.9%. Time-series data over that interval, as shown in Figure 5.3, makes it clear that the greatest increases in the unemployment rate are almost always correlated with periods of recession. The counter-intuitive fact is that "[a]s more people enter the labor force, more people get jobs" (Nowrasteh and Powell 2021, p. 21).

What about the second claim, that immigrants who enter the labour market drive down wages such that native workers are paid less for the same job? This would seem to be an entirely predictable consequence of the basic law of supply and demand from Economics 101: as the supply of labour increases, the amount paid for each unit of labour will decrease, if the demand for labour remains the same. But is it really the case that the naïve supply-and-demand analysis holds up under scrutiny?

According to Nowrasteh and Powell (2021) (emphasis added):

> when economists measure the impact of immigrants on the wages of the native-born population, they don't find any general decrease in wages *in the long term* when capital and other factors of production in the economy adjust to the increase in immigration. Nowrasteh and Powell (2021, p. 22)

The answer about wage effects depends on the point in time we are concerned with; as before, economies are dynamic entities and react to changes. But the overall effect turns out to be rather less than what one would initially expect, given the law of supply and demand. Nowrasteh and Powell (2021, p. 22) claim that, in the economic literature, "the debate on the effect of immigration on wage rates of native-born workers has narrowed to debate the effects on the wages of high school dropouts in the long run".

Figure 5.4 shows plots comparing the effects of immigration on wages from two important studies, the first by Borjas (2014) and the second by Ottaviano and Peri (2012). Each study looks at how immigrants with certain work experience and educational qualifications affect the wages of native workers with similar experience and education. In addition, each study supplements its analysis by combining it with other research that estimates how capital adjusts to changes in the labour market. The two different studies, then, involve a blend of empirical and theoretical findings, which explains why they occasionally disagree.[7] Regarding the wages of native workers, only Borjas (2014) finds one category severely affected: high school dropouts, with their wages falling

Figure 5.4: Comparison of the long-term effects of immigration on wages for native and immigrant workers

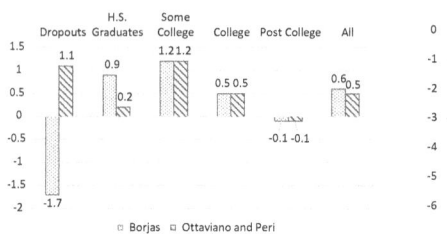
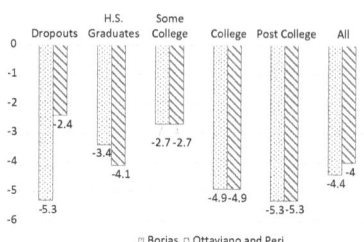

(a) Long-term effect of immigration on the wages of native workers

(b) Long-term effect of immigration on the wages of immigrant workers

Source: Figures 2.2 and 2.3 in Nowrasteh and Powell (2021, p. 24). Reproduced with permission of The Licensor through PLSclear.

by an estimated 1.7%. Aside from that, the two studies find – again, counter-intuitively – that the average effect over all categories of native workers is an *increase* in their wages of about half a percent.

The people whose wages are most affected by immigration are those immigrant workers who are already embedded in the economy. Here, the wage effects can be quite large, with postgraduate workers (and high school dropouts, as Borjas 2014 noted) experiencing a long-term decrease of 5.3% in their wages. This effect has the potential to reduce the attractiveness of further immigration over time.

The takeaway message is that, contrary to many people's expectations, the wages of native workers are not severely affected by immigration. Nowrasteh and Powell (2021) explain this slightly paradoxical finding by pointing to the heterogeneous nature of labour: immigrant workers tend to *complement* the native workforce rather than serve as outright substitutes. And while it is true that high-school dropouts are predicted to be the most severely affected, it is worth noting that high-school dropouts, as a category of worker, have increasingly struggled as economies shift towards knowledge-based work. As before, I suggest that the correct reaction to this finding is to see it as identifying the need for appropriate redistributive economic policy, shifting some of the economic gains from immigration to the category of workers most severely affected.

Finally, what about the third argument, that immigrants are a drain on the public resources from the community, taking places in schools and increasing demand for local services? Assessing the impact of immigrants on public services – the "fiscal impact" of immigration – is challenging because, as Vargas-Silva *et al.* note:

> Many of the contributions and costs that need to be included in estimates of the net fiscal impact of migration cannot be calculated directly, because the data do not exist or are not publicly available. Vargas-Silva *et al.* (2022, p. 3)

What this means is that different studies make different assumptions, and the different assumptions often lead to different estimates of the fiscal impact of immigration. For example, consider the question about whether to include the cost of education for children born inside the country. (In those countries with *jus soli* citizenship laws, this is further complicated by the fact that a child born inside the country is a citizen even if their parents are illegal immigrants.) If the definition of a "migrant" is someone born outside of the country, then a child born inside the country to immigrant, non-citizen parents does not count as a migrant. In countries without *jus soli* citizenship, one could argue that a child who is not a citizen would not have been born inside the country if their parents were not in the country, and so they should be classified as a migrant even if they don't officially satisfy the definition. Further complications exist if the child has mixed parentage, with one parent being a citizen of the country and another parent not a citizen. How do you include such children in the measurements? Some studies split the difference.

Another methodological question Vargas-Silva *et al.* (2022) mention is whether the measurement of fiscal impact should be in *absolute* terms (i.e., the total amount immigrants contribute or cost the government) or in *relative* terms compared to the native population. This choice can make a huge difference in how the results are perceived, for in years when the government runs a deficit, even native citizens are a net fiscal cost. If the immigrant population costs less than the native population – say, by being more economically productive – then they are *more* beneficial to the government than the native population.

In what follows, I'll consider two reports by Vargas-Silva *et al.* (2022) and Blau and Mackie (2017), the former discussing the estimated fiscal impact of immigrants in the UK and the latter, the US. The result of the reports will provide some general guidance as to the fiscal impact of immigration but, of course, no definitive answer can be provided for all of the qualifications cited above.

In the UK context, most measurements of the fiscal impact of immigrants agree that immigrants from the European Economic Area (EEA)[8] have a more positive impact than immigrants from non-EEA countries. According to Vargas-Silva *et al.* (2022, p. 4, Table 1), a number of studies over 2013–18 indicate that immigrants from the EEA paid more in income tax and national insurance contributions[9] than non-EEA immigrants. Recent immigrants were found to have more of a positive fiscal impact than immigrants who had been in the UK for longer. (One reason for this is that people often wait a few years after they settle into a place before they decide to have children.) Overall, though, Vargas-Silva *et al.* (2022, p. 4) find that "in all cases, the [fiscal] impacts have been estimated at less than +1% or −1% of GDP".

You might wonder how to square that finding with the earlier claim that increasing immigration can have such a huge positive impact on world GDP. At first blush, the fact that the fiscal impact of immigrants in the UK is in the interval −1% to +1% makes it sound as though immigrants make a minimal contribution to the UK economy. Yet recall the definition of fiscal impact: it is the amount that a person contributes to public finances (e.g., by paying tax) minus that person's cost to public finances. Suppose an immigrant pays £10,000 in income tax and costs the UK government £12,000 due to healthcare expenses incurred in that tax year. That's a net fiscal impact of −£2,000. But there are additional economic contributions made by the immigrant to the overall economy, which fiscal impact doesn't measure. Let's suppose that the immigrant spent £10,000 on food, clothing, entertainment, and other consumables in a given year.[10] That is £10,000 of economic activity generated, which wouldn't have been if the immigrant wasn't living in the country. Such spending increases overall economic activity and helps boost GDP.

Let us turn now to the US context. One interesting difference in measuring the fiscal impact of immigrants between the US and the UK occurs in an unexpected form: how to factor in spending on pure public goods – like national defence – into the measurement. The US national defence budget in 2022 was set at $782 billion. In contrast, the UK government defence budget in 2021–22 was £46.0 billion (HM Treasury 2021). This accounting question matters because it's hard to imagine that the US or UK governments would significantly alter their spending on national defence even if they didn't have any immigrants.

A key finding of Blau and Mackie (2017, p. 11) is that "viewed over a long time horizon (75 years in our estimates), the fiscal impacts of immigrants are generally positive at the federal level and negative at the state and local levels". Why is that? Because educating the children of immigrants is paid for by state and local governments, but the methods of taxation used by states and local governments don't really succeed in recovering those costs from the educated children when they become taxpayers in later life. Suppose, for example, that the child moves to an entirely different state (in the US) for work once they complete their education. Then, the contributions to state and local taxes paid by the educated child will help fund schools in the state that is their new home rather than the state that educated them. But, that said, an important finding is that "An immigrant and a native-born person with similar characteristics will likely have about the same fiscal impact" (Blau and Mackie 2017, p. 11).

Rowthorn (2008) attempts to estimate the fiscal impact of immigrants on a number of advanced economies. The broad findings are in line with what we have found in the UK and US context:

> In countries where there has been mass immigration over a fairly long period of time, the stock of migrants and their descendants

normally contains a fairly wide spread of different types and age
groups. This explains why estimates of the fiscal contribution of
the immigrant population are typically quite small. The positive
contributions of some migrants is largely or wholly offset by the
negative contribution of others. [...] Estimates of the net fiscal
contribution of past immigration normally lie within the range
±1 per cent of GDP. (Rowthorn 2008, p. 577)

Rowthorn does note that there are a few exceptions to the ±1% rule, but these tend to be in countries that are experiencing a demographic collapse due to the joint effect of three factors: a rapidly ageing population, declining birthrates, and unrealistic assumptions about how the fiscal burden will be allocated across generations. However, even in these cases, Rowthorn finds that when more realistic assumptions are made that the net fiscal impact of immigration, even for the countries experiencing demographic collapse, is much smaller.

And so it seems that the third argument against immigration – that immigrants are a drain on the public finances – can also be seen as more-or-less refuted. I say "more-or-less" because, as with any measurement problem this overwhelmingly complex, it will be impossible to reach universal agreement on the conclusion.[11] What we have seen real evidence of is that the net fiscal impact of immigration, despite all the measurement problems, despite all the variation across countries and immigrant populations, tends to be pretty small. I suggest that the takeaway lesson about the fiscal impact of immigrants is that it should have no real bearing on the overall decision about whether greatly increasing immigration is a good thing or a bad thing. Perhaps the best way to draw this part of the discussion to a close is in the words of Rowthorn (2008, p. 577): "The above findings suggest that, in general, there is no strong fiscal case for or against sustained large-scale immigration. The desirability or otherwise of mass immigration should be decided on other grounds."

The three economic arguments against immigration that we have just considered have been around for a long time. More recently, however, an argument known as the "new economic case for immigration restrictions" (NEC) has been put forward by a number of academics.[12] The NEC is worth considering because it challenges the economic gains predicted from opening up borders from a new perspective, although some of the ideas it draws on have been around for a very long time as well.

The core idea of the NEC is straightforward: many of the economic gains predicted from opening up borders are generated by workers moving from low-productivity countries to high-productivity countries. But what is it that makes a country a *low-productivity* country? Generally speaking, a country can have low productivity for a number of different reasons: perhaps it has a shortage of natural resources or insufficiently many skilled workers. But sometimes a country will be a low-productivity country because it lacks properly functioning institutions that enable economic productivity, such as the rule of law, stable political organisations, appropriate cultural practices (e.g., a strong "work ethic"), and so on. Institutions, both formal and informal, and cultural practices are the products of human behaviour, built on the beliefs and attitudes of the people involved. According to the NEC:

> If immigrants harbor beliefs, attitudes, ideologies, or other factors that are, in part, responsible for the formal and informal institutions and norms that cause low productivity in their origin countries, then they could bring these ideas with them when they immigrate. (Nowrasteh and Powell 2021, pp. 273–4).

If that were the case, then the enormous economic gains predicted by the models described earlier would not actually be found because immigration on a large scale would lower the productivity of the destination countries. If the productivity of destination countries were lowered enough, the predicted benefits of immigration could be wiped out entirely.

Some might detect a hint of casual racism built into the assumptions underlying the NEC. And, indeed, history is replete with the writings of people worrying about whether – and, if so, how – immigration will corrupt the social fabric of their country. But proponents of the NEC will stress that there is no such intended interpretation to their models; instead, they are simply making the following point: if low productivity results from certain social practices in source countries, will those social practices be imported, to any extent, into the destination country? Viewed dispassionately, the NEC can be seen as asking whether immigration has negative externalities that affect the productivity of the destination country. That is an empirical question.

In their book *Wretched Refuse? The Political Economy of Immigration and Institutions*, Nowrasteh and Powell provide an extremely detailed and scrupulously researched investigation into whether any such negative externalities can be found to support the NEC. They proceed by looking at detailed case studies of immigration in three countries (the US, Israel, and Jordan) and running regressions on various cross-country data sets to see whether any correlation can be found between immigration and social practices which matter for productivity. In particular, they investigate whether immigrants (i) have an impact on the institutions in destination countries that support economic freedom,[13] (ii) increase the rate of corruption in destination countries,[14] (iii) increase the risk of terrorism in destination countries,[15] and (iv) have an impact on measures of generalised trust in destination countries.[16]

Nowrasteh and Powell's findings are surprisingly strong:

> Overall, our findings fail to detect the presence of the negative externality posited by the new economic case against immigration and sometimes indicate an opposite, positive, institutional externality in improvements in economic freedom. (Nowrasteh and Powell 2021, p. 279)

They find no evidence of the posited negative externalities. They do add a slight qualification (emphasis added):

> However, neither our cross-country findings, nor our case studies, *can rule out the possibility that, in particular cases*, immigration from one or more origin countries to a particular destination country *could* generate the negative externality posited by the new economic case for immigration restrictions. (Nowrasteh and Powell 2021, p. 279)

I think that's important enough to repeat: they could not rule out the *possibility* that *in some cases* negative externalities *could* be generated. Given how difficult it is to rule out the possibility of any social phenomenon occurring, this is not surprising. And they offer a simple suggestion for how to deal with such negative externalities if they are found to occur: impose targeted quantitative limits on migrant flows from the relevant source countries, leaving immigration from the rest of the world untouched.

When people first hear about the possibility of opening borders and increasing the amount of immigration permitted, it is only natural to worry about the potential economic consequences. What we have seen is that, contrary to most people's expectations, the potential economic consequences are vast and positive. This is important because we have already encountered excellent *moral* reasons for opening borders. It turns out that there are very good to excellent *economic* reasons for opening borders as well. In a way, this is a welcome finding: in our globalised world, there is a large amount of free movement of capital across borders. Why should capital have more freedom than people?

6. Nowhere, man

During the UK Conservative Party conference in October 2016, then-Prime Minister Theresa May took a swipe at cosmopolitan elites: "If you believe you're a citizen of the world, you're a citizen of nowhere." It was a deliberate nod to populism in a post-Brexit world. It was an easy attack on globe-trotting globalists, whom many felt were to blame for the ills at home.

It, unfortunately, also had more sinister echoes. In November 1933, in a speech given to workers at the Siemens Dynamo Works in Berlin, Adolf Hitler attacked a "small, rootless, international clique". He elaborated:

> It is the people who are home both nowhere and everywhere, who do not have anywhere a soil on which they have grown up, but who live in Berlin today, in Brussels tomorrow, Paris the day after that, and then again in Prague or Vienna or London and who feel at home everywhere. (Wikiquote 2024)

I don't mean to suggest that Theresa May intended to channel Hitler, but her suggestion that what really matters is being a citizen of *somewhere*, of being rooted in a place, unfortunately also plays into the next few lines of Hitler's vitriolic speech. He continued: "The people are bounded to its soil, bounded to its fatherland, bounded to the possibilities of life that the state, the nation, offers" (Wikiquote 2024).

Here's one attempt at a charitable interpretation of what Theresa May said that captures a major worry about the cosmopolitan conception of the Open Society. If we open up borders and allow high levels of migration, isn't there a risk that all the local aspects of life you know and love will be displaced? This complaint is like what people say about gentrification of neighbourhoods but at a national scale. In 2014, the film director Spike Lee launched into an amazing rant[1] against gentrification in New York, of which some selected portions, quoted below,[2] make it very clear what his objections were:

> Here's the thing: I grew up here in Fort Greene. I grew up here in New York. It's changed. [...] My father's a great jazz musician. He bought a house in nineteen-motherfuckin'-sixty-eight, and the motherfuckin' people moved in last year and called the cops on my father. He's not — he doesn't even play electric bass! It's acoustic! We bought the motherfuckin' house in nineteen-sixty-motherfuckin'-eight and now you call the cops? In 2013?

Get the fuck outta here! Nah. You can't do that. [...] You have to come with respect. There's a code.
I mean, they just move in the neighborhood. You just can't come in the neighborhood. I'm for democracy and letting everybody live but you gotta have some respect. You can't just come in when people have a culture that's been laid down for generations and you come in and now shit gotta change because you're here?

Spike Lee's complaint was that the local culture had grown up over many years. It had its unique traditions and practices. The people who lived there cared about their community's traditions and practices. It was *somewhere* that people called home, and they wanted to carry on with that form of life. The worry is this: how is the cosmopolitan conception of the Open Society compatible with communities maintaining their unique form of life? Won't embracing the cosmopolitan conception of the Open Society result in all of our *somewheres* ending up, like, *nowhere*, man?

A cautionary tale is provided by Venice, Italy. Venice has always been popular with tourists and was part of the Grand Tour taken by young aristocrats in the 17th to early 19th centuries. With the advent of international air travel after World War II, followed by the invention of the mega-cruise ship, the number of tourists visiting Venice skyrocketed. With that growth in tourism, the permanent population in Venice's historic city centre declined precipitously. Since 1950, the permanent population of Venice's city centre declined by two-thirds, from being upwards of 175,000 to about 50,000. In a typical year, almost 30 *million* tourists visit. And while tatty gift shops abound, replacing your sofa is tricky.

The concern about whether it is possible to maintain a unique sense of local community in the face of increased migration is perfectly valid. In this chapter, I am going to argue for two points. First, that this concern, rather than being a knockdown argument *against* it, provides powerful reasons for careful, measured policy decisions about implementing the cosmopolitan conception of the Open Society *in the right way*. Second, that the cosmopolitan conception of the Open Society is compatible with the existence of two duties regarding assimilation by migrants. These two duties, which follow from the existentialist foundation argued for in earlier chapters, serve to mitigate the Nowhere, Man problem.

To begin, I want to make one thing perfectly clear: although some of the economic analyses cited in the previous chapter assume all the migration resulting from open borders occurs in the first year, *there is no reason* the cosmopolitan conception of the Open Society requires such a policy. It would be foolish to think that a sudden, radical opening up of borders to high levels would result in anything except social chaos as cities struggled to adapt to undeliverable demand for housing, food, and jobs.

What the economic analyses from the previous chapter make clear is the potential economic benefit from opening up borders to levels greater, perhaps far greater, than we are doing at present. If that is the case, it becomes an evidence-based policy question about how to proceed. It would be rationally prudent to adopt a gradualist approach: begin by opening up borders for migration a bit more than they are at present, keeping that increase in place year-on-year so long as the economy and local communities remain healthy and adapt to the influx of people. That migration should be managed with programmes to help new residents integrate. If the predicted economic growth materialises, the additional resources it provides could be used to mitigate any negative consequences that arise. Why tolerate *any* negative consequences? Because the fundamental moral arguments for opening borders suggest this is an obligation we all have. But adopting a gradualist approach to opening borders would help ensure that any problems remain within the ability of societies to adapt. The reason why it is in the interest of societies to do so is the amount of economic growth possible: the trillion-dollar bills currently being left on the sidewalk would fund a lot of necessary services.

Why is it reasonable to think a gradualist approach would make a difference to the Nowhere, Man problem? It is worth reflecting on two natural experiments in open borders, one that has lasted for over 245 years and the other that has lasted for over 65 years. The first natural experiment is the US; the second natural experiment is the suprapolitical organisation now known as the European Union. Both natural experiments have complex histories and important legal differences, but they serve as the closest attempt we have seen in recent history to provide a partial realisation of the cosmopolitan conception of the Open Society.

In the US, freedom of movement appears in the Privileges and Immunities Clause of the Constitution (Article IV, Section 2, Clause 1). It states: "The Citizens of each State shall be entitled to all Privileges and Immunities in the several States." The intended interpretation of the clause was to prevent one state from discriminating against citizens of another state and provide a right of interstate travel. But specific details as to what that meant precisely did not receive a definite answer from the US Supreme Court for quite some time. The difficulties in providing a clear interpretation of the Privileges and Immunities Clause can be seen as arising from the inevitable conflict resulting from the coexistence of states where slavery was legal and states where it was illegal. It wasn't until after the Civil War and the ratification of the Fourteenth Amendment that the Supreme Court ruled in the 1869 case of *Paul v. Virginia* that:

> It was undoubtedly the object of the clause in question to place the citizens of each State upon the same footing with citizens of other States, so far as the advantages resulting from citizenship in those States are concerned. It relieves them from the disabilities of alienage in other States; it inhibits discriminating legislation against them by other States; it gives them the right of free ingress into other States, and egress from them; it insures to them

in other States the same freedom possessed by the citizens of those States in the acquisition and enjoyment of property and in the pursuit of happiness; and it secures to them in other States the equal protection of their laws. (US Supreme Court 1869)

The first point is that, since its founding, the US has had freedom of movement, in some sense, across state borders. Since the *Paul v. Virginia* decision, the right of freedom of movement was clearly recognised by the Supreme Court. With the development of railways and then, later, the automobile, that freedom of movement became accessible to all. If you live in Arkansas and want to move to Utah or California, you can. There is no need to apply for permission to travel across state borders or to file your intent. You don't even need to have a job in the destination state. You can simply pack up and go and try your luck elsewhere. As you drive across the border into the next state, no one will check your finances or ask if you are able to return from where you came, if things don't go to plan.[3]

The second point is that even with all this freedom of movement in the US, there are huge differences in local communities, their traditions and practices, and their unique sense of place. New Orleans, Louisiana, has a very different vibe from Fort Lauderdale, Florida, which differs from Washington, DC; Portland, Oregon; Seattle, Washington; Las Vegas, Nevada; Oklahoma City, Oklahoma; and Billings, Montana, and so on. Unique local culture is compatible with freedom of movement once an equilibrium has been achieved. The local ingress and egress of people naturally track periods of economic growth and decline, the perceived desirability of the location, and so on. Each city, having had to deal with the ingress and egress of persons over the years, would have accrued experience in dealing with the shifting population over time. Of course, there has been change over time, in each of these communities, but some degree of change is compatible with each place retaining its *je ne sais quoi* that makes it the *somewhere* that people value.

The EU provides another example, although with more recent origins and a more complex legal structure. After World War II, there was a general interest in establishing greater economic integration between the countries of Europe so as to reduce the likelihood of war in the future. At the time, because coal and steel were necessary industries for war preparations, the Treaty of Paris of 1951 established the European Coal and Steel Community (ECSC). The ECSC consisted of Belgium, France, Italy, Luxembourg, the Netherlands, and West Germany. Originally, freedom of movement was limited to those working within these industries. In 1957, the Treaty of Rome brought forth the European Economic Community (EEC), whose remit was to create a common market and customs union for its member states, which, at the time, was just the same six ECSC members. Over time, the EEC grew in importance, and in 1965 the Treaty of Brussels merged the separate executives of the ECSC, the EEC, and the European Atomic Energy Community (EAEC) into a single entity known as the European Communities (EC).

Growth of the EEC occurred in fits and starts over the decades. Here is an incomplete list of examples, just to give a sense of the messy, organic nature of the process. Greece was the first country to join the EEC in 1961 (in a limited capacity known as "associate member") but was suspended after a right-wing dictatorship took control of the country in 1967 in a military coup. The UK also applied for membership in 1961, but its application was vetoed by the French President Charles de Gaulle out of fears that British membership would give the US too much control over the EEC. (The UK later joined in 1973.) Spain's application for membership was rejected in 1964 on the grounds that the dictatorship of Francisco Franco was incompatible with the democratic ethos of the EEC. (Spain later joined in 1986.) Greenland was a member of the EEC for a while, as a territory of Denmark, but after being given limited home rule in 1979, Greenland voted in 1982 to leave the EEC due to a dispute over fishing rights.[4]

For our purposes the crucial event is the Maastricht Treaty of 1992 – the founding treaty of the EU. The EU provides yet another layer of political organisation on top of the EC. The Maastricht Treaty introduced the concept of a shared "European citizenship" for citizens of its member states. Membership of the EU provided freedom of movement, allowing individuals to move between member states and take up residence and work where they liked. And many people did.

The freedom of movement provided by the EU gave great opportunities to its citizens, with enormous flows of labour across borders.[5] But the freedom of movement provided by the EU has not erased the character of its member states. Each member state of the EU still retains its rich cultural identity, with great diversity across the local districts. France feels very different from Italy, Germany, Spain, and so on. This suggests the Nowhere, Man objection may have been overstated in general. Free movement of people hasn't led to a mass homogeneity of environs and a loss of local culture. To be honest, I suspect a greater threat to local culture comes from the spread of international corporations, offering the same generic chain stores and restaurants on every corner, making available in Italy the same products, like coffee and hamburgers, that you can get in Alaska.

Not everyone agrees with that view. Some have argued that, like Spike Lee, their local community has been transformed with the freedom of movement provided by the EU. There are three points I wish to make in response. The first point is that I am not denying that some places have been very greatly affected by the EU's free movement of people. In any social experiment of that magnitude, it will surely be the case that there are some places that have been transformed far more than the local residents feel comfortable with. I am speaking about the overall level of cultural homogenisation, in general. The second point is that people have a natural tendency to interpret any change as for the worse. In *Phaedrus*, Plato complained about the invention of *writing*, for god's sake. Change can be unsettling, and people vary both in their ability to tolerate it and how much change is acceptable. The third point is that the concern is really about the *rate of change*. Opening borders needs to be done carefully and gradually. The US had many years to reach equilibrium with its free movement of people. (And, don't forget, the free movement of people was much harder before the invention of the automobile.) The EU is attempting a similar experiment but in a much shorter period of time.

The Nowhere, Man problem concerns how migration may change the local culture of a place. Those who find the problem persuasive think that closing borders and stopping or reducing migration will solve it. It is worth noting that in some cases, counterintuitively, attempts to *restrict* the movement of people across borders can actually exacerbate the problem people are trying to address. This is nicely documented in a detailed discussion by Massey *et al.* (2016), who show how the crackdown on migration across the US–Mexico border after 1960 turned a small amount of cyclical, seasonal migration affecting three states into a permanent population of 11 million people living in all 50 states.[6] Let us consider this in some detail so as to see how, sometimes, the best response to the Nowhere, Man problem can be to allow *greater* freedom of movement.

In 1942, the US entered into the Mexican Farm Labor Agreement with Mexico. This agreement initiated what was known as the Bracero Program, whereby Mexican labourers were brought into the US to help alleviate the labour shortage caused by the number of Americans deployed in World War II. Although the number of braceros admitted into the US was initially quite small, the number of Mexican workers grew over time in response to the growing demand for labour. After the end of the war, the Bracero Program remained in place, with various amendments, until it was eventually terminated in 1964 out of concern that the braceros were suppressing the wages earned by native workers.

At the same time, US attitudes towards immigration were changing. In 1965, the US Congress passed the Immigration and Nationality Act, which imposed strict limits on immigration from the Western Hemisphere. Over time, the already strict initial limits were decreased further until

> by the late 1970s Mexico was placed under a quota of just 20,000 legal resident visas per year and no temporary work visas at all, as compared with 50,000 permanent resident entries and 450,000 temporary work entries in the late 1950s. (Massey *et al.* 2016, p. 1559)

Since people still entered the US from Mexico to meet the demand for labour, the primary effect of this legislation was to make most labourers entering from Mexico illegal. By the early 1980s, the fact that most Mexican labourers entering the southwestern US were illegal immigrants, gave politicians and pundits ample material to whip up fears. In 1985, Ronald Reagan declared illegal immigration to be a "threat to national security" (see Massey *et al.*

2016, p. 1561), and the political rhetoric became increasingly heated. By 2006, Patrick Buchanan could claim in his book *State of Emergency* that Mexico was following a strategy that aimed

> directly at a reannexation of the Southwest, not militarily but ethnically, linguistically, and culturally, through transfer of millions of Mexicans into the United States and a migration of 'Anglos' out of the lands Mexico lost in 1848. (Buchanan 2006, p. 125)

Buchanan also invoked the standard conspiracy theory of the "enemy within" by claiming Mexico was urging the immigrants to seek US citizenship in order "to advance the agenda of the mother country". Mexico's aim, Buchanan asserted, was to "attain that leverage over U.S. policy toward Mexico that the Jewish community has over U.S. policy towards Israel and Cuban-Americans have over U.S. policy toward Castro" (Buchanan 2006, p. 125). Massey et al. (2016) describe these pundits and politicians as deliberately cultivating a state of "moral panic". This moral panic legitimated calls for stricter border enforcement policies, which continue today, echoed in Trump's call to "build the wall".

Yet the truth of the matter is that much of the migration across the border was *circular*. Mexican workers would cross the border, legally or illegally, and then after a period of time would return home. Not all, but many. In a detailed study that looks at migration from 1965 to 1980 – the years before Reagan branded illegal immigration a national security threat – Massey and Singer (1995, p. 211) find that "over the 25-year period under study, 86% of all entries were offset by departures". After 1980, some years had more Mexicans *leaving* the country than entering. By the late 1980s, in a typical year, 3.1 million illegal immigrants would enter the country and 2.9 million would leave, for a net increase of about 200,000 people. To put that into perspective, in a typical year across 1990–2010, the US would admit *one million* legal immigrants (data from Migration Policy Institute 2024).

When public sentiment demanded ever-stricter border enforcement, it led to a change in the strategic calculation of the incoming immigrants. Although strict border enforcement did increase the rate of apprehension, the effect was minimal. As Massey *et al.* (2016, p. 1581) observe, "The massive increase in enforcement spending had only a modest effect on the probability of apprehension and virtually no effect on the ultimate likelihood of entry." But what *did* change for the illegal immigrants was the cost of getting into the US and the risks they had to take. Smugglers would charge more and the increased policing meant that people needed to attempt more dangerous routes into the country. So although there was little change to the overall probability of getting *into* the US, the cost and risk faced by immigrants was such that circular migration was no longer an attractive option. Strict border enforcement thus served to take a relatively minor problem of illegal immigration[7] and transform it into a greater one. Massey *et al.* (2016, p. 1592) sum up the result nicely: "In the end, a circular flow of male workers going to a handful of states was transformed into a settled population of families dispersed throughout the nation." Had the US kept the border *porous* so that circular migration remained possible, it is arguable that the US would face a much smaller problem regarding the Dreamers. And if that is true for illegal immigrants crossing a *porous* border, imagine what could have been the case if the US had adopted a more open border policy, such as retaining the Bracero Program. Perhaps the greatest irony of all is that the 1965 termination of the Bracero Program, which kicked off this whole sequence of events, was found to have made no real difference to the wages of native workers (see Clemens *et al.* 2018).

At this point I have argued that opening up borders, contrary to what some might think, does not necessarily generate the Nowhere, Man problem. We have seen this to be the case in two natural experiments – the US and the EU. We have also seen how the attempt to strictly enforce borders can backfire in unexpected ways. This matters because critics of open borders tend to concentrate only on the fact that they allow people to *enter* the country easily, but open borders also virtually eliminate the cost of *leaving* the country as well. With an open border policy, people will be much more willing to leave because they know that, should events not work out as they foresee, they can return.

In addition, I think a proper understanding of the existentialist foundations of the cosmopolitan conception of the Open Society I am defending yields two duties for immigrants in the destination country. Discharging these two duties will further serve to mitigate the Nowhere, Man problem. How so? Fundamentally, the Nowhere, Man problem results from local communities changing dramatically as the result of new arrivals. But the two duties I will now discuss would temper the effect of new arrivals on the local community.

When philosophers talk about duties, they typically distinguish between *perfect* and *imperfect* duties. A perfect duty is something you must do, always. A failure to perform a perfect duty is morally blameworthy. A standard example of a perfect duty is the prohibition against murder: there is no time when murder is permitted, and under no circumstances would there be a morally permissible way to murder someone.[8] An imperfect duty, in contrast, is something that you do not always have to do, but you are not allowed to ignore it entirely. A standard example of an imperfect duty is the requirement to help others. We recognise that you do not *always* have to help others because life is complicated and sometimes what I have to do is not compatible with helping someone at that time. If I am rushing to an important job interview, which has the potential to transform my life, and someone on the street asks for complex directions, I do not have to stop and assist *on that occasion*. However, we think that you should help others when and how you can, to the extent you are capable. Imperfect duties allow flexibility in how individuals perform them and when they judge it appropriate to do so.

The existentialist foundations of the cosmopolitan conception of the Open Society yield one perfect duty and one imperfect duty for new immigrants. The perfect duty is this: do not (initially) interfere with members of the community carrying on with their time-honoured and cherished traditions or social practices. This follows from the basic respect for individual freedom that is the cornerstone of existentialism. The people of that community are exercising their individual freedom to engage in social practices in which they have collectively engaged. A new arrival to a community is, in a manner of speaking, entering into a conversation between other people that has been ongoing for a long time. And, just like it would be rude for someone joining an ongoing conversation to immediately try to change the topic, it is inappropriate for a new arrival to attempt to change or block a cherished tradition or social practice. Let us call this the *perfect duty of non-interference*.

It will have been noted that the perfect duty of non-interference includes the temporal qualifier *initially*. The reason for this is that all communities have norms or procedures for how their traditions and social practices can be revised over time. Not everyone in a community agrees on all aspects of that community's practices. As a new arrival becomes embedded into a community, perhaps ultimately being accepted as "one of our own", the immigrant becomes – to continue the metaphor – increasingly able to participate in the conversation and exercise conversational protocols for the changing of topic. At that point, the perfect duty of non-interference will cease to bind, for the new arrival will have effectively made the transition from an immigrant to a fully-fledged member of the community.[9]

Complementing the perfect duty of non-interference is the *imperfect duty to assimilate*. It is an *imperfect* duty because respect for individual freedom means that no person can be *forced* to assimilate into a community: even native-born members of a community have, as I've previously observed, the right to go their own way and opt out of traditions or practices as they see fit, as long as they comply with the law. Every community needs to respect the right of an individual to say, "I don't feel comfortable with that." The imperfect duty of assimilation places upon the immigrant the ability to choose in what ways they wish to assimilate and the extent they will do so.

Why is there an imperfect duty to assimilate at all? It follows from the respect owed to the community by the immigrant, for being allowed into the community in the first place. Previously, I described how respect for individual freedom means that we need to respect each person's freedom to associate with those whom they choose. This is, ultimately, what allows groups, communities, and societies to form: people choosing to associate with one another and enter into a common form of life. But the freedom of association also entails the freedom to exclude: a football club is free to exclude someone from being a member if they hate football and refuse to play. Two people cannot be forced to be friends if neither wish to be. Given that, if a community is willing to allow a person inside when they did not have to do so, it is only fitting to reciprocate by trying to enter into their form of life, to some extent.

The perfect duty of non-interference and the imperfect duty to assimilate work together to mitigate the Nowhere, Man problem. Discharging both duties means that immigrants in a community will strive to respect the ongoing traditions of that community. As Spike Lee said: "You can't just come in when people have a culture that's been laid down for generations and you come in and now shit gotta change because you're here?"

7. Concluding remarks

What, then, is the overall assessment of the cosmopolitan conception of the Open Society? Is it something to be assigned to the scrap heap of history, as populist politicians are wont to argue? Or is there enough value in it to warrant rehabilitating the idea?

As I have argued, the cosmopolitan conception of the Open Society has been greatly maligned. Instead of being a threat to national security, economic stability, or national identity, it can transform the world for the better in many ways. Opening up borders would provide an important corrective to the natural injustice inflicted upon so many as a result of the birthright lottery. It would also generate great economic benefits. And more open borders, if implemented properly, need not threaten the national identity and character of local communities.

There is one last objection to consider: one might grant the natural injustice of the birthright lottery yet think that the correct response is not to allow the free movement of people but, rather, working towards international development. This view argues that by helping developing countries build their economies and institutions, the inequities generated by the birthright lottery can be alleviated without the need for opening borders. While it is true that international development has improved the material conditions of many over the past three decades (a point we will revisit in Chapter 22), the fact that we can still speak of the natural injustice of the birthright lottery today shows that development has only partially alleviated the inequities. Development is necessary to improve the lives of future generations, but opening borders, even if only slightly, provides a way to mitigate, even if imperfectly, the injustice of the birthright lottery for those alive today.

Furthermore, while it is surely important to improve the material conditions in developing countries, let us not forget that economic development is only one contributor among many to the well-being of a person's life. No country can be all things to all of its citizens, and some people born into a particular state may fundamentally disagree with its politics or values. Respect for individual freedom and the right of self-determination means allowing people the opportunity to go their own way if they choose. When faced with a misalignment between an individual's values and the larger society, some people will choose to leave, but not all. As we have seen, sedimentation is a powerful force and so some will choose to stay, working to try to bring their country into alignment with their values.

There is one further implication of the cosmopolitan conception of the Open Society worth mentioning. Perhaps it ought to be easier for new countries to be formed. When people differ fundamentally in their worldview and conception of morality, it can be difficult to maintain a stable, coherent political union in the face of such polarisation. (We will cover the subject of polarisation in detail in Part IV.) In such cases, it could be beneficial to allow new units of political self-determination to arise. If that were to happen, and borders were open, then there would be no need for extended arguments about which form of life was the "right" one. Let people move as they like, provided that they comply with the perfect duty of non-interference, the imperfect duty of assimilation, and the consistency principle. Then the division of the world into states would result in a proper group competition, with successful states being those where people choose to live and unsuccessful states being those where people flee. That would also help redress an imbalance of power between people and corporations. It is a curious fact that, in the modern world, we allow corporations to shop around countries, looking for the best deal they can get, when ordinary people cannot.

Notes to Part I: Don't come around here no more

1. Consider the wall

[1] According to US Customs and Border Protection, at the end of October 2020 only 15 miles of new "primary barrier" had been completed, with 350 miles of replacement and/or "secondary barrier" built. At the time, 221 miles of additional barrier – some primary, some secondary – was under construction. But since the US–Mexico border is over 1,900 miles long, the majority of the border remains without any barrier in place at all, other than the naturally inhospitable environment. (See Rodgers and Bailey 2020, for a more lengthy discussion.)

[2] The fact that these children had no say in a decision that affected their life prospects more than those of the people who participated in the vote is worth stressing. While I suspect few would join the political scientist David Runciman in calling for the voter age to be lowered to the age of six (Runciman 2021), the general point about age bias and how long-term and future concerns are reflected in political decision making is clear. We shall explore this point in greater detail in Chapter 3 when we consider the "All-Affected" principle of democratic participation.

[3] It will be argued by those in favour of Brexit that the reduction in the opportunities available to those children will be compensated by greater opportunities in the future that are yet to be realised, opportunities that would have not existed if it had not been for Brexit. Determining the truth of such counterfactual claims is notoriously difficult, but I think at least the following can be said: the set of opportunities available to the children of the UK pre-Brexit is not only different but partially non-overlapping with the set of opportunities post-Brexit. From a moral perspective, this gives rise to the following criticism. I venture that it will often, but not always, be accepted that there is nothing wrong with enlarging the set of opportunities available to a child such that the set of opportunities available at a later time contains all the opportunities previously available, plus some more, provided that the additional opportunities included are, on average, primarily positive and/or morally permissive. (No one would think that enlarging a set of opportunities to include only additional explicit harms is a good thing. Matters become difficult when the enlarged set of opportunities includes both harms and benefits, and the additional benefits cannot possibly be added without also adding some harms. For example, the greater communicative benefits provided by the internet are undoubtedly an all-things-considered benefit, but it is also undoubtedly the case that the internet makes possible new forms of harm.) In this case, anything the child could have chosen before is still available for them to choose later. However, when the later set of opportunities removes items from the earlier set, we have clear grounds for possible complaints, for the child may now be unable to choose something that they would have preferred. What the

Brexit vote did was change the set of opportunities for future generations in the second manner, which is morally problematic.

[4] The 12 countries were Belgium, Denmark, France, Germany, Greece, Ireland, Italy, Luxembourg, the Netherlands, Portugal, Spain, and the UK.

[5] How are we to make sense of this paradoxical result? Dennison and Geddes suggest that support for anti-immigration parties increases depending on the salience of immigration as a political issue, which is not the same thing as people's actual attitudes towards immigrants.

[6] For example, do we have special duties and obligations to family and friends that potentially trump our duties and obligations to others? Or are we required to treat all of our moral obligations to members of the community as equally demanding? Consider the following thought experiment, inspired by the famous example of the drowning-child-in-a-pond, by Singer (1972, pp. 231–32). Suppose it is your child's birthday tomorrow, and you have a spare US$10 bill that you can include in their birthday card. You know that they will use this money to buy something that will give them a modest amount of transient happiness (i.e., a comic book or some candy). Alternatively, you also can donate the US$10 to the Red Cross, who will use that money to vaccinate five children against measles, potentially saving their lives (see American Red Cross 2022). Are you morally obligated to donate the money to the Red Cross, potentially saving the lives of five children, or can you give it to your child so that they can buy a modest amount of transient happiness?

[7] Although few people argue for the most extreme form of political cosmopolitanism, it was defended by Anacharsis Cloots (originally Jean-Baptiste du Val-de-Grâce, baron de Cloots), who was born to Dutch parents and raised in Prussia but moved to Paris after inheriting great wealth from his father. In Paris, Cloots became known as a free-thinker, writing sceptical tracts against religion and arguing that the logic of social contract theory required nothing less than the formation of a single world state. Despite his privileged upbringing, Cloots was a staunch supporter of the French revolution and used his foreign status to his advantage, suggesting that the revolution was not just about the liberation of France, but the liberation of humanity from tyrants everywhere (Kleingeld 2006, p. 56). Cloots' luck ran out, though, when the French revolutionaries turned against cosmopolitanism for political reasons. He was executed by the guillotine in March 1794.

[8] I shall argue that this is a mistake and that the real problem is not globalisation, or economic cosmopolitanism, per se but, rather, how it has been realised.

[9] One peculiar aspect of this claim is that it is actually a meme that originated in the US in the 1940s, moving over to the UK shortly thereafter. Barry O'Neill, a professor of political science at the University of California, Los Angeles, wrote a short memo tracing the history of the "Great Cabbage Myth" (O'Neill 1995). According to O'Neill, the myth derives from a directive regulating the price of

cabbage seed that was issued by the US in 1943. The reason for the directive was that a California speculator attempted to make excessive profits during a shortage in the supply of cabbage seed in the US, which was caused by the Nazi occupation of the Netherlands. Although the document was only 2,000 words, it contained a number of examples of phrasing typical of a document drafted by committee. Allegedly, because one supervisor insisted that all key terms had to be defined, a *cabbage seed* was helpfully defined as a "seed used to grow cabbage". Over time, both the source and subject of the regulation began to drift and the number of words increased by a factor of ten. Why 26,911 words? No one knows why, but the precision suggests evidential backing. Numerous articles have been written attempting to debunk this urban legend, all to no effect (see Gray 2016).

[10] This stands in sharp contrast with the views of those political cosmopolitans, like Cloots, who think that the world would be better off if we rid ourselves of all individual nations, moving towards a single world state.

[11] A male oyster releases sperm into the environment that is then collected by female oysters through respiration. Once the eggs have been fertilised, they remain in the female oyster for approximately 10 days until they are released into the environment – millions at a time, depending on the species. The released eggs drift through the water until they attach to a hard surface and then continue to develop.

2. You should have picked different parents

[1] It is important to distinguish being a citizen from one's national identity. Although the two concepts overlap in many cases, some of the most difficult practical and philosophical problems arise when the two become decoupled. For example, in the US, at least hundreds of thousands of children (and potentially millions, see Nakamura 2018) of illegal immigrants (the "Dreamers") have been raised and educated in the US after being brought into the country at a very young age by their parents. They are, for all intents and purposes, culturally American, despite not having citizenship. They present an anomaly for those who argue that immigration needs to be sharply restricted due to concerns about diluting or changing the national identity by an influx of foreign nationals who, through naturalisation, increase the pool of citizens. In the case of the Dreamers, they already *have* the national identity but lack the citizenship. (And that's before we even consider the question of whether a *national identity* is the sort of thing for which it makes sense to speak of in such a monolithic sense.)

This formal decoupling of citizenship and national identity can occur for a variety of other reasons. Sometimes the decoupling is voluntary, for instance, when foreign nationals move abroad for employment reasons and later choose to apply for naturalisation. But it can also occur involuntarily, for instance, when a territory with a given national identity is incorporated into the political organisation of another. Consider, for example, the reunification of East and West Germany after the Cold War. During the slightly less than 41 years of East Germany's existence, enough cultural drift had occurred between the two states that reunification created problems regarding the respective identities of each group, which persist to this day (see Bennhold 2019). The decoupling of citizenship and national identity can also result from a combination of both voluntary and involuntary reasons, for instance, when persons flee a region of political conflict and rationally see seek asylum in another state. The millions of Ukrainians who fled after the Russian invasion in February 2022 are an example.

[2] On the extent of birth tourism in the US, Nori (2016) provides a short overview of the business. Lewin (2015) reported that one company boasted on its website of having helped 8,000 pregnant women gain access to the US.

[3] There were three conditions under which birthright citizenship would be denied but they would apply in very rare cases. First, children born to foreign diplomats with diplomatic immunity, as we have seen before in the US context; second, children *born on a ship or aircraft registered to another country*; and third, children born to parents who were *enemies of New Zealand* who had *occupied territory*. This last condition had never obtained in practice.

[4] Indeed, it is this very aspect of the acquisition of citizenship that led Ayelet Shachar to name her book analysing the global inequality generated by our current citizenship scheme *The Birthright Lottery* (Shachar 2009).

[5] Even talk of *potential* needs to be treated with caution, for a person does not have a potential *simpliciter* but, rather, has a potential relative to the environment they happen to inhabit. But, even so, we can usefully speak about differences in the potential between persons A and B. How so? Given some particular realisation of the environment E, we can then talk about the differences in capabilities between A and B in E. Identifying this difference can be helpful even if there is some alternative environment E', such that the capability of A in E' is the same as the capability of B in E.

[6] Whether this intuition is ultimately defensible is unclear. In order for innate differences in potential to be unfair, there needs to be a possible world in which the same persons would have different potentials, where that alternate world is viewed as more desirable than the actual world. (If no such possible world exists, it would perhaps be better to describe the differences in potential as *unfortunate*.) Yet whether this makes sense depends on how we understand the identity conditions for persons when we make comparisons across possible worlds. For example, if we accept Leibniz's Law, then x and y are different if and only if there is at least one property which x has that y lacks (or vice versa). So, if we imagine comparing a person x in the actual world, who has a certain potential, with a person y in an alternate world, who has a different

potential, it would seem that x cannot be identical to y *because* of the difference in potential. (Actually, the problem arises even earlier because if x and y are in different possible worlds and we think of *the-world-an-object-is-in* as a property, then no two objects in different possible worlds can be identical, according to the identity of indiscernibles.) If so, then how can we make sense of the claim that it is unfair for x to have the potential that she has because it would have been better for x to have a different potential? We would then be talking about a different person than x. There are many ways one might try to address this issue, such as by distinguishing between *essential* and *accidental* properties of a person, but all solutions to trans-world identity are philosophically contentious.

[7] For example, by calling attention to the environmentally relative nature of potential that I've noted before. Thirty years ago it was commonplace to hear people with dyslexia or dyspraxia being described as having a "learning disability". Now, it's much more common to hear talk of *neurodiversity*. Why the shift in language? Because talk of "learning disability" presupposes that there is *one correct way to learn*. If changes in the environment allow people to learn, then what we have is really just variation in learning styles.

3. The room where it happens

[1] However, New Zealand has quite strict rules on who can become a permanent resident. It is first necessary to obtain a visa, and many routes for getting a visa require the applicant to be under 55 and have an offer of employment.

[2] Even if you are a citizen of a country that is predicted to not be particularly badly affected by climate change, there is still an overall net incentive to prevent climate change over the short- to medium-term due to the global political instability and economic shocks that will result from it. Over the long-term, concerns about intergenerational justice should prompt all those with children to worry about the world that their great-grandchildren will inherit.

[3] Although the boundary problem most naturally arises in the context of democratic theory, the problem applies generally to all decision-making entities. It is always possible to ask what legitimates any particular decision-making body. The *paradoxical* nature of the boundary problem, though, is unique to democratic theory. No paradox arises, for example, if we answer the question "who decides?" by saying "the king" where the justification for the monarch is based on the divine right of kings.

[4] Strictly speaking, the Identity of Indiscernibles states that if A and B have every property in common, then A and B are identical; the version used in the text is the contrapositive of the conditional, which is logically equivalent.

[5] There is a deep philosophical literature concerning the precise relation holding between properties and predicates. Here I am assuming – as it seems is required by Geach's definition – that any definable predicate in a language picks out some property.

⁶ These are standard examples used to illustrate intrinsic properties, assuming Newtonian physics. Once we assume relativistic physics, even these standard examples become problematic: length contraction means that height is not invariant across all contexts and the observed mass of an object increases with its velocity. Life is complicated.

⁷ It doesn't have to be this particular relational property: any relational property will work. I have selected this particular relational property because it will play a role in the subsequent discussion of possible solutions to this problem.

⁸ At the time I wrote this, the US was undergoing social upheaval from a leaked document regarding the Supreme Court's imminent decision concerning Roe v. Wade, which they overturned in 2022. As an illustration of the point under discussion, consider the question of whether abortion should be legal. Who has an "interest actually affected" by this decision? Does a biological male, incapable of having children, who has no children, count? (Children affect the future economic viability of the country and make a difference for the sustainability of pension schemes.) What about a hermit removed from society, who lives alone, has no family, and primarily interacts with society via the internet, passively consuming news? We can readily imagine an "interest" held by both – say a concern in the general functioning of society – but how does this abstract, theoretical interest weigh against the very real and material interest of a female who is capable of getting pregnant?

⁹ The basic problem is that the running of modern society requires too many decisions, which affect too many people, to allow the general application of the All-Affected principle in its broadest form.

¹⁰ One question, which I will not address here, concerns whether the new types of identifiable change have *always existed* or whether they have *recently become possible*. I think, in some instances, it makes sense to say that we are finally able to identify types of change that have always existed but have been beyond the expressive capabilities of our language. In other instances, it will be more accurate to say that new types of change have become possible. Which applies, in a given case, is a deep and difficult question concerning the discursive processes of social constructivism.

4. Go your own way

¹ I include this list because I don't want to take a stand on what the appropriate unit of organisation is for establishing a moral or social norm. Bicchieri (2005, 2017) defines a *social norm* in terms of an individual's *reference network* – the people that person treats as their community who have some influence over their behaviour – as follows: "A social norm is a rule of behavior such that individuals prefer to conform to it on condition that they believe that (a) most people in their reference network conform to it […] and (b) that most people in their reference network believe they ought to conform to it" (Bicchieri 2017, p. 35). A social norm can be thought of as a person P's *conditional preference*

to behave in a certain way, given that enough other people of their reference network behave similarly, and expect P to conform.

The relationship between moral norms and social norms is complex. Bicchieri thinks that moral norms go beyond the conditional preferences which characterise social norms. In particular, Bicchieri (2017, p. 33) states: "Our commitment to these moral norms is independent of what we expect others to believe, do, or approve/disapprove of. Social norms instead are always (socially) *conditional*, in the sense that our preference for obeying them depends upon our expectations of collective compliance." But moral norms *do* shift over time: they co-evolve with values of the moral community in which one is embedded under the influence of key "thought leaders". Perhaps the greatest sleight-of-hand performed by moral education is that people are *socialised* under the influence of their *reference network* to acquire a *commitment* to something which they take to be "independent of what we expect others to believe, do, or approve/disapprove of". An illustration of how moral norms can shift over time under the influence of other shifts in social norms is revealed by a recent discussion of the history of the pro-life movement in the US by the *Washington Post* (Frank and Young 2022).

[2] Taking *utility* to be individual well-being determined by an objective set of criteria has the virtue of ensuring a common conception of the good across all persons. If utility is understood as individual preference satisfaction, as is common in economics and other social sciences, there is always the chance that two people may have maximally incompatible preferences: that the good for one person counts as the bad of another. (Think of the difficulty in trying to satisfy the preferences of a mixed population evenly split between sociopaths and saints.) However, even under an objectivist conception of individual well-being, conflict can still arise; Nozick's marriage problem, again, providing a salient example. The point is that an objectivist conception of individual well-being is anticipated to have fewer conflicts requiring resolution.

[3] Although there are a number of points of overlap in the moral beliefs held by different communities (e.g., obey your parents, respect your elders, always tell the truth), there are also stark disagreements. I am not assuming that moral pluralism is in fact the case but, rather, noting that the distribution of moral beliefs throughout the world is consistent with moral pluralism. Given that, it seems desirable, if we are aiming at a descriptively accurate theory, to take as a working assumption the possibility of moral pluralism.

[4] Note that this thought experiment does not solely consist of the act of taking a job with Exxon, allocating one's time there instead of, say, being an Extinction Rebellion protester. There are many ways to construct coherent reasons that make sense of a climate change protester taking a job with Exxon: to act as a consultant with the aim of helping shift the company's business model away from fossil fuels, or, more sinisterly, to act as a saboteur. Rather, this thought experiment asks us to consider a climate change activist who simply chooses

to walk away from that aspect of their life without giving another moment's thought to it, taking a job with Exxon and throwing themselves completely behind the project of extracting and selling fossil fuels. And, again, the point of this thought experiment is not to suggest it is difficult to construct reasons that rationalise such a choice, for that, too, would be easy. We can readily imagine a climate change protester who is fed up with living a hand-to-mouth existence and needs money to support and raise their family. The point is that we would not describe someone who would simply drop a decade's worth of climate change activism for a high salary as someone who had actually been *committed* to climate change activism, for presumably there are other means to obtain a high salary that would not involve selling fossil fuels.

5 To stress: by "price" Sartre means the psychological cost of making adjustments. He is not concerned with economics.

6 There are interesting differences in how Merleau-Ponty and Beauvoir conceive of sedimentation. For Merleau-Ponty, the concept is *epistemic*; for Beauvoir, the concept is *motivational*. We can find the epistemic sense of sedimentation in the following examples:

> When I move about my house, I know without thinking about it that walking towards the bathroom means passing near the bedroom, that looking at the window means having the fireplace on my left [...] When I chat with a friend whom I know well, each of his remarks and each of mine contains, in addition to the meaning it carries for everybody else, a host of references to the main dimensions of his character and mine, without our needing to recall previous conversations with each other [...] there is a 'world of thoughts', or a sediment left by our mental processes, which enables us to rely on our concepts and acquired judgements as we might on things there in front of us, presented globally, without there being any need for us to resynthesize them. (Merleau-Ponty 1958, pp. 149–50)

Here, sedimentation serves as an epistemic shortcut: as I move about the house, I do not need to re-infer from my knowledge of the floor plan how my current position changes my relative position to other rooms in the house. My friend's comments immediately signify, to me, meaning which is beyond that available to other participants in the conversation, without my having to make explicit inferences. That said, there are places in *Phenomenology of Perception* where Merleau-Ponty hints at a broader use of the concept (italics in the original):

> If it were possible to lay bare and unfold all the presuppositions in what I call my reason or my ideas at each moment, we should

always find experiences which have not been made explicit, large-scale contributions from past and present, a whole 'sedimentary history' which is not only relevant to the *genesis* of my thought, but which determines its *significance*. (Merleau-Ponty 1958, p. 459)

Here, Merleau-Ponty states that sedimentation *determines*, for me, the current significance of my ideas. This evaluative use of the term is closely connected to Beauvoir's motivational understanding; however, the motivational interpretation is less developed in Merleau-Ponty's work.

[7] By "weight" I do not mean our degree of belief but, rather, how responsive that belief is to contrary evidence. If believe that some proposition p is likely but I then encounter evidence to the contrary, how likely I think p is can shift a lot or a little.

[8] Two recent books that provide detailed first-person accounts of the efforts required to overcome sedimented values and beliefs are *Educated: A Memoir*, by Tara Westover, and *Unfollow: A Journey from Hatred to Hope*, by Megan Phelps-Roper. Both books detail how people born into closed communities eventually rejected values and beliefs that were originally deeply held. And both books show how undoing sedimentation involves critique originating from within the individual as well as contingent exogenous shocks, which provided an initial destabilisation, either epistemic or evaluative.

[9] Popper was aware of the challenges of striking the right balance. He wrote:

> I do not imply, for instance, that we should always suppress the utterance of intolerant philosophies; as long as we can counter them by rational argument and keep them in check by public opinion, suppression would certainly be most unwise. But we should claim the *right* even to suppress them, for it may easily turn out that they are not prepared to meet us on the level of rational argument, but begin by denouncing all argument; they may forbid their followers to listen to anything as deceptive as rational argument, and teach them to answer arguments by the use of their fists.
> (Popper 1945, p. 226)

We shall investigate some of the challenges raised by the phenomenon of *epistemic closure*, where a group is not willing to engage in rational argument, in Parts III and IV.

[10] This is one benefit of informational transparency at the level of institutions or organisations, a topic which we will turn to in Part II.

5. It's the economy, stupid

[1] Value obtained using WolframAlpha.

[2] It must be acknowledged that difficulties exist in identifying the precise conditions when robustness analysis works and when it can be used as a reliable inferential guide. Frigg (2023) provides an excellent summary of the philosophical debate up to the present day.

[3] This technique is named after the Nobel laureate physicist Enrico Fermi, who was well-known for being able to quickly generate approximate solutions to difficult problems, often based on little known information and accurate to an order of magnitude. Fermi's technique relies on being able to make reasonable estimates of the necessary variables, taking into account their variance and likely upper and lower bounds. Perhaps the most famous example of Fermi's skill took place during the Trinity nuclear test on 16 July 1945. Fermi, who worked on the Manhattan Project and was one of the observers of the Trinity detonation, slowly dropped six pieces of paper as the blast wave was passing. Since there was no wind at the time, this allowed Fermi to measure the displacement of the pieces of paper by the blast wave. Since the displacement was about 2.5m, Fermi calculated that the Trinity explosion was equivalent to approximately 10,000t of TNT (Fermi 1945). Estimates of the actual yield of the Trinity explosion have varied over the years. Most recently, Selby et al. (2021) determined that the yield was 24.8 ± 2kt of TNT, which is considerably higher than the first official estimate of 21kt. The important point is that the Selby et al. result, based on a detailed radiochemical analysis of trinitite from the blast site, shows that Fermi's estimate was accurate to within a factor of three.

[4] A recent example of brain drain in action occurred after the Russian' invasion of Ukraine in 2022. A number of news organisations reported that many young workers with highly sought-after and transferable skills (i.e., IT specialists, journalists, researchers, and analysts) were leaving Russia and taking jobs elsewhere, since they no longer felt safe in the increasingly authoritarian political climate. *Al Jazeera* reported (Vorobyov 2022) that more than *four million* workers left during the first three months of 2022 and *The Japan Times* reported (Bedwell and Champion 2022) that 80,000 Russians had moved to Georgia (the country, not the US state).

[5] For example, economist Paul Krugman credits the lump of labour fallacy as underlying the French government's 1999 decision to try to create more jobs by reducing the length of the working week. He also identifies the fallacy as being used by apologists of the George W. Bush government's failure to deliver decent job growth in its recovery from the early 2000s recession (see Krugman 2003). The apologists blamed the poor growth in jobs on structural factors in the US economy rather than on the inability of tax cuts for the rich to deliver job growth via trickle-down economics.

⁶ In 1950, only 29.6% of the US workforce was women, numbering slightly more than 18 million. In 2000, that figure had increased to 46.6%, numbering over 65 million women (see Toossi 2002).

⁷ But, as noted in our discussion regarding robustness analysis, the important point here is that the two studies are generally in agreement with both the *direction* of effect and its *magnitude*.

⁸ The EEA consists of the EU countries, plus Iceland, Liechtenstein, and Norway. Membership in the EEA allows these three countries to participate in the single market even though they don't have the full benefit of being an EU member state. Switzerland is neither a member of the EU nor the EEA but has access to the single market.

⁹ For US readers: national insurance contributions are a bit like social security payments except that they are used to fund the National Health Service in addition to providing for a small state pension when one retires.

¹⁰ I am excluding cost of housing from this quick example because it could be argued that spending on housing crowds out possible spending activity by native workers. If the immigrant wasn't renting a flat, another native worker forced to live at home with their parents would have rented that flat instead. Concentrating on food and such explicit consumables circumvents this problem: the amount of money spent by the immigrant on food isn't crowding out possible spending on food by a native worker.

¹¹ Harry Truman once asked to be sent a one-armed economist because he was fed up with his advisers always hedging their advice by saying, "On the one hand, this" and "on the other hand, that" (Buttonwood 2010).

¹² Borjas (2015) presented the first formal model of the NEC, drawing upon ideas suggested by Collier (2013). In a later work, Clemens and Pritchett (2019) developed their own formal model, attempting to improve on the work of Borjas. However, it should be noted that Clemens and Pritchett do not actually endorse the NEC.

¹³ This effect is measured using the 2013 version of the *Economic Freedom of the World Annual Report*. The Economic Freedom of the World (EFW) index is constructed from 43 variables across the following 5 areas: size of government, legal system and property rights, sound money, freedom to trade internationally, and regulation (Gwartney *et al.* 2013). Data on immigration was taken from the United Nation's *International Migrant Stock by Destination and Origin* data series.

¹⁴ Nowrasteh and Powell (2021, p. 100) state that they measure corruption using the inversed Control of Corruption indicator from the Worldwide Governance Indicators (WGI) project by the World Bank. The WGI index is constructed from 30 data sources, which track 6 indicators of governance: voice

and accountability, political stability and absence of violence/terrorism, government effectiveness, regulatory quality, rule of law, and control of corruption. Data on migration is from the years 1995 to 2015 and looks at immigrants as a percentage of the population.

[15] The risk of terrorism is measured using the annual terrorism murder rate, which gives the chance of being killed in a terrorist attack as a proportion of the population (i.e., 1 in N, for some N). Only deaths were used as an indicator on the grounds that it was clearly comparable across countries. Data on the number of people killed in terrorist attacks was taken from two sources: for all countries *other* than the US, the Global Terrorism Database from the National Consortium for the Study of Terrorism and Responses to Terrorism at the University of Maryland, College Park; for the US, a more fine-grained data was used, constructed by Nowrasteh (2019).

[16] There is a large trust-growth literature in economics, leading to a great availability of data. As Nowrasteh and Powell (2021, p. 162) note, "surveys like the World Values Survey, EuroBarometer, the American General Social Survey, the Latinobarómetro, and others have all asked similar questions about trust for decades in many different countries."

6. Nowhere, man

[1] Lest people think I am being disrespectful towards Spike Lee, this is how the speech was described by many papers. See, for example the headlines from the Guardian (Michael and Bramley 2014), CNN (Sanchez and Almasy 2014), and the Huffington Post (Oh 2014).

[2] Coscarelli (2014) includes the full text in his brief report.

[3] By way of contrast, a non-citizen isn't even allowed to visit the UK *as a tourist* unless they can prove that they will be returning to their country and that they have enough money for their trip.

[4] Greenland still retains some connection to the EU as one of 13 Overseas Countries and Territories of the EU.

[5] Indeed, before the UK voted to leave the EU, it was frequently joked that it was easier to find a Polish plumber in the UK than in Poland because so many had moved to work in the UK.

[6] This phenomenon was also covered in Malcolm Gladwell's *Revisionist History* podcast, in the episode "General Chapman's Last Stand" (Season 3, episode 5).

[7] Recall that the workers were needed and were only classified as illegal because the arbitrarily strict quotas made it difficult for them to obtain a work permit.

[8] You might wonder about killing people during war or capital punishment. The standard way to handle these cases is to introduce a conceptual distinction so that these acts, although instances of *killing*, do not count as *murder*. I won't broach the question of whether or not that response is ultimately defensible.

[9] It's important to realise that communities may place limits on the possibility of immigrants making this transition, at least with respect to some aspects of the community. Consider a thought experiment inspired by Spike Lee's remarks on gentrification: suppose a white family moved into a predominantly Black neighbourhood. After period of time of sincere community engagement, done in good faith and with a real desire to fit, its reasonable to think that they would be able to broach the topic of playing music at certain times of the day. However, it's also reasonable to think that there would be certain aspects of the community on which, because they are not Black, the new residents would not be able to shape the conversation.

References

Alexander, J. McKenzie. (2007). *The Structural Evolution of Morality.* Cambridge University Press. https://doi.org/10.1017/CBO9780511550997

American Red Cross. (25 April 2022). "World Immunization Week: Red Cross Fights to Erase Measles & Rubella." https://www.redcross.org/about-us/news-and-events/news/2022/red-cross-fights-to-erase-measles-rubella.html

Anderson, Rindy C. and Casey A. Klofstad. (2012). "Preference for Leaders with Masculine Voices Holds in the Case of Feminine Leadership Roles." *PLOS One* 7 (12):e51216. https://doi.org/10.1371/journal.pone.0051216

Bedwell, Helena and Marc Champion. (6 July 2022). "Russia's brain drain is officially under way." *The Japan Times.* https://www.japantimes.co.jp/news/2022/07/06/world/russia-brain-drain-underway/

Bennhold, Katrin. (8 November 2019). "Germany Has Been Unified for 30 Years. Its Identity Still Is Not." *The New York Times.* https://www.nytimes.com/2019/11/08/world/europe/germany-identity.html

Bicchieri, Cristina. (2005). *The Grammar of Society: The Nature and Dynamics of Social Norms.* Cambridge University Press. https://doi.org/10.1017/CBO9780511616037

Bicchieri, Cristina. (2017). *Norms in the Wild: How to Diagnose, Measure, and Change Social Norms.* Oxford University Press. https://doi.org/10.1093/acprof:oso/9780190622046.001.0001

Blau, Francine D. and Christopher Mackie (eds.). (2017). *The Economic and Fiscal Consequences of Immigration.* The National Academies of Sciences, Engineering, Medicine. https://doi.org/10.17226/23550

Borjas, George J. (2014). *Immigration Economics.* Harvard University Press.

Borjas, George J. (2015). "Immigration and Globalization: A Review Essay." *Journal of Economic Literature* 53 (4):961–974. https://doi.org/10.1257/jel.53.4.961

British Broadcasting Corporation. (10 March 2019). "North Koreans vote in 'no-choice' parliamentary elections." *BBC News.* https://www.bbc.co.uk/news/world-asia-47492747

Buchanan, Patrick J. (2006). *State of Emergency: The Third World Invasion and Conquest of America.* Thomas Dunne Books.

Buttonwood. (7 June 2010). "One-armed economists." *The Economist.* https://www.economist.com/buttonwoods-notebook/2010/06/07/one-armed-economists

Case, Anne and Christina Paxson. (2008). "Stature and Status: Height, Ability, and Labor Market Outcomes." *Journal of Political Economy*

116 (3):499–532.
https://doi.org/10.1086/589524
Clemens, Michael A. (2011). "Economics and emigration: Trillion-dollar bills on the sidewalk?" *Journal of Economic Perspectives* 25 (3):83–106.
https://doi.org/10.1257/jep.25.3.83
Clemens, Michael A., Ethan G. Lewis, and Hannah M. Postel. (2018). "Immigration restrictions as active labor market policy: Evidence from the mexican bracero exclusion." *American Economic Review* 108 (6):1468–87.
https://doi.org/10.1257/aer.20170765
Clemens, Michael A. and Lant Pritchett. (2019). "The new economic case for migration restrictions: an assessment." *Journal of Development Economics* 138:153–164.
https://doi.org/10.1016/j.jdeveco.2018.12.003
Collier, Paul. (2013). *Exodus: How Migration is Changing Our World*. Oxford University Press.
Coscarelli, Joe. (25 February 2014). "Spike Lee's Amazing Rant Against Gentrification: 'We Been Here!'" *New York Magazine*.
https://nymag.com/intelligencer/2014/02/spike-lee-amazing-rant-against-gentrification.html
Dennison, James and Andrew Geddes. (November 2018). "A Rising Tide? The Salience of Immigration and the Rise of Anti-Immigration Political Parties in Western Europe." *The Political Quarterly* 90 (1):107–116.
https://doi.org/10.1111/1467-923x.12620
Desilver, Drew. (May 2019). "Despite global concerns about democracy, more than half of countries are democratic." Pew Research Center.
https://www.pewresearch.org/short-reads/2019/05/14/more-than-half-of-countries-are-democratic/
Desmet, Klaus, Dávid Krisztián Nagy, and Esteban Rossi-Hansberg. (2018). "The Geography of Development." *Journal of Political Economy* 126 (3):903–983.
https://doi.org/10.1086/697084
di Giovanni, Julian, Andrei A. Levchenko, and Francesc Ortega. (February 2015). "A Global View of Cross-Border Migration." *Journal of the European Economic Association* 13 (1):168–202.
https://doi.org/10.1111/jeea.12110
Erlanger, Steven. (13 June 2016). "Britain's 'Brexit' Debate Inflamed by Worries That Turkey Will Join E.U." *The New York Times*.
https://www.nytimes.com/2016/06/14/world/europe/britain-brexit-turkey-eu.html
Feldscher, Karen. (4 January 2022). "Why more stringent regulation is needed for 'forever chemicals'." *Harvard School of Public Health*.
https://www.hsph.harvard.edu/news/features/why-more-stringent-regulation-is-needed-for-forever-chemicals/
Fermi, Enrico. (1945). "My Observations During the Explosion at Trinity on July 16, 1945." U.S. National Archives, Record Group 227, OSRD-S1

Committee, Box 82 folder 6, "Trinity". Transcription and document scan by Gene Dannen.

Frank, Gillian and Neil J. Young. (16 May 2022). "What everyone gets wrong about evangelicals and abortion." *The Washington Post.* https://www.washingtonpost.com/outlook/2022/05/16/what-everyone-gets-wrong-about-evangelicals-abortion/

Fricker, Miranda. (2006). "Powerlessness and Social Interpretation." *Episteme: A Journal of Social Epistemology* 3 (1–2):96–108. https://doi.org/10.3366/epi.2006.3.1-2.96

Fricker, Miranda. (2007). *Epistemic Injustice: Power & the Ethics of Knowing.* Oxford University Press.

Frigg, Roman. (2023). *Models and Theories: A Philosophical Inquiry.* London and New York: Routledge.

Geach, Peter. (1969). *God and the Soul.* London: Routledge & Kegan Paul.

Gray, Laura. (6 April 2016). "The great cabbage myth." *BBC News.* https://www.bbc.co.uk/news/magazine-35962999

Gwartney, James, Robert Lawson, Joshua Hall, Alice M. Crisp, Bodo Knoll, Hans Pitlik, and Martin Rode. (2013). "Economic Freedom of the World." Technical report, Fraser Institute. https://www.fraserinstitute.org/sites/default/files/economic-freedom-of-the-world-2013.pdf

Hacking, Ian. (1999). *The Social Construction of What?* Harvard University Press.

Hains, Tim. (14 September 2016). "Trump in Flint: It Used To Be That We Built Cars In Michigan And Didn't Drink Water In Mexico, Now It's The Opposite." *RealClearPolitics.* https://www.realclearpolitics.com/video/2016/09/14/trump_in_flint_it_used_to_be_that_we_built_cars_in_michigan_and_didnt_drink_water_in_mexico_now_its_the_opposite.html

Heinsalu, Alo, Arne Koitmäe, Leino Mandre, Mihkel Pilving, and Priit Vinkel. (2016). *Elections in Estonia: 1992–2015.* Talinn: National Electoral Committee. Translated by: Galina Ader and Mari Ets and Helve Trumann and Mari Vihuri.

HM Treasury. (27 October 2021). "Autumn Budget and Spending Review 2021: A Stronger Economy for the British People." Technical report, House of Commons. https://assets.publishing.service.gov.uk/government/uploads/system/uploads/attachment_data/file/1043689/Budget_AB2021_Web_Accessible.pdf

Judge, Timothy A. and Daniel M. Cable. (2004). "The Effect of Physical Height on Workplace Success and Income: Preliminary Test of a Theoretical Model." *Journal of Applied Psychology* 89 (3):428–441. https://doi.org/10.1037/0021-9010.89.3.428

Kleingeld, Pauline. (October 2006). "Defending the Plurality of States: Cloots, Kant, and Rawls." *Social Theory and Practice* 32 (4):559–578. https://doi.org/10.5840/soctheorpract200632428

Kleingeld, Pauline and Eric Brown. (2019). "Cosmopolitanism." In Zalta, Edward N. (ed.), *The Stanford Encyclopedia of Philosophy*. Metaphysics Research Lab, Stanford University, winter 2019 edition. https://plato.stanford.edu/entries/cosmopolitanism/

Kopan, Tal. (29 June 2018). "Government never had specific plan to reunify families, court testimony shows." *CNN*. https://edition.cnn.com/2018/06/29/politics/family-separations-reunification-never-plan-court/index.html

Krugman, Paul. (7 October 2003). "Lumps of Labor." *The New York Times*. https://www.nytimes.com/2003/10/07/opinion/lumps-of-labor.html

Levins, Richard. (1966). "The strategy of model building in population biology." *American Scientist* 54 (4):421–431.

Lewin, Tamar. (March 2015). "California Apartments Raided in Federal Investigation of Chinese 'Birth Tourism.'" *New York Times*. https://www.nytimes.com/2015/03/04/us/california-homes-raided-in-federal-crackdown-on-chinese-birth-tourism.html

Massey, Douglas S., Karen A. Pren, and Jorge Durand. (2016). "Why border enforcement backfired." *American Journal of Sociology* 121 (5):1557–1600. https://doi.org/10.1086/684200

Massey, Douglas S. and Audrey Singer. (1995). "New estimates of undocumented Mexican migration and the probability of apprehension." *Demography* 32 (2):203–213. https://doi.org/10.2307/2061740

Merleau-Ponty, Maurice. (1958). *Phenomenology of Perception*. Routledge & Kegan Paul. Translated by Colin Smith.

Michael, Chris and Ellie Violet Bramley. (26 February 2014). "Spike Lee's gentrification rant — transcript: 'Fort Greene park is like the Westminster dog show.'" *The Guardian*. https://www.theguardian.com/cities/2014/feb/26/spike-lee-gentrification-rant-transcript

Migration Policy Institute. (6 January 2024). "U.S. Immigration Trends." https://www.migrationpolicy.org/programs/data-hub/us-immigration-trends

Moyer, Melinda Wenner. (1 December 2016). "How Drug-Resistant Bacteria Travel from the Farm to Your Table." *Scientific American*. https://www.scientificamerican.com/article/how-drug-resistant-bacteria-travel-from-the-farm-to-your-table/

Nakamura, David. (23 January 2018). "In debate on 'dreamers,' an unresolved question: How many should benefit?" *The Washington Post*. https://www.washingtonpost.com/politics/in-immigration-debate-on-dreamers-an-unresolved-question-how-many-are-there/2018/01/23/72713072-0053-11e8-9d31-d72cf78dbeee_story.html

Newson, Adlai and Francesco Trebbi. (November 2018). "Authoritarian Elites." *Canadian Journal of Economics* 51 (4):1088–1117. https://doi.org/10.1111/caje.12362

Nori, Mehera. (2016). "Asian/American/Alien: Birth tourism, the racialization of Asians, and the identity of the American citizen." *Hastings Women's Law Journal* 27 (1):87–108.

Nowrasteh, Alex. (7 May 2019). "Terrorists by Immigration Status and Nationality: A Risk Analysis 1975-2017." *Cato Institute Policy Analysis* (866). https://www.cato.org/sites/cato.org/files/pubs/pdf/pa_866_edit.pdf

Nowrasteh, Alex and Benjamin Powell. (2021). *Wretched Refuse? The Political Economy of Immigration and Institutions.* Cambridge University Press. https://doi.org/10.1017/9781108776899

Nozick, Robert. (1974). *Anarchy, State and Utopia.* Basic Books.

Oh, Inae. (26 February 2014). "Spike Lee's Incredible Gentrification 'Rant' Is Backed By Solid Facts." *Huffington Post.* https://www.huffingtonpost.co.uk/entry/spike-lee-gentrification_n_4856847

O'Neill, Barry. (1995). "Cabbages and Tobacco." http://www.sscnet.ucla.edu/polisci/faculty/boneill/cabbages.html

Ottaviano, Gianmarco I. P. and Giovanni Peri. (2012). "Rethinking the effect of immigration on wages." *Journal of the European Economic Association* 10 (1):152–197. https://doi.org/10.1111/j.1542-4774.2011.01052.x

Owen, David. (2012). "Constituting the polity, constituting the demos: On the place of the all affected interests principle in democratic theory and in resolving the democratic boundary problem." *Ethics & Global Politics* 5 (3):129–152. https://doi.org/10.3402/egp.v5i3.18617

Phelps-Roper, Megan. (2020). *Unfollow.* riverrun.

Pierce, Chester. (1970). "Offensive Mechanisms." In Barbour, Floyd B. (ed.), *The Black Seventies,* 265–282. Porter Sargent Publisher.

Popper, Karl R. (1945). *The Open Society and Its Enemies: Volume One — The Spell of Plato.* Routledge & Kegan Paul.

Rodgers, Lucy and Dominic Bailey. (31 October 2020). "Trump wall: How much has he actually built?" *BBC News.* https://www.bbc.co.uk/news/world-us-canada-46824649

Rousseau, Jean-Jacques. (2019). *On the Social Contract.* Hackett. Originally published in 1762.

Rowthorn, Robert. (2008). "The fiscal impact of immigration on the advanced economies." *Oxford Review of Economic Policy* 24 (3):560–580. https://doi.org/10.1093/oxrep/grn025

Roy, Eleanor Ainge. (16 May 2019). "'One day we'll disappear': Tuvalu's sinking islands." *The Guardian.*

https://www.theguardian.com/global-development/2019/may/16/one-day-disappear-tuvalu-sinking-islands-rising-seas-climate-change

Runciman, David. (16 November 2021). "Votes for children! Why we should lower the voting age to six." *The Guardian.* https://www.theguardian.com/politics/2021/nov/16/reconstruction-after-covid-votes-for-children-age-six-david-runciman

Sanchez, Ray and Steve Almasy. (27 February 2014). "Spike Lee explains expletive-filled gentrification rant." *CNN.* https://edition.cnn.com/2014/02/26/us/new-york-spike-lee-gentrification/index.html

Sartre, Jean-Paul. (2003). *Being and Nothingness.* London, England: Routledge, 2nd edition. Translated by Hazel Estella Barnes.

Scholz, John Karl and Kamil Sicinski. (2015). "Facial Attractiveness and Lifetime Earnings: Evidence from a Cohort Study." *The Review of Economics and Statistics* 97 (1):14–28. https://doi.org/10.1162/REST_a_00435

Selby, Hugh D., Susan K. Hanson, Daniel Meininger, Warren J. Oldham, William S. Kinman, Jeffrey L. Miller, Sean D. Reilly, Allison M. Wende, Jennifer L. Berger, Jeremy Inglis, Anthony D. Pollington, Christopher R. Waidmann, Roger A. Meade, Kevin L. Buescher, James R. Gattiker, Scott A. Vander Wiel, and Peter W. Marcy. (2021). "A New Yield Assessment for the Trinity Nuclear Test, 75 Years Later." *Nuclear Technology* 207 (sup1):321–325. https://doi.org/10.1080/00295450.2021.1932176

Semyonov, Moshe, Rebeca Raijman, and Anastasia Gorodzeisky. (June 2006). "The Rise of Anti-foreigner Sentiment in European Societies, 1988-2000." *American Sociological Review* 71 (3):426–449. http://dx.doi.org/10.1177/000312240607100304

Shachar, Ayelet. (2009). *The Birthright Lottery: Citizenship and Global Inequality.* Cambridge, Massachusetts: Harvard University Press. https://doi.org/10.4159/9780674054592

Sifri, Ziad, Aastha Chokshi, David Cennimo, and Helen Horng. (2019). "Global contributors to antibiotic resistance." *Journal of Global Infectious Diseases* 11 (1):36. https://doi.org/10.4103/jgid.jgid_110_18

Singer, Peter. (1972). "Famine, Affluence, and Morality." *Philosophy & Public Affairs* 1 (3):229–243.

Summers, Deborah. (30 January 2009). "Brown stands by British jobs for British workers remark." *The Guardian.* https://www.theguardian.com/politics/2009/jan/30/brown-british-jobs-workers

The World Bank. (11 February 2024). "GDP (current US$)." https://data.worldbank.org/indicator/NY.GDP.MKTP.CD

Toossi, Mitra. (May 2002). "A century of change: The US labor force, 1950-2050." *Monthly Labor Review* 125:15–28.

US Bureau of Labor Statistics. (24 April 2024). "Unemployment Rate [UNRATE]." *Federal Reserve Bank of St. Louis.*
https://fred.stlouisfed.org/series/UNRATE
US Central Intelligence Agency. (4 January 2024). "CIA World Factbook."
https://www.cia.gov/the-world-factbook/field/life-expectancy-at-birth/country-comparison/
US Department of State. (4 January 2024). "Acquisition of U.S. Citizenship at Birth by a Child Born Abroad."
https://travel.state.gov/content/travel/en/legal/travel-legal-considerations/us-citizenship/Acquisition-US-Citizenship-Child-Born-Abroad.html
US Supreme Court. (1869). "Paul v. Virginia, 75 U.S. 168."
https://supreme.justia.com/cases/federal/us/75/168/
Vargas-Silva, Carlos, Madeleine Sumption, and Peter William Walsh. (2022). "Briefing: The fiscal impact of immigration to the UK." Technical report, The Migration Observatory at the University of Oxford.
Vorobyov, Niko. (23 May 2022). "'Criminal adventure': Ukraine war fuels Russia's brain drain." *Al Jazeera.*
https://www.aljazeera.com/news/2022/5/23/many-leave-russia-as-ukraine-war-drags-on
Walmsley, Terrie L. and L. Alan Winters. (2005). "Relaxing the Restrictions on the Temporary Movement of Natural Persons: A Simulation Analysis." *Journal of Economic Integration* 20 (4):688–726.
https://doi.org/10.11130/jei.2005.20.4.688
Webber, Jonathan. (2018). *Rethinking Existentialism.* Oxford University Press.
https://doi.org/10.1093/oso/9780198735908.001.0001
Westover, Tara. (2018). *Educated.* Windmill Books.
Whelan, Frederick. (1983). "Prologue: Democratic Theory and the Boundary Problem." In Pennock, R. J. and J. W. Chapman (eds.), *NOMOS XXV: Liberal Democracy*, 13–47. New York, NY: New York University Press.
Wikiquote. (2024). "Adolf Hitler." Online, accessed 4 August 2024.
https://en.wikiquote.org/w/index.php?title=Adolf_Hitler&oldid=3548306

PART II
The panopticon of the soul
The transparent conception of the Open Society

8. The book of life

Christian eschatology holds that on the day of the Last Judgement, every person will face a final reckoning of their life's actions. A description of the consequences of the judgement, if one's life is found to be wanting, appears in the book of Revelation:

> And I saw the dead, great and small, standing before the throne; and the books were opened: and another book was opened, which is the book of life: and the dead were judged out of those things which were written in the books, according to their works.
>
> And whosoever was not found written in the book of life was cast into the lake of fire. (Revelation 20:12, 15)

The author of the Book of Life is, of course, God; omniscience is useful for fully chronicling each person's life. But even if you are not omniscient, you can still have a pretty good go at the job. Some people have recorded their own lives to such an extent that they could be drafting their entries in the Book of Life. Of these, the most famous is arguably Samuel Pepys, who from 1660 to 1669 wrote a diary of 1.25 million words. Pepys's diary provides a remarkable insight into his personal life. He describes at great length not only mundane aspects of his daily life but also his extramarital affairs. He also noted how he buried a wheel of Parmesan cheese in his garden to save it from the Great Fire of London.

Pepys might be the most famous diarist, but he falls short of being the most prolific. His diary of 1.25 million words is more than an order of magnitude shorter than the 17 million words written by the obscure poet Arthur Crew Inman,[1] and just barely 5% of that of the journalist Edward Robb Ellis, who managed 22 million words. The most extreme diarist on record is Reverend Robert Shields, who generated 37.5 million words of phenomenally boring prose by logging his life in five-minute intervals.[2]

One problem faced by extreme diarists is what Bertrand Russell called the Tristram Shandy paradox: the more assiduously they chronicle every detail,

---

How to cite this book part:

Alexander, J. McKenzie (2024) *The Open Society as an Enemy: A critique of how free societies turned against themselves*, London: LSE Press, pp. 101–171.
https://doi.org/10.31389/lsepress.ose.c. License: CC BY-NC 4.0

the further behind they fall in the task.[3] Tristram Shandy was an extreme instance of this problem, requiring one year of labour for every day recorded. Karl Ove Knausgaard improves upon this in his 3,600-page work, *My Struggle*, but even he, on occasion, needs 80 pages to describe a single evening (Kachka 2014). But suppose we could automate the recording of our lives so that our history is written in real-time. Would we want to do that? How would that change our experience of living if we knew that everything we did was not only recorded but accessible to anyone?

Some people have tried to live that way. In 1996, Jennifer Ringley began broadcasting her life from her college dorm using a webcam (British Broadcasting Corporation 2016). In doing so, she became the first person to live life on the internet in real-time. Or at least that portion of her life falling within the line of sight of her webcam. (She added three more webcams a couple of years later when she moved.) The largely uncensored images gave viewers a rare insight into the life of a complete stranger. She broadcast her life in this way for seven years, finally unplugging the webcams in 2003.

Professor Morris Villarroel started logging his life in 2010 but, unlike Ringley, shows no sign of giving up. During most of his waking hours, Villarroel wears a chest-mounted camera that takes a picture every thirty seconds, logging around 1,200 photographs a day. Many photos feature the steering wheel of his car. In an interview with Hooper (2016), Villarroel explains he was inspired to begin this project after turning forty. "I was looking back on my life", he said, "and wondering what did I have to show? I wanted for the next 40 years to have a greater sense of what I had actually done during those years."

Technology such as the internet, social media, and the smartphone enable us to record and share our thoughts and activities to an extent few anticipated. Most of us don't engage in extreme lifecasting like Ringley or Villarroel, but many who use social media are willing to disclose a surprising amount of information about themselves. Shortly after founding Facebook in his dorm room at Harvard, Mark Zuckerberg remarked on this phenomenon to a friend:

> Zuckerberg: Yeah, so if you ever need info about anyone at Harvard,
> Zuckerberg: Just ask.
> Zuckerberg: I have over 4,000 emails, pictures, addresses, SNS.
> [Friend]: What? How'd you manage that one?
> Zuckerberg: People just submitted it.
> Zuckerberg: I don't know why.
> Zuckerberg: They "trust me".
> Zuckerberg: Dumb fucks.

Reporting on this for *Business Insider*, Carlson (2010) included the following contextualising remarks from Facebook's COO, Sheryl Sandberg: "Mark really does believe very much in transparency and the vision of an open society and open world, and so he wants to push people that way [...] He hopes you'll get more open, and he's kind of happy to help you get there."

And so we turn to the transparent conception of the Open Society. Transparency is an important tool for eliminating corruption, reducing inequality, and ensuring that meritocratic aims are pursued fairly. Transparency facilitates accountability by allowing us to hold individuals responsible for their decisions. Transparency is also identified as a business virtue, providing instrumental benefits. A 2013 survey by TINYPulse (Kruse 2013) found that the most important factor in determining whether employees were happy was transparency of management, with a correlation coefficient of 0.93. Transparency was also found to make good business sense by improving customer satisfaction; in one report, Buell *et al.* (2014) found that in restaurants where customers and cooks were visible to each other, customer satisfaction increased by 17% and speed of service went up by 13%.

Yet, alongside all these virtues of the transparent Open Society, are the concomitant vices. We are social beings and, as such can feel considerable pressure to alter our behaviour and conform. In one famous experiment, Solomon Asch showed how group pressure could cause an individual to accept an explicitly incorrect group judgement about something as blatantly objective as which of three lines was longest.[4] How does living in a world in which every aspect of a person's life can be examined by others affect one's autonomy and capacity for personal growth, development, and expression?

All this raises a great many questions. How much transparency do we want in society? Is a society where the book of life is available to all a good thing? How does a transparent society rebalance the distribution of power between individuals, corporations, and the state? Does radical transparency help or hinder personal growth? What affect does radical transparency have on personal freedom and other individual liberties? Let us now turn to these questions.

9. Unwanted inferences

One problem with the transparent conception of the Open Society is that living generates *a lot* of information. In the wrong hands that information can be manipulated to reveal things about a person they might rather keep private. Given this, it's important for two reasons to think about the conditions under which that information is disclosed. First, when we think about transparency, we typically imagine the voluntary disclosure of information, such as what you say to a pollster, your doctor, or your tax accountant. In practice, much of the information generated by living is disclosed because it's impossible to avoid disclosure, or because the actions required to avoid disclosure are excessively onerous. Second, there's a problem with the metaphor; the term "transparency" suggests a symmetric relation, just like how light travels through a pane of glass in both directions. But much of the information flow concerning people lacks this symmetry. Information flows into a corporation, but that corporation tightly controls what information flows in the reverse direction. We'll consider both of these aspects in this chapter.

The involuntary nature of informational disclosure matters because it happens all the time. If you walk down the street listening to a podcast, other people can see your expression as you react to the audio. If you try to keep a poker face so as to avoid broadcasting your emotions, your poker face and emotional neutrality is on display. Walking into a shop signals that you think that that shop is (probably) worth going into, and so expresses an implicit endorsement of the establishment. Since the political leanings of newspapers are fairly well known, reading a newspaper in public suggests to observers your likely political affiliation. And so on.

Most of the time, we don't worry about this because these small amounts of information that are released seem arbitrary and insubstantial. Who cares if you are seen to go into a Starbucks with a copy of the *New York Times*, or a Wetherspoon's with a copy of the *Daily Mail*? The problem with this line of thought is that it assumes the value of any piece of information is restricted to its explicit propositional content. However, when a piece of information is considered in the wider social context in which it is embedded, those pieces of information, when aggregated, can reveal much more than we suspect.

Involuntary disclosures become all the more revealing when we consider the possibility of aggregating the drip-feed of personal information over time. Consider the act of shopping at your favourite superstore. The list of items that appear on the receipt at checkout doesn't disappear once you leave. It's useful for stores to know what items were purchased together and who purchased them. One common way of collecting this data is by encouraging people to use store loyalty cards that offer small financial incentives for their continued use. Those loyalty cards provide one way of associating a purchase history with an individual. And even if a person doesn't have a loyalty card (or doesn't use one consistently), the purchase history can still be collected if a known credit card is used to make the payment.

In principle, even using cash would not necessarily enable a person to avoid accruing a purchase history associated with them. Face recognition technology could easily be installed at any checkout register to automatically identify people even if they paid with cash. It is easy to imagine companies choosing to pool information collected this way to develop a more fully-rounded profile of their customers.[1] As a proof of concept of something not all that different, in 2017, Alibaba, the world's largest retailer, demonstrated a "smile to pay" service at a fast food joint in Hangzhou (Russell 2017). People did have to sign up for the service, so it was voluntary in this case, but accurate facial recognition technology could make anonymous purchases essentially impossible in the future.

This matters because detailed consumer histories can reveal surprising facts about people. Consider the following example involving the American retailer Target. The problem Target wanted to solve was how to increase the number of people shopping regularly in their stores. It turns out that most people's shopping behaviour is pretty habitual; they do their weekly grocery shop at the same supermarket, they shop for clothes at certain retail outlets, and they shop for household goods at others. Target, like Wal-Mart, is a superstore that offers all of these under one roof. In principle, people could do most, if not all, of their shopping there, but people often don't because their habits are already set and resistant to change.

But there are certain rare events that *do* allow a person's behaviour to change. These events typically involve a substantial life-altering event that completely shatters the old routine, such as having a baby. In many parts of America, new births are officially registered and these data are available to the public. The problem with that, from Target's point of view, is that getting the information then is too late to be helpful – the new parents would be bombarded with advertising from a bunch of companies. The challenge was to try to identify potential new parents earlier. As Andrew Pole, a statistician who worked for Target, told the *New York Times*:

> We knew that if we could identify them in their second trimester, there's a good chance we could capture them for years. As soon as we get them buying diapers from us, they're going to start buying everything else too. If you're rushing through the store, looking for bottles, and you pass orange juice, you'll grab a carton. Oh, and there's that new DVD I want. Soon, you'll be buying cereal and paper towels from us, and keep coming back. (Duhigg 2012)

By extensively trawling through the available data, some of it collected at Target, some of it purchased from other sources, Pole was able to design a measure that calculated the probability that a woman was pregnant, given what Target knew. This was possible because there are certain changes to a woman's behaviour that are likely to occur when she becomes pregnant. For example, women in the first trimester tend to stock up on certain vitamin supplements.

Pole's measure was surprisingly accurate. In his *New York Times* interview, he told the story of a man who walked into a Target store in Minneapolis and insisted on speaking with the manager. The man said: "My daughter got this in the mail! She's still in high school, and you're sending her coupons for baby clothes and cribs? Are you trying to encourage her to get pregnant?" The manager apologised profusely and, a few days later, called him at home to apologise again. The man said: "I had a talk with my daughter. It turns out there's been some activities in my house I haven't been completely aware of. She's due in August."

Perhaps the most remarkable thing about Pole's measure is that it didn't require massive amounts of data – it only needed to look at a bundle of 25 select products. With that small set of data, Target was able to issue custom direct advertising that, indirectly, notified the woman's father that she was pregnant before she told him.

Such highly specific mail advertising is legal, but is it moral? On one hand, you might argue *yes*, since the measure only placed women in a certain reference class. Simply being part of a reference class doesn't determine anything, the argument goes. No harm was done. If we want to assign a probability to a single outcome (i.e., the probability of a *particular* woman being pregnant), we start by putting the event into the narrowest reference class we can using statistical data and then take into account other non-statistical information which can further influence our judgements about that probability. This non-statistical information can easily be more important than the information about the reference class. The British economist and philosopher John Maynard Keynes specifically warned about this back in 1921:

> Bernoulli's second axiom, that in reckoning a probability we must take everything into account, is easily forgotten in these cases of statistical probabilities. The statistical result is so attractive in its definiteness that it leads us to forget the more vague though more important considerations which may be, in a given particular case, within our knowledge. To a stranger the probability that I shall send a letter to the post unstamped may be derived from the statistics of the Post Office; for me those figures would have but the slightest bearing upon the question. (Keynes 1921, p. 322)

On the other hand, you might argue *no*, it isn't moral for Target to engage in this kind of advertising. Although any pregnant woman who chooses to have a baby will eventually have to make that known (either when it becomes obvious that she is pregnant or when she gives birth), the exact moment she chooses to disclose that information, and to whom, is her right to decide and hers alone.[2] According to this line of thinking, Target's advertising committed a moral wrong by undermining the woman's control over this decision. How is her control undermined? A person seeing a brochure advertising baby clothes and baby furniture might well assume – as the father did – that there is a reason the woman is receiving such notices. That could cause uncomfortable conversations to be initiated between people. Depending on the nature of the relationship, the woman might be forced to admit something she did not want to admit. A woman may have very good reasons for wanting to keep her pregnancy secret; she may have an abusive partner she intends to leave and does not want to have his child.

Generalising the Target example, the worry about involuntarily disclosed information is that such information, when aggregated, can be used to make inferences about personal characteristics which the individual may not want to share and which, in some cases, are legally protected (Solove 2011, p. 27). In the UK, the Equality Act 2010 identifies nine "protected characteristics": age, disability, gender reassignment, race, religion, sex, sexual orientation, marriage and civil partnership, and pregnancy and maternity status. We have seen how even a not-particularly-sophisticated algorithm can make a pretty good guess about whether a woman is pregnant; it's not hard to imagine that other protected characteristics could be similarly unmasked. Protected characteristics are protected because, historically, they were frequently used as grounds for discrimination.[3] If they can be uncovered, it creates the possibility of covert discrimination under the cover of plausible deniability: someone identified as belonging, or likely belonging, to a certain reference class might just never make it to the short list. We know that this happens with respect to people's *names*: Bertrand and Mullainathan (2004) found in an experiment that when fake resumes were sent in response to help-wanted ads in Boston and Chicago, "white names [received] 50% more callbacks for interviews." More information isn't always better.

Although it might strike us as a bit creepy for a business to be able to determine from a distance when someone is pregnant, the resulting invasion of privacy might not strike us as deeply problematic, even if, all things considered, it was wrong. Had Target used the result of their inference differently, our moral qualms might have been assuaged. We might expect such self-policing on behalf of companies to take place, for it is in the self-interest of business to try and avoid aggravating and harming the consumer. The matter becomes much more problematic when we consider what could happen when the state becomes involved.

There are a number of countries where sex outside of marriage is a crime. In Saudi Arabia, flogging is a common punishment for sex outside marriage. In Iran, the punishment is 100 lashes and, occasionally, stoning to death (United

Kingdom Home Office 2016). There are many such examples. Target's pregnancy metric, developed in order to steer more customers through its doors, could instead be used as a tool of the state for identifying potential out-of-wedlock fornicators. Whereas a doctor might choose not to report a pregnant woman to the morality police out of sympathy for her plight, a computer algorithm has no such reservations.

If pregnancy can be identified by trawling through data, what about one's sexuality? According to the 2017 report from the International Lesbian, Gay, Bisexual, Trans and Intersex Association, there are 72 countries in the world that have criminalised same-sex relationships (Duncan 2017). Of those, Iran, Sudan, Saudi Arabia, Yemen, and parts of Somalia and Nigeria allow homosexuality to be punished by death. (Syria and Iraq have *de facto* death penalties for homosexuality, although they are enforced by agents other than the state.)

Estimates on the percentage of people who are gay vary. In 1948, Alfred Kinsey reported in his book, *Sexual Behavior in the Human Male*, that approximately 10% of men were gay. A later report by Janus and Janus (1993) provided a similar estimate, suggesting that 9% of men and 5% of women could be considered homosexual.[4] In an open-ended survey of Americans in 2002, Gallup found that these estimates were far too low. According to Gallup, 21% of men and 22% of women are homosexual (Robison 2002).

In a country where homosexuality is criminalised, people will either repress their sexuality or go to considerable lengths to hide it. Given the general base rates of homosexuality that social surveys have found, governments of countries where homosexuality is banned have good reason to suspect that there's still a fair bit of homosexual activity taking place. It's too expensive for an oppressive authoritarian regime to monitor *everyone* to catch homosexuals, but what if cues could be found in involuntarily disclosed data that enabled estimates of the chance that someone was homosexual? Target was able to identify pregnant women; can big data perhaps reveal cues to identify homosexual men and women? If yes, that would allow oppressive regimes to identify potential suspects and engage in cost-effective, targeted police surveillance. Lest you think this is pure speculation, Wang and Kosinski (2018) claimed that a neural network, trained from a database of 35,326 images, could distinguish between homosexual and heterosexual men 91% of the time (83% for women) when given five images of a person, exceeding the ability of human judges. That said, whether the methods used in this study could be rolled out more widely while retaining the purported accuracy has been questioned. *The Economist* wryly noted that the inclusion of dating site pictures in the training set were "likely to be particularly revealing of sexual orientation" (The Economist 2017a).

Even if we set aside concerns about how aggregated information could be used for the direct oppression of individuals, there are more subtle uses that we need to be wary of. For instance, women who buy birth control could be targeted by pro-life or pro-choice pressure groups. Temperance movements could do something similar to people who buy alcohol. Individuals who have recently lost their job due to a corporate relocation overseas could be targeted on social media with political advertisements for an anti-immigration candidate; or, more worryingly, they could be targeted by fake news campaigns attempting to skew their understanding of the social and political landscape at a time when they are psychologically vulnerable. People who live in areas affected by certain demographic or economic changes could be identified as being more susceptible to extreme ideologies (whether it be white nationalist, radical Islamist, or other extremist groups), with a stream of notifications and stories fed to them on social media. Even if there's relatively little harm done by a company such as Target attempting to shift a few more goods by smartly targeting individuals, a real concern lies with possible political uses of the information that is available in the Open Society. We'll return to this topic in Chapter 14.

The ability to identify patterns in people's involuntarily disclosed data is not necessarily a bad thing. Many people *like* receiving recommendations from Amazon and Netflix. And I suspect many would find it acceptable for stores to automatically report to the police purchase histories which suggested harmful intent, such as buying items that, when combined, could be used to make improvised explosive devices.

Yet, when so much information is available, the risk of false positives greatly increases. Chapatti flour, a key ingredient in some homemade explosives, is also a staple of Indian cuisine. Fertilisers and acetone can be used to make bombs, as well as feed plants and remove nail varnish. One news story that went viral shortly after the terror attack on the Boston marathon by the Tsarnaev brothers involved six police officers allegedly visiting a family's house because of an accidental combination of innocent Google searches. Initial reports suggested that the wife's search for a new pressure cooker, her husband's search for a new backpack, and her son's Googling for news about the Boston attacks triggered the visit (Catalano 2013). (It later transpired that what *actually* prompted the visit was the husband searching for "pressure cooker bombs" and "backpacks" on his office computer at his former employer.) Even though the story turned out to be not quite what it seemed to be, the concern it calls attention to is a valid one. No system is perfect, and so false positives will always occur.

This is closely related to a problem Daniel Solove calls *distortion*: data collected about a person fails to represent the whole individual. Consequently, inferences made about a person can yield a skewed understanding of the true situation. Solove provides a nice example:

> Suppose government officials learn that a person has bought a number of books on how to manufacture methamphetamine. That information makes them suspect that he's building a meth lab. What is missing from the records is the full story: The person is writing a novel about a character who makes meth. When

he bought the books, he didn't consider how suspicious the purchase might appear to government officials, and his records didn't reveal the reason for the purchases. (Solove 2011, p. 28)

Even if you aren't planning on writing the next *Breaking Bad*, this point should still give one pause. Each of us interacts with many people over the course of our life, with little control over how these interactions might be interpreted in the future. Here's an example from personal experience: the father of a boy I used to play with as a child turned out to be a notorious serial killer. As a lecturer at LSE I happened to teach Saif al-Gaddafi in a moral and political philosophy seminar. Neither of those have affected my life, aside from giving me some memorable examples to illustrate the "six degrees of separation" thesis (Milgram 1967). However, other people have not been so lucky. People have been banned from travelling to America simply because a student they taught in class turned out to be a terrorist. Unwanted inferences have the power to radically alter lives.

10. Lifting the veil

In the previous chapter, we considered the problem of unwanted inferences made about *ourselves* drawn from information that we have disclosed, generally involuntarily. Let's now consider a different way informational transparency can generate problems: cases where someone *wants* something to be known about them, because it works to their personal advantage, but doing so creates negative externalities for *other* people. Insurance premiums provide a nice illustration. The key idea underlying the insurance business is nothing more than risk pooling. Suppose that house fires in a certain area occur 0.01% of the time, and each house is worth £500,000. If you could persuade 10,000 people to pay £5 a month for protection, your little insurance scheme has an expected profit of £100,000 a year, and each person can sleep easy knowing that if their house burns down they don't have to find £500,000 to rebuild.

All of that sounds good, except people are remarkably sensitive to perceptions they are getting a raw deal. Someone who lives in a thatched-roof house has a much higher natural level of fire risk than someone who lives in an igloo. Why should they both pay the same amount for fire protection?

This came to a head in the EU regarding differential pricing for car insurance (Sinner and Neligan 2011). For whatever reason (some evolutionary psychologists would suggest that men and women have deeply ingrained natural differences towards risk), women are statistically better drivers than men, having fewer collisions and making fewer claims. A recent study by Laiou *et al.* (2016) found that women, despite being 51% of the EU population, account for only 24% of all road fatalities. Given this, if car insurers carved up the risk pools taking gender into account, women would stand to benefit by having lower insurance premiums than men. For a number of years, this was done. Women could purchase car insurance from companies that only sold to women drivers, and they paid lower rates than men. However, in March 2011, the European Court of Justice issued a ruling, known as the EU Gender Directive, that made it illegal for insurers to take gender into account when calculating insurance premiums. As a result, the car insurance premiums for women rose approximately 30%. (Interestingly age is a protected characteristic that is still legal to take into account for car insurance.)

Big data creates the possibility of generating extremely finely constructed risk pools for highly personalised insurance. Doing so means that insurance premiums can differ greatly from one person to another, with one person's benefit coming at the expense of another. When should this be allowed?

Car insurance provides an interesting case study, both regarding the issue about risk pools and how the technology used to adjust risk pools bleeds into other areas of moral concern. Telematics is a form of personalised insurance which uses data trackers installed in one's car to collect information about a person's driving habits. The data trackers can measure how long someone has been driving, how quickly they accelerate, how hard they brake, how tight they turn, and the location of the car. The selling point of telematics is that it allows drivers to not only *claim* that they are a safe driver but also to *prove* that they are a safe driver. Since safe drivers have reduced risk of accidents, this could allow a person to pay less for their car insurance. GPS devices fitted to cars also, in principle, would allow the automobile to be tracked if stolen, increasing the chances of recovery.

It's worth noting what else that information can be used for. Different areas of cities have different rates of vandalism and theft. If you park your car in an area with a higher than usual crime rate, the insurance company could be notified of the increased risk and correspondingly adjust your premium upwards. If you leave your car in your garage at home and don't drive it at all, the rate can be adjusted downwards. If you drive your car late at night or early in the morning when the risk of accident is higher, the rate can be adjusted upwards. Real-time adjustment of the premium sounds advantageous, in that a person can be billed according to the exact level of risk incurred.

Yet there's a hidden injustice lurking here. Crime rates tend to be higher in poorer areas. If you live in a high-crime area and are poor, telematics can result in you paying a higher insurance premium than a rich person who can afford to live in a safer area. If you are poor, you are also more likely to work unsocial hours, which means that you will drive your car during those hours identified as time of increased risk, and hence pay more. The personalisation of insurance which telematics makes possible could very easily result in the better-off benefiting at the expense of the worse-off. That doesn't seem fair.

Furthermore, telematics enables greater state surveillance. The GPS information collected would allow speeding tickets to be filed automatically, without any need for you to be caught by a speed camera or a police officer with a radar gun. That's not necessarily a bad thing; it arguably would make the roads safer. But automating the policing of speed limits in this manner could penalise people for innocent mistakes. You could be penalised if you accidentally speed while driving in a new area and are unfamiliar with the route, or if you briefly exceed the speed limit to avoid a dangerous situation, and so on. Although it's true that breaking the speed limit is against the law, we need to distinguish between intentional violations and accidental excesses. This could be accommodated by saying that a ticket would be issued only if the person was driving more than a certain amount over the limit. Yet it's worth bearing in mind that governments like revenue, especially easy revenue. One constant bone of contention in the UK has been the perceived egregious levels of fines for parking violations, on top of how expensive parking is in the first place.[1] Once a government realises how easy it is to collect money through automated fines, the temptation to reduce the threshold above which a fine is issued would be great. Furthermore, suppose you are incorrectly accused of speeding, based on an error in the telematic data. What kind of audit trail would exist to allow you to not only appeal but to have some chance of proving your innocence?

In addition, there are privacy concerns. Who would have access to the data showing where you drove, and when? Would the insurance company be able to sell that information to other interested parties? Would that information be accessible by the state? It's easy to see that making such information available has both benefits and disadvantages. Certain crimes would become easier to solve. Fans of the first season of the podcast *Serial* will recall that a significant amount of time was spent trying to determine just where Jay and Adnan were at certain times.[2] Mandatory GPS trackers in cars would, in cases like that, be a useful source of information. However, it does raise a further question of how to confirm who was driving the car or travelling in it. We are now confronted with a new challenge whereby advocating for one form of transparency creates problems for which the solution is even more transparency. How do you confirm who was driving or travelling in the car? Why not use facial recognition? Maybe this could also be a way to reduce car theft. If the car can be operated only when a registered, recognised driver is behind the wheel, car thefts might be reduced. (But we might then wonder if the number of short-term kidnap events would increase.)

From the point of view of issues closer to home, parents would surely appreciate being able to check whether their children were driving safely and going where they said they were. (This latter question is already answerable with smartphone apps such as "Find my Friends".) However, the possibility of such parental verification sits ill at ease with the goal of encouraging children to become independent and autonomous individuals. Part of the reason why Americans have a longstanding love of the automobile is the sense of freedom that comes with it. Being able to exercise that freedom is part of personal development. After all, if you are old enough to assume the responsibility of driving, shouldn't you also be trusted to do what you say you are going to do?

Trust is an interesting attitude. There's an old Russian proverb, "Trust, but verify." It became Ronald Reagan's signature phrase as president and governed his approach towards negotiating arms control agreements with the Soviet Union. It has also become a popular phrase regarding parental strategies for raising children and managing other personal relationships both within families and within the workplace.

Trust is a relational concept; it either refers to *the belief in* (the noun form) or *believing in* (the verb form) the reliability, truth, or ability of a person or thing. When we think of how the transparent conception of the Open Society enables a "trust, but verify" approach, we need to be aware of two very different instances in which that approach can be used. In the first instance, it can be effective; in the second, "trust, but verify" is potentially harmful.

An organisation such as an insurance company may use "trust, but verify" because what they primarily care about is the *outcome*: Are you driving safely? With arms control, what we care about is whether the number of nuclear weapons has been reduced or whether centrifuges capable of enriching uranium have been mothballed. As a means of enforcing outcomes, "trust, but verify" can be very effective.

However, in cases where we primarily care about a *relationship* between two people, "trust, but verify" is potentially harmful. If A trusts B, then that means that A believes in the reliability, truthfulness or ability of B. Yet the act of verifying suggests that A, in fact, does not fully believe in the reliability, truthfulness or ability of B; if A did, why would A need to verify? Consider a micro-manager who always verifies that their personal assistant puts stamps on the post. In what sense, if any, is that behaviour compatible with the state of *believing* that the personal assistant was reliable? Verification is associated with *mistrust* rather than trust. That's the whole *reason* why Reagan adopted his signature phrase with the Soviets.

One problem is that much of life involves interactions where we care *both* about the outcome and the relationship. In these instances, we need to understand the pros- and cons- of "trust, but verify". With respect to insurance companies, or your bank, we may be much less concerned about the relationship since few people have a close connection to their insurer or bank. However, in parent-child relationships, "trust, but verify" needs to be used sparingly so as to preserve the feelings of mutual respect and growing recognition of independence that happens as the child ages. The question of how to manage "trust, but verify" with respect to the state is a matter of great importance. An important component of state legitimacy in democratic societies is whether people trust the state. We can't all be present everywhere to monitor each vote in each election – much less be present in every legislative debate. If the state continuously employs "trust, but verify" with its citizens, will that signal of mistrust be reciprocated, eroding trust in the government and people's belief in the legitimacy of the state?

It may seem that we have moved quite far afield from the original question of what kind of information is acceptable to use in creating risk pools, but we really haven't. When it comes to informational transparency, the Open Society presents a multi-dimensional problem. One cannot answer questions about what information is acceptable to use for certain purposes without also addressing who may access that information and what kinds of controls and protections exist. Information collected for innocent purposes can just as well be used for nefarious purposes. This leads us towards two other classes of issues Solove identifies – problems of *exclusion* (do people know how their information is being used?) and *secondary use* (will information obtained for one purpose be used for another purpose without their consent?). Underlying all of these are questions of trust: to whom will we entrust our information and how can we ensure that our trust is not misplaced?

Let us revisit the question of personal information use in the Open Society, but from the point of view of health policy. Like car insurance, medical insurance references a number of individual factors that are under a person's control: how often they exercise, their diet, and whether they smoke or drink. However, a person's health also depends on factors that they have no control over, for instance, their genetic inheritance. Both of these interact to produce the person's health state, along with a chance component.

Genetic testing used to be something out of science fiction; today, you can order a home testing kit from a company such as 23andMe for £149. It's important to distinguish between genetic *testing* and genetic *sequencing*. Genetic testing looks at specific sites on the genome in order to identify which variants of those genes a person has. This allows us to say if the person carries the gene for Tay-Sachs disease, cystic fibrosis, beta thalassemia, and other disorders. It can also track genetic associations associated with less important traits such as earwax type, finger length ratio, your ability to perceive bitter tastes, and the photic sneeze reflex. Genetic sequencing (also known as "whole genome sequencing"), in contrast, identifies the arrangement of nucleotide base pairs which constitute each person's unique genetic inheritance. (Unless you have an identical twin.)

If genetic testing seems comparatively cheap, the decline in the cost of genetic sequencing over the past two decades is nothing less than astonishing. According to the National Human Genome Research Institute, the Human Genome Project (HGP) invested approximately $2.7 *billion* on the technology and research activities associated with the HGP. The actual cost of sequencing the first human genome in 2003, according to their estimates, was about $300 million, depending on how you do the accounting (Wetterstrand 2024).

Since then, the decline in the cost of genetic sequencing has decreased faster than Moore's law. If you consider Moore's law that computing power doubles every two years and assume that the cost of manufacturing is constant, then that would mean that the cost of a given unit of computing power halves every two years. Figure 10.1 shows a plot tracking the decline in cost for sequencing an entire genome since 2001, contrasting it with a hypothetical decline in cost corresponding to Moore's Law. The cost for genetic sequencing roughly kept pace with Moore's law until 2008, when the original method of sequencing (Sanger sequencing) was replaced with the aptly named "Next-Gen" sequencing methods. By 2015, the cost of sequencing a whole genome was approximately $1,500. According to Jay Flatley, the CEO of Illumina, "[G]etting to a $500 genome is technologically possible, and we think certainly there's potential far beyond that" (Tirrell 2015).

Sequencing an individual genome is priced at a level that makes it feasible for a developed economy to start doing that for every one of its citizens. In 2015, slightly fewer than 4 million children were born in the United States, a figure relatively constant year-on-year (Martin *et al.* 2015). Assuming a cost of genetic sequencing of $1,500 per person, it would cost $6 billion to sequence each baby born in 2015. That sounds like a lot of money until you compare it to the overall budget. In 2015, the total expenditure by the US government was approximately $3.69 *trillion*. Genome sequencing for each new citizen would have required only 0.163% of the yearly budget. To put *that* in perspective,

Figure 10.1: The decline in the cost of sequencing an individual human genome

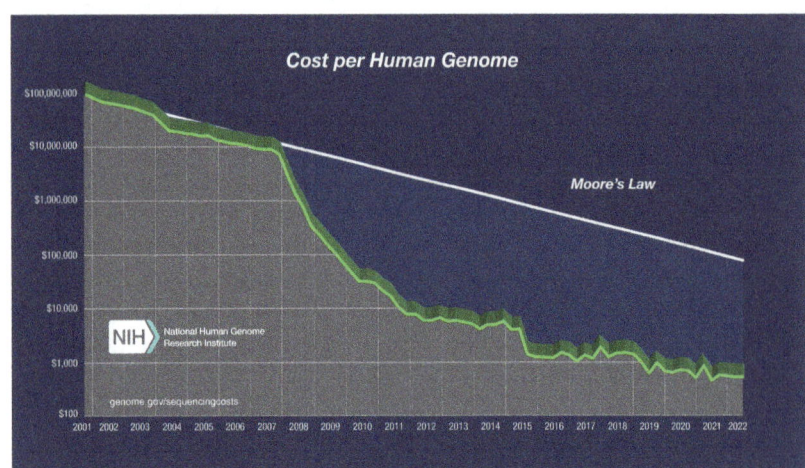

Source: Wetterstrand (2024). Courtesy: National Human Genome Research Institute, Public Domain (https://www.genome.gov/about-genomics/fact-sheets/DNA-Sequencing-Costs-Data).

the median US income in 2015 was $55,775 (Posey 2016), of which 0.163% is $90.91, or slightly shy of the price of 19 Big Macs (The Economist 2015). Future technological improvements will only make mass sequencing of the entire population cheaper.

Consequently, the following scenario is a real possibility. Medical insurance companies could require individuals to submit a genetic profile (partial or complete) so that they can be grouped into an appropriate risk pool. This information could be used along with an individual's aggregated consumer profile to determine whether someone has taken reasonable precautions to avoid triggering certain dispositions towards illnesses they might naturally have due to their genetic endowment. For example, someone with a disposition for type 2 diabetes, which can be prevented or delayed by following a healthy diet, could be determined to have not taken suitable precautions given their consumer profile. A person's consumer profile is an imperfect guide to their lifestyle; simply because someone bought eight cans of lager does not mean that they drank all or any of them. But years of data would provide enough evidence to significantly shift the balance of probabilities of whether a person maintained a healthy lifestyle.

From a philosophical point of view, one problem raised by all of the information which will become available about a person is how we (or society) assigns responsibility for what happens to them. This is a particularly acute problem in the case of healthcare, where demand is potentially limitless but resources scarce. How should we treat people in need of a liver or lung transplant where the need for that transplant is due to lifestyle choices? Should the position of a person on a waiting list be determined solely on the basis of need, regardless of the cause, or should there be a "merit" element to it, where a person partially responsible for their health condition is demoted to a lower place on the list? Should a person who drives their car into a high-crime area be subjected to higher premiums (or a higher deductible if something untoward should happen)? Similar scenarios are easily envisioned. Should the generosity of unemployment benefits be conditional on the work history of a person? The possibilities multiply.

Underlying these issues is a question concerning the aspects of one's life over which one has control. One intuition many people have is that they need less protection from things that result from factors over which they have control. For example, why should society worry about how a person's information is used if they ultimately have control over how that information is released? If you don't want expensive car insurance, then buy the right kind of car, drive safely, and keep a clean record. When it comes to healthcare, then exercise, eat healthily, and don't drink too much. Read the fine print, look out for your own interests, and take care of yourself.

But what do we mean by "control"? Let's begin with the following definition by Dennett (1984): "*A controls B* if and only if the relation between A and B is such that A can *drive* B into whichever of B's normal range of states A wants B to be in." The idea behind this definition is that A has "control" over B exactly when there is robustness under counterfactual variations of the desires of A: if A were to change her mind about the state she wanted B to be in, A would still be able to drive B into that state.

There are a couple of features to note regarding this concept of control. First, there is an implicit dependence on context. This is clear from an example Dennett gives involving a person using a "wireless radio 'remote control' system" (how quaint that description sounds, today!) to control a model aeroplane. If the radio system loses power, then the person no longer has control over the model aeroplane. The concept of control, then, does not just involve a mere relationship between the person and the aeroplane, but a *three-way* relationship between the person, the aeroplane, and the environment.[3]

A second feature is that, in many cases, whether a person has control over something depends on the resources at their disposal, which can be brought to bear on the control problem. Call this the *budget* of the person.[4] For example, at present, I have some control over where I live; if I had a higher salary or more investments, I would have more control over where I live because then the set of possibilities would be larger. Although it's natural to think of a person's budget as referring to the wealth they have at their disposal, it also includes resources such as free time and social capital.

Putting these two aspects of control together, a third feature immediately emerges: control isn't necessarily preserved under aggregation. Suppose that a person A has three areas of her life which matter to her: B_1, B_2, and B_3. It can be the case that A can control B_1 or B_2 or B_3 *in isolation* (so, in a sense, A has control over everything which matters to her), yet at the same time, A cannot control *the collection of B_1 and B_2 and B_3*. Why? When A controls B_1, it might either alter the environment in which A operates, or it might involve expenditure of some of A's budget. That then changes the conditions under which A approaches the control problem of either B_2 or B_3. A's ability to drive B_2 or B_3 into a particular desired state prior to driving B_1 into a certain state, might now be impaired. This also shows that when we think about multiple control problems faced by an agent, there can be *path dependence*.

The flip response is to say that this is nothing more than the basic fact that "you can't do everything". However, this misses the deeper point that when faced with issues such as how Target uses people's data to make inferences about their life, or how insurance companies use information to calculate rates, or what your genome reveals about your tendency to develop diabetes or dementia later in life, it's all too easy for people, organisations, or the government to view those particular cases *in isolation* and say that worries such as those I've expressed aren't a big issue because if a person feels uncomfortable they can avoid it. (That is, they can exercise control over the relevant area of their life.) But life is an *aggregate* control problem, where people are worried about controlling the *collective*. Our limited resources often mean we have to make cost-benefit calculations and relinquish control over part of our life simply because other things matter to us more. Yet the fact we *acquiesce* to something doesn't mean that we *accept* it.

We've covered a lot of ground in this chapter, but the underlying theme that has been driving the discussion is the following: a lot of the time people accept a great deal of transparency regarding their personal information because of the alleged benefits it gives them. But this is a devil's bargain for two reasons. First, social practices that require the disclosure of personal information because it benefits one category of person can create negative externalities for people from other categories. (This was illustrated in the discussion of using telematic data for car insurance.) Second, the alleged benefits of social practices that require the disclosure of personal information should be treated with scepticism, given the possibility of unexpected negative side-effects. (This was illustrated in the discussion of using genomic testing for health insurance.)

Both of these points matter because, although they raise concerns about how voluntarily disclosed personal information is used, they are generally not seen as providing decisive reasons against, in principle, rolling out social practices that use such information. Why is that? Because, in almost all cases, it can be argued that if someone is concerned about how their personal information might be used (for or against them) in particular instances, they have the ability to do something about it. As I said, people are thought to have *control* over the relevant aspect of their life, and could do something about it, if the way in which their personal information was used (or misused) was a cause of concern. However, as I then argued, even if that is true on a case-by-case basis, it probably isn't true for a person's life *in aggregate*, because control isn't necessarily preserved under aggregation. And this establishes that the argument for why use of voluntarily disclosed personal information is not so bad (because people can always do something about it if it concerns them) is actually based on a false assumption.

The mere process of living generates a lot of information, much more than we can ever really comprehend. Is it a bad thing that, in the contemporary world, we are implicitly broadcasting all the time whether we like it or not? (Or, for that matter, whether we choose to or not?) This is the topic to which we turn in the next chapter.

11. Letting it all hang out

In the second quarter of 2017, Facebook had 2 billion active users worldwide. At the same time, Instagram boasted 800 million active users, Twitter (now X) 330 million, Pinterest 175 million, LinkedIn 467 million, and the messaging service WhatsApp over 1.3 billion users. By the fourth quarter of 2022, Facebook had added almost another billion active users, growing to 2.96 billion (Statista 2023a). Instagram had 1.28 billion users at the end of 2022, Twitter 368 million (Statista 2022a), and WhatsApp 2.24 billion (Statista 2022b). With the exception of Twitter, the major social media networks saw nothing but growth during that five-year period. In China, the largest social network, WeChat, had over 1.3 billion users at the end of 2022 (Statista 2023c), with 586 million active users on Weibo, the Chinese equivalent of Twitter (Statista 2023b). That's a lot of people broadcasting information about themselves.

The extraordinary growth of social media over the past decade is one of the greatest uncontrolled experiments we have conducted on ourselves. We are a social species, but the physical environment in which humans evolved is so vastly different from the environment on social media that it's not at all obvious that our natural dispositions, developed for face-to-face interactions in small groups, translate well to the new setting.[1] Here are a number of important differences: the relative *anonymity* of interactions, the *speed* at which communication can take place, the *scale* on which interactions can take place, and the temporal *endurance* of information thus generated. Let's work through these four differences in turn.

Consider anonymity. What is different from an interaction on social media and an ordinary interaction in the real world? Suppose I am at a dinner party with a group of friends and I make an assertion about politics. Although every person at the dinner party will have heard the assertion, my act of making the assertion ceases to exist once I have finished speaking. The only remaining trace of it will be a representation in the memory of my friends. If the assertion was controversial and my friends decide to talk to others about it once the dinner party is over, all they can do is *report* what I said as they remember it. The original speech act cannot be shared or reproduced. In some cases – if I say something particularly memorable or shocking – they might remember my assertion verbatim, but for most communications such exact recall is rare. Hence, if my friends decide to share what I said, what they communicate to others can only be a paraphrased version of their understanding of what I meant.

How do we understand what a speaker means? In a famous article, the philosopher of language H. Paul Grice offered the following analysis of attributing meaning to a speaker A who makes an utterance x:

> A must intend to induce by x a belief in an audience, and he must also intend his utterance to be recognized as so intended. But these intentions are not independent; the recognition is intended by A to play its part in inducing the belief, and if it does not do so something will have gone wrong with the fulfillment of A's intentions. Moreover, A's intending that the recognition should play this part implies, I think, that he assumes that there is some chance that it will in fact play this part, that he does not regard it as a foregone conclusion that the belief will be induced in the audience whether or not the intention behind the utterance is recognized. (Grice 1957, pp. 383–84)

That is, in order to say that a person A means p by x, three conditions have to hold. First, A intends to get the audience to believe p by means of x. Second, A also intends the audience to recognise that A *wants* them to come to believe p by x. Third, the audience does, at least in part, come to believe p because they recognise this intention on A's behalf.

If we accept Grice's account of speaker meaning, a number of differences between a social media interaction and an ordinary interaction are revealed. First, in an ordinary interactive context, such as a dinner party or a board meeting, the identity of the audience is fixed. Given this, the speaker then has the ability to select his or her words with the particular audience in mind, knowing what forms of communication are judged as acceptable by that audience. Second, the intention of the speaker, in cases of ambiguity, is frequently disambiguated by context or the shared background knowledge the audience possesses of the speaker. Both of these are important in ensuring effective communication, and both help to prevent radical misinterpretation of what the speaker says.

The difficulty arises when people post some x on social media, and x becomes detached from the speaker, the intended audience, and the context of its generation. The x can also be trivially reproduced in new contexts and to new audiences. Since the audience is no longer fixed, the ability to disambiguate or clarify the intention of the speaker by appealing to context or the speaker's background is lost.

In one sense, this is nothing new; in many respects, it is similar to the traditional publishing model where an author generates a text and releases it into the world. Yet there are some important dissimilarities. First, when we consider the traditional production of texts for public consumption, the authors or artists were aware of the fact that they were relinquishing control over who will encounter their work. Second, when people generated texts for publication or presentation in the past, they were *intending* to communicate to a wide audience; they *wanted* to broadcast their message beyond a small set of people. Both of these factors would focus the mind on the form of expression used. Social media, by contrast, can encourage an illusive understanding of the nature of the audience, encouraging the adoption of an informal and unguarded tone. One may believe that one is just communicating with one's friends or followers. Yet the ability of social media to reach an audience very different than the one a person intended to address can have phenomenally damaging consequences, in two different ways.

First, national security services routinely trawl social media sites as part of their intelligence operations. This worked to the disadvantage of Leigh Van Bryan, who in 2012 tweeted a friend to say, "Free this week, for quick gossip/prep before I go and destroy America." Stripped of any context about the intention of the speaker, one faces the interpretive problem that "destroy" has a number of meanings, some innocuous, some not. We can speak of a sports team destroying their opponent (meaning, to defeat them in a match), a student destroying a test (meaning, to do well on it), a person destroying a hamburger (meaning, to eat in an uninhibited manner), or a person getting destroyed at a party (meaning, to become very intoxicated). Unfortunately, "destroy" also means "to demolish". When Van Bryan and his friend Emily Bunting arrived at Los Angeles International Airport, they were detained by the US Department for Homeland Security and questioned for five hours before being sent back to the UK (BBC 2012).

Second, posts on social media are easily transmitted, thereby changing the membership of the audience after the time of the original utterance. Since the expressed message is unchanged, each new recipient will view it as the speaker making the same utterance again, and will attempt to extract the speaker's meaning. This is problematic. Following Grice, although I may attempt to induce the belief p in audience A by uttering x, it does not follow that I would attempt to induce the same belief p in audience A' by making the same utterance x – even if every member of A is also part of A'. A form of communication, acceptable to audience A because they know the speaker and thus understand the intended interpretation of x, may not be acceptable to the wider audience A' because they lack the necessary information to know the speaker's intent. The anonymity of the speaker to the new audience thus creates a blank slate regarding the new audience's understanding of the speaker's intention, only constrained by a literal reading of the text. Statements involving irony or humour are thus particularly open to being misconstrued.

Let us now add to the mix how issues of both *speed* and *scale* affect the interaction. Jon Ronson, in *So You've Been Publicly Shamed*, discusses the role played by social media in the phenomenon of public shaming. Shame has played a part in all societies as a form of punishment and social control, but it has recently taken on a new, sinister, arbitrary, and disproportionate character when combined with social media.

In December 2013, Justine Sacco was travelling from the US to South Africa and she decided to pass time by tweeting sarcastic jokes and commentary about her experiences along the way. A typical example was her observation from Heathrow: "Chili – cucumber sandwiches – bad teeth. Back in London!" Where things went awry is when she decided to send one last tweet before boarding the plane to South Africa. She tweeted: "Going to Africa. Hope I don't get AIDS. Just kidding. I'm white!"

There are a lot of ways a person can read that last tweet. A charitable reading would interpret it as a send-up of white privilege, written by someone pretending to be an ugly American, expressing racist stereotypes. In doing so, it could also be seen as a historical allusion to a mistake made in the US when the AIDS epidemic first emerged there. (This might be an overly charitable reading.) How so? Because the AIDS epidemic in America was initially written off by many as a "gay cancer" (Kerr 2020). It was only when AIDS made inroads into the heterosexual population that it began to be taken seriously. Reading these historical allusions into the subtext of Sacco's message would have been a charitable interpretation.

When Justine landed in South Africa, she found the internet had not been charitable. In the space of 11 hours, her tweet had moved from being seen by her 170 followers to being the *top worldwide trend* on Twitter. Some of the commentary quoted by Ronson is disturbing for the sheer glee some people took in holding her feet to the fire:

> 'In light of @JustineSacco disgusting racist tweet, I'm donating to @care today' and, 'How did @JustineSacco get a PR job?! Her level of racist ignorance belongs on Fox News. #AIDS can affect anyone!' and, 'No words for that horribly disgusting, racist as fuck tweet from Justine Sacco. I am beyond horrified' and, 'I'm an IAC employee and I don't want @JustineSacco doing any communications on our behalf ever again. Ever' and, 'Everyone go report this cunt @JustineSacco' and, from her employers, IAC, 'This is an outrageous, offensive comment. Employee in question currently unreachable on an intl flight' and, 'Fascinated by the @JustineSacco train wreck. It's global and she's apparently *still on the plane*' and, 'All I want for Christmas is to see @JustineSacco's face when her plane lands and she checks her inbox/voicemail' and, 'Oh man, @JustineSacco is going to have the most painful phone-turning-on moment ever when her plane lands.' (Ronson 2015, p. 65)

Justine was fired from her job.

There are a couple of important things to note about this. First, interpreting the tweet as a "horribly disgusting, racist as fuck tweet" is making a claim about speaker meaning. During the 11 hours that Justine was on the plane, the rapid expansion of the audience from her original pool of 170 followers to an audience of *millions*, the vast majority of who did not know her, meant that the speaker's intention was largely unknown. In the absence of any knowledge of the speaker or further contextual understanding, people were free to attribute to her whatever intention they wished due to the absence of evidence. And, once the tweet went viral, crowd dynamics and herding behaviour took over.

Second, it's worth remembering that the vast majority of us *never* address an audience of several million people. Because we never expect our words to be heard, read, or listened to by an audience of millions, we don't usually choose our words with that in mind. Most of us have, at one time or another, made a comment which, taken out of context and broadcast to several million people, could result in a fate similar to Justine's. But most of us haven't suffered that kind of public scrutiny of our carelessly chosen words, and most of us will continue to be lucky in the future. In this way, public shaming seems both arbitrary and disproportionate.

The important lesson to be drawn from this, is how the phenomenon of public shaming is a predictable consequence of how speaker meaning can be misattributed when the anonymity of the speaker is combined with a rapid scaling up of the size of the audience. Figuring out what a person intends is difficult, and we rely on a lot of contextual knowledge, along with background knowledge of the speaker, to do so. And, most importantly, in our day-to-day social interactions, if a friend says something rude or unkind or unpleasant, but is otherwise thought to be a good person, we look to environmental or external factors to explain the behaviour, rather than appealing to character flaws. Context, then, is crucial.

Yet Twitter almost seems to be designed to *encourage* people to take things out of context. There's only so much you can say, after all, in 140 (later, 280) characters.[2] Twitter isn't the only form of social media susceptible to the charge; comments on Facebook and photographs on Instagram or Snapchat can similarly mislead. The danger in all of these instances is that we experience the world and understand our actions through the omnipresent background context provided by our own internal narrative. Because *we* typically understand what we intend to mean by what we say and do, it's not normal for us to step back and reflect on how our statements and actions could be misinterpreted. However, when the background context exists only within our head, that gets lost over the internet.

What this chapter illustrates is yet another way that the radical transparency offered by the Open Society can be problematic. Digital communication via social media differs sufficiently from ordinary methods of face-to-face communication that our informal understanding of how to determine a speaker's meaning (e.g., Grice's theory) cannot simply be carried over without modification. This means that it is very easy for miscommunication to occur, with unusually harmful consequences for persons involved given the four factors that distinguish communication via social media from other forms (i.e., anonymity, speed, scale, and endurance).

It is important to note that the concerns raised here about miscommunication are ones that occur in the context where I am explicitly restricting attention to cases where people are engaged in *good faith* communication. Good faith communication already presents a number of problems regarding interpretation of meaning because of the possible uses of humour and irony (and other rhetorical devices), which are well-known to present risks of being misunderstood. *Bad faith* communication, in contrast, involves people deliberately attempting to mislead or spread misinformation. The problem of bad faith communication is, in some sense, not new. There have always been liars and hucksters and people willing to say anything you want to hear in order to get you to do something for them. What the internet and social media enable is for this bad faith communication to occur on a scale which was previously unimaginable. One interesting question this presents is, how do we decide who to trust? As that question is, I believe, deeply connected to the re-emergence of tribalism and the rejection of the communitarian conception of the Open Society, that investigation will be postponed until Chapter 24 of Part IV.

12. Don't you forget about me

In *Funes the Memorious*, Jorge Luis Borges tells the story of Ireneo Funes, who, after injuring his head in a fall from a horse, develops the ability to remember everything that happens to him. Such an ability at first blush sounds desirable. Think about how much time you would save! Passing the written test at the local department of motor vehicles would be a cinch, you'd be the most sought-after team member for the next pub quiz, and filing your taxes would be trivial.

Except, in these fantasies, there's one crucial assumption: we only remember the things we *want* to remember. We envision ourselves like a modern-day John von Neumann, who purportedly could recall every book he'd ever read (Goldstine 1980). We don't envision our memories polluted with all the *faux pas* we have ever made, all the rejections we have experienced, and all the suffering of loved ones in their last moments. When those memories are included, Funes' gift no longer seems quite as attractive.

A select group of people actually do have the ability to remember everything that happens to them. The first person to be diagnosed with Highly Superior Autobiographical Memory (HSAM) was Jill Price, who emailed Dr James Mc-Gaugh, the director of UC Irvine's Center for the Neurobiology of Learning and Memory, on 8 June 2000 to complain about a problem with her memory. The problem? She remembered too much. From her point of view, the memories inserted themselves into her consciousness in a manner beyond her control and often against her will (McRobbie 2017).

Since McGaugh's discovery of HSAM, around 60 people worldwide are now thought to have the condition. One common reaction, although not universally shared, is that HSAM is both a blessing and curse. In an interview with the BBC, Nicole Donohue, who has HSAM, said: "It can be very hard to forget embarrassing moments. You feel the same emotions – it is just as raw, just as fresh […] You can't turn off that stream of memories, no matter how hard you try." Another person with the condition, Nima Veiseh, agreed: "It is like having these open wounds – they are just a part of you" (Robson 2016). Yet, at the same time, Nima put forward an interesting theory about how having HSAM has made him a better person: "Some say 'forgive and forget', but since forgetting is a luxury I don't have, I need to learn to genuinely forgive. Not just others, but myself as well."

The idea that forgetting is advantageous has been around for a while. Back in 1890, William James wrote in *The Principles of Psychology* that "If we remembered everything, we should on most occasions be as ill off as if we remembered nothing." The virtues of forgetting have perhaps been underappreciated, though, since we generally tend to undervalue that which we experience in excess. Furthermore, the virtues of having a good memory have been noted for ages; Socrates, in *The Phaedrus*, argued that the invention of writing was bad because "this discovery of yours will create forgetfulness in the learners' souls, because they will not use their memories; they will trust to the external written characters and not remember of themselves."

If forgetting is a virtue, what are we to make of an Open Society in which our personal information will be always available, instantly discoverable, and impossible to forget? Removing information from the internet has become the modern-day analogue of a Sisyphean task. Nima's challenge of learning how to live when forgetting is not an option is one which all of us increasingly face. And although the "right to be forgotten" has recently begun to appear in legislation of the EU and elsewhere,[1] whether there is, in fact, a right to be forgotten is a contested issue. In the US, some have argued that the right to be forgotten sits uneasily, or outright conflicts, with the freedom of speech guaranteed by the First Amendment.

What will it be like to live in a world where nothing can be forgotten? If, as Nima suggests, the inability to forget requires the ability to genuinely forgive, are we capable, as a society, to be so forgiving? Let's broach that question from the point of view of one society: the US. There is good reason to think that, in some sense, the US has become a less forgiving society over the past few decades. Truth in sentencing laws, which began to appear in the mid-80s, restricted chances for prisoners to be paroled for good behaviour. Increasing numbers of people were locked up as part of the "war on drugs," even for non-violent crimes. The penal code became a lot tougher, as well. The first "three strikes and you're out" law was passed in California on 7 March 1994. If a felon with two prior convictions for serious or violent felonies was found guilty of a third offence, the law required that they be sentenced for a period between 25 years and life. Three strikes laws are popular with voters, as they give the appearance of being tough on crime; some version of the three strikes laws can be found in 28 states. However, these laws also generate remarkable injustices. In 1995, Curtis Wilkerson, a 33 year-old Californian man who had prior convictions from 1981 (he had served as a lookout in a number of robberies when he was 19), was caught attempting to shoplift a pair of white tube socks valued at $2.50. He was sentenced to 25 years to life. A number of other examples of disproportionate sentencing exist.[2]

In addition to longer prison sentences and the growing elimination of judicial discretion on sentencing (that is, the greater use of "mandatory minimums"), there are further punishments people experience even if they aren't locked up for life. A criminal record in the US hampers one's ability to start again due to restrictions on the kinds of work former convicts are able to get. The *Economist* noted that a number of jobs in the US require a licence of some sort, and licences are typically denied to convicted felons. Being a firefighter in California, for example, requires certification as an emergency medical technician, which not many felons achieve. Any licence which includes a "good moral character provision" rules out a person with a felony conviction. Oklahoma's restrictions are particularly onerous: "state licensing boards completely banned convicted felons from almost 40 professions ranging from asbestos-abatement contractor to embalmer, and from landscape architect and podiatrist to wrecker, a job which usually entails removing debris from building sites" (The Economist 2017b).

Social policy towards people convicted of crimes provides one perspective on the *zeitgeist* of the US. It suggests people aren't particularly willing to forget and forgive the sins of others. How does that attitude manifest itself when we consider the permanent record of people's past left on social media? Remember, a behaviour doesn't have to be *illegal* for people to disapprove and act differently towards a person. It turns out that even though social media tends to involve the personal aspects of one's life, that can have negative consequences for people in a variety of ways. Let us call this phenomenon "the policing of the personal". It can take several forms: organisations and individuals using available information about a person's private life to penalise them in ways they wouldn't be inclined to if that information wasn't available, and – more worryingly – people recognising this possibility and *internalising* these expectations and altering their behaviour in ways which they would not otherwise.

In 2013, *The New York Times* reported a Kaplan survey of 381 college admissions officers. Over 30% admitted to having looked up applicants on Facebook or other forms of social media. Of those, 30% said that they had found negative information which affected the individual's application. The results of Facebook searches by admissions officers have led to applications being rejected, even though it was almost certain that other individuals who were admitted had engaged in similar behaviour, but just didn't leave a detectable record. In response to this phenomenon, high school students are now frequently advised to clean up their social media profiles by removing posts related to alcohol and to use personal email addresses that are appropriate for a general audience.

Things don't get appreciably better once you leave university and go to work. *Time* magazine reported in 2015 that over 50% of companies check the social media profiles of job applicants (Kumar 2015). Once you make it over the various hurdles and secure a job, the trawling doesn't end there. A 2012 report from the IT research firm Gartner predicted that the proportion of corporations monitoring the behaviour of employees on social media will rise to 60% by 2015. Such monitoring, as you might expect, occasionally results in the business discovering that their employees aren't always saying positive things about their employer. A number of people have been fired for "inappropriate" remarks made on social media.

The problem here is that whereas it's one thing to hold someone accountable for behaviour that violates the law or clearly stated guidelines, such as rules regarding procurement, what counts as an "inappropriate" remark is a judgement call. Inappropriate to whom, and for what reason? In 2013, Stephanie Bon learned that the new chief executive of Lloyds Banking Group could earn up to £8.3 million in their first year of employment. That evening she posted the following remark on Facebook: "New boss gets £4,000 an hour. I get £7 an hour. That's fair." The next day she was fired. In 2017, Juli Briskman was fired from her job as a marketing and communications specialist for Akima, a federal contractor, after using a photograph of herself flipping off Trump's motorcade as her profile picture on Twitter and Facebook (Walters 2017). Should an off-hand remark or gesture result in a person losing their job, simply because their employer doesn't like it? Bon's comment could be viewed as a critique of social inequality and pay differences, especially in light of the financial crisis. Briskman's gesture, made while cycling and off work, is legally protected speech, even if a bit rude.

The cases have important differences in their legal contexts because Bon was working in the UK whereas Briskman was working in the US, but they both illustrate the phenomenon of a person experiencing retribution for expressing legal speech in their personal life. The difficulty is that social media allows speech within one's personal sphere to intersect with the public sphere in ways which "normal" speech does not. Given that social norms have changed and opting-out of social media is increasingly less feasible, we need to ask if it is acceptable for corporations and organisations to use their power over us to restrict personal expression simply because they dislike it. (It's worth noting that these corporations and organisations have no problem using social media to push *their* own interests,[3] so it's not like they have a principled objection against their brand appearing in social media, generally.) The economic power exercised by companies and organisations is possible because most of us need to work to feed ourselves and afford a place to live; and this economic necessity exists because we were born into a pre-existing economic system at a particular place in the structure over which we had no control. (Think of this as an economic variant of the birthright lottery, from Chapter 2.) Is it right that something I have no control over explicitly restricts my freedom of speech and ability to express myself? The rich and powerful have many advantages which the rest of us do not. Should those advantages be expanded to include not just fancy hotels and fine wines but also the ability to express themselves with impunity?[4]

One line of argument some people advance is that the freedom of speech does not mean the freedom to speak without consequences. In the case of Juli Briskman, she was employed in Virginia which has "at-will" employment. States with such laws allow private-sector employers to fire people at any time, for any reason. We need to ask whether such broad laws are fit for purpose. One consequence of "at-will" employment is that it leads to the second aspect of policing the personal – the internalisation of the expectations of others. When a company can fire a person for any reason (e.g., when a social media mob demands it), any online speech act becomes fraught with danger. Any speech, no matter how innocuous on the surface, will be run through a content filter which not only asks "Is this what I really think? Does this express the point I am trying to make?" but, in addition, "How will my employer respond? What will someone who knows nothing about me think?"

It is true that freedom of speech does not mean the freedom to be a jerk or, worse, without consequences. But it *does* mean the freedom to express religious or political beliefs (among others) in many contexts with protection against certain sorts of reprisals. The issue at stake is whether one can speak freely *within* the limits of socially acceptable discourse without fear of reprisal.[5] A right which cannot be exercised without fear of reprisal undermines the very idea of that being a *right* in the first place. (Here, it is important to distinguish between fear of reprisal due to people violating the law and fear of reprisal due to people acting entirely within the law.)

One worry about the transparent Open Society and its inescapable memory is that it does not seem to fit well with how many people actually evaluate the character of individuals. If we consider the phenomenon of public shaming, the unforgiving attitude demonstrated by the criminal justice system in the US, and the uncompromising attitude of many employers (and admissions officers) towards social media posts, it seems that the way many people evaluate others shares a lot in common with the following biblical quote from Matthew:

> Every good tree bringeth forth good fruit; but a corrupt tree bringeth forth evil fruit. A good tree cannot bring forth evil fruit, neither can a corrupt tree bring forth good fruit. Every tree that bringeth not forth good fruit is hewn down, and cast into the fire. Wherefore, by their fruits ye shall know them. (Matthew 7:17–20, KJV)

Why are so many so willing to engage in public shaming, deny criminals rehabilitation opportunities, and reject or fire people based on social media revelations? Because of the underlying assumption that people have stable and binary characters; small samples of a person's behaviour are treated as revealing the whole. In addition, people commit the fundamental attribution error (Ross 1977), where they explain the behaviour of *others* via character traits downplaying environmental influences. Thus, when we see something we dislike, we tend to explain it as that person being a bad person instead of some other cause. People falling for the fundamental attribution error would interpret Justine Sacco's tweet as indicative of racist beliefs rather than a bad joke tweeted unthinkingly.

This matters because people are complex aggregates of both good and bad, subject to environmental influences more than we think (Doris 2002). Good people can do bad things, and *vice versa*. Hitler was a vegetarian who loved dogs. Gandhi, in addition to liberating India from colonial rule, tested his ability to resist sexual temptation by sleeping naked with his teenage grandniece (Connellan 2010). Virginia Woolf has been accused of anti-Semitism, and Pablo Picasso and J. D. Salinger were misogynists. When it comes to famous individuals, we seem better at separating judgement of their achievements, both good and bad, from their personal attributes. Yet when it comes to ordinary individuals, maintaining that division is harder. This is another challenge presented by the transparent conception of the Open Society: the omnipresent availability of our past providing a voyeuristic window into a person's life, in a world unwilling or incapable of accepting the complexity of people.

13. Returning to the past

Some have claimed that the loss of privacy in a transparent society is nothing more than a return to the natural state of humanity. In small hunter-gatherer societies – the original position of *homo sapiens* – there was no "right to privacy". In a small society, everyone knew what everyone else was doing. There was more emphasis on the community and less on the individual. Jared Diamond calls attention to the contrast quite vividly:

> [Privacy is] an unusual concept by the standards of world cultures, most of which provide little individual privacy and don't consider it a desireable ideal. Instead, common traditional living arrangements consist of an extended family inside a single dwelling, or a group of huts or shelters around a single clearing, or a whole band sleeping in one communal shelter. Unthinkably to most modern Americans, even sex between a couple traditionally goes on with a minimum of privacy. The couple's hammock or mat is visible to other couples, and the couple's young children may be sharing the same mat but are merely expected to close their eyes. (Diamond 2012, p. 224)

As an aside, it's worth noting that this anthropological fact challenges Hannah Arendt's claim that "from the beginning of history to our own time it has always been the bodily part of human existence that needed to be hidden in privacy, all things connected with the necessity of the life process itself" (Arendt 1959, p. 72). Privacy has not nearly been so central to the human condition.

Yet even if life in small-scale societies is typically lived under the watchful eyes of others, we should not assume that people don't find that grating and, hence, that the modern conception of privacy is not something worth safeguarding. In his ethnography of the life of the Kragur on Kairiru island in Papua New Guinea, Smith argues:

> I believe even villagers find their small-scale social world a strain at times. Families sometimes build second houses near their gardens […] not only to save time when there is so much work to be done, but also, some told me, so that they can occasionally escape from the noise of dogs and children, the frequent public gatherings, and the lack of privacy of life in the closely packed village. (Smith 1994, pp. 60–61)

This suggests a more nuanced understanding of the value of privacy in traditional societies than Diamond suggests.

If the Open Society threatens to undermine people's ability to live private lives, is that necessarily a bad thing? After all, what is the value of privacy? Josh Cohen, author of *The Private Life*, offers one answer to this question: "Privacy, precisely because it ensures we're never fully known to others or to ourselves, provides a shelter for imaginative freedom, curiosity and self-reflection. So to defend the private self is to defend the very possibility of creative and meaningful life" (Preston 2014).

How does privacy provide shelter for "imaginative freedom, curiosity and self-reflection"? It doesn't seem obvious that privacy is *necessary* to pursue those ends. Imagine an artists' commune where everyone lives openly in an environment of tolerance, mutual respect, and intellectual freedom. For the sake of argument, let's assume the commune was also founded in perpetuity by a large foundation grant so that it was financially self-sufficient, removing the need for members to worry about economics. Such a place would seem to be one where "imaginative freedom, curiosity and self-reflection" could co-exist with an absence of privacy.

I venture that Cohen's claim about the value of privacy relies on the empirically contingent fact that people, in social settings, can be pressurised to behave in ways contrary to how they would otherwise, in the absence of others. The Asch experiments, mentioned in Chapter 8, provide one vivid example. More generally, the phenomenon we are discussing is people's willingness to conform to a *social norm*. Part of the value of privacy, then, is its ability to protect people's autonomy by reducing the influence of others.

Bicchieri (2005) introduced an influential definition of a social norm. The following definition from her later work, *Norms in the Wild*, is an updated version:

> A *social norm* is a rule of behaviour such that individuals prefer to conform to it on condition that they believe that (a) most people in their reference network conform to it (empirical expectation), and (b) that most people in their reference network believe they ought to conform to it (normative expectation). (Bicchieri 2017, p. 35)

From this definition, one problem with Cohen's defence of the value of privacy becomes apparent. If individuals *prefer* to conform to a particular rule, given that the empirical and normative expectations are met, how can we say a person's autonomy is undermined by their conforming to the norm? Being able to act in accordance with one's *preferences* seems, in part, a requirement of autonomy.

Perhaps what is at stake concerns the source of an individual's preference. A heroin addict's preference for heroin might have been acquired through a free and autonomous choice of the person, yet at the same time, the preference created by the addiction prevents the addict from exercising autonomy. Similarly, a preference to conform to a particular norm can undermine a person's autonomy unless that preference to conform to a norm is the right kind of preference (i.e., not like that of the addict) and acquired in the right way (i.e., not through coercion). The difficulty with this line of defence is that it makes the value of privacy turn on a distinction between legitimately and illegitimately acquired preferences and how they are generated through one's social existence. If there is a value to privacy, and I believe that there is, it should admit a more direct and substantive defence.

A different line of argument can be found in John Stuart Mill's seminal work *On Liberty*:

> As it is useful that while mankind are imperfect there should be different opinions, so it is useful that there should be different experiments of living, that free scope should be given to varieties of character short of injury to others, and that the different modes of life should be proved practically. (Mill 1859)

Here, the idea is that privacy provides a degree of protection for persons to engage in "experiments of living". The difference between this defence and Cohen's defence is that, here, *society* is the beneficiary of a right to privacy; for Cohen, it was the individual. Another advantage of this defence of privacy is that it doesn't require an appeal to any *specific* values, such as "imaginative freedom, curiosity and self-reflection" or the pursuit of a "creative and meaningful life". If you didn't believe those were important, should you still value privacy? I think so; even philistines can value privacy.

There's another reason we should be sceptical of the claim that the transparent Open Society is nothing to worry about because it's just the natural state of humanity. The small bands and tribes that were the dominant form of social organisation for most of human existence were relatively *egalitarian*.[1] This matters because one fact about people is that our happiness not only depends on absolute outcomes (e.g., am I getting enough food?) but also on *relative* outcomes (e.g., how much is my opinion valued?). Life in a transparent Open Society may be unproblematic when the society is small and egalitarian because my life, compared to others, is about as good as everyone else's. However, when the basis of comparison in an Open Society expands to include millions or billions with great levels of inequality, the widespread knowledge of relative inequality can cause us to feel very differently about our lives than we would have otherwise.

One much-discussed example of how relative perceptions matter for people's perception of happiness is the Easterlin paradox. In 1974, Richard Easterlin argued that, despite the growth in income in the US over the past 50 years, there had been no corresponding increase in happiness (Easterlin 1974). Figure 13.1 illustrates this for both the US and five European countries for the

30-year period from 1973 to 2004. In both cases, happiness levels remained flat despite considerable increases in income in all countries. Why is this? Layard (2005, p. 45) explains the phenomenon as follows: "People are concerned about their relative income and not simply about its absolute level. They want to keep up with the Joneses or if possible to outdo them."

Easterlin's claim has not gone unchallenged. It has been suggested that a link between happiness and income does exist in developing countries which began with a low level of GDP per capita. Easterlin's original observations have been reconciled with this by theorising that once a country has become wealthy enough to satisfy the basic needs of its people, happiness starts to level off, with other life matters becoming more important. Clark et al. (2008, p. 96) note that, "It has been argued that once an individual rises above a poverty line or 'subsistence level,' the main source of increased well-being is not income but rather friends and a good family life." Stevenson and Wolfers (2008, p. 9) go further, disputing the existence of a satiation level at all: "new large-scale datasets covering many countries point to a clear, robust relationship between GDP per capita and average levels of subjective well-being in a country. Furthermore, we find no evidence that countries become satiated – the positive income-happiness relationship holds for both developed and developing nations." In response, Easterlin et al. (2010) rejects the Stevenson and Wolfers findings on the grounds that it rests "almost entirely on the short-term positive association between life satisfaction and GDP" in certain transition countries.

One concern is that much of this debate is taking place at too high a level of abstraction to be truly useful. Setting aside the question over whether any link between happiness and income is meaningful over a 30-plus year period, given all the cultural and political shifts that occur,[2] we might ask what happens if we shift the focus from wealth to types of consumption. In an interesting study, Hsee et al. (2009) investigate the connection between happiness and how it is generated by money, acquisition, and consumption. Intuitively, you might think that a person who receives a certain amount of money experiences happiness by reflecting on her expected consumption. However, Hsee et al. found that this isn't always the case.[3] They write:

> We posit that utility of money has two rather independent components: its value *per se* (monetary experience) and its consumption consequence (consumption experience). These two types of happiness obey different hedonic principles: Monetary experience depends on relative monetary value, whereas consumption experience depends on absolute consumption level. (Hsee et al. 2009, p. 400)

Something similar was found if one measured the happiness associated with the *acquisition* of a good, separate from its consumption. But it would be too quick to conclude that happiness produced by consumption only depends on

RETURNING TO THE PAST 141

Figure 13.1: Two illustrations of the Easterlin paradox

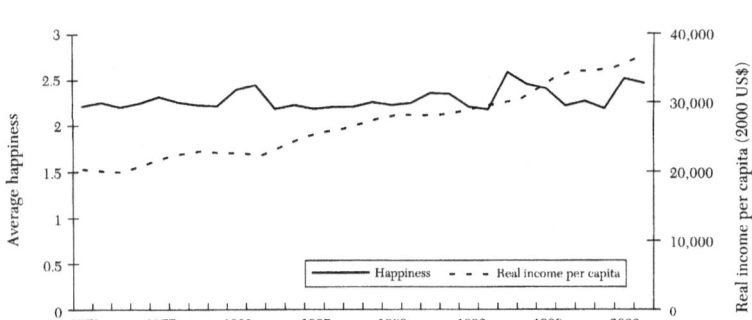

Notes: Happiness is the average reply to the question: "Taken all together, how would you say things are these days? Would you say that you are...?" Responses were coded as (3) Very Happy, (2) Pretty Happy, and (1) Not too Happy.

(a) Happiness and Real Income Per Capita in the United States, 1973–2004

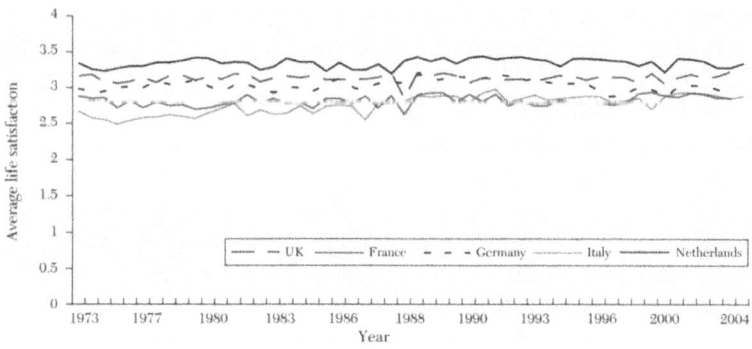

Notes: Happiness is the average reply to the question: "On the whole how satisfied are you with the life you lead?" Responses were coded as (4) Very Satisfied, (3) Fairly Satisfied, (2) Not Very Satisfied, and (1) Not at all Satisfied.

(b) Life Satisfaction in Five European Countries, 1973–2004

Source: Figures 1 and 2 in Clark et al. (2008). Copyright AEA, reproduced with permission from the authors.

absolute levels of the good being consumed; it also depends on the kind of good. Goods such as a warm house or a delicious cup of coffee will produce happiness corresponding to an absolute evaluation, whereas a good such as expensive jewellery will produce happiness according to relative evaluations.

The point is this: relative comparisons matter greatly for human happiness, regardless of whether we are talking about the receipt of money, the acquisition of a good, or even the *consumption* of certain types of goods (such as the wearing of jewellery). Constant exposure to the Rich Kids of Instagram can cause a person who would otherwise be content to become unhappy. This matters because the role played by relative comparisons is often lost in the narrative of capitalism, with the rhetoric of a rising tide lifting all boats. Reflecting on the US, Andy Warhol put the point well:

> What's great about this country is that America started the tradition where the richest consumers buy essentially the same things as the poorest. You can be watching TV and see Coca-Cola, and you know that the President drinks Coke, Liz Taylor drinks Coke, and just think, you can drink Coke, too. A Coke is a Coke and no amount of money can get you a better Coke than the one the bum on the corner is drinking. All the Cokes are the same and all the Cokes are good. Liz Taylor knows it, the President knows it, the bum knows it, and you know it. (Warhol 1975)

Warhol is right that all the Cokes are the same and all the Cokes are good, but you won't enjoy your Coke as much in your one-bedroom shotgun shack if you are looking at a billionaire drinking one on his megayacht. With the top 1% of global wealth holders now possessing 50.1% of all wealth, according to a 2017 Credit Suisse report, we have moved very far away indeed from the equality of the natural state of humankind.

Interestingly, this problem of perception gets worse as you get richer. Catherine Rampell argues that one reason why many rich people don't feel particularly rich is because of how *unequal* the wealth distribution is, even at the very top (Rampell 2011). Figure 13.2 plots the log of income for the various percentiles in the US for 2010. What's striking is how rapidly inequality *increases* towards the upper end of the plot. An income of $10,000 puts one just below the 10th percentile, but *quintupling* the income to $50,000 would move that person to just above the 54th percentile. However, when a person with an income of $250,000, right above the 96th percentile, increases their income to $1,250,000, they would just climb above the 99.5th percentile. Paul Krugman elucidates this well with the following metaphor: imagine society "as being something like a long street running up a hill, in which rising altitude goes along with rising income" (Krugman 2011). This street metaphor offers a psychological explanation for why the rich don't feel as happy as we might expect: people don't consider their overall position with respect to the entire

Figure 13.2: Natural log of income versus percentiles for 2010 US

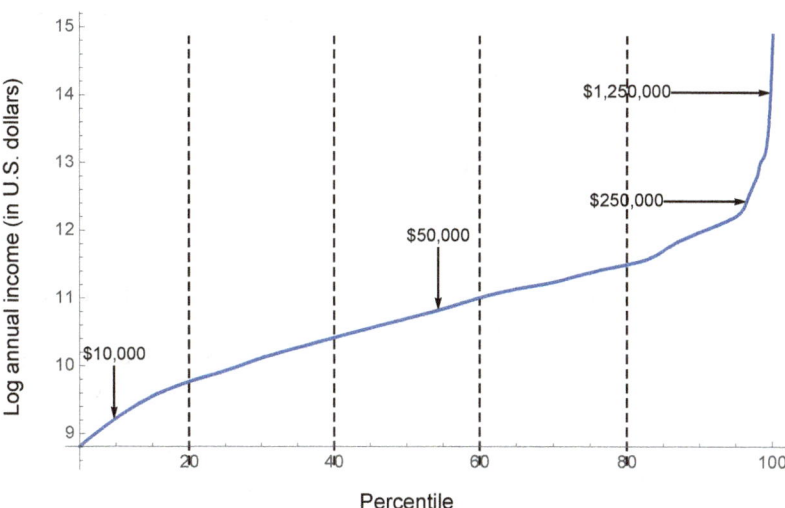

Source: created by the author using data from Rachel Johnson, Urban-Brookings Tax Policy Center Microsimulation Model (version 0509–7).
Notes: the idea to plot log income rather than just income versus percentiles is due to DeLong (2011).

street but only compare themselves to their neighbours on either *side*. For people in the lower percentiles, the difference in income (altitude) on either side is about the same: your worse-off neighbour differs from you about as much as you differ from your better-off neighbour. Yet when you look at people on the upper percentiles, that symmetry is lost; your worse-off neighbour differs from you much less than you differ from your better-off neighbour. If happiness is based on relative comparisons, this is a precarious position to be in; it will be perceived as much easier to slip down the ladder than to climb up because the distance between the rungs increases the higher you climb.

And so another problem with the transparent Open Society is that it can lead to greater levels of unhappiness because of the constant awareness of relative inequality, *regardless of what level one is at*. In addition to the decrease in happiness, there's another problem that's been identified – social anxiety. The constant exposure to news and images of other people's experiences on social media has given rise to a new term, *Fear of Missing Out* (FOMO). Przybylski *et al.* (2013) define FOMO as: "a pervasive apprehension that others might be having rewarding experiences from which one is absent." Although it hasn't yet made it into that great catalogue of mental illnesses published by the American Psychiatric Association, the DSM, Oxford Dictionaries Online added "FOMO" in 2013 (Dirda 2013).

There are a couple of reasons why the fear of missing out has become so salient. The first has to do with the immediacy and detail with which people can chronicle their experiences. Fifty years ago, photography was slow or expensive. You either sent film away to be developed, or you developed it yourself, or you used an instant camera. In 1972, the Polaroid SX-70 instant camera cost $180, with film costing $6.90 for a pack of ten pictures. In 2017 dollars, that would be $1,031 for the camera and $40 for ten pictures. Home videos were a rarity, and telephone calls were expensive. As a result, sharing details of experiences was difficult.

Now fast-forward to April 2023 (when I am writing this); the cheapest iPhone costs $429. That phone gives you virtually unlimited digital photographs and video, all of which can be shared immediately. Voice and video calls can still be expensive if you aren't on the right data plan (some things never change), but that's trivially avoidable with an internet connection and apps. As a result, people don't need to carefully select what experiences they share; anything they want to share can be shared.

This ease of sharing interacts with the second reason why FOMO is so salient: people don't generally want to broadcast all aspects of their life, but only the better parts, carefully curated. In a society where personal identity is a commodity and people are urged to develop their personal brand, people want to present themselves positively – although context-dependency can make this tricky. For example, photographs of someone having a fantastically hedonistic experience in Magaluf may not be well received by a potential future employer, as we have seen. But those photographs would, at least, show the person to be having a good time. It is much rarer to find someone sharing details of their misery in the moment without it being part of a larger narrative arc tending towards positivity.[4] There are the occasional ironic outliers, of course. "Sad desk lunch" does exist as a Tumblr site (Fisher 2015), but hasn't been updated since October 2015.

The ease of sharing experiences, along with a selection bias towards the positive, combines with a third cause of FOMO. When people engage with social media, they tend not to be in the midst of a positive experience of their own at the time of engagement. Instead, they are commuting, attempting to study in the library, in a lecture, at their desk at work, or bored at home. If they *are* engaging with social media while in the middle of an experience – at a club or at a concert – they are typically looking at experiences *different in kind* from the one they are having. In the first case, the contrast between one's banal existence with the positive experience seen will obviously be striking. In the second case, one might well wonder if the person's current experience, although nice enough, is still not quite as good as what the others are experiencing. These comparisons will not always be negative, of course; my point is that the comparisons will often be enough to plant a kernel of doubt – the fear of missing out.

What we have seen in this chapter and the previous one are some of the individual consequences of making so much information about our private lives readily available. We focused on issues surrounding our inability to escape our past and carve out a new identity for ourselves (e.g., Chapter 12) and the psychological effects of being constantly exposed to information about *other* people (e.g., this chapter). The focus of these chapters has primarily been on how information about ourselves and other people can affect us in a variety of ways. However, another obvious consequence of making information about ourselves available is that people can *use* that information to *manipulate* us without us being aware of it. That is the topic of the next chapter.

14. We'll be watching you

Jeremy Bentham, the co-founder of utilitarianism with James Mill, is remembered for many things – the idea that the measure of right and wrong was "the greatest happiness of the greatest number", his work in economics and the law, his commitment to gender equality and reforming attitudes towards homosexuality, and the fact that his body was preserved after his death and put on permanent display in University College London.[1] Yet, perhaps the idea most closely associated with him is one related to an obsessive 20-year project on prison reform: the Panopticon. Bentham's Panopticon has become synonymous with surveillance, monitoring, and social control. The basic design is a building in which all prisoners are housed in cells observable by a single person (see Figure 14.1) without the prisoners *knowing* that they are being watched. This was meant to instil constant fear in the prisoners so that they had to behave all the time.

What we have seen is how the transparent Open Society creates a panopticon of the soul. Your desires are knowable by tracking what you buy or what you read and watch on the internet. GPS in mobile phones makes your movements knowable whenever you leave the house. The ability of any microphone-equipped device, whether it is a mobile phone or a virtual assistant, to be turned on silently means that, in principle, your personal conversations could be recorded and shared without your knowledge. And the explosion of social media means that people's beliefs and interests, hopes and fears are logged in real time. Add in the risk of public shaming, losing your job because your employer spots something they don't approve of (or of not being hired in the first place), all confounded by the indelible shadow of the past. In many ways, this is more troubling than Bentham's Panopticon because, there, only your *body* was being watched; now, people can get inside your head. The ability to pressure people to conform is great. But there is a greater problem.

The greater problem is that we know people's behaviour systematically fails to be rational in a number of ways. This was first revealed in a joint work by Daniel Kahneman and Amos Tversky in the early 1970s which led to Kahneman getting the Nobel Prize in Economics in 2002,[2] followed a few years later by Richard Thaler receiving the 2017 Nobel Prize in Economics for his work in behavioural economics. People's systematic deviation from rational behaviour goes well beyond framing effects, confirmation bias and nudging, extending into political behaviour. When people's choices are strongly influenced by things other than facts, the more you know about what someone believes and wants, the more power you have to influence that person's behaviour indirectly, without them knowing.[3]

Figure 14.1: Bentham's Panopticon

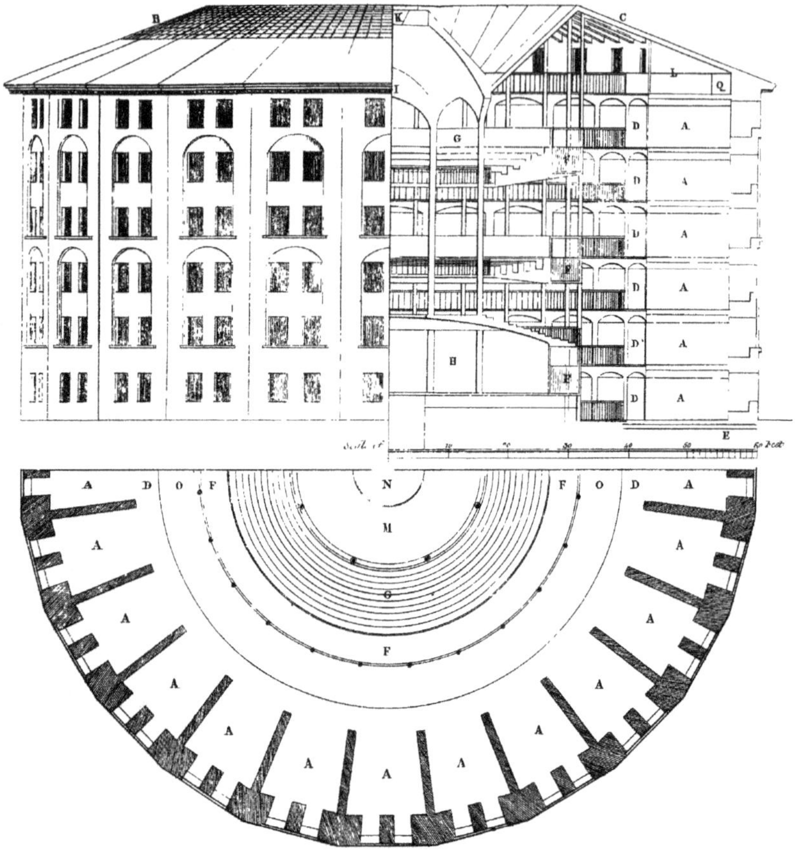

Source: Reveley (1791). Available under CC BY-SA 4.0 via Wikimedia Commons.

Democracies have long posed a problem in how to explain people's voting behaviour using the rational actor model. For starters, it's not clear why anyone would bother to vote. In large populations, the chances of any single voter being pivotal in an election are essentially zero. (That said, examples of single voter pivotality do exist – the ironically named Marcus "Landslide" Morton was elected governor of Massachusetts in 1839, receiving 51,034 of 102,066 votes.) Since voting costs time and effort, why would anyone turn out to vote if it probably won't make a difference? A lot of ink has been spilt trying to show, despite appearances to the contrary, that voting is rational.[4]

There's another assumption lurking in the background: that people are generally responsive to reasons when they decide for whom to vote. This is why democracies have held political debates where candidates discuss and argue about policy and why politicians have worried about their stance on certain issues and articulated an overarching coherent worldview to ground their positions. People, according to rational voter theory, listen to debates, weigh reasons for and against, and ultimately plump for the side they find most persuasive. Unfortunately, research suggests this model is far from the truth.

Westen (2008) conducted an experiment on partisan voters in the US, in the run-up to the 2004 election. Each voter was presented with six pairs of statements by John Kerry, six by George W. Bush, and six by "politically neutral" persons (e.g., Tom Hanks). The pairs of statements consisted of an initial assertion, followed by a second one which contradicted the first. After being presented with the conflicting information, voters were asked to rate on a scale of 1 to 4 the extent to which they thought the two statements were contradictory.[5] The point of the experiment was to identify how partisan voters, and their brains, reacted when exposed to such information.

The findings were what you might suspect. Partisan voters clearly identified the conflicts as contradictions for those on the *other* side of the political spectrum, but they were much less likely to see contradictions in statements made by people on *their* side. In addition, Westen found that "the neural circuits charged with regulation of emotional states seemed to recruit beliefs that eliminated the distress and conflict partisans had experienced when they confronted unpleasant realities." Interestingly, this was done with little activation of those parts of the brain that are involved in explicit reasoning. The most striking result was the following:

> Once partisans had found a way to reason to false conclusions, not only did neural circuits involved in negative emotions turn off, but circuits involved in positive emotions turned *on*. The partisan brain didn't seem satisfied in just feeling *better*. It worked overtime to feel *good*, activating reward circuits that give partisans a jolt of positive reinforcement for their biased reasoning. (Westen 2008)

So not only did partisan voters not see the contradictions made by their own side, they felt *good* when they didn't see them.

A lot of other research has reported on the less-than-rational aspects of how voters behave. Here's a small sample. Klor and Winter (2018) draw upon experimental and empirical evidence to argue for a "bandwagon effect" from polling data. That is, people who believe the election is close and are on the side with the slight majority are significantly more likely to turn out to vote.[6] Payne *et al.* (2010) suggest, based on survey data, that implicit racial prejudice might have affected the 2008 US presidential election, in that "even explicitly rejected attitudes can influence important political decisions." They found that "Americans higher in implicit prejudice were less likely to vote for Obama, but not more likely to vote for McCain." (After Trump's 2016 election, we might also wonder whether people are much better at hiding explicit racial prejudice than we thought: see Stephens-Davidowitz 2017 for a discussion of how Google searches cast light on the seedy underbelly of the American psyche.)

The tendency to feel disgust also turns out to be a predictor of how people vote. Inbar *et al.* (2009) find that the tendency to feel disgust is correlated with people's political and moral attitudes; in particular, persons more likely to feel disgust are more likely to self-describe as conservative. Inbar *et al.* (2012) provide further evidence that the connection between being sensitive to disgust and political conservatism holds even when you control for other factors such as personality traits. Bloom (2014) found that when subjects are primed with associations of harm and the emotion of disgust, they evidenced greater moral conviction on political issues.

Finally, what are some factors connected with why voters prefer a candidate? Caprara and Zimbardo (2004) examined the self-reported personalities of voters and how they aligned with the public presentation of candidates amongst centre-right and centre-left candidates in Italy. They found a degree of affinity between the two: voters' personalities were more similar to the politicians they preferred than the politicians they didn't. Reflecting on this finding, they speculate:

> Either citizens' political preferences are in accord with their self-reported personality, with voting serving an expressive function with regard to self-perception, or that citizens assimilate their preferred candidates' personalities to their own. In both cases, personality characteristics that are reported and inferred may be critical to strengthening the bond between voters, parties and candidates. (Caprara and Zimbardo 2004, p. 586)

This is one reason why, in American elections, pollsters ask questions such as, "Which candidate would you most like to have a beer with?" Establishing an emotional connection with a candidate matters because, once someone has picked a candidate, that colours their interpretation of subsequent information.

Furthermore, when a person's behaviour doesn't conform to the rational actor model, knowing about things that *do* influence them allow for carefully crafted, targeted advertising to be aimed at them. Westen suggests:

> If you're running a campaign, you shouldn't worry about offending the 30 percent of the population whose brains can't process information from your side of the aisle unless their lives depend on it (e.g., after an attack on the US mainland). If you're a Republican, your focus should be on moving the 10 to 20 percent of

the population with changeable minds to the right and bring your unbending 30 percent to the polls. (Westen 2008)

If you can identify people who are likely single-issue voters, you then saturate their social media with ads showing how your candidate is better on that issue. Eric Greitens, the Republican nominee for the governor of Missouri in 2016, released an advertisement consisting of nothing more than him firing a Gatling gun while a voice-over uttered a few platitudes. Such an ad wasn't designed to win over fence-sitters with subtle argumentation: it was a direct appeal to the gut of gun lovers. And one reason stories of Hillary Clinton's handling of official government emails while Secretary of State featured endlessly in 2016 was because, even though the FBI said there was nothing to it, repeated mentions of the emails eroded Clinton's perception of trustworthiness amongst fence-sitters. The thing about emotional judgements is that they don't need to be supported by *reasons*, much less *good* reasons. If getting a voter to feel a way towards a candidate is the primary thing that matters, then any method of forming that association is as good as another.[7] Given this, the real danger of fake news is that it can plant seeds of doubt in an undecided voter's mind, tipping them one way or another, and then legitimate news stories will be interpreted as providing *retrospective* reasons offered by a person to explain why they voted the way they did.

In addition, while elections are decided by who gets the most votes, we mustn't forget the electioneering tactic of trying to *suppress* the other side's vote. It doesn't matter if your candidate is less popular, all things considered, than the other person if enough of the *other* person's supporters stay at home.[8] Carefully targeted negative advertising seeks to depress voter turnout by lowering the enthusiasm of voters for candidates they might otherwise support. In Western democracies with low voter turnout, this can have important effects on the outcome and perceived legitimacy of the purported mandate.[9]

In 2017, reporters uncovered some of the methods pioneered by Cambridge Analytica to influence voter behaviour in the 2016 Brexit referendum, the 2016 presidential campaign in America, and elections in other countries around the world. These methods involve combining many of the sources of data we've discussed in this part of the book, and then targeting specific individuals. Cambridge Analytica acquired data from Facebook, constructed psychological profiles of individuals, and then combined that information with data purchased from other sources – "everything from magazine subscriptions to airline travel" (Cadwalladr 2017). These detailed psychological profiles allowed them to identify likely trigger issues for individuals: effective pressure points for nudging them in one direction or another. A former employee described their operations in 2013 as being similar to psychological warfare:

> That's what it is. Psyops. Psychological operations – the same methods the military use to effect mass sentiment change. It's

what they mean by winning 'hearts and minds'. We were just doing it to win elections in the kind of developing countries that don't have many rules. (Cadwalladr 2017)

And that, of course, is the real problem. In the best of times, elections are a crude instrument for crafting future policy. Politicians aren't held accountable (at least, until the next election) for promising something they fail to deliver.[10] Voters project onto a candidate their beliefs about what that candidate stands for. A candidate becomes a Rorschach concept for each individual voter, and how a voter perceives a candidate is based partly on fact and partly on gut response. From a campaign manager's point of view, all that matters is whether you can get someone to prefer your candidate (or issue, if we are talking about a referendum) more than the alternatives. And that preference doesn't have to be based on true beliefs, because elections aren't about whether people have *good* reasons for their preferences. The transparent Open Society risks creating a world where we, the electorate, have our own information used against us, manipulating us like pawns in a political game.

Although I have focused on how our personal information can be used by others to manipulate us for explicitly *political* ends, the point is easily generalised. How many times have you had a conversation with a friend at a party and then, soon afterwards, seen an advertisement for the very thing you were speaking about? (See McNutt & Partners 2021 for a discussion of this phenomenon.) The point is that all of our mental attitudes – our beliefs, feelings, and desires – are vulnerable to being shaped by someone who has access to our information. Even when we think we are acting autonomously, making a decision based on evidence from the world around us, it doesn't hurt to keep a degree of critical awareness and ask *who benefits* from our choice? The fact that we *believe* we made our own decision is entirely compatible with that decision also having been shaped to further someone else's interest.

15. Concluding remarks

What, then, is the overall assessment of the transparent conception of the Open Society? The first point is that when faced with all these issues it is easy to feel a sense of despair at reversing the trend. The technological drive is towards ever more information transparency and more collection of data, creating more opportunities for our personal information to be misused. There is simply too much money at stake and too many powerful institutions (governmental or otherwise) with a vested interest in collecting as much information as possible about individuals by any means possible. The Stasi would have loved the information gathering methods which now exist.[1]

However, a second point is that our age of information transparency, in many other instances, provides social goods worth preserving. Many people want to know whether our pension funds are being invested in tobacco companies or armaments industries. We would like to see *all* of the trials performed by drug companies, not just the ones showing a drug performed better than placebo with sufficiently few side effects that it could be approved for the market. We want to know who funded certain studies or policy papers, who paid for political advertisements, and who gave what to politicians or judges. And it is important, sometimes, to know whether people with certain criminal records live in the neighbourhood or have applied for certain jobs. Any attempt to prevent potential abuses of informational transparency needs to be weighed against the potential benefits such transparency can provide. But one message which emerges from our investigation is that the current realisation of the transparent conception of the Open Society is too much in favour of making the lives of ordinary people transparent to companies and governments, and too little in favour of making the operations of companies and governments transparent to ordinary people.

Do we want to live in a panopticon of the soul? As we have seen, the abuse of personal information means that in countries with lax labour protections, individuals can be fired from their job for engaging in *legal behaviour* during *out-of-work hours* as a *private citizen*. And the way information was handled in the past allowed companies such as Cambridge Analytica to use personal information to craft fine-tuned campaign advertisements targeting hot-button issues likely to trigger an emotional response in the viewer, who would not know that they were being deliberately manipulated. When it is impossible to prevent our information from being collected, we need protection to stop our information being weaponized against us.

Striking the right balance will not be easy. It requires a public discussion about the kind of society we want to live in, and how the power conferred by the possession of information should be distributed across society. For example, should it be the case that social media companies can retain the information they collect indefinitely? In asking that question, let's set aside what the actual terms and conditions said when you agreed to use the platform: those terms and conditions were often written during the Wild West period of the internet, when services were developing faster than social norms or the law could adapt. Should it be the case that companies can access the information – anonymised or not – which people voluntarily disclose? It would be possible for social media companies to use end-to-end encryption so that *they* were unable to access the information stored on their servers even though users could. But that would prevent companies from monetising the information of its users, and it would no longer be possible for them to provide the service for free. Would advertisers be less willing to advertise on a service if they cannot aim highly targeted ads at users, given the already poor rate at which ad impressions are converted into useful outcomes?[2] Would users be willing to pay for it? If social media provides a valuable public service – the digital equivalent of a public square (albeit often a shouty, misanthropic one) – should that kind of service be brought into public ownership and regulated by an independent, politically neutral body?

If we want to rebalance transparency in the Open Society, what kind of regulation should be put in place, and what kind of trade-offs are we willing to accept regarding our privacy and the material benefits generated? One worry I have is that conversation is not being held. Another worry concerns the move from *regulation* to *enforcement*. Although it is all well and good to pass laws regarding how companies can use our information, laws provide no protection if they are not enforced. And even if they are enforced, the punishment for violation needs to be sufficiently severe so as to avoid companies simply pricing in fines as part of the "cost of doing business".[3]

But we have faced bleak situations in the past and have managed to turn things around. The economic advancements of the Industrial Revolution led to atrocious working conditions for many, yet laws were introduced, and the most egregious evils of that system were curtailed. Food safety standards were introduced, and environmental protection legislation was passed. These advances need continuous protection, but advances *were* made. And although many parts of the world still suffer from the excesses of exploitative capitalism, it is worth remembering the following statement from Popper's philosophical colleague: "no social tendency exists which could not be altered if the individuals concerned both wanted to alter it and possessed the appropriate information" (Watkins 1953). When faced with deepfake videos and troll factories using AI to carpet-bomb the internet with misinformation, there are options. We could, for example, choose as a society to have less technology in our lives. Why we will probably not choose that outcome is an interesting question, and one which I address in the final chapter of this book.

It could be argued that it is not possible to curtail the transparent conception of the Open Society simply because there is too much money to be made and too much power at stake. But I think that conclusion is wrong for two reasons. First, although economics is a hugely important determinant of social practice, it is not the *sole* determinant. A nice historical example to illustrate the point can be found in the abolition of slavery by the British empire.[4] At the time slavery was abolished, there were still vast sums of money to be made from the institution. The abolitionists were able to push through radical change even though this was against the economic interests of a great many people and cost the government of the time a lot of money.[5] The abolitionists, through effort and moral persuasion, eliminated a practice which had existed for several hundred years *despite* its continued profitability.[6] This shows that, in principle, it is possible to change social practices for the betterment of humanity even in the face of economic interests. If we were take a principled stand and resist the panopticon of the soul, the fact that there are enormous profits to be made by mining our information does not mean resistance is futile.

Second, I think there are good moral reasons to think that, even though there are vast sums of money to be made through the collection, analysis, and sale of personal information, this is not the kind of world we should want. I've outlined a number of reasons to think this in this part of the book, but let me mention one last reason to bring this chapter to a close. The reason involves a transformation in the way we think about human beings, and a human's ultimate source of value.

You might have thought it was bad enough when capitalism brought about the transformation of individuals into *consumers*. Instead of conceiving of people as agents with hopes, ambitions, goals, and projects they want to see realised, we shifted the focus to the products and resources used along the way. As long as people consumed, increasing economic activity and helping GDP grow, we paid less attention to the side effects of all that consumption. Data mining, unleashed upon the boundless quantities of information about individuals, runs the risk of transforming *consumers* into mere *commodities*. The second form of the Categorical Imperative resonates here: "Act in such a way that you treat humanity, whether in your own person or in the person of any other, never merely as a means to an end, but always at the same time as an end." Human beings should not *just* be commodities in an economic game, where our information is collected, analysed, and sold so that we can be manipulated. The fundamental values of democracy, the Enlightenment, and civil society risk being undermined when we allow our information to be turned against us, transforming us into a mere means to bring about another person's end, often at our own expense.

Notes to Part II: The panopticon of the soul

8. The book of life

[1] Published as *The Inman Diary: Volumes 1–2: A Public and Private Confession*, Harvard University Press (1990). I suggest an electronic version, if possible, as the hardback is 1,600 pages.

[2] The *New York Times* published an obituary shortly after his death in 2007 (Martin 2007). Those interested in reading the contents of his diary will be disappointed, as the terms and conditions of Shields' bequest to Washington State University include the requirement that no one be permitted to read the diary until 2057. However, if you search Google you can find excerpts, hence my claim about the "phenomenally boring prose".

[3] Bertrand Russell introduced the Tristram Shandy paradox in his 1903 book, *The Principles of Mathematics*. The original purpose of the paradox was to illustrate one of the antinomies of set theory: that an infinite collection can be put into a one-to-one correspondence with a proper subpart. According to the paradox, Tristram Shandy writes his diary very slowly, taking one year of his life to record the events of one day. However, if Shandy lives for an infinite length of time, he will complete his diary even though he always falls further behind. How is this possible? Shandy finishes the diary entry for the Nth day of his life at the end of the Nth year. If he were to fail to complete his diary, there must be some day M whose events are not adequately reported. But we can say with certainty when he finishes writing about the Mth day, and since he lives infinitely long each day gets recorded.

[4] In the original experiment, Asch (1951) put a single experimental subject in a group with seven confederates and asked each member of the group to match a given line with one of three other lines of unequal length. When the confederates stated their beliefs about the match, they were all *unanimously wrong*, with the margin of error ranging between half an inch (1.27cm) and one and three-quarters of an inch (4.44cm), in various trials. The error was thus clearly, *obviously*, recognisable. The point of the experiment was to see what people did when they were in a *minority of one* pitted against a *unanimous majority*. Asch found that, while some subjects defied the majority, one-third changed their judgements to the majority view in one-half or more of the trials. These results were confirmed in a later paper (Asch 1956).

9. Unwanted inferences

[1] Face recognition technology is already used throughout the world for security purposes and to increase ease-of-entry in public venues. Football stadiums are using it to prevent known hooligans from entering matches. On a more entertaining note, Cohen (2023) reported that James Dolan, the owner of Madison Square Garden, uses face recognition technology to identify lawyers representing people suing him to prevent them from entering the venue.

² Although, on this point, recall our discussion of Nozick's objection to the All-Affected principle in Chapter 4.

³ For example, my mother was denied a job as a schoolteacher in northern Minnesota in the late 1960s because the official policy was that they didn't hire married women.

⁴ One point of imprecision with this statistic is how to define what it means to be homosexual. In their survey, Janus and Janus (1993) found that 22% of men and 17% of women reported having had at least one homosexual experience. However, of this subset, only 39% of men and 27% of women said that they "frequently" had homosexual experiences or had ones which were "ongoing". These latter estimates are what generate the 9% and 5% estimates, respectively.

10. Lifting the veil

¹ To provide some context, there is a worry that when a society cracks down hard on minor, unintended violations of the law by generally law-abiding citizens while, at the same time, allowing criminals to get away with egregious violations, public attitudes towards the law and the police change. For example, in the UK, "from 2020, not a single personal, vehicle or bike theft was solved by police in between half and two-thirds of the 30,100 neighbourhoods in England and Wales" (Hymas 2023). At the same time, UK local councils "issued 19,631 parking fines per day in 2022, up 12 per cent from 2021 and a surge of 36 per cent from 2020" Saunders (2023).

² Modern smartphones, with inbuilt GPS, give a totally different solution to this problem.

³ Dennett does talk about the environment in a later example involving a person attempting to control an automated fuel refinery by intervening in the environment where the refinery operates by depressing the aviation fuel market. But this is better read as an illustration of how the relation of control can, in some instances, be transitive. An agent A, by controlling B, who controls C, can thus be said to control C. However, the passage isn't presented as an example of how the control relationship has implicit contextual dependence.

⁴ One could treat the budget as part of the environment. Yet, I wish to distinguish them. I take environmental dependency to refer to features outside of A or B that matter *at a particular moment in time* for A to control B, such as whether a remote has working batteries or not. The budget, on the other hand, involves resources that can be used or exchanged to make it possible for A to control B in the future.

11. Letting it all hang out

¹ In a famous study, Dunbar (1992) investigated a correlation between the size of the neocortex and the size of the social group in primates. The basic idea is

that maintaining stable social relations is cognitively expensive, which places an upper limit on the size of a social group. By examining data from 38 genera of social primates, Dunbar proposed that if humans follow the same trend, we can typically maintain around 150 stable relationships.

[2] In 2023, Twitter expanded the character limit to 4,000 if you were a US-based Twitter Blue subscriber.

12. Don't you forget about me

[1] It is closely related to the "right to erasure", and appears in Recitals 65 and 66 of the European Union's General Data Protection Regulation (GDPR). Recital 65, on the right of erasure, specifies that "a data subject should have the right to have his or her personal data erased and no longer processed where the personal data are no longer necessary in relation to the purposes for which they are collected or otherwise processed, where a data subject has withdrawn his or her consent or objects to the processing of personal data concerning him or her, or where the processing of his or her personal data does not otherwise comply with this Regulation." Recital 66, on the right to be forgotten, states: "To strengthen the right to be forgotten in the online environment, the right to erasure should also be extended in such a way that a controller who has made the personal data public should be obliged to inform the controllers which are processing such personal data to erase any links to, or copies or replications of those personal data."

[2] In recent years, California has attempted to address the most egregious injustices generated by the "three strikes" law. In 2012, Proposition 36 was passed, which reformed the law by requiring the third strike to be a serious or violent felony rather than any crime.

[3] In 2014, the UK's Advertising Standards Authority criticised Mondelez, the owner of Oreo brand biscuits, for paying vloggers in the UK to promote Oreos without labelling the videos as an advertisement. This shows that companies are clearly willing to exploit loopholes in regulation regarding social media when it's to their advantage.

[4] In the UK, the wealthy have a greater ability to exercise control over the Open Society than the rest of us through the use of injunctions to prevent the media reporting stories which they dislike. Furthermore, there has been increased use in what are known as "super-injunctions" that prevent the media from disclosing the fact that a wealthy individual has obtained an injunction preventing news organisations from reporting a story.

[5] Here we encounter, once again, the importance of Popper's observation that the Open Society should tolerate everything except intolerance. Firing someone from their job simply because they expressed a reasonable point is a high order of intolerance. Such intolerance deliberately cultivates a climate of fear, preventing discourse required as part of the Enlightenment conception of the Open Society, which we consider in Part III.

13. Returning to the past

[1] Service (1962) introduced four categories of human social organisation: bands, tribes, chiefdoms, and states. The smallest form of organisation, the band, typically consisted of about 10–30 individuals, often one or two extended families. The next form, the tribe, consisted of about 200 individuals. Each stage in the transition from bands to states is accompanied by a corresponding increase in size, political centralisation, and social stratification. The first state came into existence only around 3,400 BC, in the Fertile Crescent (see Diamond 2012, p. 12).

[2] For example, during the 30-year period from 1973 to 2004, US society experienced (a) the legalisation of abortion with the Roe v. Wade decision in 1973; (b) the end of the Vietnam war in 1975; (c) a significant push by the women's movement attempting to ratify the Equal Rights Amendment (which failed in 1982); (d) the growing conservative backlash against the counterculture movement of the 60s; (e) longstanding problems concerning inflation; (f) Reagan's election, followed by a recession; (g) the end of the Cold War and the collapse of the Soviet Union; (h) the first Gulf War; (i) the bursting of the the dot-com bubble; and (j) the 9/11 attacks and subsequent "war on terror". (That's just a subset of the major events.) Why focus on just GDP?

[3] In one experiment, they divided a pool of subjects into two groups: a "poor" group and a "rich" group, where members of the poor group received coupons worth either one or two points, and members of the rich group received coupons worth either five or ten points. (Notice that this divides each group into two: you could be a poor member of the poor group, with a coupon valued at only one point, or a rich member of the poor group, with a coupon valued at two points.) The coupon could be exchanged for a 100ml glass of milk, with the number of teaspoons of milk powder used to make the glass of milk corresponding to the number of points on the coupon. Subjects were asked to assess their happiness first upon receipt of the coupon, and then after drinking the glass of milk. What Hsee et al. found was that the happiness reported after receipt of the coupon didn't depend on whether a person was a member of the rich or poor group – it just depended on their relative positioning *within* that group. However, when people reported their happiness after consumption, the happiness level depended just on absolute properties of the milk.

[4] I want to distinguish between different kinds of negative valence and the forms it can take. People do post about family funerals or experiences of surviving abusive relationships or dysfunctional families. My point is that these stories often belong to a larger positive narrative of survival, endurance, and overcoming. Or they can illustrate involvement in individual or collective acts of protest against injustice. A person engaging in self-harm may post photos of the act, but that is generally viewed as a call for help. The act I am claiming to be rare is the sharing, by a person, of the kind of ordinary, day-to-day negative experiences which leave one feeling overwhelmed, out of control, alienated, disquieted, unhappy or helpless, without a concomitant attempt to seek

redress. From the point of view of managing your personal brand, failure, depression, anxiety, alienation, and anomie make poor copy.

14. We'll be watching you

[1] *Most* of it is still available for viewing by the public. The one exception is his head, which didn't respond to the embalming nearly as well as the rest of his body and went cheesy shortly after his death. Bentham's head was thus replaced by a wax replica. If you search the internet, you can find images of the current state of Bentham's preserved head, but I don't recommend it.

[2] Amos Tversky died in 1996 and the Nobel Prize cannot be received posthumously.

[3] Much has been written recently about the ethics and appropriateness of using "nudges" to shape people's behaviour (see Thaler and Sunstein 2009). While I think there are some cases where nudging is not ethical, my concerns here are with much more invasive and troubling applications.

[4] The main contending theories invoke additional concerns of the voter that make voting instrumentally rational despite the low probability of being pivotal. For example, if you believe that you have a *duty* to vote, then you will make an effort to vote because it is rational to do your duty (Mackie 2014). Alternatively, there is the expressivist theory of voting, which says that a person casts a vote in order to signal that they have certain values or belong to a certain group (Brennan and Lomasky 1993). This second point relates to issues we'll cover in Part IV.

[5] Yes, I know; two statements can be contradictory *to a degree* in the same way a woman can be a little bit pregnant. The statements weren't *literal* contradictions. They conflicted in that their natural interpretation, which required filling in some hidden assumptions, would be contradictory, yet they admitted other interpretations which reconciled the conflict.

[6] The explanation they give is that in such circumstances people overestimate their chances of being pivotal. One might also wonder if there is some regret aversion at work, too; imagine how bad you would feel in a close election where your side was ahead, but you *didn't* vote, only to have the other side squeak through to victory.

[7] In Chapter 16 of Part III, I'll explore this point further, looking at how laws protecting freedom of speech can be exploited by the unscrupulous for this purpose.

[8] Insidious methods of voter suppression include putting bureaucratic hurdles in place to discourage certain classes of people from voting, or denying people the right to vote due to prior convictions. As an example of the former method, Hebert and Lang (2016) report: "In North Carolina, the legislature requested racial data on the use of electoral mechanisms, then restricted all

those disproportionately used by blacks, such as early voting, same-day registration and out-of-precinct voting. Absentee ballots, disproportionately used by white voters, were exempted from the voter ID requirement [...] The documents acceptable for proving voters' identity in North Carolina were the ones disproportionately held by whites, such as driver's licenses, US passports, and veteran and military IDs, and the ones that were left out were the ones often held by poor minority voters, such as student IDs, government employee IDs and public assistance IDs. The Texas voter ID law was designed the same way: There, officials accepted concealed-weapon licenses but not student or state employee IDs." An example of the second method is what is known as felony disenfranchisement. Lai and Lee (2016) note that 10% of the voting population in Florida, a major swing state, is disenfranchised due to prior felony convictions. However, my interest here lies with less blatant methods of attempting to influence voter turnout.

[9] The UK Brexit referendum may provide an illustration of this. The Brexit verdict was delivered by a 52% to 48% win (BBC News 2016), or 17,410,742 votes to 16,141,241. The population of the UK in 2016 was 65.4 million people, of which 46,501,241 were in the electorate. Of those eligible to vote, 72.2% participated, or approximately 33.6 million. The number of people who *could* have voted, but didn't, was more than 25 times the winning margin of Vote Leave.

[10] I will return to this point in Chapter 29.

15. Concluding remarks

[1] Space constraints have prevented me from covering more than a mere fraction of what is possible and what has been done. For example, consider Pegasus, the software originally designed by the NSO Group to track terrorists and members of organised criminal networks. Pegasus allowed governments to circumvent the security protections that were built into the software of smart phones, allowing the user's emails, text messages, photos, appointments, to be harvested. Pegasus even allowed governments to record the keystrokes of users *while using applications that provided encrypted communication.*

There's no doubt that this power gave police an advantage in the fight against crime. Pegasus led to the arrest of the Mexican drug lord El Chapo, and was used to break up a number of child-abuse rings (Kitroeff and Bergman 2023). However, interest in Pegasus spread well beyond what one might consider its reasonable use. Pegasus has been implicated in the assassination of Jamal Kashoggi. It was proven to have been installed on the phone of his wife, Hanan Elatr, months before his murder. In addition, the FBI purchased the Pegasus software "for product testing and evaluation" purposes *after* the software was blacklisted by the Biden administration (Mazzetti and Bergman 2023). Although there is, at the time I write this, no evidence that the FBI has used Pegasus against the US population, the FBI has given demonstrations of other software, known as Phantom, that could hack American phones. A brochure obtained by the *New York Times* advertised Phantom to US law enforcement claiming that it could "turn your target's smartphone into an intelligence gold mine" (Levenson 2022).

[2] Measuring the efficacy of online advertising is tricky, but two standard key performance indicators are used – the click-through-rate (CTR), and the click-conversion rate (CCR). Because people do not click on an advertisement every time they see it, you need to first measure, on average, how many times you need to show an advertisement to people before someone eventually clicks on it. The CTR, a percentage, is defined as follows:

$$\frac{\text{Total number of ad clicks}}{\text{Total number of ad impressions}} \times 100 = \text{CTR}.$$

The CTR varies across social media platforms and the kind of ads we are talking about. For instance, the average CTR in 2023 for Facebook was 0.9% (Gardner 2023). So just over one hundred ad impressions were required in order to get a single user to click.

But not every click by a user results in a positive outcome for the company that placed the ad, be it a sale, a new contract, or whatever. (This is known as a "conversion".) This is where the CCR comes in. The CCR attempts to measure how many clicks are required in order to generate an outcome the company wants. It is defined as:

$$\frac{\text{Total number of ad coversions}}{\text{Total number of ad clicks}} \times 100 = \text{CCR}.$$

Again, taking Facebook as an example, the average CCR across industries is 9.31%. That means that just under one in every ten people who click on an ad takes further action to the company's benefit. So even *with* highly specific targeted advertising, it takes about 1,000 impressions in order to get one positive result.

[3] We will revisit some of these questions in Chapter 29.

[4] The abolition of slavery in the British empire took several decades. The slave *trade* was officially abolished by the Slave Trade Act in 1807, but existing slaves were not freed in colonies of the British empire until years later. The Slavery Abolition Act 1833 paved the way for the gradual elimination of slavery in most parts of the British Empire, with exceptions for territories controlled by the East India Company, Ceylon, and St. Helena. The 1833 Act freed slaves younger than six years of age, but converted slaves older than six to apprentices, with the apprenticeships ending in two stages: one lot ending on 1 August 1838 and the second lot ending on 1 August 1840. In addition, the 1833 Act set aside twenty million pounds (equivalent to nearly £2.2 billion in 2023) for the financial compensation of slave-owners. Slavery was not abolished in areas

controlled by the East India Company until the Indian Slavery Act 1843 was passed. However, *even then* slavery was replaced by other forms of indentured labour (see Dingwaney 1985).

[5] It has been argued (see Williams 1944) that the institution of slavery was already in decline as a result of industrialisation, and the abolitionist movement merely hastened its end. However, the modern consensus is that this was far from the case. Drescher (2010) argued that abolition of slavery actually occurred at a time when it was still very much economically viable, and that ending the slave trade imposed great expense on the government. A detailed discussion of this topic can be found in Macaskill (2022) (see, in particular, the section "The Contingency of Abolition").

[6] Although it is worth noting that the practice of slavery persisted longer than most people know: Mauritania was the last country to officially abolish slavery, in 1981.

References

Arendt, Hannah. (1959). *The Human Condition*. Anchor Books.

Asch, S. E. (1951). "Effects of Group Pressure Upon the Modification and Distortion of Judgments." In Guetzkow, Harold (ed.), *Groups, Leadership and Men: Research in Human Relations*, 177–190. Rutgers University Press.

Asch, Solomon E. (1956). "Studies of independence and conformity: I. A minority of one against a unanimous majority." *Psychological Monographs: General and Applied* 70 (9):1–70.
https://doi.org/10.1037/h0093718

BBC. (8 March 2012). "Caution on Twitter urged as tourists barred from US."
https://www.bbc.co.uk/news/technology-16810312

BBC News. (2016). "EU Referendum Results."
https://www.bbc.co.uk/news/politics/eu_referendum/results

Bertrand, Marianne and Sendhil Mullainathan. (2004). "Are Emily and Greg More Employable than Lakisha and Jamal? A Field Experiment on Labor Market Discrimination." *The American Economic Review* 94 (4):991–1013.
https://doi.org/10.1257/0002828042002561

Bicchieri, Cristina. (2005). *The Grammar of Society: The Nature and Dynamics of Social Norms*. Cambridge University Press.
https://doi.org/10.1017/CBO9780511616037

Bicchieri, Cristina. (2017). *Norms in the Wild: How to Diagnose, Measure, and Change Social Norms*. Oxford University Press.
https://doi.org/10.1093/acprof:oso/9780190622046.001.0001

Bloom, Pazit Ben-Nun. (2014). "Disgust, Harm, and Morality in Politics." *Political Psychology* 35 (4):495–513.
https://doi.org/10.1111/pops.12053

Brennan, Geoffrey and Loren Lomasky. (1993). *Democracy and Decision: The Pure Theory of Electoral Preference*. Cambridge University Press.
https://doi.org/10.1017/CBO9781139173544

British Broadcasting Corporation. (18 October 2016). "Jennicam: The first woman to stream her life on the internet."
https://www.bbc.co.uk/news/magazine-37681006

Buell, Ryan W., Tami Kim, and Tsay Chia-Jung. (2014). "Cooks Make Tastier Food When They Can See Their Customers." *Harvard Business Review* 92 (11):34–35.

Cadwalladr, Carole. (May 7 2017). "The great British Brexit robbery: how our democracy was hijacked." *The Guardian*.
https://www.theguardian.com/technology/2017/may/07/the-great-british-brexit-robbery-hijacked-democracy

Caprara, Gian Vittorio and Philip G. Zimbardo. (2004). "Personalizing Politics: A Congruency Model of Political Preference." *American Psychologist* 59 (7):581–594.
https://doi.org/10.1037/0003-066X.59.7.581

Carlson, Nicholas. (13 May 2010). "Well, These New Zuckerberg IMs Won't Help Facebook's Privacy Problems." *Business Insider*. https://www.businessinsider.com/well-these-new-zuckerberg-ims-wont-help-facebooks-privacy-problems-2010-5

Catalano, Michele. (1 August 2013). "My family's Google searching got us a visit from counterterrorism police." *The Guardian*. https://www.theguardian.com/commentisfree/2013/aug/01/government-tracking-google-searches

Clark, Andrew E., Paul Frijters, and Michael A. Shields. (2008). "Relative Income, Happiness, and Utility: An Explanation for the Easterlin Paradox and Other Puzzles." *Journal of Economic Literature* 46 (1):95–144. https://doi.org/10.1257/jel.46.1.95

Cohen, Andrew. (16 February 2023). "Facial recognition in sports: The biometrics technology shaping ticketing, payments, security, more." *Sports Business Journal*. https://www.sportsbusinessjournal.com/Journal/Issues/2023/01/09/Technology/facial-recognition-technology-sports-stadiums.aspx

Cohen, Josh. (2013). *The Private Life: Why We Remain in the Dark*. Berkeley: Counterpoint.

Connellan, Michael. (27 January 2010). "Women suffer from Gandhi's legacy." *The Guardian*. https://www.theguardian.com/commentisfree/2010/jan/27/mohandas-gandhi-women-india

DeLong, Brad. (12 January 2011). "On the Richness of the Rich Once Again." https://delong.typepad.com/sdj/2011/01/on-the-richness-of-the-rich-once-again.html

Dennett, Daniel C. (1984). *Elbow room: The varieties of free will worth wanting*. MIT Press.

Diamond, Jared. (2012). *The World Until Yesterday*. Penguin Books.

Dingwaney, Manjari. (1985). "Unredeemed Promises: The Law and Servitude." In Patnaik, Utsa and Manjari Dingwaney (eds.), *Chains of Servitude: Bondage and Slavery in India*, chapter 9, 283–347. Sangam Books.

Dirda, Michael. (28 August 2013). "Oxford Dictionaries adds 'twerk,' 'FOMO,' 'selfie,' and other words that make me vom." *The Washington Post*. https://www.washingtonpost.com/lifestyle/style/oxford-dictionaries-adds-twerk-fomo-selfie-and-other-words-that-make-me-vom/2013/08/28/678ddd48-102c-11e3-8cdd-bcdc09410972_story.html

Doris, John M. (2002). *Lack of Character: Personality and Moral Behavior*. Cambridge University Press. https://doi.org/10.1017/CBO9781139878364

Drescher, Seymour. (2010). *Econocide: British Slavery in the Era of Abolition*. The University of North Carolina Press, 2nd edition.

Duhigg, Charles. (16 February 2012). "How Companies Learn Your Secrets." *The New York Times Magazine*.
https://www.nytimes.com/2012/02/19/magazine/shopping-habits.html
Dunbar, Robin IM. (1992). "Neocortex size as a constraint on group size in primates." *Journal of Human Evolution* 22 (6):469–493.
https://doi.org/10.1016/0047-2484(92)90081-J
Duncan, Pamela. (27 July 2017). "Gay relationships are still criminalised in 72 countries, report finds." *The Guardian*.
https://www.theguardian.com/world/2017/jul/27/gay-relationships-still-criminalised-countries-report
Easterlin, Richard A. (1974). "Does Economic Growth Improve the Human Lot? Some Empirical Evidence." In David, R. and M. Reder (eds.), *Nations and Households in Economic Growth: Essays in Honor of Moses Abramovitz*, 89–125. New York: Academic Press.
https://doi.org/10.1016/B978-0-12-205050-3.50008-7
Easterlin, Richard A, Laura Angelescu McVey, Malgorzata Switek, Onnicha Sawangfa, and Jacqueline Smith Zweig. (2010). "The happiness—income paradox revisited." *Proceedings of the National Academy of Sciences* 107 (52):22463–22468.
https://doi.org/10.1073/pnas.1015962107
Fisher, Kira. (13 October 2015). "Sad Desk Lunch."
https://saddesklunch.com
Gardner, Madelyn. (17 February 2023). "Social Advertising Benchmarks for 2024."
https://www.brafton.com/blog/social-media/social-advertising-benchmarks/
Goldstine, Herman. (1980). *The Computer from Pascal to von Neumann*. Princeton University Press.
Grice, H. Paul. (1957). "Meaning." *The philosophical review* 66 (3):377–388.
https://doi.org/10.2307/2182440
Hebert, J. Gerald and Danielle Lang. (3 August 2016). "Courts are finally pointing out the racism behind voter ID laws." *The Washington Post*.
https://www.washingtonpost.com/posteverything/wp/2016/08/03/courts-are-finally-pointing-out-the-racism-behind-voter-id-laws/
Hooper, Richard. (3 November 2016). "The man who records his entire life." *BBC*.
https://www.bbc.co.uk/news/magazine-37631646
Hsee, Christopher K, Yang Yang, Naihe Li, and Luxi Shen. (2009). "Wealth, warmth, and well-being: Whether happiness is relative or absolute depends on whether it is about money, acquisition, or consumption." *Journal of Marketing Research* 46 (3):396–409.
https://doi.org/10.1509/jmkr.46.3.396
Hymas, Charles. (25 June 2023). "Police solve no thefts at all in most neighbourhoods." *The Telegraph*.

https://www.telegraph.co.uk/news/2023/06/25/theft-decriminalised-two-thirds-neighbourhoods-police/

Inbar, Yoel, David Pizarro, Ravi Iyer, and Jonathan Haidt. (2012). "Disgust sensitivity, political conservatism, and voting." *Social Psychological and Personality Science* 3 (5):537–544. https://doi.org/10.1177/1948550611429024

Inbar, Yoel, David A. Pizarro, and Paul Bloom. (2009). "Conservatives are more easily disgusted than liberals." *Cognition and emotion* 23 (4):714–725. https://doi.org/10.1080/02699930802110007

Inman, Arthur Crew. (1985). *The Inman Diary: A Public and Private Confession*, volume 1 and 2. Harvard University Press.

James, William. (1890). *The Principles of Psychology*, volume 1. New York, NY: Holt.

Janus, Samuel S. and Cynthia L. Janus. (1993). *The Janus Report on Sexual Behavior*. John Wiley & Sons, Inc.

Kachka, Boris. (27 May 2014). "Why One Norwegian Author's 6-Volume, 3,600-Page Book Is on the Verge of Breaking Out in America." *New York Magazine*. https://www.vulture.com/2014/05/karl-ove-knausgaard-boyhood-profile.html

Kerr, Ted. (2 July 2020). "39 Years Later, The New York Times' 1981 'Gay Cancer' Story Continues to Distort Early AIDS History." *The Body*. https://www.thebody.com/article/new-york-times-1981-gay-cancer-story-distorts-aids-history

Keynes, John Maynard. (1921). *A Treatise on Probability*. London: Macmillan.

Kinsey, Alfred C., Wardel B. Pomeroy, and Clyde E. Martin. (1948). *Sexual Behavior in the Human Male*. Philadelphia and London: W. B. Saunders Company.

Kitroeff, Natalie and Ronen Bergman. (18 April 2023). "How Mexico Became the Biggest User of the World's Most Notorious Spy Tool." *The New York Times*. https://www.nytimes.com/2023/04/18/world/americas/pegasus-spyware-mexico.html

Klor, Esteban F. and Eyal Winter. (2018). "On Public Opinion Polls and Voters' Turnout." *Journal of Public Economic Theory* 20 (2):239–256. https://doi.org/10.1111/jpet.12274

Krugman, Paul. (12 January 2011). "Why Does Inequality Make the Rich Feel Poorer?" *The New York Times*. https://archive.nytimes.com/krugman.blogs.nytimes.com/2011/01/12/why-does-inequality-make-the-rich-feel-poorer/

Kruse, Kevin. (2 December 2013). "Transparency Eats Culture For Lunch." *Forbes*.

https://www.forbes.com/sites/kevinkruse/2013/12/02/transparency-eats-culture-for-lunch/

Kumar, S. (22 May 2015). "Why Monitoring Employees' Social Media Is a Bad Idea." *Time*. https://time.com/3894276/social-media-monitoring-work/

Lai, K. K. Rebecca and Jasmine C. Lee. (October 6 2016). "Why 10% of Florida Adults Can't Vote: How Felony Convictions Affect Access to the Ballot." *The New York Times*. https://www.nytimes.com/interactive/2016/10/06/us/unequal-effect-of-laws-that-block-felons-from-voting.html

Laiou, Alexandra, Katerina Folla, George Yannis, Robert Bauer, Klaus Machata, Christian Brandstaetter, Pete Thomas, and Alan Kirk. (2016). "Comparative analysis of road accidents by gender in Europe." *Injury Prevention* 22 (Suppl 2):A305–A305. https://doi.org/10.1136/injuryprev-2016-042156.856

Layard, Richard. (2005). *Happiness: Lessons from a New Science*. London: Penguin.

Levenson, Michael. (28 January 2022). "F.B.I. Secretly Bought Israeli Spyware and Explored Hacking U.S. Phones." *The New York Times*. https://www.nytimes.com/2022/01/28/world/middleeast/israel-pegasus-spyware.html

Macaskill, William. (2022). *What We Owe The Future: A Million-Year View*. Oneworld Publishing.

Mackie, Gerry. (2014). "Why It's Rational to Vote." In López-Guerra, Claudio and Julia Maskivker (eds.), *Rationality, Democracy, and Justice: The Legacy of Jon Elster*, 21–49. Cambridge University Press. https://doi.org/10.1017/CBO9781107588165.005

Martin, Douglas. (29 October 2007). "Robert Shields, Wordy Diarist, Dies at 89." *The New York Times*. https://www.nytimes.com/2007/10/29/us/29shields.html

Martin, Joyce A., Brady E. Hamilton, Michelle J. K. Osterman, Anne K. Driscoll, and T. J. Mathews. (2015). "Births: Final Data for 2015." *National Vital Statistics Reports* 66 (1):1–69.

Mazzetti, Mark and Ronen Bergman. (2 April 2023). "A Front Company and a Fake Identity: How the U.S. Came to Use Spyware It Was Trying to Kill." *The New York Times*. https://www.nytimes.com/2023/04/02/us/politics/nso-contract-us-spy.html

McNutt & Partners. (25 January 2021). "Why We See Digital Ads After Talking About Something." https://www.mcnuttpartners.com/why-we-see-digital-ads-after-talking-about-something/

McRobbie, Linda Rodriguez. (8 February 2017). "Total recall: the people who never forget." *The Guardian*.

https://www.theguardian.com/science/2017/feb/08/total-recall-the-people-who-never-forget

Milgram, Stanley. (1967). "The small world problem." *Psychology Today* 2 (1):61–67. https://doi.org/10.1037/e400002009-005

Mill, John Stuart. (1859). *On Liberty*. London: John W. Parker and Son, West Strand.

Payne, B Keith, Jon A Krosnick, Josh Pasek, Yphtach Lelkes, Omair Akhtar, and Trevor Tompson. (2010). "Implicit and explicit prejudice in the 2008 American presidential election." *Journal of Experimental Social Psychology* 46 (2):367–374. https://doi.org/10.1016/j.jesp.2009.11.001

Posey, Kirby G. (2016). "Household Income: 2015 — American Community Survey Briefs." Technical report, United States Census Bureau. https://www.census.gov/content/dam/Census/library/publications/2016/acs/acsbr15-02.pdf

Preston, Alex. (3 August 2014). "The death of privacy." *The Guardian*. https://www.theguardian.com/world/2014/aug/03/internet-death-privacy-google-facebook-alex-preston

Przybylski, Andrew K., Kou Murayama, Cody R. DeHaan, and Valerie Gladwell. (2013). "Motivational, emotional, and behavioral correlates of fear of missing out." *Computers in Human Behavior* 29 (4):1841–1848. https://doi.org/10.1016/j.chb.2013.02.014

Rampell, Catherine. (11 January 2011). "Why So Many Rich People Don't Feel Very Rich." *The New York Times*. https://archive.nytimes.com/economix.blogs.nytimes.com/2011/01/11/why-so-many-rich-people-dont-feel-very-rich/

Robison, Jennifer. (8 October 2002). "What Percentage of the Population Is Gay?" *Gallup*. https://news.gallup.com/poll/6961/what-percentage-population-gay.aspx

Robson, David. (26 January 2016). "The blessing and curse of the people who never forget." *BBC Future*. https://www.bbc.com/future/article/20160125-the-blessing-and-curse-of-the-people-who-never-forget

Ronson, Jon. (2015). *So You've Been Publicly Shamed*. Riverhead Books.

Ross, Lee. (1977). "The intuitive psychologist and his shortcomings: Distortions in the attribution process." *Advances in Experimental Social Psychology* 10:173–220. https://doi.org/10.1016/S0065-2601(08)60357-3

Russell, Bertrand. (1937). *The Principles of Mathematics*. London: George Allen & Unwin, Ltd., 2nd edition.

Russell, Jon. (4 September 2017). "Alibaba debuts 'smile to pay' facial recognition payments at KFC in China." *TechCrunch*. https://techcrunch.com/2017/09/03/alibaba-debuts-smile-to-pay/

Saunders, Hayley. (12 January 2023). "Councils issue nearly 20,000 parking fines per day." *DirectLineGroup*. https://www.directlinegroup.co.uk/en/news/brand-news/2023/12012023.html

Service, Elman R. (1962). *Primitive Social Organization: an Evolutionary Perspective*. Random House, New York.

Sinner, Michele and Myles Neligan. (1 March 2011). "EU court bans insurers from pricing on gender." *Reuters*. https://www.reuters.com/article/uk-europe-insurance/eu-court-bans-insurers-from-pricing-on-gender-idUKTRE72O1O720110301/

Smith, Michael French. (1994). *Hard Times on Kairiru Island: Poverty, Development, and Morality in a Papua New Guinea Village*. University of Hawaii Press: Honolulu. https://doi.org/10.1515/9780824843267

Solove, Daniel J. (2011). *Nothing to Hide: The False Tradeoff between Privacy and Security*. Yale University Press.

Statista. (December 2022a). "Number of Twitter users worldwide from 2019 to 2022." https://www.statista.com/statistics/303681/twitter-users-worldwide/

Statista. (May 2022b). "Number of unique WhatsApp mobile users worldwide from January 2020 to June 2022." https://www.statista.com/statistics/1306022/whatsapp-global-unique-users/

Statista. (February 2023a). "Number of monthly active Facebook users worldwide as of 4th quarter 2022." https://www.statista.com/statistics/264810/number-of-monthly-active-facebook-users-worldwide/

Statista. (March 2023b). "Number of monthly active users of Weibo Corporation from 1st quarter of 2014 to 4th quarter of 2022." https://www.statista.com/statistics/795303/china-mau-of-sina-weibo/

Statista. (March 2023c). "Number of monthly active WeChat users from 2nd quarter 2011 to 4th quarter 2022." https://www.statista.com/statistics/255778/number-of-active-wechat-messenger-accounts/

Stephens-Davidowitz, Seth. (2017). *Everybody Lies: What the Internet Can Tell Us About Who We Really Are*. Bloomsbury Publishing.

Stevenson, Betsey and Justin Wolfers. (2008). "Economic Growth and Subjective Well-Being: Reassessing the Easterlin Paradox." *Brookings Papers on Economic Activity* 2008:1–87. https://doi.org/10.1353/eca.0.0001

Thaler, Richard H. and Cass R. Sunstein. (2009). *Nudge: Improving Decisions about Health, Wealth and Happiness*. Penguin.

The Economist. (16 July 2015). "A few dollars less." *The Economist*. https://www.economist.com/finance-and-economics/2015/07/16/a-few-dollars-less

The Economist. (2017)a. "Advances in AI are used to spot signs of sexuality." *The Economist.*
The Economist. (26 October 2017)b. "Preventing ex-convicts from working is silly." *The Economist.* https://www.economist.com/united-states/2017/10/26/preventing-ex-convicts-from-working-is-silly
Tirrell, Meg. (14 December 2015). "Unlocking my genome: Was it worth it?" *CNBC.* https://www.cnbc.com/2015/12/10/unlocking-my-genome-was-it-worth-it.html
United Kingdom Home Office. (November 2016). "Country Policy and Information Note — Iran: Adulterers."
Walters, Joanna. (7 November 2017). "Woman who gave Donald Trump the middle finger fired from her job." *The Guardian.* https://www.theguardian.com/us-news/2017/nov/06/woman-trump-middle-finger-fired-juli-briskman
Wang, Yilun and Michal Kosinski. (2018). "Deep Neural Networks Are More Accurate Than Humans at Detecting Sexual Orientation From Facial Images." *Journal of Personality and Social Psychology* 114 (2):246–257. https://doi.org/10.1037/pspa0000098
Warhol, Andy. (1975). *The Philosophy of Andy Warhol: From A to B & Back Again.* Harcourt Brace Jovanovich.
Watkins, J. W. N. (May 1953). "Ideal Types and Historical Explanation." *The British Journal for the Philosophy of Science* 3 (9):22–43. https://doi.org/10.1093/bjps/III.9.22
Westen, Drew. (2008). *The Political Brain: The Role of Emotion in Deciding the Fate of the Nation.* Public Affairs.
Wetterstrand, Kris A. (1 February 2024). "DNA Sequencing Costs: Data from the NHGRI Genome Sequencing Program (GSP)." National Human Genome Research Institute. https://www.genome.gov/sequencingcostsdata
Williams, Eric. (1944). *Capitalism and Slavery.* Chapel Hill: The University of North Carolina Press.

PART III
Safe spaces
The Enlightenment conception of the Open Society

16. Generation Wuss?

One might expect Bret Easton Ellis, author of *American Psycho*, to have no truck with the overly sensitive. How else would he have been able to think himself into the headspace of a chainsaw-wielding psychopath? And there's some truth to that: Ellis attracted a fair bit of attention over his critical comments in a *Vice* interview, where he complained about what he saw as the excessively delicate nature of the Millennials, who he dubbed "Generation Wuss". In a later follow-up piece published in *Vanity Fair*, he elaborated on why he thought that the Millennials had a number of traits that made them not as robust as his own Generation X. What collection of traits was Ellis concerned with? Here's a brief list:

> My huge generalities touch on their over-sensitivity, their insistence that they are right despite the overwhelming proof that suggests they are not, their lack of placing things within context, the overreacting, the passive-aggressive positivity, and, of course, all of this exacerbated by the meds they've been fed since childhood by over-protective 'helicopter' parents mapping their every move.

If his characterisation is correct, one problem is that the Millennial attitude isn't well-adapted to a Hobbesian world where life is "nasty, poor, brutish and short". The overly sensitive nature of Generation Wuss, said Ellis, leaves them exposed and vulnerable and less able to negotiate an unfriendly world. When faced with harsh truths, "Generation Wuss responds by collapsing into sentimentality and creating victim narratives rather than acknowledging the realities of the world and grappling with them and processing them and then moving on."

Setting aside the question of whether Ellis's characterisation of Generation Wuss is correct, there's no doubt that the *zeitgeist* features the idea that younger generations have a lot of "snowflakes". In March 2016, students at Emory University woke up to find "Trump 2016" written in chalk on some sidewalks and walls. One student was quoted as saying, "I think it was an act of violence, I legitimately feared for my life" (Haidt and Haslam 2016). Related to

How to cite this book part:

Alexander, J. McKenzie (2024) *The Open Society as an Enemy: A critique of how free societies turned against themselves*, London: LSE Press, pp. 173–221.
https://doi.org/10.31389/lsepress.ose.d. License: CC BY-NC 4.0

the "snowflake" critique is the idea that some people are less willing (although not necessarily less able) to engage with ideas they find unsettling.[1] Examples of this phenomenon have been much talked about, such as the increased use of "trigger warnings" in the classroom, demands for "safe spaces", moves to "no-platform" controversial speakers, and increased concern about "extremist speech" and its connection to radicalisation.

The demand for safe spaces of various kinds highlights a sense in which the Enlightenment conception of the Open Society is seen as an enemy. This conception involves the free exchange of ideas, marked by participation in the ideal of free inquiry and rational debate and of the willingness to defend the expression of ideas with which one profoundly disagrees.[2] Is the free exchange of ideas under threat by Generation Wuss, who just can't cope with troubling ideas? Or does the very characterisation of some people as "snowflakes" disregard legitimate concerns through the use of a disparaging *ad hominem*? As we'll see, the answer is a little bit of both.

17. Trigger warnings

A "trigger warning" (also known as a "content advisory warning") is a statement included at the beginning of a text, video, song, or performance alerting people that the content contains material that some might find disturbing. Anyone purchasing music in the US from 1985 onwards would be familiar with warning labels from the Parents Music Resource Center, alerting the consumer that the content might be objectionable.[1] Television programmes often include notices warning that the content might be unsuitable for younger viewers, and various film boards around the world rate films as suitable for certain groups based on local cultural criteria. All of these can be seen as trigger warnings of varying degrees of usefulness.

There has been considerable discussion about the use of trigger warnings in the classroom. This reached a high point in 2015 with the publication in *The Atlantic* of an essay by Greg Lukianoff and Jonathan Haidt titled "The Coddling of the American Mind" (extended to a book in 2018). In that essay, the authors link the movement urging trigger warnings with the idea of turning campuses into "safe spaces" where students are "shielded from words and ideas that make some uncomfortable". They connect this movement with an underlying psychological attitude, which they call "vindictive protectiveness", that "seeks to punish anyone who interferes with that aim, even accidentally". This movement and the culture it seeks to create, they claim, poses a *significant danger* (their phrase) to the quality of American universities and scholarship. Heady stuff.

What's the concern about trigger warnings? Let's begin by acknowledging some perfectly legitimate uses of trigger warnings. If you are about to show a video containing flash photography or strobe effects in a lecture, you *should* tell people in advance. Why? Because flash photography and strobe effects can trigger seizures in people with photosensitive epilepsy. Warning people about the content of a video containing strobe effects isn't mollycoddling students, it's simply being a responsible educator by trying to prevent avoidable harm that is not required by the learning process.

As a general principle, I think that's one we can all get behind – one should try to prevent avoidable harm that is not required by the learning process. That principle is one reason it's no longer acceptable to beat students who fail a test. The difficulty is that, as with all general principles, people can reasonably disagree on how to interpret every one of the key terms in it.

In saying that one "should try to prevent" harm in certain contexts, there is an implicit cost-benefit calculation in the background. One only need to take reasonable steps to prevent harm and not do everything possible, because that would not be cost-effective. I *will* mention that a video I am about to show contains strobe lighting, but I *won't* check all the video cables in the lecture theatre, even if a loose video cable could cause effects visually similar to strobe lighting.

There's also a debate to be had about what constitutes *harm*.[2] Part of what underlies the debate over trigger warnings and safe spaces is a disagreement about the concept of harm and what harms educators should work to prevent. The difficulty here is that talking about harm will move us very quickly from *universally* recognised harms (such as seizures) to *generally* recognised harms (such as post-traumatic stress disorder)[3] to notions of harm that are more controversial (such as microaggressions).[4] I'll return to the issue of harm and microaggressions below, as they appear prominently in the critique made by Lukianoff and Haidt.

Finally, in our purported principle, there is the question of whether some harms are required by the learning process. The unpleasant physicality of basic training is a requirement of joining the military because a certain threshold of fitness is required for being a soldier. If you find calculus boring and tough, you are just going to have to cope if you want to become a physicist. Any course in international relations requires a person to get to grips with a sea of acronyms regarding international organisations. It seems that, occasionally, some learning does require having unpleasant experiences. But harm, though?

One worry people express about trigger warnings is that once you start listing things people might find upsetting, it's hard to know where to stop. This is illustrated by examples such as the following: requests that *The Great Gatsby* feature trigger warnings for "suicide", "domestic abuse", and "graphic violence", and students reading Chinua Achebe's novel *Things Fall Apart* be warned that the novel is "a triumph of literature that everyone in the world should read. However, it may trigger readers who have experienced racism, colonialism, religious persecution, violence, suicide, and more."[5] Other examples, noted by Lukianoff and Haidt (2015), include Virginia Woolf's *Mrs. Dalloway* (with warnings about "suicidal inclinations") and Ovid's *Metamorphoses* (with warnings about "sexual assault").

All things considered, worrying about where to stop when listing warnings is a pretty minor one for the following reasons. First, few people suggest trigger warnings are supposed to be *exhaustive* – just an exercise in basic common sense about things people might find deeply troubling. Second, when it comes to identifying things people "might find deeply troubling", a natural benchmark already exists – a benchmark that educators should already be aware of, given the duty of care we have towards our students – established for diagnosing the condition of post-traumatic stress disorder. This is a clinically recognised mental disorder that has a fairly specific set of diagnostic criteria. Here is the list of stressors and intrusive symptoms, as listed on the website for the *US Department of Veterans Affairs* (not an organisation that can be plausibly said to pander to snowflakes):

Criterion A (one required): The person was exposed to: death, threatened death, actual or threatened serious injury, or actual or threatened sexual violence in the following way(s):

- Direct exposure
- Witnessing the trauma
- Learning that a relative or close friend was exposed to a trauma
- Indirect exposure to aversive details of the trauma, usually in the course of professional duties (e.g., first responders, medics)

Criterion B (one required): The traumatic event is persistently re-experienced in the following way(s):

- Intrusive thoughts
- Nightmares
- Flashbacks
- Emotional distress after exposure to traumatic reminders
- Physical reactivity after exposure to traumatic reminders

(I omit criteria C through H for reasons of brevity.) If we just focus on those conditions that are part of a clinically recognised medical disorder for which reasonable adjustments should be made, we already have a decent list of subjects to flag: physical or sexual violence, death, and serious injury. That's not too many nor difficult to identify texts where those feature.

Furthermore, this just adds to a pre-existing list of things that instructors already need to consider as part of their duty of care towards students. For instance, students with visual or hearing impairments need to have materials provided to them meeting accessibility requirements. Students with certain medical conditions are given rest breaks when taking exams to allow them to perform at their full capacity. We adjust the teaching calendar so as to accommodate different religious traditions. More recently, the growing recognition of neurodiversity has caused instructors to reflect on whether the traditional lecture-based mode of education is really the best for all students. (It's not.) The debate about trigger warnings thus needs to be situated within the wider context of how best to teach people with diverse backgrounds and complex circumstances but who are all there to learn.

I think there's another important point to keep in mind, one often overlooked – many of these "warnings" would be unnecessary if students were presented with an informative syllabus including not only the author and the title of the text but also a brief explanation of what they were being asked to read and why. Would anyone object to the notice about Achebe's novel if it had been phrased as follows: "This novel is a triumph of literature that everyone in the world should read because of its relevance for understanding racism, colonialism, religious persecution, violence and death." That minor reformulation doesn't explicitly use the words "trigger warning", but it makes it clear what some of the content of the book is and, hence, the frame of mind one should have when approaching the text. This is simply a matter of managing expectations.

Another argument I've heard regarding trigger warnings is that their use interferes with academic freedom regarding teaching pedagogy. The difficulty with this argument is that the number of instances where there are good pedagogical reasons for not informing students, in advance, of what they will be exposed to are few. I imagine that classes in creative writing or in film school will benefit from having students approach material from a state of complete ignorance. After reading a novel or watching a film, students could discuss the theory and methods that made those particular pieces of work so effective. But how often will that kind of issue arise in the natural or social sciences, or philosophy, for that matter?

I suspect that part of what underlies the visceral rejection of trigger warnings is that they partially invert the traditional power dynamic of the classroom. Student need, not faculty interests, are seen as determining or influencing (in part) how content should be presented, which directly challenges those traditionally in power and control of the classroom. But, if so, this seems to ignore the basic point of education, which is to facilitate student learning. If a practice helps facilitate student learning by allowing them to engage more fruitfully with challenging material, what is wrong with that?

I think the real worry people have about trigger warnings is what we might call the *Bartleby objection*, after Herman Melville's short story, *Bartleby the Scrivener*, published in 1853. The story concerns a newly hired clerk who increasingly refuses to do work, saying only, "I would prefer not to" as his reason. The Bartleby objection, then, is that trigger warnings provide a means by which students can opt out of engaging with certain content they deem offensive, troubling, or upsetting. Rather than read an assigned text on a certain topic, a student can instead say, "I would prefer not to", on the grounds that it would upset them. Regardless of whether alternative work is assigned in its place, the resulting intellectual package is *different* from that originally intended, and the lesson is not the same. That could be an important difference.

One reason this concern feels compelling is that much of what people learn at university *can* be offensive, troubling, or upsetting – especially when it challenges us to rethink deeply held beliefs or confront unpleasant facts that we would otherwise not encounter. But the mere fact something is upsetting is not, on its own, sufficient reason for refusing to engage with the material. What matters is *why* something is upsetting. We need to work through several different reasons why material may be upsetting, as there are different responses that are required.

First, let's acknowledge that learning about the Holocaust, genocide, ethnic cleansing, wars, crime, social deviance, mental disorders, racism, the horrors of slavery and colonialism, and so on, is upsetting because those are nasty and horrid facts about the world. Learning about them does force one to engage with disturbing ideas. But there are good reasons why we ask students to do so. Knowing about history and the many horrid injustices that have occurred is necessary for both trying to avoid them in the future and to try to make amends, where possible. This is part of helping people to become informed citizens able to participate in a well-functioning society. A willingness to engage with ideas that one might find troubling is part of the deal one makes when one goes to university.

A second reason why material might be upsetting is because it contradicts the deeply held beliefs of a person. For example, when I was in high school, a deeply religious fellow student objected to studying evolution because it contradicted his religious beliefs. The teacher held his ground and informed the student that if he didn't know the material on evolution and wasn't able to answer the questions related to it in the exam, he would receive a lower grade. The student eventually relented and passed the test, although I strongly suspect that he only went through the motions of learning evolutionary theory rather than adopting any beliefs. The point here is that the mere fact a person has religious or other ideological beliefs that are contradicted or questioned by the material being taught shouldn't count as a reason for opting out. A flat-earther in an astronomy class (or someone who believes the Earth is only 5,000 years old in a geology class) can't get special permission to opt out due to his or her incorrect beliefs. Yet the reason why it is appropriate to deny the opt-out here is that the conflict between individual beliefs and the taught material is one that can be approached while remaining intellectually detached. Someone who deeply believes God exists should still be able to study arguments for why God doesn't exist without feeling personally threatened. If they cannot, that's an important diagnostic tool in assessing the mental fragility of the person.[6]

Where things get complicated is when it isn't possible to maintain intellectual detachment from the material. As a third case, imagine a student who had recently been raped and, hence, objects to being asked to read Alice Walker's *The Color Purple* in a literature class as it contains multiple descriptions of rape and sexual violence. This strikes me as a reasonable instance of when an opt-out should, in principle, be allowed. Unless one is specialising in the work of Alice Walker or writing a PhD thesis about the importance of *The Color Purple* in American literature, it isn't *necessary* to read *The Color Purple*. It could be possible to arrange for an alternative assignment. In this case, I think using a trigger warning with an opt-out permitted would be perfectly acceptable and possibly even required out of a duty of care.

As a fourth case, imagine a Black American taking a course on the history of the slave trade, or a Hispanic person taking a course on immigration in the US after 1950. These examples are ones I assume where intellectual detachment is also likely to be difficult, but where the reactions are likely to be less immediately *visceral* than in the third case. The texts read would likely contain statements that attack, devalue, depersonalise, or otherwise disrespect the racial, ethnic, or social group to which the student belongs and thus might seem candidates for trigger warnings. But, here, the issue about trigger warnings seems *unlikely to arise* in the first place. How could someone take a course on the history of the slave trade without knowing that the course content would contain potentially offensive material given historic attitudes of racism, colonialism, and so on? Regardless of whether trigger warnings are used or not, the difference between the third and fourth case seems to be the following: there are perfectly valid reasons for *why* the materials might be found upsetting in both cases, but that it would be possible, through appropriate classroom management techniques, to introduce and contextualise the materials in the fourth case so as to create an overall positive learning experience.[7]

From this, I conclude that even the Bartleby objection to the use of trigger warnings is largely a non-issue. People take courses because they generally *want* to read and engage with the texts on offer. In those instances where trigger warnings prompt concern and requests for an opt-out, they either yield helpful information about the person revealing other aspects of concern (case two), a legitimate issue that needs to be handled appropriately (case three), or instances where greater care needs to be exercised in the presentation, contextualisation, and explanation of the pedagogical reasons underlying the choice of material (cases one and four).

That said, what if a student *were* to follow Bartleby and sincerely assert "I would prefer not to" when presented with a text, and none of the four cases discussed previously applies? What is the appropriate response? On one hand, this goes against the spirit of the Enlightenment conception of the Open Society. On the other, it would seem to follow from the minimal core discussed in Chapter 4 that we should respect the right of a person to choose to go their own way. The solution to this apparent conflict is to note that this is one instance where the perfect duty of non-interference applies. Choosing to attend university is analogous to entering a new community, a community of scholars, and that means that a student agrees to follow certain rules about the terms of engagement with material, at least initially.[8] The university cannot force a person to engage with material when they refuse; but when they do, the informal contract between the person and the university is broken. The person has the freedom to go their own way, but doing so will either mean a life outside the university or a life with a worse grade on their transcript.

Educational organisations, whether they be schools, colleges, or universities, are dedicated to cultivating a life of the mind and an attitude of critical rationalism. If the goal is to educate students as best as possible and help them become well-informed, resilient, and robust, then judicious use of trigger warnings is just another tool in the pedagogical toolkit. Can they be misused? Sure, but *everything* can be misused. You can die from drinking too much water. Everything in moderation.

18. Safe spaces

Let us now turn to safe spaces. Lukianoff and Haidt saw trigger warnings as part of a broader movement seeking to generate spaces where students are "shielded from words and ideas that make some uncomfortable." I think there's a lot more to the idea of safe spaces than just words and ideas. It also involves addressing behaviours that are sexist, racist, homophobic, transphobic, and bullying or harassing, and how to deal with environments that are shaped, directly or indirectly, by the legacies of colonialism, slavery, and great economic and social inequality.[1] The issue of safe spaces not only concerns how we seek to address past injustices, some of them deeply embedded in structural and cultural aspects of society, but also how we adjudicate disputes between groups of people acting within their legal rights, yet at the same time, who have radically divergent attitudes about what constitutes acceptable norms of speech and behaviour. In short, how do we negotiate the collision of horizons that inevitably takes place in diverse societies?[2]

There are a number of different ideas that fall under the term "safe space" and can easily be conflated. Here are a few: (i) classrooms or seminar rooms should be environments where people do not feel uncomfortable, insecure or threatened; classroom discussions need to be held in an environment of mutual respect and understanding; (ii) universities (or other quasi-autonomous groups, such as student organisations) should quash racism, sexism, and all of the other -isms that are anathema to a modern and tolerant society; (iii) universities (or other organisations) should provide certain spaces, as part of public events, that people can go to if they find the event disturbing; or (iv) universities should make campus a space where no one feels threatened, unsettled, or uneasy; they should aim to provide an environment where everyone feels at home and welcome. The key question is this: *where* should be safe, *for whom*, and *from what*?

Despite the discussion of safe spaces being formulated as if it was a recent invention, the idea has existed for a while. The concept of "safe spaces" can be traced back to at least second-wave feminism when a shift in focus occurred from the pursuit of explicit political ends (the right to vote, the right to own property, and so on) to broader social matters. One part of widening participation in the feminist movement involved what became known as "consciousness-raising" sessions; these were meetings, typically only involving women, where they could congregate and discuss matters of mutual interest and concern. These "safe spaces" provided an environment where women could not only speak freely but, through the sharing of experiences, realise how individual experiences fit into a larger pattern of structural oppression.

One thing that's interesting about the consciousness-raising sessions of second-wave feminism is that they were *explicitly* conceived of as an arena of protected discourse, a "safe space". But other important examples of safe spaces existed prior to that, even if people didn't explicitly conceive of them in that manner. Prior to the decriminalisation of homosexuality in the US and elsewhere, gay bars provided a similar function. In their history of gay culture around San Francisco Bay, Stryker and Van Buskirk (1996) observe, "A gay bar was like a hothouse for nurturing and building a sense of community in a time when there were no gay newspapers or other social centers."

From this perspective, one uncontroversial sense of a "safe space" is simply a place where people sharing common interests can meet in an environment shielded from people outside the group who do not share those interests. Although being able to negotiate a diverse society with people having views different from one's own is important, as we saw in Chapter 4 it's important for a group to be able to meet on its own. That is how groups can reflect on their nature and purpose and mobilise to pursue certain ends. It also provides a place where people can explore how their individual identity relates to that of the group. In this way, the Republican and Democratic National Primaries function as a safe space. In the UK, meetings of Green, Labour, Tory, or UKIP activists are similar kinds of spaces. And what is the annual meeting of the World Economic Forum in Davos other than a safe space for elites?

On this understanding, a safe space is nothing controversial or unusual. Clubs and societies have always had spaces for their members to meet. Yet one crucial feature of these examples is that clubs and societies are institutionalised entities, ones recognised by the wider society – or, at least, those in power – as entities worth supporting (or, at least, not worth suppressing). Hence, the need for such spaces to be "safe" was never really an issue, for these groups, even if marginalised, were not perceived by their members to be under threat.[3] There are a number of instances where things become more complicated. As a crude first attempt to articulate some ideal types, consider the following: (i) when the group, although recognised by the larger society,[4] experiences an imbalance of power with respect to a number of other groups;[5] (ii) when the group is recognised by the wider society, but only as a liminal entity;[6] and (iii) when the group is inchoate, and hence not recognised by the wider society and perhaps not even by its members who understand their identity relative to the group as though through a glass, darkly.[7]

Keeping these ideal types in mind, let us now turn to consider three cases where discussions over safe spaces entered the public consciousness. Each of these cases attracted considerable media attention and, sometimes, considerable secondary commentary. The first case examines the student protests that took place at Yale University during Halloween 2015, initially prompted by an email reflecting on a recent recommendation to be considerate when choosing a costume. These protests led to the resignation of the Head and Associate

Head of Silliman College. The second case examines the student protests at the University of Missouri during the latter half of 2015 following a series of racial incidents. These protests led to the resignation of the University of Missouri System President Tim Wolfe and the Chancellor of the Columbia branch of the University of Missouri, Richard Loftin. The third case examines the decision to offer a special room "equipped with cookies, coloring books, bubbles, Play-Doh, calming music, pillows, blankets and a video of frolicking puppies, as well as students and staff members trained to deal with trauma" (Shulevitz 2015) to anyone who might feel traumatised when Wendy McElroy spoke at Brown University in November 2014. Although these events are a little dated, they are worth considering in some detail, in my opinion, because of the disconnect between how they were represented in much of the media and competing interpretations.

In the autumn of 2015, the Intercultural Affairs Committee at Yale circulated an email asking students to be sensitive when considering their Halloween costumes. In particular, the email pointed out that certain items, such as turbans, feathered headdresses, and blackface, might be seen as culturally insensitive. There had been previous instances of white students wearing blackface during Halloween within the past few years (see Cox and Love 2007), contributing to concerns about racism on campus. Shortly after the email was circulated, Erika Christakis, the Associate Head of Silliman College and a lecturer, sent an email questioning the advice from the Intercultural Affairs Committee. Her email was lengthy, reflective, and carefully written (I suggest you track down a copy on the internet). Near the end of the email, she quoted the Head of Silliman College (her husband):

> Nicholas says, if you don't like a costume someone is wearing, look away, or tell them you are offended. Talk to each other. Free speech and the ability to tolerate offence are the hallmarks of a free and open society.

This email was not received well. Despite the inclusion of a number of self-effacing remarks, such as "I don't wish to trivialize genuine concerns about cultural and personal representation" and "I don't, actually, trust myself to foist my Halloweenish standards and motives on others," a student group was formed in protest. People argued to remove both Erika and Nicholas from campus. One video featuring a group of students surrounding and shouting at Nicholas went viral. In that video, a student can be heard saying: "In your position as master, it is your job to create a place of comfort and home for the students who live in Silliman. You have not done that. By sending out that email, that goes against your position as master. Do you understand that?!" When Nicholas Christakis disagreed, the student responded vitriolically,

> Then why the fuck did you accept the position?! Who the fuck hired you?! You should step down! If that is what you think about

being a master you should step down! It is not about creating an intellectual space! It is not! Do you understand that? It's about creating a home here. You are not doing that!

Much of the discussion in the media was highly critical of the students. Consider the following excerpt from *The Atlantic*:

> The Yale student appears to believe that creating an intellectual space and a home are at odds with one another. But the entire model of a residential college is premised on the notion that it's worthwhile for students to reside in a campus home infused with intellectualism, even though creating it requires lavishing extraordinary resources on youngsters who are already among the world's most advantaged. (Friedersdorf 2015b)

It continued:

> According to *The Washington Post*, 'several students in Silliman said they cannot bear to live in the college anymore.' These are young people who live in safe, heated buildings with two Steinway grand pianos, an indoor basketball court […a lot more…] But they can't bear this setting that millions of people would risk their lives to inhabit because one woman wrote an email that hurt their feelings? (Friedersdorf 2015b)

Lastly, after quoting an open letter signed by hundreds of people at Yale stating that "We [students] were told to meet the offensive parties head on, without suggesting any modes or means to facilitate these discussions to promote understanding," the article said:

> Yale students told to talk to each other if they find a peer's costume offensive helplessly declare that they're unable to do so without an authority figure specifying 'any modes or means to facilitate these discussions,' as if they're Martians unfamiliar with a concept as rudimentary as disagreeing in conversation, even as they publish an open letter that is, itself, a mode of facilitating discussion. (Friedersdorf 2015b)

There's much to say about this. It *is* true that "the entire model of a residential college is premised on the notion that it's worthwhile for students to reside in a campus home infused with intellectualism." Yet what this does is generate a potential conflict because the campus is trying to perform several functions simultaneously, and these functions, on occasion, have conflicting requirements. Insofar as the campus serves as a *home*, the administration has duties of pastoral care; insofar as the campus serves as a *university*, the administration has duties of fostering intellectual inquiry. And while residing "in a campus home infused with intellectualism" has many virtues, we must acknowledge that few people want to spend every moment of their lives as if they were in the middle of a debating society, justifying their choices and defending their way of life. At the end of the day, students – just like everyone else – will often want to go *home* to someplace where they can find respite and solace. Providing such a space is part of the duty of pastoral care. The challenge facing residential colleges lies in defining and delineating the boundaries of the home and educational environments. That they occur in close and possibly overlapping spaces does not mean that the boundary does not exist and should not be respected.

I think Erika's email, and Nicholas's public statements, went awry in two places. First, there was a lack of appreciation of these two sets of potentially conflicting duties (or, at least, a failure to articulate them) and what was required of them in their role as Associate Head and Head of Silliman College. Since Nicholas was a Professor at Yale, and Erika a lecturer, I suspect they were often used to attending to those duties attached to the educational mission of the university – the fostering of intellectual inquiry. Yet the point of concern lay with their responsibilities acquired while wearing their *other* hat as Head and Associate Head of the college: the duties of pastoral care. This is why the student argued (emphasis added)– "*In your position as master*, it is your job to create a place of comfort and home for the students who live in Silliman." Rather than being a rejection of the norms and expectations of free inquiry at university, this statement shows students' awareness of the responsibilities attached to certain institutional roles.

Second, it is important to remember that Yale University is an institution with a history of longstanding racial tensions. One point of concern going back many years was the name of Calhoun College, named after John C. Calhoun, an alumnus of Yale who was a slave owner and a white supremacist.[8] And it wasn't just the *name* of the college that upset people, but the images as well – stained-glass windows in the college showed slaves carrying bales of cotton on their heads. It is against this background of concern for racial inclusivity that we must consider the signal sent by the Head of College saying, "If you don't like a costume someone is wearing, look away or tell them you are offended." Whereas that could be taken as advice when offered by a friend or a peer, when that is offered by the leading administrator in charge of pastoral care at college, that can *also* be seen as *abdicating* responsibility for enforcing norms of what is appropriate or morally required. I suspect it was this perceived abdication of responsibility, leaving the enforcement of certain norms to the group of people most affected by their violation, which generated outrage.

To see why this second point matters so much, we need to expose a critical underlying assumption of the Head of College's statement. Universities encourage an egalitarian ethos where all students are social and political equals.

Yet, in reality, no matter how hard a university tries to maintain this noble illusion, it remains a myth. Social and economic inequalities existing outside the university continue to exercise influence inside the university as students carry with them the attitudes and expectations formed prior to arrival. Someone born into a family of great wealth and power and used to acting with impunity will not suddenly change their behaviour upon enrolling. The imperative "if you don't like a costume someone is wearing, look away or tell them you are offended," *might* make sense in a situation where all are social equals and where all care about the effect they have on others; but this is rarely the situation in practice. If you are Black and see someone wearing blackface, and you tell them that it offends you, but are met with a brush-off or an insult or worse, that exchange only reinforces your lack of power to rectify racial injustice. This is why, in the open letter, students complained about being told to "meet the offensive parties head on, without [the Head of College] suggesting any modes or means to facilitate these discussions."

Some interpreted the students' request for mediation as a curious kind of doublespeak: "Up is down. The person saying that adult men and women should work Halloween out among themselves is accused of infantilizing them" (Friedersdorf 2015b). Yet, on the contrary, I see this as a clear act of *realpolitik* by minority students at Yale. If you are in a minority group attempting to negotiate a hostile environment, you will want to use to your advantage all the institutional levers of power that are available. Given that the First Amendment of the US Constitution permits very few *legal* restrictions on freedom of expression, minority groups who wish to combat racist, sexist, homophobic, transphobic, and other types of offensive speech or behaviour *need* to be able to invoke institutional procedures when personal expressions of opprobrium fail to curtail the offending behaviour due to First Amendment protections.[9] That is why the abdication of responsibility was so grating to the students.

What we see then is that this is an incident about safe spaces involving the first kind of ideal type (introduced earlier), which is a group (minority students) recognised by the larger society, but one which experiences an imbalance of power. The kind of safe space the group sought to create was a space where racist or culturally offensive material was prohibited, a desire entirely understandable and appropriate for the home environment of the college. What this incident was *not* about was an attempt to prevent, curtail, or inhibit the discussion of ideas in the *educational environment* of the college. When Erika Christofakis wrote, "American universities were once a safe space not only for maturation but also for a certain regressive, or even transgressive, experience; increasingly, it seems, they have become places of censure and prohibition," the *safe space* she had in mind was the intellectual, educational, and public space of a university. What she neglected was that, as Associate Head of Silliman College, she was charged with fostering and cultivating the home of the students, a different *kind* of safe space. That distinction matters.

A second case involving safe spaces occurred around the same time in 2015 at the University of Missouri (UM). There, student protests emerged as a result of the convergence of a number of different issues[10], eventually coalescing around long-standing and unresolved grievances about racism on campus. The watershed moment was an incident on 11 September, when racist slurs were yelled at the Missouri Students Association President, Payton Head. A Facebook post he wrote after the event went viral. However, the fact that Richard Lifton, the Chancellor of the University of Missouri-Columbia, didn't respond until six days later (in a message that condemned "bias and discrimination" without using the word "racism") prompted students to hold a "Racism Lives Here" protest on 24 September. Two more "Racism Lives Here" protests were held on 1 October and 11 October. Growing concern about the administration's inability to respond effectively to a number of race-related events led to the student group, Concerned Students 1950 (named after the first year that Black students were admitted to the University of Missouri), to demand the resignation of Tim Wolfe, the president of the entire University of Missouri system. On 24 October, a swastika drawn in faeces in a bathroom of a hall of residence served to highlight the students' concerns – especially since this was the second time in 2015 that anti-Semitic graffiti had appeared in a hall of residence. On 2 November, Jonathan Butler, a graduate student, began a hunger strike, which he claimed would either end in his death or Wolfe's removal from office. After that, events moved quickly. On 4 November, the English Department at UM-Columbia passed a vote of no confidence in Chancellor Lifton by 26-0. On 5 November, the Faculty Council expressed serious reservations about the leadership of both UM-Columbia and the leadership of the University of Missouri system more generally. It seems that these reservations were well-deserved, for in a disastrous interview with students at UM-Kansas City, in response to a request for a definition of "systematic oppression", Wolfe answered: "Systematic oppression is because you don't believe that you have the equal opportunity for success" (Knott and Prohov 2015). People immediately pointed out that this laid the blame for systematic oppression on the *oppressed* because they didn't have the right beliefs. Within hours of this statement, Black football players for the university announced that they would boycott all football-related activities until Wolfe resigned. Despite releasing a public statement on 8 November insisting that he would remain, President Wolfe resigned on 9 November, followed shortly by Chancellor Lifton's resignation.

It was after these two resignations that the issue of safe spaces came to the foreground. A student reporter, Tim Tai, attempted to enter Carnahan quad, which the protesters had turned into their unofficial camp. He was prevented from doing so by protesters forming a human chain, blocking his ability to access the public space. Tai's repeated requests to be able to access the quad and take photographs were denied on the grounds that doing so would be disrespectful to the protesters – the quad was a self-declared safe space. The disagreement soon turned ugly. Amid repeated chants of "No comment", there was scuffling and pushing, with some shouting, "Push them all out!" A video of the conflict went viral, with perhaps the most striking part being when an assistant professor shouted, "Who wants to help me get this reporter out of here? I need some muscle over here!"

Much of the media coverage was negative. *The Atlantic* wrote: "it is as if they've weaponized the concept of 'safe spaces'" (Friedersdorf 2015a). An editorial in the *New York Post* declared "'Safe space' fascists now rule the University of Missouri" (Post Editorial Board 2015). Setting aside the over-the-top rhetoric, there is an important difference between this call for a safe space and that of the students at Yale. Whereas the Yale students wanted to create a space free from offensive *behaviours*, the University of Missouri students wanted to create a space that prevented certain *people* from entering on the grounds that their presence would be disrespectful or upsetting.

What exactly did people find unsettling about this call for a safe space? Was it that certain individuals were banned from entering the quad simply by virtue of belonging to a certain profession without *those individuals* having done anything to warrant exclusion? Or was it the physicality of the exclusion – the shoving, the call for "some muscle over here!" – which raised people's ire? Or was it also that the quad was a public space that the reporters had a legal right to be able to access, which they were denied?

To begin with, let's acknowledge that part of how this particular event unfolded was due to the inflamed passions at the time. The shoving and bullying were clearly inappropriate but were also clearly at odds with the overarching aims of the protest, which was meant to combat racial harassment and create a more welcoming and inclusive environment on campus. Once tempers calmed down, the protesters realised this. The group behind the protests, Concerned Students 1950, handed out flyers the next day with the text, "Media has a 1st amendment right to occupy campsite. The media is important to tell our story and experiences at Mizzou to the world. Let's welcome and thank them!"

That said, it's also understandable why the protesters reacted to the media with suspicion and wanted to exclude them – the media doesn't always get the narrative right. With a history of bias in its portrayal of Black communities, many of the protesters had good reason for believing that the media was not to be trusted in covering this story. As Terrell Starr observed in the *Washington Post*, students wanted to create a space free from "the insensitivity they encounter in the news media: Newspapers, Web sites and TV commentary had already been filled by punditry telling Black students to "toughen up" and "grow a pair". If we reflect on how the students at Yale were portrayed in the media, and how the specific nature of their requests was lost in the resulting furore, it's not surprising that students at the University of Missouri wanted to exercise greater control over how their protest was reported.

There's no inconsistency in saying that the crowd's treatment of Tim Tai was wrong, that the student movement's attempt to ban the press was unwise (since the resulting negative coverage did more harm than good), *and* that the student movement should have been able to restrict reporters from the "safe space" on the quad. Reporters in pursuit of a story have a known history of intruding on people in ways that make them uncomfortable. The issue at stake here is essentially how to balance people's desire to be left alone, even in a public space, with the media's desire to report on an issue of general concern. That's a complicated question to answer, and one which I suspect can't be answered by appealing to a general principle. Cases such as this provide an illustration of the attraction of *moral particularism*: the view that moral judgements depend on all the contextually relevant features of a situation and not general moral principles.

Finally, consider the third case of safe spaces that commanded attention in 2015: Brown University and the recuperation room. In 2014, a student group at Brown invited Jessica Valenti and Wendy McElroy to participate in a debate concerning sexual assault on college campuses. When Katherine Byron, a student member of the Sexual Assault Task Force heard about the scheduled debate, she was concerned about the effect it might have on some people. In an interview with a reporter from *The New York Times* (Shulevitz 2015), Byron expressed particular concern about how McElroy, a libertarian, might be received: "Bringing in a speaker like that could serve to invalidate people's experiences."

Out of concern that some might find the debate too much to bear, Byron and a few other students created a room that people could retire to if they found the debate disturbing. The room had "cookies, coloring books, bubbles, Play-Doh, calming music, pillows, blankets and a video of frolicking puppies, as well as students and staff members trained to deal with trauma" (Shulevitz 2015). Over the course of the event, it was estimated that a few dozen people visited the space.

The media's reaction was generally critical and negative. The *New York Times* article, mentioned above, that reported on the event was titled "In College and Hiding from Scary Ideas," concisely summarising the reaction of many. Critics charged that the safe space was infantilising and disempowering, and suggested that students were becoming incapable of engaging with ideas challenging their beliefs. If the kind of safe space demanded by the Yale students made sense (e.g., seeking to ban racist and sexist behaviours), and the kind of safe space demanded by the University of Missouri activists was understandable (e.g., attempting to shield protesters from the media), the kind of safe space offered at Brown was, for many, one step too far; this safe space was seen as contrary to the mission of a university – it allegedly provided a place for students to flee to when discomforting ideas were raised.

To begin with, we need to recognise that describing the room as a place for students to hide from "scary ideas" misrepresents the situation. It wasn't as though the debate concerned the merits of a flat rate of income tax and the students needed the space because their liberal views about redistribution of wealth were being challenged. The debate concerned the issue of sexual assault on college campuses. It is reasonable to assume that some of the people attending the debate had been sexually assaulted, and among them, there would likely be variations in terms of their stages of recovery and psychological resilience. Someone might have believed they would be fine listening to the debate, yet react unexpectedly to something that was said. Offering a place where people could go to recover, if necessary, is just a basic act of human decency.

What I think *really* drove people's reactions was the fact that the recovery room was filled with colouring books, Play-Doh, bubbles, and more. Since those items are what children play with, offering the same thing to college students seemed to treat them as children, hence the objection that the safe space was infantilising or disempowering.

It strikes me that there's a condescending and paternalistic element to criticising the contents of the room. The critique assumes that there is a *right way* to deal with emotional trauma and, whatever the right way might be, *that* room didn't provide it. I suspect fewer complaints would have been raised if students upset by the debate chose to deal with it by going kickboxing or to a noisy bar. Yet why are violent sports or drinking seen as more socially acceptable ways of dealing with emotional trauma than a room filled with bubbles and videos of puppies? Is it because engaging in violent sports and drinking, being stereotypically *adult male* ways of responding to stress, are seen as the archetype of acceptable responses? What should really matter in our assessment of that safe space is the effect it had on the people who utilised it. It makes no sense to say, of the space itself, that it was infantilising – something is infantilising only if it brings about the corresponding behavioural changes in people who encounter it. But that is an empirical question. If that space made people feel better and helped them cope, isn't that what counts?

There's another aspect of the media outcry worth noting. Here we have a case of a concerned student making a sincere effort to provide a service for people experiencing emotional stress. Regardless of whether you think that the specific features of the room were appropriate or not, Katherine Byron's desire to help and the action she took was commendable. The vituperative response by the media and on social media only serves to discourage similar good-faith efforts by others in the future – if you try and the mob disapproves, there is hell to pay, so why bother trying?

Recall Mill's defence of "experiments in living" from Chapter 13. We know that safe spaces are social goods playing an important role in society. We also know it's highly implausible to think that we've obtained the optimal design regarding how to structure society and provide social goods (a point I'll return to in the final chapter of the book). Given this, the specific nature of the safe spaces we think society should provide is under continual revision. The *safe spaces* we create depend not only on the kind of *society* we want to have and the kind of harms we want to mitigate, but they also depend on what we *conceptualise* as harms in the first place. Following the argument from Chapter 4, we should encourage experimentation in the kinds of practices used to address harm. If the sharply critical response by the media towards the safe space at Brown reduces future efforts at Brown or elsewhere to try to address harm, then society is worse off as a result.

What about the criticism that the room disempowered students? Here I think it is important to distinguish several different functions that a safe space may provide. Sometimes, a safe space has a *therapeutic* function. Many schools and universities offer quiet rooms where people with social anxiety disorder can go when necessary. The Brown University room functioned as a therapeutic space. Many other examples exist: several colleges at the University of Cambridge have made available rooms with animals to help students cope with exam stress (BBC News 2018). We must recognise that the policies behind these spaces target very real concerns. According to the Office for National Statistics in the UK, approximately 100 students (18 and over) commit suicide each year (Coughlan 2016). In the US, the figure is considerably higher, even controlling for the larger population size, with 7,126 people between 10 and 24 committing suicide in 2021 (Centers for Disease Control and Prevention 2023). These therapeutic spaces are simply one more tool for addressing problems such as these.

Another function of safe spaces is to facilitate political *mobilisation*. Student groups and organisations of activists need spaces to coordinate and plan activities (although the communication abilities provided by the internet mean that much of this can now take place virtually). And, importantly, some spaces are dual-purpose and provide both kinds of functions. Gay bars and the consciousness-raising sessions of the feminist movement are spaces that were *both* therapeutic and facilitators of mobilisation.

The worry that safe spaces like the one offered at Brown serve to *disempower* students only makes sense if the therapeutic function provided crowds out opportunities or the desire for political mobilisation. What would be the mechanism by which such crowding out occurred? One might argue that therapeutic, safe spaces encourage an "inward turn", causing people to become solipsistic, solely focused on their emotional security or feeling good instead of being politically engaged. But that argument applies quite generally to a *lot* of human activities. One might avoid psychoanalysis, or therapy more generally, for the same reason.

On the contrary, far from disempowering people, safe spaces could encourage more political engagement by preventing "learned helplessness". The concept of learned helplessness first originated in animal experiments in the late 1960s (see Overmier and Seligman 1967; Seligman and Maier 1967) and was later extended to humans in the early 1970s. The core idea is that an agent, having experienced a number of outcomes over which they have no control (typically with adverse effects), will, in the future, fail to act in instances when they do, in fact, have control. Early work on learned helplessness in humans found results analogous to those in the first animal experiments (Hiroto and Seligman 1975). Later research, though, found that people's ability to theorise about our agency and efficacy required a more nuanced account in order to distinguish between transient forms of learned helplessness and more enduring forms. This led to the "attributional reformulation" of the theory (Abramson *et al.* 1978). According to this version, the type of learned helplessness that humans exhibit depends on how the person affected sees it, depending on three attributes: (i) whether it derives from internal or external factors (e.g., personal traits or the environment); (ii) whether it derives from stable or unstable factors (e.g., things that are hard to change or not); and (iii) whether it derives from global or local factors (e.g., factors that are widespread or specific). When a person's helplessness is attributed to global and stable factors, the passivity acquired readily transfers to other areas. Safe spaces provide an environment where some of the factors underlying learned helplessness are absent, potentially helping to combat the phenomenon.[11]

Given all these considerations, what are we to conclude about safe spaces? I suggest the following: many of the concerns raised were prompted by issues that are only indirectly related to the concept of safe spaces. In the Yale case, the concerns were about proper conduct and behaviour on campus when expressing disagreement. At the University of Missouri, the concerns were about the intimidation and bullying of a reporter and the apparent attempt to suppress the freedom of the press. At Brown, it concerned perceptions of what was an appropriate way to deal with psychological distress. The merit, function, and value of safe spaces were called into question simply as collateral damage. What I hope to have defended in this chapter is that safe spaces, far from being controversial, actually fulfil a number of important social needs, not only for the most vulnerable but for all of us.

Let us return to the key question about safe spaces: *where* should be safe, *for whom* and *from what*? Any group of freely associating individuals can collectively choose to adopt norms of conduct that require its members to refrain from behaviours or speech that are otherwise legal. This is an application of the right of self-determination and freedom of association, which form the minimal core, from Chapter 4. Any group of people can choose to self-regulate in ways to make the space they occupy "safe" as they see fit. (At this point, perhaps it would be best to drop the adjective "safe" altogether and reframe the issue as a debate over norms of appropriateness.) There are two problems that can arise. First, what happens when a group occupies a shared public space and they no longer have exclusive control over what happens in the area? Second, what happens when the group's membership is relatively fixed over time and there is internal disagreement over norms? Here, the fixed nature of the group means that structural reorganisation to neutralise the disagreement is not a feasible option. In both cases, conflict can arise between two sets of people over what is permissible to do or say. This, then, is one real underlying worry about "safe spaces": that one group's conception of permissibility or appropriateness collides with another, and there is no way to adjudicate the dispute without creating negative externalities. As it makes sense to situate this discussion within the context of polarised communities, we will revisit this topic in Chapter 28, "The collision of horizons".

19. No-platforming

When, if ever, should a person be stopped from giving a public lecture on a university campus? This practice, known as "no-platforming", has been used to target a number of people, although not always successfully. A very brief list of some of those targeted include Ayaan Hirsi Ali, a member of the Dutch Parliament, screenwriter, and a feminist critic of Islamic law;[1] Julie Bindel, a feminist writer and activist;[2] Richard Dawkins, evolutionary biologist and author of *The Selfish Gene* and *The God Delusion*;[3] Germaine Greer, author of *The Female Eunuch*;[4] Boris Johnson, at the time, former Mayor of London, Member of Parliament and Brexit campaigner;[5] Nick Lowles, director of Hope Not Hate; Peter Tatchell, an LBGT activist;[6] Marine Le Pen, leader of the French far-right party Front National;[7] Condoleezza Rice, former US Secretary of State;[8] and Milo Yianopoulous, former senior editor for *Brietbart News*.

In working through some of the concerns that no-platforming raises, I will argue that, despite there being some *prima facie* reasons supporting the practice, there are ultimately no defensible intellectual reasons for denying speakers a platform *provided that* they satisfy a certain standard of intellectual merit or public interest. The reasons for this are varied, but in brief: (1) any attempt to delineate sufficient criteria for no-platforming speakers will be self-undermining as there will be false positives that deny a platform to speakers who support causes advocated by those in favour of the no-platform policy; (2) that no-platforming also serves to alienate and antagonise those holding differing opinions in ways that are not conducive to changing beliefs, and thereby fuels polarisation in society; (3) that no-platforming misapplies Mill's Harm Principle by assigning too much weight to immediate, local harms and assigning too little weight to long-term harms; and (4) that no-platforming, as a policy, is inconsistent with attempting to inculcate the necessary values for a civil, diverse, democratic society, namely, how do we live with those who have deeply divergent but sincerely held views about what constitutes a life worth living. (That is, we should tolerate everything except intolerance.)

Let's begin by acknowledging some basic facts. Given the constraints on space, budgets, and time, it is not possible to accommodate all of the speakers a university would like to invite. Furthermore, not every speaker who would like to speak at a university should be given a platform because what they say might not meet the required standards. The relevant question then becomes, what are those standards? How do we navigate the space between speech permissible under law and speech granted a platform to address a wider university audience? For example, could one justify inviting Steve Bannon or Marine

Le Pen while excluding US white supremacist David Duke or UK far-right campaigner Tommy Robinson? And what about academics whose published work has strayed beyond the pale, like Charles Murray or Richard Herrnstein, whose controversial book, *The Bell Curve*, argued that IQ differences between certain racial and ethnic groups had (at least in part) a genetic basis?

As a rough first approximation, let's take the scope of universities to consist of some combination of educating students plus discovering or constructing new knowledge through research.[9] One minimal requirement an invited speaker has to satisfy is that the talk can be reasonably expected to satisfy a certain threshold of intellectual merit in service of at least one of those two goals. Although that might sound like a trivial point, the fact that only *one* of those two goals needs to be satisfied has important implications. If it were only the creation of new knowledge that mattered, a number of topics could easily be excluded on the grounds that the *novelty* criterion isn't satisfied. For instance, one topic often appearing in public lectures concerns arguments for the existence (or nonexistence) of God and whether the findings of natural science are compatible (or incompatible) with certain conceptions of God. Were novelty the only criterion that mattered, one would be hard-pressed to say that those topics need to feature as often as they do. Given the amount of attention and debate these issues have received over hundreds of years, there is very little left to be said which properly counts as "new", unless one waters down the concept of novelty substantially.[10] The reason these topics appear as frequently as they do is because they contribute to the *educative* mission of the university and reflect the interest of students or members of the public in the topic. A talk or debate can be worth having, even given scarce resources, if it brings something to the table outside of that found in the lecture, classroom, or seminar setting, even if it does not, in fact, create new knowledge.[11]

How are we to understand the requirement that "a certain threshold of intellectual merit" is met? One way to operationalise this would be to say that the purpose of universities, in addition to the creation of new knowledge, is to teach students how to analyse and criticise ideas and theories, how to assess evidence, and how to argue in support of a position. Could a baseline threshold of merit be that the speaker attempts to argue for a particular view through providing reason and evidence? This view is consistent with the mindset advocated by George and West (2017), when they write: "All of us should be willing – even eager – to engage with anyone who is prepared to do business in the currency of truth-seeking discourse by offering reasons, marshaling evidence, and making arguments." That attitude nicely resonates with Popper's critical rationalism. In his book, *Conjectures and Refutations*, Popper asks the question, "How can we hope to detect and eliminate error?" His answer: "by *criticizing* the theories or guesses of others and – if we can train ourselves to do so – by *criticizing* our own theories or guesses" (Popper 1963, p. 53). One reason we should be eager to engage with others, trading arguments, and offering reasons as George and West describe, is that no view should be treated as sacrosanct, especially our own. In particular, "in searching for the truth, it may be our best plan to start by criticizing our most cherished beliefs". (Popper 1963, p. 8)

That proposal is a good starting point, but reflection quickly reveals a number of inadequacies. First, it is at best a *necessary* rather than a sufficient condition. Not all views for which a person offers reasons, marshals evidence, and makes arguments merit a platform. Consider a member of the flat-Earth society who sincerely believes that the Earth is not roughly spherical, or someone who sincerely believes that the Earth is only 5,000 years old. Suppose that both individuals have arguments in support of their views. Both of these views are false. The reason these views do not merit a platform is not because they are false, nor because there are no good arguments to be made in support of them, but because these are no longer *significant* points of intellectual concern for most people. But even the claim that they are no longer significant points of intellectual concern needs to be qualified, because one can readily envision both the claims and the arguments appearing in a talk. For example, a sociologist discussing why people believe odd things would be a perfectly able to *mention* the claims and arguments, as illustrations of the phenomenon. The key distinction is that the claim and arguments are not being endorsed *in themselves*, but are being used to illustrate and investigate a wider sociological or psychological phenomenon.

Is it ever possible that a speaker intending to endorse a known false claim, having only bad arguments, might merit a platform to discuss the claim and the arguments *in themselves*, in the right circumstances? To provide a concrete example, consider someone who sincerely believes that Barack Obama was not born in the US. In this case, there is a very reasonable concern about why such a speaker might *not* merit a university platform – a concern that, again, has little to do with the fact that the claim is false and the arguments are bad. Here, the concern is that speaking at a university campus confers *legitimacy* to a topic, signalling it as one worth taking seriously. Since the "birther" movement was founded on the false belief that Barack Obama was not the legitimate president, this view, as the product of a conspiracy theory, does not deserve to be *endorsed* as a topic meriting discussion. However, even here there is an important qualification: when the issue of Obama's birth and US citizenship *first* surfaced, there *may* have been sufficient interest in the topic as a matter of public concern for informed individuals to engage with the claim and set the record straight on what was known. (What I am suggesting is not having a "birther" being given a platform solely on his or her own, but rather facing a critical interlocutor prepared to interrogate the claim.) Yet I suggest we need to recognise there is a limited window of time when such a debunking service would merit regular discussion in a university setting. Why? Because frequent revisitation of matters debunked in the past serves only to *re-legitimate* the issue as one deserving attention.[12] The educational mission of the university is not well served when it misleads people by suggesting something deserves attention when it, in fact, does not.

In the "birther" example, despite the claim being false and the arguments being bad, the topic may have been seen as one of *significance* because it was a point of interest to the public. But this on its own is an insufficient reason – that the public is interested in something does not make it a matter of public interest. Responsible news organisations confront this dilemma all the time. Furthermore, if all that was needed to merit a platform was something in which the public was interested, that creates opportunities to skew the discourse of a university by gaming the media. The growth of "fake news" – stories that are little more than emotionally provocative clickbait – are an unfortunate side effect of the attention economy. Likewise, as we saw with the initial reporting on Watergate, the fact that most people *aren't* talking about something doesn't mean that it is worth ignoring. In short, popularity is no reliable guide to which topics merit a platform.

What about the idea that regardless of the veracity of the claim there is at least a claim being defended? Unfortunately, such a criterion would preclude extending a platform to people asked to speak about their experiences. One could easily envision former ambassadors, heads of state, CEOs, and social, ethnic, or religious leaders being invited to talk about their *experiences* in their particular role. Such talks would likely satisfy the requirement of intellectual merit, as they would provide interesting information about the challenges and demands faced by an individual in certain settings. It would be difficult to construe such a talk as defending a *claim*, in the sense normally meant, given the dependence upon subjective first-person experiences that cannot be independently assessed.

Finally, what about the idea that the person speaking must be an *expert*, even if just in terms of just reporting on their own subjective experiences? There can be experts on a variety of topics of dubious veracity (e.g., astrology) and people are generally taken to be experts about their own experiences. Yet, given what we know about how unreliable memory can be, this too is problematic. But even the requirement for expertise is too restrictive. Consider, for example, if President Trump had been invited to talk about climate change. Given his reaction to the Paris Agreement on climate change, Trump had strong opinions about the matter. However, it strains credulity to claim that he be counted as an *expert* on the topic. Yet the reason why Trump would have merited a platform had nothing to do with the intellectual virtues of anything he would say; it would derive entirely from his role as President of the United States. That alone would merit a platform for his views on climate change.

All these considerations suggest that the issue of "sufficient intellectual merit" does not admit a straightforward answer. We face an entanglement of concerns: engaging with pre-existing academic topics, the discussion or disclosure of new information or ideas, engaging with timely political and social issues, duties towards acting in the public interest, the pursuit of matters of intrinsic intellectual interest, and listening to individuals occupying certain roles and stations. This list is by no means exhaustive.

One helpful way to think about this entanglement of concerns is to consider the concept of *intellectual merit* as constituted by what Mackie (1980) called *INUS conditions*. In his wonderfully named book, *The Cement of the Universe*, Mackie was concerned with how we identify causes. Consider a very simple event – say, the lighting of a match – and ask yourself, what caused the match to light? Our first intuition would be to say that the match was lit because someone struck the match on the side of the box. But this ignores a host of other conditions that also need to be satisfied for the match to light, like the fact that matches burn only in the presence of oxygen. If the match had been struck in a room filled with pure nitrogen, the match would not have lit. Similarly, the lighting of the match required that the match was dry, not wet.

What Mackie proposed was that there is no single *thing* that caused the match to light. What needed to occur is a set of conditions $S = \{\,c_1, \ldots, c_n\,\}$ where each c_i is *insufficient*, on its own, to bring about the lighting of the match, but each c_i is a *non-redundant* part of S. That is, if we consider the smaller set obtained by removing c_i from S, that smaller set of conditions would no longer result in the lighting of the match. Furthermore, even though S does bring about the lighting of the match, S is an *unnecessary* but *sufficient* set of conditions. S is unnecessary because there are many other ways to light the match. The person could have struck it on the side of a rock, for example, or used a blowtorch. A cause, then, is an Insufficient but Non-redundant part in an Unnecessary but Sufficient set of conditions (an INUS condition, for short).

The point Mackie wanted to make about causation was that singling out one *thing* as the cause of an event was really a statement about what we took to be important or unusual. The presence of oxygen in the air is just part of the normal background conditions, and so we don't identify the presence of oxygen as a cause of the match lighting, although we all know that matches don't burn in the absence of oxygen. What's unusual is that the match was struck and so we pick out that one item of the set S and label it the "cause" even though all of S is needed for the match to light.

I propose something similar holds for why certain individuals talking on certain subjects merit a university platform. Here, the set of INUS conditions involves *who* is speaking, about *what*, and *why*. Occasionally it matters *when* and *where* they are talking. Is the issue, like the "birther" example, particularly timely? Are they speaking to a small group of people or on the main stage of the university's largest lecture theatre? Sometimes we need to take into account *who* they are addressing (the audience[13]) and *how* the speaker intends to address them. And sometimes we need to consider what the expected *consequences* of the talk might be, given the audience. Most of the time, when we consider giving a person a platform, we concentrate on just one of these items because all the rest are uncontroversial and – like the presence of oxygen for the lighting of the match – simply folded into the background conditions.

What I have argued for in the preceding pages is that great flexibility exists in how the individual parts of the INUS condition can be satisfied when deciding who merits a platform. Disagreement over whether to grant a platform in controversial cases exists because no calculus exists for how to weigh these respective factors at any particular time, and disagreement may exist on the relative weights of each of them. Yet articulating this framework – as general as it is – and pointing out that intellectual merit is best understood in terms of INUS conditions does two things. First, it provides a framework for structuring an analysis of what makes a talk or debate worth having. Second, it helps us see one common source of controversy: fixing any *one* of those values, call it c_1, almost surely allows $c_2, \ldots, c_n$ to be filled in, in some way, resulting in a decision of meriting a platform. But holding c_1 constant, there is often *another* way $c'_2, \ldots, c'_n$ of filling in the parameters that yields a verdict of not meriting a platform. This can generate controversy, especially with speakers or subjects at particularly inopportune places or times. What I want to suggest is that, provided people act in good faith, the balance should more likely tip in favour of platforming rather than no-platforming.

This "presumption to platform" can be seen as a consequence of Popper's principle that the only thing we should not tolerate is intolerance. If a speaker is sincere, acting in good faith, not breaking the law, and an audience of people wish to hear what they say, it would be intolerant for one group to try to prevent the event from taking place. This also accords with the requirements of the minimal core underlying the cosmopolitan view developed in Chapter 4. It also connects with notions of epistemic humility that we will touch upon in Chapter 27. If we acknowledge there is some chance we might be wrong, we should be willing to have others subject our beliefs to critical scrutiny.[14]

Let us return to the original question: are there ever instances where no-platforming is appropriate? Of course. Hate speech that nevertheless falls within the boundaries of what is legal. Speech that makes no useful contribution to either the educative or research mission of the university. Some topics might prove so recherché as to never be of sufficient interest to enough people. But these statements, which I think are largely unproblematic, do not give much guidance on whether a particular instance of alleged "hate speech" really does count as such. Rarely do controversial cases fall neatly within these boundaries.

Reflecting on cases that have led to demands for no-platforming, it will prove helpful to consider three ideal types of speaker for whom concerns can be raised: the Provocateur, the Shill, and the Crank. Ben-Porath (2017, p. 39) provides a useful characterisation of the Provocateur: "speakers who intend merely to be provocative rather than to inform, challenge, or generate dialogue." By this, I don't mean an *agent provocateur*, someone who entices another individual to commit an illegal act. In my sense, the Provocateur aims to inflame the passions, to get people riled up, or to make people angry or exhilarated. The aim is not rational debate but incitement. Note that I don't assume anything about whether the Provocateur sincerely believes in what is said.

The Shill is someone trying to make a buck, to become famous, or in pursuit of some other end. Whatever is said is of secondary importance, as the only point of the speech is to achieve that goal. The Shill is a snake-oil salesperson, only trading in repartee rather than remedy. Politicians often come across as Shills, with their flexible relationship with principles in pursuit of office. Perhaps the best encapsulation of the attitude of the Shill appears in the Groucho Marx quote: "Those are my principles and if you don't like them, well, I have others." This instrumentally rational approach means that the theoretical commitments of the Shill are suspect since the aim is not to reach the *truth* but for *you* to reach a certain mental state with respect to the end the Shill is trying to achieve. Oreskes and Conway (2011) provide examples of academic guns-for-hire employed by corporations to generate research supporting the company's aims.

Our final ideal type is the Crank. Whereas our other two types may or may not believe what they say, it is the nature of the Crank to sincerely, often fiercely, believe what they say. The problem is that the Crank is committed to a view that is either false, extreme or so improbable that they exist beyond the pale in academic circles. Think of a Holocaust denier or someone who believes that the 9/11 attacks were an inside job coordinated by a US governmental cabal. The Crank has gone so far down the rabbit-hole that they have constructed an internally coherent account that resists evidence to the contrary.[15] Yet in defending this view, the Crank insists that they alone are the person objectively pursuing the truth, the one person challenging orthodoxy.

Are there defensible reasons for no-platforming any of these types on the grounds of principle? Of the three, the most obvious candidate for exclusion is the Provocateur. Recall that, as Ben-Porath (2017) says, the Provocateur "[intends] merely to be provocative rather than to inform, challenge or generate dialogue." Although it is unclear what good would come about from granting such a person a platform, we face two interrelated problems. The first difficulty is that Ben-Porath's criterion involves attributing a mental state to a person. Can one really know if the individual merely intends to be provocative? Also, we might ask why it matters if someone intends merely to be provocative – shouldn't the only criteria for judging whether someone merits a platform be what they *say*? (There are good and bad ways to be provocative.) The second difficulty is that good outcomes can result regardless of the speaker's intent. What about the case where someone *really does* intend to be merely provocative yet is informative and generates discussion as an unintended consequence of their actions? A Provocateur can wind up making a contribution, even if accidentally. Benefits may also result when a Provocateur's statements motivate *others* to do good intellectual work on either side of the divide. Those who agree could develop the theoretical foundations underlying the view, and those who disagree could develop arguments as to why the view is wrong, misguided, or dangerous. Lastly, regardless of whether one's political aims are progressive or conservative, Provocateurs exist all along the political spectrum. We might wish to avoid Provocateurs whose views we disagree with, but banning all

Provocateurs means banning those on *our team* as well. As Laurel Thatcher Ulrich's much-quoted phrase says, "Well-behaved women seldom make history." Sometimes, it's the Provocateur who initiates the next revolution.

The defence provided for the Provocateur in the previous paragraph works best when the Provocateur speaks sincerely. A sincere Provocateur is, at least, addressing things they believe in, even if they might not behave in the most productive way for advancing understanding. The *disingenuous* Provocateur, though, seems like a sociopath. Why would someone want to rile people up to provoke a reaction about something they don't care about? One benefit of the framework suggested earlier is that, using the concept of INUS conditions, we can distinguish these two cases. As I said before, a university platform needs to be managed carefully as it signals that certain views are worth taking seriously. A controversial speaker, expressing views that provoke and may cause distress, might nevertheless merit a platform on the grounds that they speak sincerely about what they believe (presumably reflecting a view shared by other people as well), yet be denied a platform if they were speaking disingenuously (perhaps not representing views held by themselves nor other people). Flipping the value of that single parameter can, in some cases, be the deal-breaker.

The concern about disingenuous speech extends to the Shill, who by definition is less concerned about the content of what is said than the end it achieves. An important difference between the Shill and the Provocateur is that the Shill at least provides *arguments* whereas the Provocateur may not. Does that mitigate the concerns raised by disingenuous speech? In one sense, it seems to make matters worse. The Provocateur's speech, at least, has the virtue of lacking subtext – it is all about inflaming the passions. In the case of the Shill, there's an ulterior motive; the speech is a performance to bring about another, unstated end. But what end?

In a university context, we often assume, as Robert P. George and Cornel West wrote, that everyone values "the cultivation and practice of the virtues of intellectual humility, openness of mind, and, above all, love of truth." The love of truth is important because that has further implications regarding shared standards of how to assess evidence, how to reason, and so on. When the love of truth is subordinated to the advancement of social, political or personal ends, those implications don't necessarily follow. But even if this suggests that the starting presumption should be denying a platform to the Shill, other factors can still tip the balance in favour. When would we want climate change deniers and tobacco company apologists given a platform? We might want to give them a platform for the purpose of exposing and debunking their arguments. Ignoring bad science and disingenuous theories is dangerous because, when unchallenged, they can easily attract followers.[16] Even if we know a Shill is acting in bad faith, it can be important to engage in defence of the public interest.

Lastly, what about the Crank? Conspiracy theorists rarely appear on university platforms because their views rarely meet the required standard of academic quality. Yet, as with the "birther" example, occasionally, there could be a public interest argument to engage with them. Another reason to platform a Crank is that serious, accomplished scholars transform into Cranks from time to time. One example of this is the so-called "Nobel disease", where winners of the Nobel prize occasionally go on to endorse bizarre ideas. In cases like that, it could be important to give the person a platform because, without subjecting the view to serious academic scrutiny, there's a risk that the person's prior justly-deserved reputation would lend credibility to their later bizarre view.

The upshot of these considerations is that there are few good general arguments for no-platforming speakers. We need to engage with controversial speakers, showing why their arguments are flawed or why their conclusions do not mean what they suggest. Attempting to shut down controversial speakers can actually do *more* harm than allowing them to speak because they not only benefit from the free media coverage generated by being denied a platform, but then their views are not subjected to scrutiny and not shown to be flawed. In the age of the internet, where anyone can publish material online and distribute it worldwide, denying a speaker a platform will not make a controversial view go away.

There is one other argument that we need to consider – the argument that some speakers should be denied a platform because their speech does harm to people in the audience. The particular example I would like to engage with concerns the feminist theorist Germaine Greer, who has attracted considerable criticism as a result of her views on transgender issues. Greer has argued that post-operative transgender men are not women. She has *not* argued that people should be denied the option of gender-reassignment surgery; she just thinks that surgery doesn't transform a biological male into a woman. As a result of comments such as these, a number of activists have called for Greer to be denied a platform on the grounds that she is a "TERF" (trans-exclusionary radical feminist).

These no-platforming controversies are part of a much larger debate over how society should understand the terms "women" and "men", the social practices associated with those terms (e.g., sporting competitions), and what kind of support, at what age, should be provided to people who identify as trans. These are complex topics intersecting with moral and political philosophy, developmental psychology, as well as biological and medical science. Let us briefly consider these points in order.

One helpful way of framing the debate, articulated by the transgender philosopher Sophie-Grace Chappell is as follows: trans-women are women in a way analogous to how adoptive parents are parents (Chappell 2018). The analogy is imperfect, like all analogies, but it reminds us how society has expanded its concept of *parent* to include those who did not initially satisfy its original, more narrow, biologically determined meaning. In most contexts, the fact that adoptive parents are not biological parents makes no difference whatsoever.[17] But, in a few special circumstances, whether or not a parent is a biological or adoptive parent can matter. For example, a long-term medical study investigating the relationship between the health of parents and children, looking to uncover how certain genetic predispositions are manifested, would rightfully exclude adoptive parents from participating in the study.

The way in which we understand the terms "man" or "woman", with all of their social implications, requires thinking through the pragmatic consequences of adjustments in usage carefully. For example, what policies should be put in place for domestic violence shelters for vulnerable women, the vast majority of whom are cisgender?[18] The concern here is not that some transgender women aren't vulnerable and don't deserve protection in domestic violence shelters, but rather that if *all* it takes to count as a transgender woman is an act of self-declaration, then this creates new avenues through which the safety of vulnerable persons can be threatened, as criminals are always looking for ways to exploit the system. Similarly, what policies should be put in place regarding transgender women and men competing in professional sports? The primary reason we split between women's events and men's events is not because of misogyny or transphobia but rather to ensure a level playing field; physiological and development differences (such as the presence of testosterone and its contribution to muscular development) between men and women are such that men, on average, tend to have different physical capabilities than women. The question of whether a transgender woman, who may have had a typical biologically male development, should compete in women's sporting events is again not a question motivated by discrimination but pragmatics. It is, to invoke another analogy, similar to the concern about whether Oscar Pistorius, the infamous "blade runner", should have been allowed to compete in the men's 400-metre race using artificial legs since his legs were amputated below the knee when he was less than a year old. And, finally, another example concerns how we should form policies for medical treatment. Given that much medical care has been predicated on the assumption that there is a general alignment between a person's gender and their sex, how do we accommodate transgender persons in overall medical policy? For example, transgender women don't need to be tested for ovarian cancer, and transgender men don't need to be tested for prostate cancer. But a policy that says that transgender women should be treated *exactly* identical to cisgender women in all respects overlooks these cases. Addressing these issues is not by any means insurmountable, but they require an open conversation so that all perspectives can be considered and a reasonable approach developed. Closing down a conversation by asserting a speaker to not be "on the right side of history" is counterproductive, and dangerous.[19]

This points to the underlying reason bans on speakers like Greer are problematic: underlying all of these issues about whether to platform or not is a complexity buried within Mill's Harm principle, namely, how we adjudicate the balance between the reduction of short-term harms versus the reduction of long-term harms. Coupled with this is a further question of whether an attempt to reduce a *known* harm may itself generate *unknown* harms in the future. This is one of the reasons why people have urged caution with respect to medical treatment of young children who identify as transgender (Cass 2024).

Let us assume, for the sake of argument, that a talk by Greer will offend or cause harm to some persons, transgender or not, in the audience. Assuming that gender is a social construct, a claim about the conceptual relationship between being a transgender person and being a woman is a claim about how the boundaries of a socially constructed term are delineated. But when it comes to socially constructed terms, no single individual or group of individuals has *exclusive* ownership of the term, although some people are clearly more invested than others. I italicised the word "exclusive" for a simple reason: when you consider some social category X, the definition used to determine what counts as an X also determines what counts as a non-X as well. That doesn't mean that the non-X's necessarily get an equal say in how X is defined or understood, but it's why exclusive ownership might be an issue, on occasion.

When it comes to how to understand the term "woman", I make no substantial claim; men have been telling women how to understand themselves for far too long. My interest here only concerns procedure. The boundaries of gender categories, what they mean and who they apply to, are understood and negotiated, and constantly re-negotiated, by *society as a whole*, with bargaining power unequally distributed amongst the participants. Any change to the meaning and boundaries of gender categories – especially any *beneficial* change – in the long-run will require people working through various issues over time, in their own way. Reducing long-term harms by arriving at an enlightened understanding of gender categories requires having an open conversation about gender categories, allowing people to ask questions, explore ideas, and interrogate beliefs, all of which may cause short-term harm. The important point is that the short-term harm is not caused *for its own sake*, but that it occurs as an unavoidable by-product to bring about a greater good over the long run. This is the *doctrine of double effect* in action. Sometimes one may permissibly bring about a harm as an unintended but foreseeable side-effect of bringing about a good.

Drawing all of this together, I suggest the important lesson to take away about the debate over no-platforming is this: clearly, we don't want to give a platform to hate speech or speech below a certain level of quality. Life is too short to listen to bad talks. But, otherwise, we should be tolerant and open to what we allow, especially with material we find challenging and difficult. When faced with views that are diametrically opposed to our own, views we fundamentally disagree with and think are utterly wrong, the thing to keep in mind is the same lesson eventually learned by the Inquisition – you can't force someone to believe something. Preventing someone from talking about something they believe is probably the least effective way of persuading them otherwise. Getting people to change their beliefs is an exercise in winning both hearts and minds and requires sincere engagement and dialogue. That is why, as uncomfortable as it may be when we face challenging speech, the best response is more speech, better speech, that moves the conversation forward.

20. Concluding remarks

What, then, is the overall assessment of the Enlightenment conception of the Open Society? In this part we examined several alleged threats to it, as discussed by the media and by politicians from across the spectrum. Regarding the use of trigger warnings and safe spaces, I have argued that many of the concerns are much ado about nothing. The main concern about trigger warnings, the Bartleby objection, is overblown. The main concern about safe spaces, that they infantilise or disempower people, is paternalistic in that it assumes there is an all-things-considered right way to cope with psychological matters. Ultimately, though, this is an empirical question: are people more or less resilient than they were in the past? If people are less resilient, the question is *why*? I suspect that if people are less resilient, it isn't *because* of trigger warnings or safe spaces. Those are, at most, symptoms rather than causes.

One area where the Enlightenment conception of the Open Society was found to be threatened was the tendency by some, on both the right and the left, to deny a platform to speakers. I have argued that deciding who merits a platform when resources are scarce can be a surprisingly complicated question to answer, as there is no single principle that can be invoked to settle the matter. Instead, the matter is best analysed using the concept of INUS conditions which I have imported from the theory of causation. When scarcity of resources is not an issue, the basic principle is that, whenever possible, we should err on the side of granting a platform rather than denying it. We should be intolerant of intolerance but otherwise grant speakers a wide latitude to express their views.

When Popper wrote *The Open Society and Its Enemies*, he was rightly concerned with the *politicisation* of knowledge. In the years leading up to World War II, Popper had seen how knowledge and information were manipulated by political forces for purposes of propaganda and censorship, influencing education and research, and shaping how people understood the world. In both Nazi Germany and the Soviet Union, truth was often subordinated to political expediency or ideology.

We still need to be on guard against the politicisation of knowledge, but what our discussion about the Enlightenment conception of the Open Society reveals is another risk, which in our secular age we have perhaps neglected: the *moralisation* of knowledge. There is no precise demarcation between moralised knowledge and politicised knowledge because moral concerns frequently intersect with or become political concerns. But it is worth making a distinction between the two, even if imperfect, because the processes that generate the two can diverge significantly. Politicised knowledge is often institutionalised, embedded within government bodies or other nongovernmental organisations; it can be supported by hierarchical power structures and enforced from the top down through official sanctions. Moralised knowledge, on the other hand, can emerge organically from shifts in social values; it can be structured along any dimension of value, maintained and enforced through diffuse social norms with no clear structure. And perhaps most importantly, the enforcement of moralised knowledge can occur locally, from the bottom up via informal sanctions. As we saw in Part II, social media provides a powerful, immediate, decentralised mechanism for enforcing informal sanctions.

Knowledge can become moralised in a variety of ways, and it would take an entire book to explore the topic at length. I provide a short statement here as a framework for reflecting on topics already covered. The first way knowledge can become moralised is when certain questions or topics become taboo so that an interlocutor's attempt to raise them in good faith is viewed as a moral failing. Moralised knowledge, in this sense, is analogous to an article of faith in religious doctrine.[1] The second way is when certain questions or topics are not themselves taboo but when certain lines of enquiry are not permissible to discuss on the grounds that doing so causes, or potentially causes, harm. Moralised knowledge, in this sense, was behind the attempt to deny a platform to Germaine Greer. The third way knowledge can be moralised is when we treat people differently with respect to their ability to advance knowledge claims on certain subjects, either because of their own moral status or because of other properties they possess, such as their membership in certain social categories. We haven't encountered many examples of this third type of moralised knowledge in this part of the book, but this type frequently appears at the intersection of epistemology and identity politics.

The moralisation of knowledge presents a challenge for the Enlightenment conception of the Open Society because it interferes with the traditional ideal of the rational, free exchange of ideas among epistemic equals. The ideal is never realised in the world because differences in epistemic and expressive ability, along many dimensions, resulting from a combination of individual and social factors, always exist and prevent us from being epistemic equals. But it is worth thinking about how the moralisation of knowledge alters the process of enquiry, because sometimes we do actually want to alter the traditional ideal in that way.

The first type of moralised knowledge is not always bad because there is, even in secular societies, a category of *forbidden knowledge*. Not everything that *can* be known *ought* to be known. For example, there are a lot of facts regarding how much torture a person can endure before they die or are irreversibly harmed; that is one area of knowledge rightly excluded as a topic of enquiry, and so we know that there is a category of things one ought not enquire about. The second type of moralised knowledge is not always bad, either, because as we have become more sophisticated knowledge producers, we realise that there are some lines of enquiry that are dangerous, harmful, or simply insufficiently fruitful to warrant the cost-benefit trade-off. For example, the gold standard of medical evidence is the randomised control trial (RCT), but not all medical interventions have been proven successful with an RCT. Appendectomies and setting broken bones in casts became established practices without ever having their effectiveness proved via an RCT. It would be madness to insist on such a study now, and so that line of enquiry is rightly excluded from investigation.

The third type of moralised knowledge is also sometimes justified because, when it comes to knowledge about persons or groups, there can be important power asymmetries at play. We are all familiar about how past "knowledge claims" about certain social categories, whether they are races, religions, or sexual orientations, have led to atrocities. In saying this, I am not arguing for an extreme view that says that *only* certain people are able to advance knowledge claims on certain subjects (although there are some who think that), but rather that because this is a sensitive area, we should proceed with caution.

The point is that there are reasonable cases where the production and dissemination of knowledge is rightly subject to moral considerations. Viewed from this perspective, questions about trigger warnings, safe spaces, and no-platforming are simply questions that naturally arise at the intersection of epistemology and morality. However, because the drivers of moral sentiment are not subject to the same kinds of evidential considerations as empirical knowledge, morality provides an orthogonal and independent perspective from which to critique knowledge production. In his writings, Foucault introduced the concept of *power-knowledge* to refer to the interaction between power and knowledge in society. Perhaps we should introduce the concept of *morality-knowledge* to refer to how the evolution and advancement of moral attitudes shapes the practice of knowledge production in society.

Knowledge production has always been subject to critique and regulation by the powerful; the persecution of Galileo by the Roman Catholic church for advocating the heliocentric model of the solar system is a classic example in the history of science. What we have explored in this Part is how knowledge production is also subject to critique and regulation from moral actors. Is this a threat to the Enlightenment conception of the Open Society? Not necessarily, but it is something of which we should remain aware and vigilant.

Notes to Part III: Safe spaces

16. Generation Wuss?

[1] That said, it's worth noting that older generations are also guilty of this kind of behaviour. After the UK's 2016 EU referendum, many conservative tabloids tried to stifle debate over whether the UK should stay in the single market or customs union, not by engaging with the *arguments* made, but rather by labelling those making the arguments as "Remoaners" or "Saboteurs". Conservative MP Chris Heaton-Harris requested all universities to make available their syllabi and teaching about Brexit, presumably to ensure that left-leaning lecturers were not corrupting the youth by indoctrinating them against Brexit. (This request, widely condemned as McCarthyist, was largely ignored by universities.)

[2] This last sentiment is often expressed with a quote misattributed to Voltaire: "I wholly disapprove of what you say and will defend to the death your right to say it." The actual source of the quote is Evelyn Beatrice Hall, who used it to describe Voltaire's *attitude* when he was defending the philosopher Claude-Adrien Helvétius, whose work "De l'esprit" had been burnt in protest over its content.

17. Trigger warnings

[1] Sometimes the warning was just about the *title*. Frank Zappa's album *Jazz from Hell* received a warning label from the Parents Music Resource Center even though it solely consisted of instrumental tracks because of the inclusion of the word "Hell" in the title and a song entitled "G-Spot Tornado".

[2] This is essentially the same debate that has been going on ever since John Stuart Mill first introduced the Harm Principle in *On Liberty*: "The only purpose for which power can be rightfully exercised over any member of a civilized community, against his will, is to prevent harm to others."

[3] I label post-traumatic stress disorder (PTSD) a "generally recognised harm" rather than a universally recognised harm for two reasons. First, although features of PTSD have been recognised for hundreds of years (some have noted that Henry VI in Shakespeare's play demonstrates many features of PTSD), it first appeared in the American Psychiatric Association's Diagnostic and Statistical Manual of Mental Disorders in 1980. Second, the entry for PTSD has undergone revision since its introduction, as people argue over its specific nature. Mental disorders, unlike broken bones and cancer, have aspects that are socially constructed and hence subject to disagreement (see Hacking 1995, 1998).

[4] The concept of a microaggression was introduced by Chester Pierce in 1970 as follows: "Most offensive actions are not gross and crippling. They are subtle

and stunning. The enormity of the complications they cause can be appreciated only when one considers that these subtle blows are delivered incessantly. Even though any single negotiation of offense can in justice be considered of itself to be relatively innocuous, the cumulative effect to the victim and to the victimizer is of an unimaginable magnitude. Hence, the therapist is obliged to pose the idea that offensive mechanisms are usually a *micro-aggression* as opposed to a gross, dramatic, obvious *macro-aggression* such as lynching."

[5] The warnings for *The Great Gatsby* were suggested by a student at Rutgers in a letter to the administration arguing in support of trigger warnings. The comment regarding Achebe's novel is an example from a draft policy by Oberlin College, which later withdrew the policy requiring such warnings (Flood 2014).

[6] In saying this, I don't mean to single out religious belief. Something similar could be said for an atheist asked to study arguments for the existence of God, or about people who don't believe climate change.

[7] If you are teaching a class on the history of slavery, or the civil rights movement, and you are going to show a photograph of a lynching, you *should* be able to justify it on pedagogical grounds. If you can't, there is an important question about the value it has in the classroom. There is no point in showing shocking and upsetting materials *just* to be shocking and upsetting. Trainee doctors encounter dead bodies and photographs of horrific injuries and conditions all the time because those are *necessary* for learning; they aren't shown violent pornography or dark web torture videos.

[8] To the extent universities are self-governing bodies, the rules are always in-principle open to revision by its members. That means that a student progressing through the ranks and eventually joining the community of scholars will be able to argue for revisions to its social practices.

18. Safe spaces

[1] Let's also not forget that *words* are powerful and can inflict great harm. Emotional abuse is a form of domestic violence whose psychological effects can last longer than the damage caused by physical abuse and can result from words alone.

[2] On this point, see also the discussion in Chapter 28.

[3] At least not under threat in a way that *literally* concerns the safety and well-being of the individual members. Political parties often describe themselves as "endangered" or facing an "existential threat" when their base declines rapidly or shifts to support another party. Yet such language, although evocative, does not correspond to the same kind of very real threat faced by people living in racist, sexist, homophobic, or transphobic societies.

[4] By "recognised", I do not mean that the group necessarily has any official protected status by the government, or that the characteristics determining group

membership are well-defined, but that the group's existence is more-or-less understood or understandable by a typical member of the society. Examples of this include ethnic groups, alumni organisations, employment-based groups, societies defined around mutual interests, athletic collectives, and so on.

[5] Depending on the nature of the group, this imbalance of power can arise from a variety of causes, with some imbalances of power not being morally insignificant. A Latvian-American society would lack power, in some respects, since its membership base would be extremely small compared to that of the overall society. (According to the 2000 US Census, there were around 87,000 people in the States claiming Latvian heritage.) Yet that group would, at the same time, largely inherit all of the advantages of being white in America. Now contrast that group with a political organisation of Black women teachers in the US. (Black women constituted 5.3% of the US teacher population in 2013, or approximately 180,000 people, according to Thomas-Carver and Darling-Hammond 2017.) Even if both groups had roughly equal amounts of power, and hence faced the same *relative* power asymmetry compared with other social groups, we would probably not view the first group's lack of power as morally significant, whereas we would more likely view the second group's lack of power to be so, due to its intersection with racial and gender considerations and the fact it represents a larger constituency.

That said, thinking of "power" as if it were an absolute attribute attached to a group (or a person) is misleading. Power, understood as the ability to see desired outcomes realised, is particular to each individual outcome. A group or person may be particularly powerful with respect to a single outcome while, at the same time, utterly lacking in power with respect to other desired outcomes. Referring, in general terms, to the power of a group or an individual is to refer to their expected ability to realise any outcome falling within their set of desired outcomes.

[6] Describing an entity as "liminal" means that it straddles a boundary or threshold; here, I think of the liminality of the group as referring to its perceived social legitimacy. Examples of such groups would be gays and lesbians after the decriminalisation of homosexual behaviour (but before social attitudes shifted to conceive of sexual orientation as just one aspect of ordinary variability among human traits), the civil rights movement in 1960s America, the various waves of feminism, and perhaps socialist or communist parties in the US. The important point is that the group is undoubtedly recognised by the wider society, but attitudes vary considerably regarding its social status. This does not necessarily correspond to a lack of power, although it may be correlated with it. After the financial crisis, investment bankers (or financiers, more generally) took on a liminal status as many viewed them disfavourably and at best a necessary evil, yet they still held enormous power.

⁷ In this case, the criteria for group membership is still being negotiated, both at the group and the individual level. Here I have in mind the socially constructed nature of the kind terms lying behind group labels (see Hacking 1996, 1999, 2007)

⁸ In 1837, Calhoun said: "I hold that the present state of civilization, where two races of different origin, and distinguished by color, and other physical differences, as well as intellectual, are brought together, the relation now existing in the slaveholding states between the two, is, instead of an evil, a good. A positive good." The following year, he stated: "Many in the South once believed that slavery was a moral and political evil. That folly and delusion are gone. We see it now in its true light, and regard it as the most safe and stable basis for free institutions in the world." (See Wikiquote 2024, for these quotes, and others.)

⁹ In the US, although a number of restrictions can be placed on speech with regard to the time, place, and manner of the speech (e.g., protesting loudly outside someone's window at midnight), those restrictions need to be content-neutral. Content-based restrictions need to meet far stricter criteria, such as advocating "imminent lawless action" or obscenity or making a "true threat". Hate speech, insofar as it does not violate these criteria, is protected under the First Amendment. This was affirmed by the Supreme Court in their 2011 decision on *Snyder v. Phelps*, when they ruled that the picketing of a military funeral by the Westboro Baptist Church was protected speech, even though the placards saying "God hates you", "Fag troops", and "Thank God for dead soldiers" intentionally caused emotional distress in the gay father of one of the dead soldiers.

¹⁰ According to *The Maneater*, the University of Missouri student newspaper, the protests were originally about changes made to graduate student healthcare and the threat to remove the provision of abortion services. The discussion in the text was drawn from a timeline originally published at http://www.themaneater.com/special-sections/mu-fall-2015, but which appears to be no longer available. (The discussion here is not intended to be complete, and some events have been omitted for the sake of brevity.) Another history is available at the Wikipedia page discussing the 2015–16 protests: https://en.wikipedia.org/wiki/2015-2016_University_of_Missouri_protests.

¹¹ In a way, safe spaces can be seen as helping to mitigate the loss of control under aggregation, as discussed in Chapter 10.

19. No-platforming

¹ Ali was invited by Brandeis University in 2014 to receive an honorary degree and speak at the commencement. After an online petition collected more than 6,000 signatures, Brandeis withdrew the offer of an honorary degree and disinvited Ali on the grounds that some of what she had said was, "inconsistent with Brandeis University's core values" (Leef 2014).

[2] Invited to speak at the University of Manchester in October 2015, Bindel was later disinvited on the grounds that her views could "incite hatred towards and exclusion of our trans students" (Bell 2016).

[3] Dawkins was scheduled for a live interview on the Berkeley radio station KPFA, followed by a book signing in support of his book, *Science in the Soul: Selected Writings of a Passionate Rationalist*. The radio station cancelled the event after discovering some of Dawkins' more controversial public statements, stating that he had hurt people with "his tweets and other comments on Islam" (Fortin 2017).

[4] Greer was invited to give a talk at Cardiff University in October 2015. A petition gathering over 3,000 signatures was circulated in attempts to bar her from speaking due to her views about transgender women. During an interview with BBC *Newsnight*, Greer stated that she would not be going to Cardiff, regardless of whether the petition was successful, as she was "getting a bit old for all this" (Dearden 2015). Despite the protest and her earlier statement that she would not speak she wound up giving the lecture. She later characterised the university's public statement defending her invitation, "We in no way condone discriminatory comments of any kind," as "weak as piss" (Packham 2016).

[5] Although he was reported in several papers as having been "no platformed," this was in error for two reasons. First, Johnson *was* invited to speak at a debate over the EU Referendum at King's College, London, but he never accepted the invitation. Second, the reported email disinviting Johnson was unofficial, written by a volunteer at the King's Think Tank who included a fake title in his signature. The email was not actually approved by the President, Vice-President, or Student Committee of the think tank (Packham 2016).

[6] Tatchell was invited to give a talk at a public event titled "Re-Radicalizing Queers? Should we toe the line or cause a stir?" at Canterbury Christ Church University on 15 February 2016. Fran Cowling, the LGBT Officer of the National Union of Students, refused to speak at the same event unless Tatchell was dropped from the bill, alleging he was both transphobic and racist (Johnston 2016). However, Tatchell appeared in the event, with Cowling choosing not to participate.

[7] Le Pen was invited to address the Oxford Union on 5 February 2015. The speech went ahead, but was delayed by over an hour by approximately 300 protesters outside the event (Henley and Ullah 2015).

[8] Invited to give the commencement address at Rutgers University in May 2014, but declined after student protests (Fitzsimmons 2014).

[9] Many universities now have subsidiary entities with connections to the business world, charged with the task of transforming the outcomes of pure research into commercial applications. Some have entities that facilitate academics engaging in consultancy work for governments or other organisations. Some have faculty wholly or partially dependent on "soft money" research

grants. The purpose of the modern university is thus only imperfectly described as "teaching and research". In the UK, the recent push to including "impact" in the assessment of research quality forces academics to also think about the short-term social or policy implications of their research. Although these considerations introduce a number of complexities that matter – such as the possible political consequences of academic research – I assume that unlike in other parts of the world (viz., Turkey under the Erdoğan regime), a general commitment to the principle of academic freedom means that we can, for the present purposes, ignore these complexities and speak abstractly just about the pursuit of research.

[10] Those interested in seeing a masterful summary of classical arguments for and against the existence of God should read the appendix to Rebecca Goldstein's novel, *36 Arguments for the Existence of God*.

[11] If one interprets the mission of "creating new knowledge" to refer to creating knowledge in *other people* – i.e., causing someone to know something that they did not know before – then the novelty criterion would be satisfied in this case as well. But then the problem becomes that the novelty criterion is all-too-easily satisfied. There are infinitely many truths, most of which are fundamentally boring but which would satisfy the novelty criterion. When we talk about the creation of new knowledge, what we want is the creation of new *significant* knowledge. Good luck trying to give an analysis of what that means, though.

[12] Debates on the reality of climate change provide another illustration of this phenomenon. Climate change deniers try to create a false sense of debate over issues generally settled by scientists in order to maintain, in the eye of the public, a sense that their concerns are real and legitimate. This technique, previously used by tobacco companies in their efforts to resist the link between smoking and cancer is well-documented in the book, *Merchants of Doubt* (Oreskes and Conway 2011).

[13] Recall our discussion of Grice's theory of speaker meaning and the role played by the audience from Chapter 11.

[14] Popper (1963) puts this point nicely as follows: "in searching for the truth, it may be our best plan to start by criticizing our most cherished beliefs". Notice that this holds even when we talk about socially constructed practices for which the notion of objective, all-things-considered truth doesn't apply. Even in that case, a group that is searching for *its truth* may still benefit from critically scrutinising its cherished beliefs.

[15] On this point, see the discussion of epistemic closure in Chapter 27.

[16] On this point, see the discussion of epistemic deference in Chapter 25 and how beliefs can serve as signifiers of group identity in Chapter 27.

[17] In general, use of the word "real" should be avoided when discussing adoptive parents, transgender individuals, and a great many other topics. Talk

about "real parents" or "real men" or "real women" is an imprecise, lazy construction that explicitly suggests that one interpretation of the term (e.g., "parent" or "men" or "women") should be favoured over all others. But there is no such all-things-considered favoured interpretation. There is a factual, historical question of how the term was generally understood in the past (but this, too, may not have a single, unique answer). There is also the question of what the salient property is for the discussion at hand, which may not overlap with the historical usage of the term. (For example, one could ask whether someone found guilty of felony murder is a "real murderer".) And then there is a purely stipulative sense of the term "real" as in the title of the 1980s book *Real Men Don't Eat Quiche*. Understanding any particular use of the word "real" will depend on the conversational context. In any event, greater precision would be obtained by avoiding the word altogether.

To see this, think about the question of whether a biological parent is a "real parent". Historically, being a biological parent involved participating in the act of fertilisation, carrying the fetus to term, and giving birth. But most steps of this process can be carried out differently, given modern technology. What about parents who could not conceive naturally but were able to through IVF treatment? What about a woman who was unable to carry a foetus to term and so relied on a surrogate mother? What about a woman who was able to carry a foetus to term but relied on an egg from a donor? What about the child who was born with DNA from three different people: the mother's nuclear DNA, a donor's mitochondrial DNA, and the father's DNA? (For a discussion of this fascinating case, see Hamzelou 2016.) Is there a difference between natural childbirth and Caesarean section, as to whether someone counts as a "real parent"? What about a sperm donor who isn't involved in raising the child? Or is being a biological parent only relevant for being considered a "real parent" if they are involved in raising the child as well? If you think that, what if one does the best job they can but nevertheless does such a bad job that the child has to be put into foster care? In none of these cases does invoking the word "real" add anything illuminating to the discussion.

Saying that some person P isn't a *real* X, for some X, is nothing more than a rhetorical strategy for denying the application of the term X to P – raising P's defensive hackles and putting them on the back foot – on the grounds that they lack some property, or set of properties, deemed essential for being an X. But, whereas it might make sense to speak of metaphysically essential properties for something like *being an electron*, it strains credulity to think that there can be anything metaphysically essential to a social property like *being a parent*. For more on this topic, see the discussion of *authenticity* in Part IV, Chapter 25.

[18] "Cisgender" refers to those individuals whose gender identity aligns with their birth-assigned sex. Some find the term "cisgender" objectionable ("political correctness gone mad!") but there is good sense behind it. The prefix "cis" in Latin means "on this side of". So, the natural contrast to "transgender", where the prefix "trans" (also Latin) means "across from" is thus "cisgender".

[19] How many tens of millions of people were killed as a result of actions taken by Lenin, Stalin, and Mao to be on the "right side of history"?

20. Concluding remarks

[1] One possible example of this type of knowledge might be the existence of anthropogenic climate change. It is increasingly the case that people who express a sceptical attitude to this claim receive a reaction highly charged with moral valence. (And I make this observation as someone who is a firm believer in anthropogenic climate change.) I suspect that this is because the evidential support behind anthropogenic climate change is so great that, when someone expresses scepticism, the most natural explanation is not that the person is, in fact, a sceptic, but rather than that they are adopting the *persona* of a sceptic in order to advance other morally objectionable interests. However, even if this explanation is correct, it does have the side effect of repressing any good faith challenge to received wisdom.

References

Abramson, Lyn Y., Martin E. Seligman, and John D. Teasdale. (1978). "Learned helplessness in humans: Critique and reformulation." *Journal of Abnormal Psychology* 87 (1):49–74. https://doi.org/10.1037/0021-843X.87.1.49

BBC News. (20 May 2018). "Cambridge University's animals help students de-stress." https://www.bbc.co.uk/news/uk-england-cambridgeshire-44137717

Bell, Sarah. (25 April 2016). "NUS 'right to have no platform policy'." BBC News. https://www.bbc.co.uk/news/education-36101423

Ben-Porath, Sigal R. (2017). *Free Speech on Campus*. University of Pennsylvania Press.

Cass, Hilary. (April 2024). "The Cass Review: Independent Review of Gender Identity Services for Children and Young People." Technical report, National Health Service.

Centers for Disease Control and Prevention. (29 November 2023). "Suicide Data and Statistics." https://www.cdc.gov/suicide/suicide-data-statistics.html

Chappell, Sophie-Grace. (20 July 2018). "Trans Women/Men and Adoptive Parents: An Analogy." Blog of the APA. https://blog.apaonline.org/2018/07/20/trans-women-men-and-adoptive-parents-an-analogy/

Coughlan, Sean. (25 May 2016). "Student suicide figures increase." https://www.bbc.co.uk/news/education-36378573

Cox, Joshua and Sharifa Love. (November 1 2007). "White Yalies in blackface reveal racism on campus." *Yale News*. https://yaledailynews.com/blog/2007/11/01/white-yalies-in-blackface-reveal-racism-on-campus/

Dearden, Lizzie. (24 October 2015). "Germaine Greer will not give Cardiff University lecture because of abuse over views on transgender people." *The Independent*. https://www.independent.co.uk/news/people/germaine-greer-will-not-give-cardiff-university-lecture-because-of-abuse-over-views-on-transgender-people-a6707236.html

Ellis, Bret Easton. (26 September 2014). "Generation Wuss." *Vanity Fair*. https://www.vanityfair.fr/culture/voir-lire/articles/generation-wuss-by-bret-easton-ellis/15837

Fitzsimmons, Emma G. (3 May 2014). "Condoleezza Rice Backs Out of Rutgers Speech After Student Protests." *The New York Times*. https://www.nytimes.com/2014/05/04/nyregion/rice-backs-out-of-rutgers-speech-after-student-protests.html

Flood, Alison. (19 May 2014). "US students request 'trigger warnings' on literature." *The Guardian*.

https://www.theguardian.com/books/2014/may/19/us-students-request-trigger-warnings-in-literature

Fortin, Jacey. (24 July 2017). "Richard Dawkins Event Canceled Over Past Comments About Islam." *The New York Times.* https://www.nytimes.com/2017/07/24/us/richard-dawkins-speech-canceled-berkeley.html

Friedersdorf, Conor. (10 November 2015a). "Campus Activists Weaponize 'Safe Space.'" *The Atlantic.* https://www.theatlantic.com/politics/archive/2015/11/how-campus-activists-are-weaponizing-the-safe-space/415080/

Friedersdorf, Conor. (9 November 2015b). "The New Intolerance of Student Activism." *The Atlantic.* https://www.theatlantic.com/politics/archive/2015/11/the-new-intolerance-of-student-activism-at-yale/414810/

George, Robert G. and Cornel West. (14 March 2017). "Sign the Statement: Truth Seeking, Democracy, and Freedom of Thought and Expression — A Statement by Robert P. George and Cornel West." James Madison Program in American Ideals and Institutions. https://jmp.princeton.edu/news/2017/sign-statement-truth-seeking-democracy-and-freedom-thought-and-expression-statement

Hacking, Ian. (1995). *Rewriting the Soul: Multiple Personality and the Sciences of Memory.* Princeton University Press. https://doi.org/10.1515/9781400821686

Hacking, Ian. (1996). "The Looping Effects of Human Kinds." In Sperber, Dan, David Premack, and Ann James Premack (eds.), *Causal Cognition: A Multidisciplinary Debate.* Oxford University Press. https://doi.org/10.1093/acprof:oso/9780198524021.003.0012

Hacking, Ian. (1998). *Mad Travelers: Reflections on the Reality of Transient Mental Illnesses.* Harvard University Press.

Hacking, Ian. (1999). "Making Up People." In *The Science Studies Reader,* 161–171. Routledge.

Hacking, Ian. (2007). "Kinds of People: Moving Targets." *Proceedings of the British Academy* 151:285–318. https://doi.org/10.5871/bacad/9780197264249.003.0010

Haidt, Jonathan and Nick Haslam. (10 April 2016). "Campuses are places for open minds — not where debate is closed down." *The Observer.* https://www.theguardian.com/commentisfree/2016/apr/10/students-censorship-safe-places-platforming-free-speech

Hamzelou, Jessica. (27 Month 2016). "Exclusive: World's first baby born with new "3 parent" technique." *New Scientist.* https://www.newscientist.com/article/2107219-exclusive-worlds-first-baby-born-with-new-3-parent-technique/

Henley, Jon and Areeb Ullah. (5 February 2015). "Marine Le Pen's Oxford university speech delayed by protesters." *The Guardian.*

https://www.theguardian.com/world/2015/feb/05/marine-le-pen-front-national-oxford-union-university-speech-delayed-protesters

Hiroto, Donald S. and Martin E. Seligman. (1975). "Generality of learned helplessness in man." *Journal of Personality and Social Psychology* 31 (2):311–327. https://doi.org/10.1037/h0076270

Johnston, Ian. (14 February 2016). "Peter Tatchell hits back at LGBT student leader's 'witch-hunt.'" *The Independent*. https://www.independent.co.uk/news/uk/home-news/peter-tatchell-hits-back-at-lgbt-student-leader-s-witchhunt-a6873991.html

Knott, Katherine and Jennifer Prohov. (7 November 2015). "Tim Wolfe, student protesters meet in Kansas City." *The Maneater*. https://themaneater.com/wolfe-student-protesters-meet-kansas-city/

Leef, George. (14 April 2014). "Brandeis Caves In To The 'No Platform For Our Opponents!' Crowd." *Forbes*. https://www.forbes.com/sites/georgeleef/2014/04/14/brandeis-caves-in-to-the-no-platform-for-our-opponents-crowd/?sh=28e9d7e51a4b

Lukianoff, Greg and Jonathan Haidt. (September 2015). "The Codding of the American Mind." *The Atlantic*. https://www.theatlantic.com/magazine/archive/2015/09/the-coddling-of-the-american-mind/399356/

Mackie, John L. (1980). *The Cement of the Universe*. Clarendon Press Oxford. https://doi.org/10.1093/0198246420.001.0001

Oreskes, Naomi and Erik M. Conway. (2011). *Merchants of Doubt: How a Handful of Scientists Obscured the Truth on Issues from Tobacco Smoke to Global Warming*. Bloomsbury Publishing.

Overmier, J. Bruce and Martin E. P. Seligman. (1967). "Effects of inescapable shock upon subsequent escape and avoidance responding." *Journal of Comparative and Physiological Psychology* 63 (1):28–33. https://doi.org/10.1037/h0024166

Packham, Alfie. (5 May 2016). "Boris, Tatchell, Greer: were they actually no-platformed?" *The Guardian*. https://www.theguardian.com/education/2016/may/05/boris-tatchell-greer-were-they-actually-no-platformed

Pierce, Chester. (1970). "Offensive Mechanisms." In Barbour, Floyd B. (ed.), *The Black Seventies*, 265–282. Porter Sargent Publisher.

Popper, Karl. (1963). *Conjectures and Refutations: The Growth of Scientific Knowledge*. Routledge.

Post Editorial Board. (10 November 2015). "'Safe space' fascists now rule the University of Missouri." *New York Post*. https://nypost.com/2015/11/10/safe-space-fascists-now-rule-the-university-of-missouri/

Seligman, Martin E. P. and Steven F. Maier. (1967). "Failure to Escape Traumatic Shock." *Journal of Experimental Psychology* 74 (1):1–9. https://doi.org/10.1037/h0024514

Shulevitz, Judith. (March 21 2015). "In College and Hiding from Scary Ideas." *The New York Times.* https://www.nytimes.com/2015/03/22/opinion/sunday/judith-shulevitz-hiding-from-scary-ideas.html

Stryker, Susan and Jim Van Buskirk. (1996). *Gay by the Bay: A history of queer culture in the San Francisco Bay Area.* Chronicle Books.

Thomas-Carver, Desiree and Linda Darling-Hammond. (2017). "Why black women teachers leave and what can be done about it." In Farinde-Wu, A., A. Allen-Handy, and C. W. Lewis (eds.), *Black female teachers: Diversifying the United States' teacher workforce*, 159–184. Emerald Publishing Limited. https://doi.org/10.1108/S2051-231720170000006009

Wikiquote. (2024). "John C. Calhoun." https://en.wikiquote.org/wiki/John_C._Calhoun

PART IV
Modern tribes
The communitarian conception of the Open Society

21. Joshua's question

In the 1973 film *Magnum Force*, Clint Eastwood, as detective Harry Callahan, is confronted by a group of three police officers who have committed a series of vigilante murders. The group try to persuade Callahan to join them, stating, "Either you're for us or you're against us." Callahan, displaying the moral backbone that exists alongside his maverick tendencies, declines the invitation, saying, "I'm afraid you've misjudged me." It's not clear whether Callahan's reason for refusing was accurate: by the end of the film he kills every member of the vigilante gang. If that doesn't count as being *against them*, I'm not sure what does.

This way of framing the central relation between an individual and a group, that one must either be *for* or *against* the group, is as old as humanity itself. It is given clear statement in the Book of Joshua, which in the King James' translation reads:

> And it came to pass, when Joshua was by Jericho, that he lifted up his eyes and looked, and, behold, there stood a man over against him with his sword drawn in his hand: and Joshua went unto him, and said unto him, Art thou for us, or for our adversaries? (Joshua, 5:13, KJV)

Not all translations phrase Joshua's question the same. The Common English Bible has him ask, "Are you on our side or that of our enemies?" The Good News translation asks, "Are you one of our soldiers, or an enemy?" The Lexham English Bible asks, "Are you with us, or with our adversaries?" And the New Living translation cuts right to the chase and simply asks, "Are you friend or foe?"

What these competing translations of Joshua's question highlight is the relationship between *belonging* to a group and the possession of certain *intentions* or *attitudes*. Some translations stress membership (are you "with us" or "on our side") and other translations stress intention ("art thou for us"). The Good News translation mixes the two, in that it treats being "one of our soldiers" and

---

How to cite this book part:

Alexander, J. McKenzie (2024) *The Open Society as an Enemy: A critique of how free societies turned against themselves*, London: LSE Press, pp. 223–300.
https://doi.org/10.31389/lsepress.ose.e. License: CC BY-NC 4.0

being "an enemy" as mutually exclusive, ignoring the fact that there can be enemies within. Underlying all of this is the idea that our fellow group members are *friends* and, hence, *for us*.

This brings us to the communitarian conception of the Open Society or, what I will treat as equivalent, the rejection of tribalism. What exactly does that mean? In his seminal work *Two Sources of Morality and Religion* – where the concept of the Open Society first appeared – Henri Bergson characterised the closed society as one where people viewed every interaction along the same lines as Joshua's question: are you with us or against us? For Bergson, this closure coexisted with hostility to outsiders:

> The closed society is that whose members hold together, caring nothing for the rest of humanity, on the alert for attack or defence, bound, in fact, to a perpetual readiness for battle. (Bergson 1935, p. 229)

The trouble with Bergson's characterisation of the closed society is that it cuts too crudely. While any group that "[cares] nothing for the rest of humanity" and is ready to do battle with outsiders certainly counts as a closed society, it's not the only kind of closed society. We can relax this condition, requiring only that the group's primary or predominant concern is with its own members, with the "rest of humanity" given lower priority. If we read Bergson figuratively, such that being "on the alert for attack or defence" means not just a physical attack but also a readiness to respond to a *perceived critique* of certain *beliefs or values* – possibly ones seen as *constitutive* of the group identity – we obtain a broader characterisation of a closed society.

Yet even under this broader interpretation of Bergson, something seems to be missing. A closed society isn't just a society whose members are ready to fiercely defend the group from external critique, even when the critique targets beliefs or values central to the group's identity. *That* attitude is compatible with communities committed to free and open inquiry, the pursuit of truth, and evidence-based decision-making, so long as those communities don't roll over immediately in the face of external critique. A closed society must also feature a degree of commitment to the group that borders on the irrational, is unresponsive to critique, or is resistant to revision in light of contrary evidence.

It is this combination of irrationality and recalcitrance that Popper identifies as the defining feature of his sense of the closed society, which he also refers to as the "tribal society". He writes:

> There is no standardized 'tribal way of life'. It seems to me, however, that there are some characteristics that can be found in most, if not all, of these tribal societies. I mean their magical or irrational attitude towards the customs of social life, and the corresponding rigidity of these customs. (Popper 1945, p. 184)

Combining the accounts of Bergson and Popper, we arrive at the following: a closed society is one (i) whose primary concern lies with its own members, (ii) whose members are ready to defend themselves against perceived threats – by which we mean not just *physical* threats but threats to certain beliefs or values, often seen as core to the group identity – and where (iii) the beliefs or values triggering the defensive response are rigidly held with a degree of irrationality.[1] From this, we may then trivially define an Open Society as one that is not closed.

This proposed definition is quite a mouthful, but it is useful for several reasons. First, it doesn't treat open or closed societies as being purely binary: societies admit degrees of closure, and this definition allows societies to be more or less closed. Second, it distinguishes between closed societies and cases of mere group loyalty. Take, for instance, football fans. Even if conditions (ii) and (iii) are met, it's unlikely that (i) will be met to the degree required to transform a group of football fans into a closed society. Recall that condition (i) relaxes the Bergson requirement that a closed society "[cares] nothing for the rest of humanity". The new requirement, a society "whose primary concern lies with its own members", allows trade-offs to be made between its members and nonmembers. For the majority of football fans, the new condition fails to obtain: an ardent Manchester United supporter will still come to the aid of a Liverpool fan collapsed on the street. But when the first condition *does* hold – and as the trade-offs increase in severity – we arrive at something other than the loyalty of football fans. At the extreme, we arrive at the phenomenon of the "Ultras", a type of fanatic where team loyalty alone justifies violent, thuggish behaviour against supporters of other teams (Jones 2017).

A third reason why the proposed definition is useful is that, although it is formulated in terms of closed *societies*, it applies to any group that has a strong sense of collective identity. Bergson spoke of closed societies because given his focus on morality and religion, that was the appropriate level of organisation on which to focus. Popper spoke of closed societies due to his interest in the ideological conflict underlying World War II – a conflict between alliances of nation states. These historical facts notwithstanding, I think that focusing on closed *societies* alone is too narrow. In the last few decades, we have seen increased polarisation *within* societies along a number of dimensions. This polarisation is accompanied by an inward turn, a closing off, which shares many features with the defining features of a closed society but among groups. And so we need to appreciate that contemporary societies are increasingly composed of groups sharing a commitment to certain beliefs or values, which constitutes a group identity. These are the *modern tribes*. But the interactions between modern tribes are still implicitly governed by how they answer Joshua's Question.

In what follows, we will explore how the growth of modern tribes threatens the communitarian conception of the Open Society. To begin, there is the preliminary philosophical question as to what exactly we mean by "polarisation", and then there is the empirical question of whether polarisation has, in fact, increased in contemporary society. After that, we need to ask how and why increased polarisation might matter. This requires us to engage with theories of social identity and how membership of a group can influence individual decision-making simply by virtue of belonging to a group as well as through the explicit pressure of social norms. Then we need to examine the underlying mechanisms that drive us to increasingly identify with tribes, which I think are deeply connected to concepts of authenticity and ideological purity. One concern about these drivers is how both can be exploited for political purposes, especially in the age of social media, returning to a concern we broached in Chapter 14. I then explore how the communitarian Open Society is threatened with fragmentation as we focus on what divides us instead of what unites us. Then I shall turn to the phenomenon of epistemic closure and how it relates to the formation and persistence of extreme groups. And, finally, we end with the question of what it means to live in an open society defined by diversity and difference of opinions and how to negotiate the collision of horizons this yields.

22. On polarisation

Polarisation exists when a population is divided into two or more groups with strong differences between the groups. This intuitive idea can be made more precise by drawing on the work of Esteban and Ray (1994), who studied measures of income polarisation. (We'll be interested in many types of polarisation, but polarisation of income is a good place to start because incomes, unlike ideas, are more easily measured.) As a starting point, they proposed such a measure should satisfy three criteria. First, there must be a high degree of homogeneity *within* each group; second, there must be a high degree of heterogeneity *across* groups; and third, there must be a small number of significantly sized groups.

Consider how the three criteria characterise the polarisation of different societies. Figure 22.1 reproduces three examples from Esteban and Ray's original paper. In 22.1(a), a society is split into 10 equally sized groups by income bracket. In 22.1(b), we see a society split into two equal-sized groups. In each case, there is essentially the same amount of homogeneity *within* each group. However, in 22.1(a) there is a smoother gradation between the poor and the rich, with a number of people in intermediary classes. This yields less heterogeneity *across* groups than in 22.1(b). Finally, in 22.1(b) the society is just two big groups. These observations fit our intuition that the society of 22.1(b) is *more polarised* than the society of 22.1(a). This also shows that the concept of polarisation is different from the concept of *inequality*. As Esteban and Ray noted, the society shown in 22.1(b) is more polarised than the society in 22.1(a), but under any reasonable measure of inequality, the society of 22.1(b) is *more equal* than that of 22.1(a). Now compare 22.1(c) with 22.1(b). The size of the two groups is unchanged, but in 22.1(c) the first group has become much poorer and the second group much richer, so inequality has increased as we move from 22.1(b) to 22.1(c). Intuitively, polarisation has also increased from 22.1(b) to 22.1(c). This shows that while an increase in polarisation can go hand in hand with a *decrease* in inequality, it may also be the case that an increase in polarisation *increases* inequality. The two concepts are distinct.

These observations about polarisation generalise beyond income distributions. The plots in Figure 22.1 can be reinterpreted as referring to the distribution of political beliefs. This interpretation invokes what is known as the spatial theory of voting. According to this theory, people's political stance corresponds to a point in an "issue space". The simplest model treats the issue space as one-dimensional, with liberal on the left and conservative on the

Figure 22.1: Comparisons between three different societies as an intuition pump for a measure of polarisation

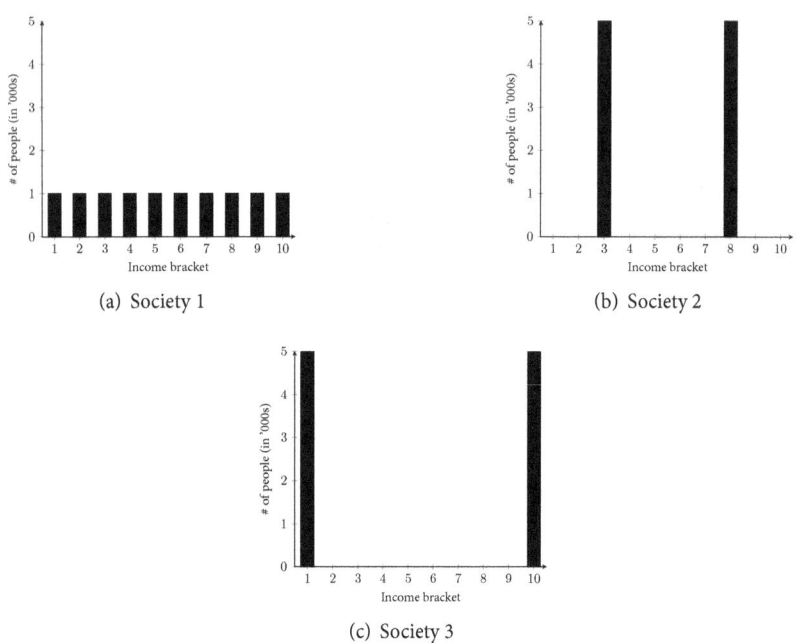

(a) Society 1

(b) Society 2

(c) Society 3

Source: adapted from Esteban and Ray (1994). Redrawn based on Figures 1A, 1B, and 2B.

right. More complex models increase the number of dimensions. In two dimensions, we might distinguish between economic policy (liberal or conservative) on one dimension and social policy (liberal or conservative) on the other. Increasing the number of dimensions increases the number of distributions, which might count as a form of polarisation. This turns out to be quite a complicated topic: Bramson *et al.* (2017) identify no fewer than *nine* different senses of polarisation in just the one-dimensional case.

In thinking about polarisation, we need to appreciate that polarisation, like many English nouns ending in *-tion*, exhibits what is known as process-product ambiguity. A word like "observation" can refer to the *process* of looking out the window – the act of observing – and the *product* of what that process yields – a person's spotting of a bird. It is important to attend to this distinction because mistakes can arise from conflating the two different meanings: things that hold for the process interpretation may not hold for the product interpretation, and *vice versa*. For example, some have suggested that a person's *perception* – understood as a process – should be treated as an unquestionable fact because, as a first-person subjective experience, how can anyone be in a position to dispute another's experience? Yet it does not follow from this that the *perception* – understood as a product – is necessarily veracious. This distinction enables us to tell someone, "You didn't actually see what you think you saw", without denying that the person *thought* they saw what they claimed to have seen. Given this process-product ambiguity, when we speak of polarisation we need to distinguish between a process that divides people and the outcome of people being divided. This yields three questions to consider: first, are societies more polarised today than before (the product interpretation)? Second, what causes polarisation (the process interpretation)? Finally, is the type of polarisation (product and process interpretations) produced undesirable?

This last question matters because not all types of polarisation are bad. Strong differences in taste are exactly what one would expect to find in a diverse society. Strong opinions motivate people to follow their interests, to specialise in chemistry or literature, opera or rock-and-roll. Strong differences in values can prompt reflection about the kind of society we want to live in and why, helping us avoid complacency by simply continuing with current practice. But strong differences in values can lead to conflict if people feel unable to compromise on those issues that matter most to them. The overall point is that polarisation, in and of itself, is not *necessarily* bad. Polarisation may function as an engine driving a diverse and vibrant society, or it can lead to endless conflict and political gridlock.

Let us now turn to the question of whether polarisation has been increasing over the past few decades. In particular, consider whether *political* polarisation been increasing. Political differences tend to be correlated with other kinds of differences due to the close relationship between identity and politics, so this is not an unreasonable place to begin. Anecdotal evidence suggests political polarisation has increased. The 2016 US presidential election, with two competing visions offered by Clinton and Trump, elicited sharp and negative reactions from both camps when they thought of the other side winning. In the UK, the 2016 referendum on whether the UK should leave the EU similarly inflamed emotions, with a narrow margin of victory for the Leave campaign. The subsequent 2017 UK general election likewise saw no clear overall winner in Parliament, with Theresa May having to strike a deal with Northern Ireland's Democratic Unionist Party to maintain power. In both cases, the nearly equal split of the vote masks the deep ideological divide on the underlying issues. In France in 2017, Emmanuel Macron, an independent centrist, won a resounding 66–33 victory over Marine Le Pen. But the fact that Le Pen was in the final election at all, surprised people, just as when her father ran against Chirac in the final election in 2002. In Germany, the Alternative für Deutschland won over 90 seats in the 2017 election, putting a far-right, anti-Islam party – which has been accused of employing rhetoric with Nazi overtones – in parliament for the first time since World War II.

Obtaining precise measurements of polarisation for cross-country comparisons is difficult because of variations across political systems. If we restrict attention to the US, Hare and Poole (2014) used a measure known as DW-NOMINATE to show that the polarisation of the two major political parties in 2013 was at its highest level since the end of the Civil War. The Hare and Poole method of gauging polarisation has two advantages. First, it measures the ideological position of legislators on the liberal–conservative spectrum using their entire roll-call voting record.[1] Second, it uses overlapping membership to provide a way of comparing the relative ideological positions of individuals who didn't serve in government at the same time.

Figure 22.2 illustrates the variation in polarisation for both the US House of Representatives and the Senate from 1879 to 2013. The vertical axis represents political orientation using a one-dimensional model, where -1.0 corresponds to highly liberal and 1.0 to highly conservative. The figure shows time-series data for how the 10th and 90th percentiles of both the Republican and Democratic parties have shifted over time. That is, the 10th percentile for the Republican party tracks the point on the political spectrum such that 10% of elected Republicans are more *liberal* than that, with the 10th percentile for the Democratic party tracking the point where 10% of elected Democrats are more *conservative* than that. In the Senate, there was considerable overlap for the 40-year period from 1935 to 1975, with a number of Democrats being more conservative than Republicans and a number of Republicans being more liberal than Democrats. In the House, the period of overlap was roughly similar, although not as great. The important thing to note is how from 1975 onwards, there has been a steady divergence of the two parties.

For the UK, evidence of increasing polarisation also exists. Jonathan Wheatley examined the responses of people living in England to survey questions[2] in 2015 and 2017 (i.e., right before two general elections) and from their responses constructed a map of the ideological dimensions associated with each party's voters. Unlike the American context, in the UK it was necessary to add a second dimension to capture the full variety of individual attitudes. One dimension was familiar, measuring the extent to which a voter was economically liberal or conservative. The second dimension, rather than being indicative of whether a person was socially liberal or conservative, was instead characterised by Wheatley (2015) as a "cosmopolitan-communitarian" dimension.

What Wheatley found was striking. Figure 22.3 illustrates the ideological drift that occurred between 2015 and 2017 for all of the major political parties in the UK. What we see is a clear polarisation: the Greens, Labour, and the Liberal Democrats became more cosmopolitan and economically liberal, while UKIP and the Conservatives became more communitarian and economically conservative. Most notably, areas of overlap between the Liberal Democrats and Conservatives have disappeared, and the close proximity between some Labour voters and some Conservative voters has likewise vanished.

Although Wheatley's study only provides evidence of increased polarisation in the UK over a two-year period, other evidence suggests this is part of

Figure 22.2: Ideological polarisation within both houses of the US Congress, 1879–2013

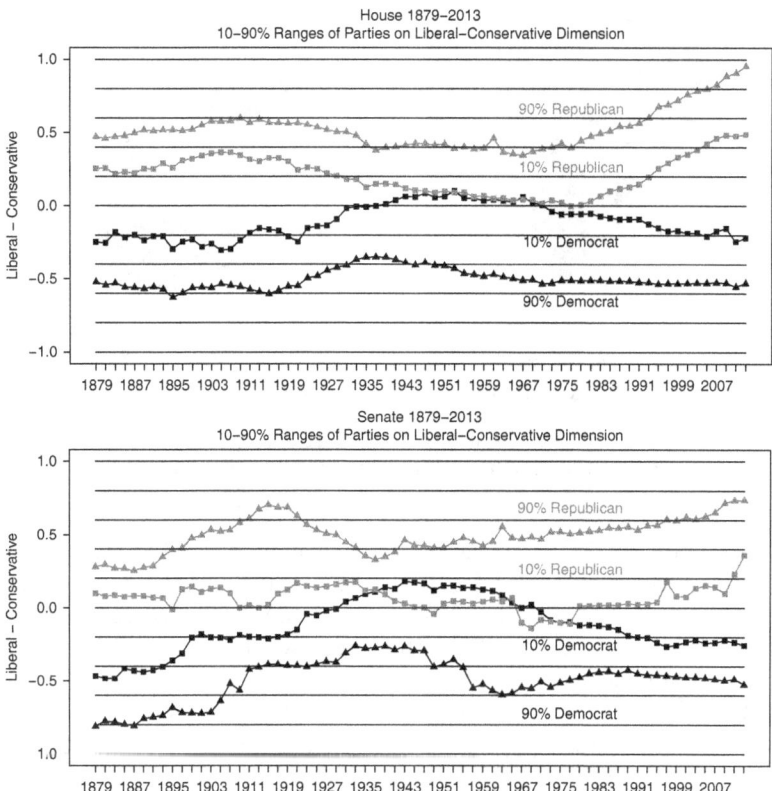

Source: Figure 1 in Hare and Poole (2014). Reproduced with permission from the University of Chicago Press.

a larger trend. Figure 22.4 shows the regional outcomes for two different referendums on whether the UK should remain part of the EC (as the EU was known prior to 1993). In 1975, the only parts of the UK to vote in favour of leaving the EC were the Outer Hebrides and the Shetland Islands, which perhaps makes sense because you already could not get much further away from the EU – physically – than those two parts of the UK. By 2016, opinion had shifted considerably towards the other end of the spectrum, with most of middle England, the south-west and part of Northern Ireland voting to leave.

These studies, although restricted to the US and the UK, are consistent with the impression that society is more polarised now than in the past. If we accept that, the next question to ask is *why*? What are the factors driving people apart?

Figure 22.3: Ideological grouping of UK political parties before the 2015 and 2017 general elections

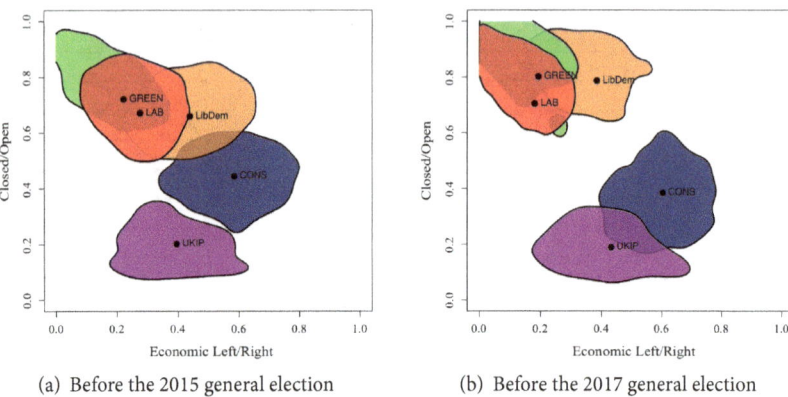

(a) Before the 2015 general election   (b) Before the 2017 general election

Source: Diagrams 1 and 2 in Wheatley (2017). Available under a Creative Commons Attribution-NonCommercial-NoDerivs 3.0 Unported License.

Three possible causes of polarisation come to mind. The first is economic: since the 1980s, globalisation has become an increasingly disruptive force, displacing entire industries in the US, the UK, and elsewhere. As peoples' income in real terms stagnates or declines, they become increasingly self-interested and local in their outlook, seeing the world as a zero-sum game. This resonates with the themes covered in Part I. The second is informational: echo chambers, customised news feeds, and filter bubbles reduce the diversity of information to which individuals are exposed. This resonates with the themes covered in Part II. The third is cultural: the social identities of people have become increasingly salient, perhaps as a result of the two previous causes. And these social identities call attention to the dimensions along which people differ, rather than points of commonality.

Of these three factors, there is good evidence to support the claim that when it comes to middle-income persons living in the US, the UK, and other parts of the West, they have lost out from globalisation. Evidence regarding the effect of filter bubbles and social media is mixed, as we will see below. The last factor, of how our social identity influences our behaviour in modern tribes, shall occupy our attention for the remaining chapters in this part.

In 2012, the World Bank published a report on global inequality, examining who the winners and losers were, under globalisation. The primary beneficiaries were the very rich and the middle classes in developing economies. Figure 22.5 shows the real increase in income (measured in 2005 international dollars) versus the percentile of global income between 1988 and 2008. The largest increases occurred at the median: an 80% increase in real terms with increases of over 70% for points nearby. The report noted (emphasis added):

Figure 22.4: Regional outcomes for the two UK referendums on whether to remain part of the EC (1975) or the EU (2016)

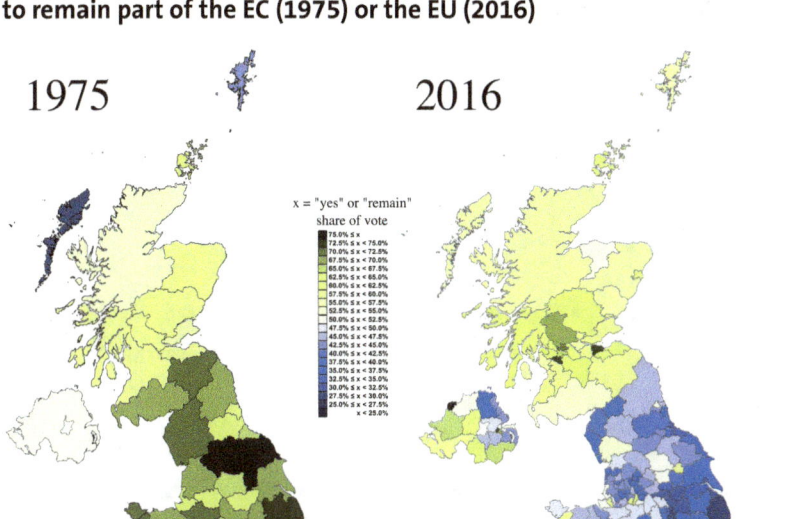

Source: Wikimedia Commons (2016). Available under a Creative Commons Attribution-Share Alike 4.0 International Licence (CC BY-SA 4.0) (https://en.m.wikipedia.org/wiki/File:United_Kingdom_European_Communities_membership_referendum,_1975_compared_to_United_Kingdom_European_Union_membership_referendum,_2016.svg).

The most interesting developments, though, happened among the top quartile: the top 1%, and somewhat less so the top 5%, gained significantly, while the next 20% either gained very little or faced stagnant real incomes. *This created polarization among the richest quartile of world population,* allowing the top 1% to pull ahead of the other rich and to reaffirm in fact – and even more so in public perception – its preponderant role as winners of globalization. (Milanovic 2012, p. 14)

In other words, for people in the middle to upper-middle classes in developed economies, those among the richest top 15%–17% of the global population, global income distribution was *more inequal* in 2008 than 20 years prior.

What about informational contributors to growing polarisation? Sunstein observed in *#Republic* that the ability to customise online news so that each

Figure 22.5: Change in real income between 1988 and 2008 at various percentiles of global income distribution

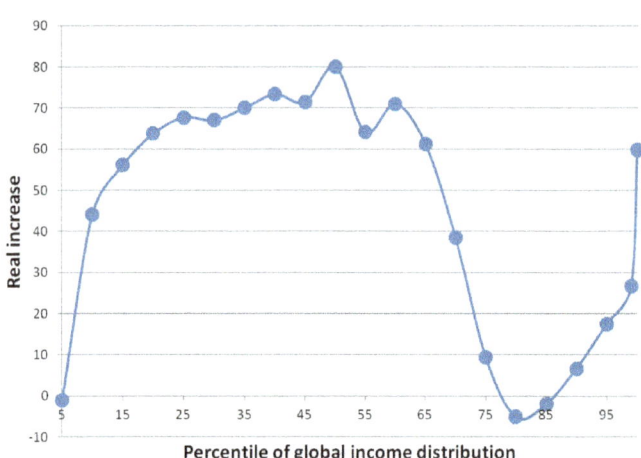

Source: Figure 4 in Milanovic (2012). Available under Creative Commons License CC BY 3.0 IGO DEED.

person receives a "Daily You", displaying only that news which interests you from those sources that appeal to you, threatens to transform a well-informed citizenry, acquainted with the issues of the day, into a partisan, polarised populace where each individual is largely unaware of any perspective other than their own. How concerned should we be about that possibility?

Back in 2007, online news viewing was in its infancy. According to Baum and Groeling (2008, p. 347), "the total volume of traffic to political web sites in May 2007 was about 9 million unique viewers (Wheaton 2007), about the same as the typical audience for a single broadcast of *ABC World News Tonight*." Yet even then, worries existed that online sites were starting to show a bias towards certain kinds of news stories. Baum and Groeling analysed 1,782 AP and Reuters news stories between 24 July and 14 November 2006, along with stories from the wire services' "top news" webpages and the websites of Fox News, Free Republic, and Daily Kos. They found that concerns about one-sided coverage were warranted, as "Daily Kos on the left and Free Republic and Fox News on the right demonstrate clear and strong preferences for news stories that benefit the party most closely associated with their own ideological orientations" (Baum and Groeling 2008, p. 359). In short, online news sites were acting like a filter, selecting content based on certain ideological leanings. Recent developments with generative AI using large-language models, like ChatGPT, will only exacerbate this problem.[3]

In contrast, a few years later (Gentzkow and Shapiro 2011, p. 1801) reported "no evidence that the Internet is become more segregated over time" regarding online news consumption. How do we account for the discrepancy between the two studies? In part, it's down to the use of different data sets and a different item of measurement: what Baum and Groeling (2008) looked at was whether *websites* displayed an ideological orientation. What truly matters, though, for the process of polarisation is the consumption of news by individuals, and this is what Gentzkow and Shapiro measured. Essentially, the reason why they found that the internet might be less effective at driving polarisation, even though many websites have an ideological orientation, is that people were varied consumers: they visited a number of different websites of different orientations, and that served to neutralise the overall effect. That said, it's worth noting that this paper was published in 2011, using data from 2004 to 2009. The world has changed a lot since then. Breitbart News wasn't launched until 2005 and didn't become a major player in the online news media until after the period of this study. For example, Robert Mercer donated $11 million to Breitbart in 2011, and Steven Bannon didn't take over as executive chairman of Breitbart until 2012. It's also worth noting that the Gentzkow and Shapiro study shows what might now strike us as a quaint concern for the importance of facts and a failure to anticipate what advances in AI might make possible:

> It is true that the Internet allows consumers to *filter* news relatively freely, but it has not changed the fact that *reporting* or *writing* stories that are tailored to a particular point of view is costly. There is no computer program that can take a story written with liberal slant as input, and output an account of the same facts written with conservative slant. (Gentzkow and Shapiro 2011, p. 1831-32)

Whereas the point about tailor-made news being costly *was* true back in 2011, that is no longer the case: AI can easily generate news on demand. And ChatGPT can easily generate new ideological perspectives on pre-existing text. For example, you might try asking it to rewrite the opening of the *Communist Manifesto* from the point of view of a free-market economist.[4] In addition, we also know that one way in which the internet polarises people is not through writing factual stories from a different point of view but, rather, through the much more effective method of "fake news", a.k.a., "making shit up."

Fast-forward to the present age and things have changed in two important ways, which make inventions like ChatGPT even more problematic. First, the amount of news that people consume online has greatly increased. In a blog post published by the Brookings Institute, Bleiberg and West (2015) wrote, "Many Americans get a significant portion of their news from Facebook and in effect the social network is the largest news platform in the U.S." Second, there has been a shift in how much news people see from certain perspectives. Bleiberg and West found that the Facebook News feed algorithm, which took a user's history of clicking on past stories into account when ranking news,

Figure 22.6: Time-series plots of polarisation by predicted internet use

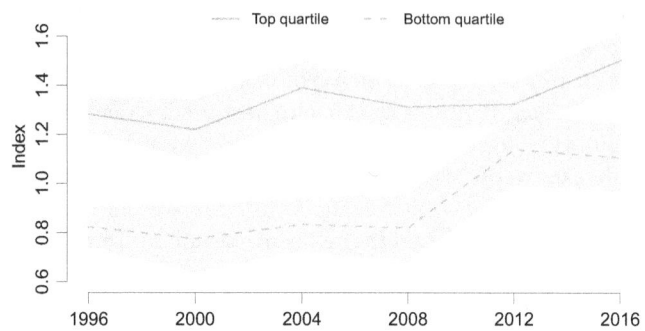

Source: Figure 4 in Boxell et al. (2017). Reproduced with permission from the Proceedings of the National Academy of Sciences.

reduced the amount of news that people saw from the other side of the political divide by 5% for conservatives and 8% for liberals. When the disposition of users to click on links was taken into account, they found that exposure to cross-party news decreased by 17% for conservatives and 6% for liberals.

Yet there is reason to think that although these differences in click behaviour and news consumption exist, this is primarily a *symptom* of polarisation rather than a *driver* of polarisation. A study by Boxell *et al.* (2017) found that the largest changes in polarisation among US adults occurred amongst those over the age of 65, who were also the *least* likely to use the internet. A close examination of the data suggests that the effect of the internet and social media on polarisation is, at best, modest. Figure 22.6 plots the trend in polarisation by predicted internet use. Although the top quartile of internet users have a higher polarisation index than those in the bottom quartile, there is relatively little change in their polarisation index between 1996 (when little online news was available) and 2016 (when a lot was available). Furthermore, a much greater increase in polarisation occurred amongst the bottom quartile of internet users. The upshot seems to be this: whatever is driving the growth in polarisation, the internet seems to be a modest contributor.

To summarise: we have shown that there is good evidence to believe that polarisation has increased considerably in recent years. We have explored some of the possible drivers of this growth and seen that both economic and informational aspects have played a part, although economics seems to have been a much more powerful contributor than informational elements. What remains to be explored is how people's self-understanding of their *social identities* may be implicated in this polarisation trend.

It is important to keep in mind the conceptual distinction between a growth in the importance of one's *social identity* and a growth in polarisation. Or, to put the point slightly differently, we need to distinguish between *polarisation* and *tribalism*. People can self-identify with a modern tribe and be highly *tribal*, even if there isn't a great deal of *polarisation*. Think of two different Christian sects whose doctrines differ by just a small amount. Although there would be little polarisation between the two groups, in terms of doctrine or beliefs, there could be a high degree of tribalism. Increased polarisation may contribute to increased tribalism, but we need to realise that polarisation is not a necessary condition for tribalism.

23. Social identity, in-group bias, and norms

One important part of contemporary society's division into modern tribes is how this affects our understanding of the identity of ourselves and others.[1] Social identity theory (see Tajfel 1972; Turner 1982) examines how our self-descriptions in terms of social categories, along with the normative requirements and subsequent evaluations generated by those categories, contribute to this self-understanding. Figure 23.1, based upon a diagram from Hogg and Abrams (1988), illustrates the multiple layers at play in the social identity approach. A person's self-identity features a number of both personal and social descriptions. The personal descriptions involve concrete relations with specific people (such as siblings, friends, or colleagues) or particular objects. The social descriptions, in contrast, relate the individual to a number of social *categories*, which are formally recognised or institutionalised to varying degrees. For example, in Figure 23.1, Linda's identity as an American has rigid membership criteria established by the state, but the criteria for whether she is a Democrat are less rigidly defined. A person can self-identify as a Democrat without being officially registered as such on the voter rolls. In contrast to both of these categories, what it means to identify as a feminist is even less sharply defined because there are a variety of different theoretical views, all of which can claim the term "feminist". Most of the time, a membership relation holds between the person and a specific social category, as with Michael's being a soldier or a Catholic, but sometimes a person is defined more in terms of their *opposition* to a social category, as with Michael's identity as being anti-woke (Figure 23.1).

A person's social identity attributes a number of categories, simultaneously, but only some of these categories are salient to a person at any one time. Which categories are salient, and thus influential in how a person interacts with the world, depends on environmental and individual factors.[2] In addition, membership in a tribe often comes with obligations or expectations. The obligations may concern how one should behave generally or how one should behave towards members or non-members of the tribe.[3] The expectations we have about people belonging to social categories may be based on either experience and evidence or stereotypes and, often, both. Yet there is no guarantee that these obligations and expectations, aggregated across all of the tribes a person belongs to, will be simultaneously satisfiable, much less coherent. Continuing the example from Figure 23.1, Linda's Catholicism exists in tension with her feminism, given how deeply entrenched patriarchal values are in the Roman Catholic church. If Linda really believes in a strict version of Catholicism, this belief exists in tension with the value of freedom of religion that is deeply

Figure 23.1: The multiple layers of personal identity

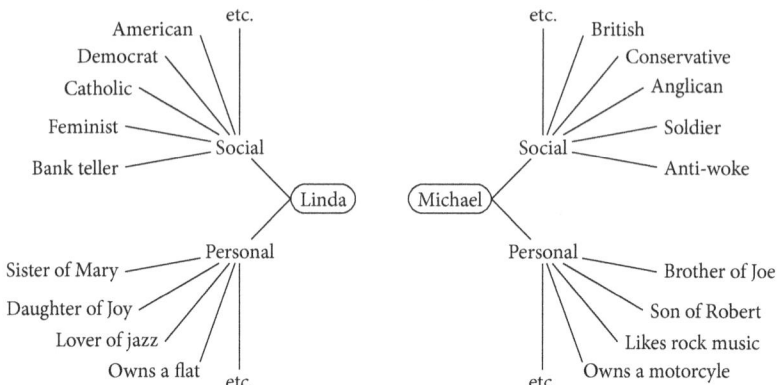

Source: author; loosely based on Figure 2.1 from Hogg and Abrams (1988).

embedded in her identity as an American because it allows other people to be *wrong* – often radically so – which would put their souls in danger.[4] Considerable conceptual gymnastics are required to resolve these tensions; sometimes it is easier to simply ignore them, hoping that they do not manifest in an explicit problem requiring resolution.

Not only does every person belong to multiple tribes but the list of tribes a person belongs to changes over the course of their life. Although relatively few people change their citizenship or religion, some do. More frequently, people change the organisations they belong to, their career, their church, and so on. And while we often think of people choosing to belong to groups because of various beliefs or the values they hold, the influence goes in the other direction as well: a person adopts new beliefs and values as a result of their membership of certain groups – beliefs and values they would not have adopted otherwise. A person's social identity thus plays an important *constructive* role in establishing a person's overall identity (Parekh 2008).

Finally, the set of obligations and expectations a person has to negotiate as a result of their membership of multiple tribes may change even if there has been no change in the *labels* that feature in a person's self-description or in the beliefs or values of that person. This can occur because of gradual *drift* in the collective tribal identity over time. Consider the following illustration, posed in the form of a trivia question: which US President created the Environmental Protection Agency (EPA) and the Occupational Safety and Health Administration (OSHA); passed the Clean Air Act and the National Environmental Policy Act (which required many federal projects to submit environmental impact reports); put in place the Philadelphia Plan (the first major federal affirmative action programme); and endorsed the Equal Rights Amendment (ERA) after the ERA passed both houses of Congress? Answer: Richard M. Nixon. If the answer surprised you – *surely it must be a Democrat!* – that is because the Republican tribal identity has moved to the right of the political spectrum over the past few decades. It is difficult to reconcile the Republican party that supported Nixon's legislative agenda with the Republican party of 2024. Given this, a person who described herself as a Republican during the Nixon period and continued to include that social category as part of her identity, would now find herself having to negotiate a world in which people behaved differently towards her as a result of changes in the public understanding of the "Republican" label. In addition, there is the question of how she would respond to these changes in the character of the Republican party. Would she feel marginalised as the political centre of the group became more extreme over time? Or would her beliefs and values change in order to track the median beliefs of the group?

All of this highlights the normative and behavioural complexities raised by our social identities in a world where all of us belong to multiple tribes. Aside from the inner conflict this generates for us, there is also the outer conflict it generates because different groups have conflicting, or only partially aligned, interests and goals they seek to realise. But are there any other phenomena we should be concerned about which arise simply in virtue of the fact that people see themselves as members of a *group*?

In a classic result from social psychology, Tajfel *et al.* (1971) showed that simply putting people into *groups* sufficed for inducing bias towards one's fellow group members, known as the *in-group*. What is striking about the phenomenon of in-group bias is that it can be created in people simply by virtue of the fact that they see themselves as *belonging to a group*, even when there is no salient collective identity that binds the group together. It seems that our disposition towards tribal thinking has a hair trigger indeed.

In one experiment, subjects were shown a series of photographs containing a number of dots and were asked to estimate how many dots were displayed. Once their estimates were collected, the subjects were divided into groups, ostensibly on the basis of whether they tended to overestimate or underestimate the number of dots on screen. In truth, subjects were put into groups at random. A second experiment altered the initial stage by showing subjects a series of two abstract paintings, without identifying the artists, and asking people to state which of the two paintings they preferred. Subjects were then divided into groups on the alleged basis of whether they tended to prefer Klee or Kandinsky (the featured artists). As before, group allocation was actually done at random.

Once subjects were assigned to groups, they were seated in isolated cubicles and given a booklet containing a number of two-person resource allocation problems. The allocation problems were stated using a matrix of numbers, with each column representing a possible outcome and the payoffs to the two players given by the numbers in the corresponding rows. Each row was labelled: "These are rewards and penalties for member N of your group" or "of the other group", with N being the code number of the person to ensure anonymity. The allocation problems fell into three types: *in-group* problems, where both recipients were from the same group as the subject; *out-group* problems, where both recipients were from the other group; and *inter-group* problems, where one recipient was from the in-group member and the other from the out-group. Subjects had to indicate which outcome they wanted by marking the appropriate column.

What Tajfel and his colleagues found was striking: when choosing allocations for inter-group problems, subjects showed a clear tendency to *favour* fellow in-group members at the expense of out-group members. This in-group bias was present despite the lack of any apparent reason for showing such favouritism: why would the mere fact that a subject was placed among fellow over- (or under-) estimators of dots prompt an aversion to fair distributions? Other experiments (see, for example, Nydegger and Owen 1974) found that in perfectly symmetric situations, people preferred to divide a resource fairly. Here, in a situation where people are essentially symmetric and the only difference is which group they belong to – this alone suffices for breaking the symmetry. Furthermore, it's important to remember that, in making these allocations, the subject's choices concerned *other* people, not themselves. And, since there was no possibility of communication with fellow group members after the allocation problems were revealed, there is no reason for subjects to think that any in-group favouritism, on their behalf, would be reciprocated. Rather, there seemed to be something merely in the act of *seeing oneself as belonging to a group* that triggered in-group bias. These results have been replicated in a number of other settings. If you harbour a worry about whether these results were truly *minimal* enough, in that the stated reason for group membership did refer to a criterion of similarity (i.e., similar tendencies to over/underestimate dots, or preference for a particular abstract artist), in a follow-up experiment, Billig and Tajfel (1973) found that in-group bias still occurred when subjects were put into groups *and told that group membership was assigned at random.*

If the mere awareness of belonging to a group – even a group with no meaningful identity – can cause people to display favouritism towards fellow group members, more extreme kinds of behaviours are easily induced when group membership is based on things people actually care about. This, of course, is no great surprise: groups of people have been killing each other in warfare throughout all of human history. What is surprising is how easily group membership, combined with a little competition, can give rise to hostilities when previously no animosity existed between individuals.

In order to understand this phenomenon, we need to realise that real-world group membership – unlike the minimal group experiments discussed previously – quickly becomes associated with a set of values and norms that regulates the expression and enforcement of those values. Interactions between people belonging to different groups then frequently cease to be seen as two people interacting *qua* individuals and are instead seen as two people interacting *qua* group representatives, with the potential conflict of values that entails. One highly influential theory of inter-group relations, known as realistic conflict theory, advances the following hypotheses:

> When a group forms it delineates itself (ingroup) from an outgroup. This categorical distinction then comes to embody value-laden content. Ingroup norms develop from interpersonal relationships within the group which define the range and content of acceptable ingroup values, and the rewards or sanctions associated with adhering to these norms. Stereotypes are then applied to outgroups, the content of which depends on the actual or perceived relations between the groups in question. Specifically, if the groups are seen as being in competition, such that something which is good for one will be bad for the other, the stereotype of the outgroup is likely to be negative and derogatory. (Hogg and Abrams 1988, p. 43)

This theory of inter-group relations was tested in a famous series of experiments conducted by Muzafer Sherif in 1949, 1953, and 1954 (see Sherif 1962, 1966).[5] In the 1949 experiment, Sherif and his collaborators arranged for 24 boys, between 11 and 12 years of age, to attend a summer camp in northern Connecticut. The boys were carefully selected so as to minimise any naturally salient attributes that could induce divisions within the group. All the boys were white Protestants from "settled American families of the lower-middle-class income group in the New Haven area" (Sherif and Sherif 1953, p. 238). They all had similar educational backgrounds and all were classified as more or less "normal". The most important point is that none of them were considered to have any behavioural problems.

The experiment had three stages. In the first stage, the boys – all strangers to one another – lived in a single large communal cabin where they were allowed to develop friendships. In the second stage, the boys were split into two groups of equal size and moved into separate bunkhouses. The groups were kept separate as much as possible, with no common activities. Over the five days of the second stage, each of the groups began to form a collective identity. They adopted names for their groups (the "Red Devils" and the "Bull Dogs", respectively), made T-shirts with their group mascots, and built private hideouts. Different behavioural norms became established in each group, ranging from how they punished social infractions by members to how they made lanyards or cleaned up trash. When the boys were asked an open-ended question about who their best friend was, with the wording indicating that they could name anyone in the *camp*, almost everyone answered by naming people within their *group*.

The final stage of the experiment involved putting the two groups into competitive situations where the aims of each group were frustrated. This began with three days of sporting competitions, with prizes given to the winners. Although the boys started with a show of good sportsmanship, their attitudes changed over the course of the competitions. A cheer which began, "2-4-6-8, who do we appreciate?" morphed into "2-4-6-8, who do we appreci-*hate*?" over the course of a match. When it became clear that the Bull Dogs were going to win the overall competition, the Red Devils were calling the Bull Dogs "cheats" and "dirty players", blaming their loss on unfair play. Other situations were engineered to generate further conflict between the groups. This led to increasingly hostile interactions, bordering on outright violence. This experiment wouldn't receive ethics approval today.

Belonging to a tribe with attitudes of group loyalty increases the likelihood of conflict occurring. Suppose, following the Sherif experiment, we have a population of 24 people, initially without any salient group identities. In this case, there are "only" 23 interactions that might get someone into a fight: one interaction for each of the other people in the population, as Figure 23.2(a) shows. Now suppose the population is split into two groups of 12, the Bull Dogs and the Red Devils, and that a person *never* gets into a fight with a fellow group member. Suppose, though, that any time a fellow group member gets into a fight, all their friends join in. Then the number of interactions that could possibly get a person into a fight increases to 144: the 12 interactions that person has with the other group, plus the twelve interactions for every one of 11 fellow group members. This is illustrated in Figure 23.2(b). The most important thing to note is that this generalises: every social group one includes as part of one's overall identity adds a whole set of new pathways for experiencing approbation or admonishment.

Sherif's work also highlights the role played by stereotypes in inter-group dynamics. In the absence of salient social categories, people must interpret their interactions with someone in *individual* terms. If I'm playing a one-on-one game of basketball and my opponent shoves me a bit too hard while trying to make a shot, I might think, "*Did he mean to do that?*" If I'm playing five-on-a-side, and I get shoved by two in quick succession, I might think,"*These guys play really rough!*" From that hasty generalisation, a stereotype emerges. The stereotype then provides a frame for interpreting future interactions for the rest of the game. As the size of the other group increases, the harder it becomes to ground one's interactions on an informed, nuanced understanding of the other person's unique character traits.

Stereotype theory has developed considerably since the early work of Allport (1954) on the nature of prejudice. Allport's original theory primarily focused on negative stereotypes built around the in-group/out-group distinction reflected in Sherif's experiment. More recent work, such as the stereotype content model of Fiske et al. (2002), treats stereotypes as having a more complex structure. According to this model, stereotypes vary along two dimensions: warmth and competence. This yields the 2×2 classification of stereotypes as shown in Figure 23.3. Stereotypes applying to the in-group or close allies

Figure 23.2: Adding group structure introduces a number of new pathways along which conflict might emerge

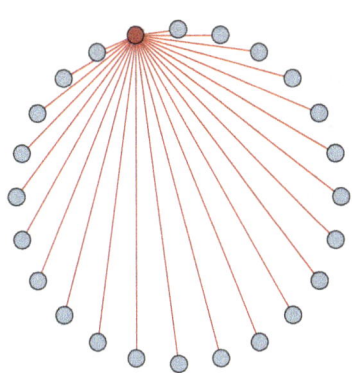
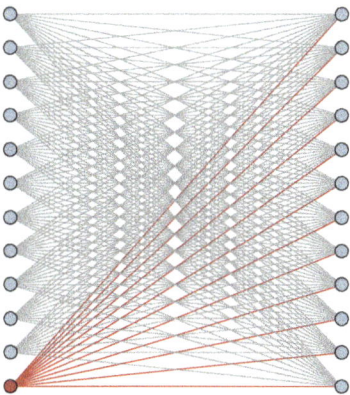

(a) The 23 interactions that might get a person into a fight when no group structure is present

(b) The 144 interactions that might get a person into a fight when a group structure is present. The interactions that the person is directly involved in are highlighted; the greyed-out interactions indicate the interactions of fellow group members.

Source: author.

tend, not surprisingly, to be high in both warmth and competence.[6] Stereotypes applying to out-groups can vary considerably depending on whether we see ourselves in competition as well as on perceptions of competence.

There's one last piece of the puzzle: the nature of norms. Group identity is often associated with norms governing members' behaviour. Bicchieri's theory of norms, which we've encountered before, distinguishes between *descriptive* norms and *social* norms. A descriptive norm "is a pattern of behavior such that individuals prefer to conform to it on condition that they believe that most people in their reference network conform to it" (Bicchieri 2017, p. 19). People won't follow a descriptive norm regardless of what others do, it depends on what other people do. If *no one* was ever fashionably late to a party, you'd probably always be on time, but since most people are fashionably late, you'll probably be fashionably late too. Second, the "other people" who matter are determined by the person's "reference network", and this may vary from person to person. As Bicchieri (2017, p. 19) notes, "A young woman in Philadelphia wearing very high heels will probably not care what other women do in India, or even New Orleans." The young woman's reference network is restricted to "the 'fashionable' crowd in her town, those who she is likely to meet" or perhaps certain celebrities or fashion icons.

Figure 23.3: A 2 × 2 categorisation of stereotypes

		Competence	
		Low	High
Warmth	High	Paternalistic prejudice Low status, not competitive Pity, sympathy (e.g., elderly people, disabled people, housewives)	Admiration High status, not competitive Pride, admiration (e.g., the in-group, close allies)
	Low	Contemptuous prejudice Low status, competitive Contempt, disgust, anger (e.g., welfare recipients, poor people)	Envious prejudice High status, competitive Envy, jealousy (e.g., rich people, feminists)

Source: Adapted from Fiske *et al.* (2002).

Recall Bicchieri's definition of a social norm, mentioned in Chapter 13:

> A social norm is a rule of behavior such that individuals prefer to conform to it on condition that they believe that (a) most people in their reference network conform to it (empirical expectation), and (b) that most people in their reference network believe they ought to conform to it (normative expectation). (Bicchieri 2017, p. 35)

Whereas a descriptive norm is a "pattern of behaviour", a social norm is a "rule of behaviour". That's an important difference: *rules* are normative in a way *patterns* are not. There's no rule saying you *must* be fashionably late to a party. In addition, with a social norm people conform to the rule because other people believe they *should*, where the "should" is a normative statement and not merely a prudential one. Social norms are rules people follow because it is the way things are done and *because other people expect you to conform*; it's not simply a matter of it naturally being in your self-interest.

Putting these elements together, it's clear how polarisation can become dangerous. The tendency to treat out-group members differently seems hardwired into our psychology. Because our concept of identity includes our *social* identity as an important constitutive part of *who we are*, we cannot avoid having our group membership – and, hence, the group membership of others – constantly made salient. The variation in social norms across groups provides multiple ways two groups can be perceived as different. Because social norms set expectations about how one *ought to behave*, differences in social norms between groups mean that members of two different groups may perceive the other as not behaving as how one ought to behave. Increased group polarisation increases the degree of perceived social distance between groups. This process of "othering" plays into our hard-wired tendency to treat out-group members differently. In extreme cases, out-group members can be dehumanised, enabling the commitment of great atrocities. This is why, in the next chapter, we consider the psychology of modern tribes.

24. The psychology of modern tribes

In modern tribes, social identity theory, in-group bias, stereotypes, and social norms interact. Social identity theory tells us that we are taught from a young age to identify with a number of tribes and incorporate that into our sense of self. As we get older and develop views about politics, morality, and other matters, we can augment that self-identity by joining additional social groups that speak to those interests. The fact of in-group bias means that we probably will, from time to time, show unwarranted favouritism towards in-group members. These acts of favouritism may be explicit or implicit. Implicit acts of favouritism are difficult to identify. If I attend a party and only engage in conversation with a few people over the course of the evening, is that an accident of social dynamics or the result of the deliberate avoidance of others? In real life, it can be a bit of both.

As we saw, the minimal group paradigm experiments show that people's tendency to favour in-group members can be invoked even when group identity isn't relevant. That's one possible source of conflict. When we are on the receiving end of out-group bias, it reinforces the negative stereotypes associated with out-groups. This matters because when we encounter an out-group member we don't know, we often frame the interaction using stereotypes. When coupled with the psychological phenomenon known as "out group homogeneity", which means people tend to view out-group members as largely undifferentiated, the negative stereotypes are readily applied. Finally, patterns of behaviour generated by these psychological processes can become encoded as social norms.

Once social norms form, group divisions and poor inter-group relations can be maintained over time, even if people dislike it. In-group members who hesitate to behave negatively towards out-group members may be sanctioned for failing to comply with the norm. In-group members who comply with a norm of discrimination towards out-group members recreate expectations of such behaviour in the future. How so? Their witnessed compliance with the norm in the *present*, reinforces *other* in-group members' belief that the empirical expectation condition is satisfied. (That is, most people in one's reference network conform to the rule.) A person's compliance with a norm also reinforces *other* peoples' beliefs that the normative expectation condition is satisfied. Why? Because when a person complies with a norm, that provides evidence that person thinks others ought to comply with the norm as well. If a person hesitated to conform with the norm, but did so after being sanctioned, that shows they didn't think nonconformity was worth the price they had to pay.

Those are the basic facts about the psychological dynamics of modern tribes. Our tribal existence faces further complexities given social media and how much of modern social life is online. Before exploring the negative aspects, let me acknowledge the important positives. One of the real advantages of social media is how easy it is to find other people like you, with your interests. Social media, and the internet, provide a forum where people can coordinate and interact, whatever their interests. That has the potential for incredibly positive and self-affirming interactions. It is useful for disadvantaged or marginalised individuals who would find it otherwise difficult to mobilise and be heard. It also has allowed powerful social movements such as #BlackLivesMatter and #MeToo to achieve international recognition more rapidly than previously possible.

Yet one downside is that when inter-group interaction takes place via social media, there are few checks and balances in place to counteract the harmful behavioural tendencies that can be triggered when group identification becomes salient. Although many social media companies provide users with the ability to control who sees their posts, many people don't exercise this control. This allows online interactions to occur between largely anonymous persons.

There is an interesting theoretical question as to what exactly "anonymity" amounts to. The main connotations are that a person is unknown, nameless, or unidentifiable. But, as Lapidot-Lefler and Barak (2012) point out, anonymity then becomes context specific. They observe that the mere absence of a name on a publication such as a newspaper article might suffice to make someone unidentifiable. But being nameless may not suffice in the context of face-to-face communication, where identifiability can result from other personal attributes. In what follows, I shall treat "anonymity" as a property, admitting of degrees, which measures how much person A knows about person B. To say that a person is "largely anonymous" means that there is very little known about that person but that there is some information available from which further inferences can be made.[1]

Consider, then, what happens when largely anonymous persons engage in an exchange regarding highly value-laden matters such as race relations, gender, immigration, economics, politics, and so on. When this happens, the interpretation of what is said by the anonymous participants often draws heavily on stereotypes triggered by the minimal information available. As we saw from the stereotype content model, out-group members can fall into one of three categories. The two competitive categories with low warmth involve stereotypes centred around either contemptuous prejudice (for low competence groups) or envious prejudice (for high competence groups), with attitudes of contempt, disgust, anger, envy or jealousy. With those stereotypes influencing how one interprets the inter-group exchange, it does not bode well for civil and charitable discourse. *Especially* when we recognise that the salient group identities will not be "minimal groups" of the kind Tajfel studied but, rather, groups expressing value-laden content where those values feature prominently in a person's identity.

We've already discussed online shaming in Chapter 11, but we can now supplement that analysis with a more informed understanding of human psychology. The eagerness of people to respond critically to online statements of others is driven by the psychology of inter-group conflict: negative stereotypes influence the interpretation of out-group members, and in-group members contribute to online shaming in order to signal commitment to the in-group. (This behaviour is closely related to "virtue signalling".) Any in-group member who expresses dissent or concern about joining Two Minutes Hate[2] may find themselves sanctioned by in-group members. These enforcement policies can themselves become a norm, what the social Scientist Robert Axelrod called a *metanorm*. Axelrod (1986, p. 1100–01) provides the following vivid illustration of a metanorm in action:

> A little-lamented norm of once great strength was the practice of lynching to enforce white rule in the South. A particularly illuminating episode took place in Texas in 1930 after a black man was arrested for attacking a white woman. The mob was impatient, so they burned down the courthouse to kill the prisoner within. A witness said,
>
>> 'I heard a man right behind me remark of the fire, "Now ain't that a shame?" No sooner had the words left his mouth than someone knocked him down with a pop bottle. He was hit in the mouth and had several teeth broken.' (Cantril 1941)

Tribal interactions on social media take place using impersonal, remote forms of communication rather than personal, direct forms of communication. That might sound like an obvious truism and thus unimportant, but some have thought this partially explains why so many people behave so badly online. Suler (2004) provided the first analysis of some causes behind what he called the "online disinhibition effect". He suggested six factors that contributed to online disinhibition: anonymity, invisibility, asynchronous communication, minimisation of status and authority, dissociative imagination (that people do not fully appreciate that what they do online is part of the "real world"), and solipsistic introjection (that people conceive of their online interlocutor as a character within their own head). Later experimental work has suggested some of these factors are more important than others. Lapidot-Lefler and Barak (2012) argue that when subjects engage in pairwise interactions controlled for anonymity, invisibility, and eye contact, the presence or absence of eye contact matters most regarding the hostility of the exchange. If the online disinhibition effect exists, and tribal identities are made salient and put into conflict, and those tribes have become more polarised over time – we have a partial explanation of the tempestuous nature of social media.[3]

There are two generally recognised mechanisms for reducing inter-group conflict. The first attempts to undo the negative stereotypes that lie at the heart of the problem. This method, due to Gordon Allport, is known as the contact hypothesis or inter-group contact theory. The contact hypothesis says that if members of two conflicting groups are able to have positive interactions with each other, under the right conditions, this reduces prejudice and mitigates stereotypes. Inter-group contact challenges the unconscious assumption of out-group homogeneity by getting a person to see out-group members as unique individuals with interests, goals, and ambitions, which may partially overlap with their own. In addition, the contact allows one to understand what the world looks like from the other viewpoint.[4]

The second method, identified by Sherif in his 1954 experiment, was for the two conflicting groups to be faced with a common threat that endangers the well-being of both groups such that only cooperation could resolve the threat. This mechanism – known as the existence of a *superordinate goal* – appeals to the self-interest of both parties, requiring cooperation to achieve it. Think of the scene from *Raiders of the Lost Ark* where Indiana Jones and a thug are choking each other during the fight in Marion's bar. When Toht says: "Shoot them. Shoot them both", Indy and the thug immediately stop choking each other and collectively fire a gun to eliminate the threat. That's a perfect example of a superordinate goal eliminating conflict.

Both the contact hypothesis and the existence of superordinate goals have been shown to be effective at reducing prejudice and inter-group conflict. However, there are several open questions about how well these experimental findings carry over into real-world situations. To begin, as noted before, there is a great difference between face-to-face contact, where each subtle aspect of human communication is visible and noticeable, and online communication. If the goal of contact is to generate a perception of "common humanity between members of the two groups" (Allport 1954, p. 281), online communication makes that difficult. That said, a number of studies have examined whether computer-mediated communication is compatible with the reduction of prejudice suggested by the contact hypothesis (see Hasler and Amichai-Hamburger 2013, for an example) with encouraging results. But the downside of these studies is that they typically use *highly controlled* online environments. When we contrast that with the wild west of unmoderated social media, different results obtain. In one study, Ruesch (2013) examined 770 groups on Facebook, each of which had over 100 members, organised around the Israel-Palestine conflict. What she found was "a highly fragmentised, polarised virtual sphere with little intergroup interaction" (Ruesch 2013, p. 22). And, perhaps not surprisingly, "Facebook groups are rather used to indicate support and opinion than to deliberate with the non-like-minded" (Ruesch 2013, p. 20). It seems that uncontrolled interaction online is more likely to bring about homophilic self-assortment than the kind of inter-group interaction required by the contact hypothesis.

As for the efficacy of superordinate goals as a means for combating inter-group conflict, the appeal to common self-interest only works as long as the threat is truly perceived as a threat to the self-interest of both parties. Depending on how the group identity is defined and how people understand their relation to the group, this might not always lead to an accurate perception of the underlying threat of the superordinate goal. The point, here, is similar in spirit to Upton Sinclair's observation that "it is difficult to get a man to understand something, when his salary depends upon his not understanding it" (Sinclair 1995 [1934], p. 109). We might similarly say that it is difficult to get a person to understand something when that person's *identity* depends upon their not understanding it.

As an example, think of the issue of anthropogenic climate change. As a superordinate goal faced by nations around the world, and by political parties within nations, it is difficult to conceive of a greater existential threat to the human species, except perhaps nuclear war. Given that, one might expect climate change to provide a superordinate goal that would reduce conflict between political parties in the US *at least on that issue*. But the problem is that denial of climate change has become a core part of the Republican group identity. The long-term time horizon of the problem allows efforts to reduce climate change to be reframed as a zero-sum game between two political parties. The action required to avert climate change can interpreted by Republicans as an attack on their political, economic, or social values. When the constituents of group identity involve commitments that impair one's ability to engage with reality accurately, superordinate goals can lose their effectiveness at mitigating inter-group conflict.

The fact that a person's group identification can, at times, impair their ability to engage with reality – and sometimes cause them to make decisions that run counter to their self-interest – is of great importance. It is especially so because, much of the time, the criteria used to determine whether a person is a "true" member of a group is set by social norms, which are not under any single person's explicit control. When a person's group identification matters greatly to the person, they can find themselves doing things in order to prove their *bona fide* membership in the group, even doing things that they would not normally be disposed to do. We turn to the subject of *authenticity* in the next chapter.

25. Authenticity and the WINOs

As we've seen, identifying with groups is an important part of a person's identity. One question that we haven't yet broached concerns the *membership criteria* that determine whether some person X belongs to some group W. Closely related to this, but conceptually distinct, is the question of what it *means* to be a W, from the point of view of X as well as other members of W and the wider society to which W belongs.

The reason why the membership criteria and what it means to belong to a group are distinct can be seen by reflecting on some of the cases discussed previously. In many of the cases we've looked at, the membership criteria are trivial: a person belongs to a group because they were simply *assigned* to it. This was true for Tajfel's minimal group paradigm experiments as well as for the Sherif experiments. The Bull Dogs and Red Devils were classified as such because Sherif's team created those groups. Yet even though the membership criteria was trivial – people belonged to the group by fiat – those groups developed a distinct identity over time. What did it mean to be a Bull Dog? Among other things, it meant that they worked well as a team and had greater organisational skills than others; this was a self-understanding that each Bull Dog came to appreciate. In real life, groups like this are found all over the place: educational classes where students are grouped by ability, working groups created by a boss, and so on.

In other cases, people aren't assigned to a group but find themselves belonging to a group because some administrator, somewhere, laid down a definition of a category and people found themselves in a group because they met the definition.[1] Here, the membership criteria are whatever the administrator declared. Whether there is any deeper meaning associated with the group depends on the role that category plays in wider society and how group members come to understand it. Sometimes the administrative category becomes part of people's identity with meanings and values that go beyond the original definition. Consider the term "middle class", for example. It was coined by the Irish statistician T. H. C. Stevenson in the 1913 Report of the UK Registrar-General. Since then, the category has acquired a number of connotations regarding normalcy that people see as desirable. It's so desirable that, in a 2015 survey, 89% of Americans considered themselves to be "middle class" (Pew Research Center 2015) even though 13.5% lived in poverty (Proctor *et al.* 2016). That's already 102.5%, and we haven't said anything about the wealthy or the rich.

Ethnic terms have begun life this way too. "Hispanic" and "Latino" entered into mainstream usage in the US as a result of their inclusion in the US Census during the late 20th century, morphing over time into quasi-racial terms with cultural associations. And this happened *despite* the US Census clearly indicating that it was an ethnicity not associated with any particular race. In a 2004 survey, 400 Dominican immigrants in New York City and Providence, Rhode Island, were asked how they defined themselves racially. The question was open ended so people could answer however they wanted. In response, 27.5% said "Hispanic" and 4.1% said "Latino" as their racial self-categorisation (Itzigsohn 2004).

In contrast, other kinds of groups are fluid with both the membership criteria and the meaning of membership. Of this latter type, consider a person's political identity. What, if anything, *must* someone be committed to if they describe themselves as liberal or conservative, Democrat or Republican, Labour or Tory? The current state of society plus recent history set general expectations about a person's beliefs and values when someone declares their political alignment, but those expectations are defeasible. We might be surprised to hear a self-declared liberal oppose abortion or the welfare state or declare support for nuclear weapons, etc., but there are reasons – principled reasons – why a sincere liberal might endorse any one of those positions. Political alignment and party affiliations are a broad church, with room for diverse combinations of opinions.

In groups of this kind, it's not uncommon for struggles to erupt over what exactly is required for someone to claim that they are a member of group W. Often the language of *authenticity* is used. A person who claims to be a W, who expresses a view on a matter relevant to, perhaps even central to, the W-identity, is criticised by other Ws for not being an *authentic* W. As such, their view as an inauthentic W is discredited, disregarded, delegitimated, or marginalised. The person is labelled a W "in name only", meaning that, although they *claim* to be a W, they aren't a *real* W.

These people are the WINOs: a "(Whatever) In Name Only". In recent years, there have been an awful lot of WINOs. In America, there are the RINOs ("Republican In Name Only") and the DINOs ("Democrat In Name Only"). In the UK, after the divisive referendum campaign regarding membership in the EU, those Brexiteers who have argued for continued membership in the Customs Union and the single market have been called BRINOs ("Brexiteer In Name Only"). If you were a moderate Republican in America, you might have thought it was bad enough being a RINO, until you met someone wearing a t-shirt saying they were a "RINO hunter". What does a RINO hunter do? Presumably root out the RINOs corrupting the rest of the party, with the implicit threat of violence not lost on anyone.

Although the term RINO is quite recent, with the first known use appearing in print in 1992, the phrase it abbreviates dates back much further. In an article entitled "A Strange Blunder", published in *The National Republican* on 26 January 1875, we find the following rant against two politicians:

Next on the list, beginning from the same end, we find Mr. William Walter Phelps, of New Jersey, and Mr. Charles Foster, of Ohio, both of whom are Republican in name only, and both of whom have proved their treachery to party principles, to party friends, and to the policy which can alone secure the success of the party.

The sentiment behind the expression hasn't changed much in over 140 years: a claim of treachery, a charge of disloyalty, and a statement of posing a threat to the success of the group. But, aside from the hostility faced by RINOs, and WINOs more generally, what further concerns are raised by charges of inauthenticity?

The first issue when a WINO is charged with inauthenticity is, who decides what it means to be an authentic W and on what authority? In thinking about this, note that there are two different concepts of authenticity in play: authenticity of the individual and authenticity of the group. One reason people care about authenticity is because of our individualistic society, with the ideal that *you should be true to yourself* and resist pressure to act otherwise. This is one reason I argued for an existentialist foundation for cosmopolitanism in Chapter 4. Yet what renders an individual authentic is different from what makes an individual an authentic member of some group W, and so the two notions may conflict.

As we have seen, a core idea of existentialist thought is freedom of choice, wherein individual choices are, in part, attempts to realise some end that person values. This doesn't mean a person has complete control over the outcome; the world places limits, sometimes severe ones, on what a person can achieve. Yet these limits do not remove the freedom of choice, although they may restrict substantially the number of options from which one has to choose. To deny this freedom and choose contrary to one's beliefs and values, perhaps by caving in to social pressure, is to act in *bad faith*. A person may feel compelled – given their beliefs and values – to act one way, while feeling compelled – through the peer pressure applied by social norms – to act differently. In such a case, the competing demands of individual authenticity and group authenticity pull in different directions.

Suppose, for purposes of illustration, you consider yourself to be Catholic but believe abortion is not necessarily wrong and should not be prohibited, as long as certain conditions are met. In particular, suppose you do not believe life begins at the exact *moment* of conception. You might not have a firm belief on when exactly life begins between conception and birth, but your inability to answer that question does not preclude you from believing that abortion is permissible in the early stages of pregnancy. Given these beliefs, you are then confronted with the fact that the official doctrine of the Catholic Church[2] requires the excommunication of Catholics who have an abortion outside the narrow conditions that render it morally permissible. Suppose that you, then, face a situation in which you have to choose whether or not to have an abortion under conditions that you believe to be morally permissible. If you choose contrary to your beliefs due to the threat of being excommunicated, you are being inauthentic and acting in bad faith. Yet if you act in accordance with your beliefs, you risk excommunication by the Church, thereby being declared not to be an authentic Catholic.

Although the source of the conflict between individual authenticity and group authenticity seems straightforward – a person's beliefs and values pitted against those beliefs and values required for group membership – social identity theory suggests that the conflict reoccurs deep within the person. In fact, social identity theory challenges the very idea of what it means to be "true to yourself" in the face of external pressure. Our social identities are incorporated into our overall identity in ineliminable ways. The flow of information and influence goes in both directions – from the person to the group and from the group to the person. Given this, where do I draw the line between *my* beliefs and values and the beliefs and values I acquire in virtue of my identifying with a group?

In order to answer this question, we first need to clarify how we think of our beliefs, desires, and values. One model, which I think many people employ, is what we might call the Library Model. According to the Library Model, a person's beliefs, desires, and values exist within their head, much as if they were books on shelves inside the library of the mind. When we introspect about whether or not we believe something, or have a desire, we check to see if that "book" is present in our mental library. If it is, we open the book and see what is written inside: the contents give our attitude towards the belief, desire, or value, along with the reasons (if any) for why we hold it and any relevant cross-references to other "books" (i.e., other beliefs, desires, or values) to which it relates. The absence of a book indicates the absence of any attitude towards that belief, desire, or value. This allows us to distinguish between having no opinion about an issue (e.g., "Gosh, I don't know. I've never thought about that before.") and having a definite opinion of no judgement (e.g., "I've thought about this long and hard and have come to the conclusion that the evidence does not settle the matter either way.").

The trouble is that the Library Model doesn't quite capture the complexity of our mental lives. First, it assumes that we only have attitudes on issues which we have actively considered at some point in time. As Pettit (1995) points out, many of our beliefs – and, I would suggest, many of our desires and values too – are ones that we only hold *virtually*. If I ask you how old you are, your belief that you are N years old will be retrieved from memory because you have actively considered it in the past. However, if I ask you whether there are more grains of sand in a 100ml jar than people living in Bob Dylan's hometown of Hibbing, Minnesota, I am willing to bet that there will be no belief stored in memory to retrieve. Rather, you will most likely infer, given *other* things that you believe, that the answer is yes.[3] Since it sounds odd to say that you didn't *believe* that, prior to being asked, Pettit introduces the concept of a virtual belief to cover this case. The Library Model doesn't easily extend to cover those virtual attitudes that readily follow from your current attitudes but which you haven't ever considered.

There's a second area where the Library Model proves to be inadequate. In "The Extended Mind", Andy Clark and David Chalmers argue for a view known as *active externalism*, wherein beliefs don't just exist in the head. Consider the following thought experiment. Suppose Otto is a person suffering from Alzheimer's disease who, in order to cope with his failing memory, records information in a notebook, which he always keeps with him. When Otto decides to go see an exhibition at the Museum of Modern Art, he consults his notebook, reads that the museum is located on 53rd Street, and goes there. Although Otto didn't have the location of the Museum of Modern Art stored as a belief inside his head, he was able to use the information stored in his notebook to get him where he wanted to go. Otto's notebook serves as a source of information which can be used to guide his actions, thus functioning essentially like his memory. The main difference is that it isn't inside Otto's head.

Although the original formulation of the Library Model wasn't designed to accommodate the extended mind, it can be easily modified to do so. Let the *books* in the Library Model represent the individual attitudes (beliefs, desires, or values) stored in the library of the mind. In addition, let's allow for slips of paper to appear on the shelves alongside the books. Each slip of paper represents an instruction redirecting the person to another source where the appropriate attitude can be found. A kind of interlending scheme for the library of the mind, if you like. The important point is that the slips of paper pointing at another source aren't restricted to referring to inanimate objects like Otto's notebook, they can point to other *persons* as well. Clark and Chalmers anticipated this extension of the extended mind thesis, noting that "In an unusually interdependent couple, it is entirely possible that one partner's beliefs will play the same sort of role for the other as the notebook plays for Otto" (Clark and Chalmers 1998, p. 17). And there's no reason to restrict the social extension of cognition to just particular persons either. Some have argued (see, for example, List and Pettit 2011) that we can speak of the attitudes held by *groups* as well as individual people. If so, socially extended cognition can include group attitudes, especially those groups with which a person identifies.

At this point, the distinction between individual authenticity and group authenticity becomes very muddled indeed. Some of my beliefs, desires, or values will be held because they are stored in memory: they will be books in my mental library. Other attitudes I have will be virtual, but they will be *my* virtual attitudes: they will be entailed by various attitudes stored in my mind even if I am not presently aware of it. But then there will be other attitudes that are part of my socially extended mind: those attitudes I have because I identify with certain groups. These attitudes will be pointed to by the slips of paper found between the books in the library of the mind. And the attitudes that appear in my socially extended mind may *also* be held either actively or virtually. Conflict can occur between all of these.

What do we do when a conflict occurs? If I choose to abdicate an attitude in *my* mind in deference to a *group* attitude – a group forming part of my social identity – does that mean I am acting inauthentically? It's not obvious how to answer this question once we move away from the limited cases of obviously acting in bad faith or choosing in full knowledge after sufficient reflection. Suppose I believe that I don't have very good reasons for my individually held attitude and that much better reasons exist for the group attitude I adopt, even if I don't know what those reasons are. This doesn't seem to be an instance of not being true to myself; it seems, rather, to be a recognition of my cognitive limitations, an expression of epistemic humility in that I am willing to learn from those whom I consider to be better informed. In general, much knowledge acquisition features this social component. But now consider a more problematic case. Suppose that I do have good reasons for my attitude, but then I adopt the conflicting group attitude out of pressure to conform. One could argue that this is a violation of authenticity, of not being true to myself. But what if I did so out of *my desire* to conform? If I conform to social pressure because I am following a norm and – following Bicchieri's theory of social norms – I am the kind of person who prefers to conditionally conform to a norm on the assumption other people do, why should that mean I am not being true to myself? What justifies treating my conditional preferences as second-class preferences, counting less than my unconditional preferences?

Essentially, the trouble with WINOs and those who berate them as such is the following conflagration of issues. First, when a person's tribal identity matters to them, it leaves them vulnerable to being manipulated and exploited by those who purport to speak for the group. Those speakers do not need to be actual group leaders in any official capacity; often it suffices that their speech has enough reach to create the impression that they are instrumental in shaping the collective identity. Second, our willingness to conform to social norms – our preference to comply with certain forms and rules of behaviour *given that* enough other people do – means that the cost–benefit calculation we perform when a conflict arises between the individual and the group may, in cases of uncertainty, tend to tip in favour of the *group*. Third, given the importance of authenticity for our self-understanding, it's easy to see how the positive psychological feedback obtained by behaving in a way publicly recognised as authentic by a group – especially a group featuring prominently in our social identity – may quash any personal reservations one may have about giving up a personal commitment. Fourth, when we allow for the possibility of socially extended cognition, the very distinction between individual authenticity and group authenticity becomes blurred. In some cases, the two concepts of authenticity may be perceived by a person to effectively collapse into one. When this happens, we arrive at the paradoxical situation where the ability to be true to one's self is no longer solely under one's control: it is ceded to the forces determining one's tribal identity. The desire to live authentically can, in this case, become subverted by groupthink and conformity.

Other grounds for concern exist. Suppose that someone is called out for being a WINO, an inauthentic group member. Rhetorically, this is a violation of what, in the legal context, would be called the presumption of innocence and a shifting of the burden of proof. The charge of inauthenticity is made public, effectively requiring a response by the person alleged to be a WINO. This places the WINO at a disadvantage for three reasons. First, authenticity is generally viewed as an all-or-nothing state; like pregnancy, a person cannot be just a little inauthentic. Refuting a charge of inauthenticity requires establishing that the WINO has never made a decision or acted in a way that goes against those characteristics required of an authentic group member. Proving a negative claim is extremely difficult. Second, the charge of inauthenticity frames the discussion in a manner unhelpful to the WINO. The status quo has shifted, so that the conversation will proceed with listeners judging whether what the WINO says suffices to persuade them to move *away* from the charge of inauthenticity. This matters because psychological experiments have shown that status quo bias wields a powerful influence on human decision-making. Third, for the vast majority of groups and organisations, what it means to be an "authentic" member of the group is not universally agreed upon. Authenticity is thus a Rorschach concept upon which every group member can project his or her understanding. The WINO then faces the near-impossible task of persuading each member of the group that, according to his or her own understanding of the group identity, the WINO actually meets those criteria.

Those are some reasons why it's bad to be called a WINO, from the WINO's point of view. Let's now consider some sociological reasons why the very concept of a WINO, of appeals to group authenticity, can be harmful to society.

When someone is said to be an *authentic W*, what does that mean? Authenticity has many connotations, but some of the important ones are as follows. An authentic W is someone whose credentials as a W are undisputed. They are seen as a loyal and reliable member. They are judged as having been faithful to whatever principles and values are constitutive to the identity of the group. Authenticity, then, suggests a principled consistency.

There are many occasions when principled consistency is to be cherished. However, when group authenticity becomes fetishised to the point where inauthenticity becomes a term of critique, we should recall Emerson's observation: "A foolish consistency is the hobgoblin of little minds" (Emerson 2005 [1841], p. 40). Labelling someone a WINO is often an attempt to control the group, an attempt to reduce the diversity of viewpoints, and an exercise of power by those who claim authority to determine what makes someone an authentic group member.[4] Requiring group members to adhere to a single worldview can be counterproductive to the advancement of the interests of the group. Groups exist in a dynamic world, and the fact that established principles or ways of being have generally functioned in the past provides no guarantee they will continue to do so in the future. Allowing for natural variation within the group provides a degree of resilience against the unexpected. This is as true for cultural groups as it is for biological groups.

An obsession with group authenticity is often closely related to concerns about ideological purity. Yet ideological purity creates potentially disastrous conditions when two groups with incompatible worldviews interact. Real-world problems are complex and messy and often cannot be solved without compromise. If individual members find themselves self-censoring, or constraining their behaviour, out of concern of being branded inauthentic, that can reduce the possibility of successful compromise. Furthermore, inter-group relations can become increasingly volatile when framed in terms of authenticity. Why? Since authenticity is an all-or-nothing concept, the combination of inter-group relations and authenticity encourages conceiving the interaction in terms of a zero-sum game. Any deviation from authenticity, on either side, is seen as an unacceptable loss. Yet such deviations may be required to achieve joint concessions, yielding an overall net gain for each group. Such deviations will be difficult, if not impossible, to entertain if they involve attitudes understood as *necessary* or *essential* to be a group member. Yet there are very few social groups where what it means to be an *authentic* member is not socially constructed and hence, in principle, subject to revision.

A further trouble with charges of inauthenticity is that it merely attacks *what* the WINO says or does, rather than the *reasons* underlying the WINO's speech or behaviour. Sometimes there might be very good reasons for a person speaking or acting contrary to what one would normally expect from an authentic group member. Nixon's trip to China in 1972, despite being deeply out of character for the strongly anti-Communist Republican party of the time, was absolutely crucial to a thawing of relations between the US and China. Despite it being open to charges of inauthenticity from those who believed a Republican president should be a strong anti-Communist hawk, it was the right thing to do. Similarly, Dwight Eisenhower – the former Supreme Allied Commander in Europe during World War II, who led the D-Day invasion of Europe in Operation Overlord – ended his two terms as US President with a warning in his farewell speech about the excessive influence accruing to the military–industrial complex.

Finally, the elephant in the room about WINOs and those who complain about them is the basic problem of who decides what counts as authentic. The collective identity of groups emerges from the beliefs, desires, values, and actions of the people who belong to them. When a person, or a set of persons, attempts to brand someone as inauthentic in the absence of clear supporting evidence or reasons, that effort should be seen for what it is: an attempt to marginalise, exclude, or delegitimate the person. But disagreements over authenticity need not always mean that. Although some might find the existence of division within the tribe over what it means to be a W frustrating, as long as the division exists because people are acting sincerely and in good faith, this disagreement should be seen as the cost of living in a free and open society.

Concerns about authenticity become especially vexed when we take into consideration the fact that a single person's social identity involves membership in multiple groups at the same time. How does a person decide what to do when they belong to several groups and the constitutive rules for membership in those groups point to different courses of action? One of the difficulties with speaking of a person being an authentic W is that almost no one is *just* a W: a person is both a W *and* an A (and a B, and a C, ...) This brings us to the concept of intersectionality, which we will consider in the next chapter.

26. Intersectionality

In thinking through these issues about modern tribes, one assumption made throughout was that a person's tribal identity was relatively straightforward. Sometimes this is true. There are people who clearly identify as conservative or liberal, Muslim or Christian, who tick all the membership criteria and fit squarely within the tribe. But, in other cases, a person's social identity is less straightforward. This can happen for a variety of reasons. Sometimes it happens because a person feels that they are at the margin of a group and just don't fit in. Sometimes it happens because no social group which the person can see themselves as belonging to exists. Of these cases, the most interesting cases occur not when people simply haven't yet organised but because the relevant *concepts* have not yet been invented or discovered. The nature of transgender individuals, before "being transgender" entered into public awareness, may provide one illustration of this. And sometimes it happens because a person not only belongs to multiple tribes but because their existence at the intersection of multiple tribes yields an experience that is more than the sum of its parts.

Up to now, when talking about tribes the working assumption has been that people's tribal identity is *additive*. Although the obligations you might have as both an X and a Y could conflict – in the sense of competing demands on your time, or in the sense of Sartre's student who was torn between joining the French resistance or staying home to take care of his mother – the actual *experience* of being both an X and a Y was assumed to be just the result of combining the experience of being an X and a Y in isolation.

Sometimes, though, social identities are not merely additive. In these cases, what one experiences as a member of *both X and Y* is not the same as merely taking the experiences of being an X and adding to it the experiences of being a Y. In these cases, the combination of the two categories creates unique experiences that are not shared by people who are X-but-not-Y or Y-but-not-X. This is the phenomenon of *intersectionality*.

The emergence of the concept of intersectionality traces back to the experiences and concerns of Black feminists in the 19th century. First-wave feminism, which ran from the 19th century to the early 20th century, was primarily focused on achieving certain legal outcomes such as women's suffrage, the right of women to own property, and the right of women to have access to their children. Although these aims were ones that concerned *all* women, the fact that the social and political movements associated with first-wave feminism were largely composed of white, middle-class women meant that the concerns of minority women were frequently sidelined. And while there is no *conceptual* reason why these two social groups necessarily need to be misaligned in this way, the specific historicity of the abolitionist movement and the women's rights movement in the US led to this tension.

Despite the phenomenon of intersectionality existing for many years, the term "intersectionality" only entered contemporary social theory in 1989, when the legal scholar Kimberlé Crenshaw published an influential paper examining the ways in which the combination of gender and race created problems for the application of anti-discrimination policies in the law. Since then, the concept of intersectionality has been generalised beyond its original application in theories of feminism and race. This is why people now speak of intersectionality concerning the complexities involved by those who are X and Y, for a wide range of values of X and values of Y.

Intersectionality has become an important conceptual resource for understanding the dynamics of power, discrimination, and marginalisation. Calling attention to the non-additive nature of social identities and the complexities that they generate for the law, public policy, and social theory is extremely valuable. At the same time, a number of criticisms have been raised about intersectionality theory, such as a tendency to theoretically privilege identity at the expense of other sociological factors, like economic class. Some have also argued that supporters of intersectionality theory have, on occasion, allowed the perfect to become the enemy of the good. The moment one acknowledges the non-additive nature of being an X and Y, it becomes easy to find apparent examples of exclusion where none was intended. Any gathering of X-types will, of necessity, fail to include a number of X *and* Y for at least some values of Y. Is this failure of inclusion an act of deliberate discrimination on behalf of the few X-types who gathered, i.e., is it an attempt to marginalise certain perspectives? Or is it simply because every person speaks from some perspective and any organised meeting has finite capacity? Helen Lewis noted:

> When Caroline Crampton and I got together our bloggers last year for a *New Statesman* debate about feminism, the response was [...] well, there were two responses. There was criticism that was *constructive* [...] And there was criticism that was *destructive*, aimed at wounding us for not representing every possible permutation of womanhood. (I laughed when one particularly enthusiastic deconstructor, when asked: 'Well, how can you possibly make a six-person panel totally representative of half of humanity?', came back with, 'Oh, that's why I don't believe in panel discussions.') (Lewis 2014)

Given the social psychology of modern tribes, there's another point of concern worth noting. Suppose we have two tribes, X and Y, such that membership in these tribes is not mutually exclusive. As we have seen, the composite

Figure 26.1: The fracturing of tribes along the lines of intersectional identities

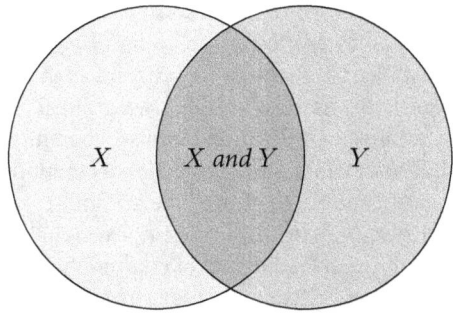

(a) Before the redefinition of tribal identities: two tribes with some overlap

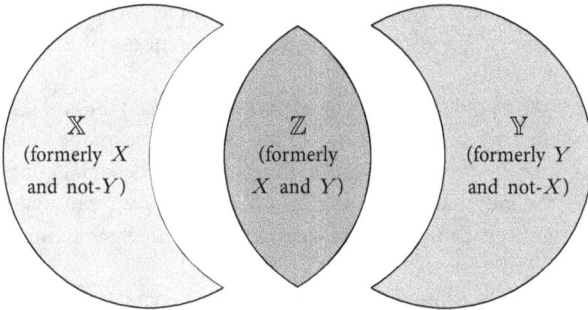

(b) After the redefinition of tribal identities: three tribes, with no overlap

Source: author.

identity of X and Y can create unique possibilities and experiences. Let us assume this is the case. It then becomes possible for those persons to convert their collective intersectional identity into a new tribe $\mathbb{Z}$, where members of $\mathbb{Z}$ are those who are both X and Y. Once this happens, the new social understanding of what remains of tribe X, call it $\mathbb{X}$, are those who are X and not-Y. And something similar holds for the new understanding of what is left of the original tribe Y. Figure 26.1 illustrates this fracturing of identities.

In reality, the fracturing of identities will rarely be neat and orderly. Some who are both X and Y may resist treating their intersectional social identity as a new tribe in itself. Others may feel liberated by such a fracturing, believing that only by declaring X and Y to be an independent tribe of its own can the X and Y avoid subordination. In this renegotiation of tribal identities, all the issues we've looked at previously reappear in new ways. Is someone who is X and Y but doesn't want to align themselves with a separate tribe – perhaps they are happy just seeing themselves as primarily an X or as a Y – not authentically embracing their intersectional identity? What happens when an X and Y and an X and not-Y disagree over what it means to be X? For example, think about the debates between different schools of feminist thought regarding the nature of transgender women or sex workers. And how does our tendency towards in-group bias and negative stereotyping of out-groups influence us once an intersectional identity becomes understood as constitutive of a group *itself*, rather than as existing in the overlap of two groups?

This last point warrants consideration because when intersectional identities become constitutive of tribes, the intersectional component has the power to cleave. As previously noted, "to cleave" means both to divide and to join. If we consider the tribes in Figure 26.1, the intersectional identity of $\mathbb{Z}$ joins it with both $\mathbb{X}$ and $\mathbb{Y}$ through the overlap of common parts. But the intersectional identity of $\mathbb{Z}$ may, on occasion, divide it from $\mathbb{X}$, for members of $\mathbb{X}$ are also not-Ys whereas members of $\mathbb{Z}$ are Ys. Whether or not the identity of $\mathbb{Z}$s is seen as joining or dividing them from members of $\mathbb{X}$ thus depends on which aspects of $\mathbb{Z}$'s identity are salient. When the Y-aspect of a $\mathbb{Z}$'s identity matters, it is possible that members of $\mathbb{X}$ will be seen as the *out-group*. Similarly, when the X-aspect of a $\mathbb{Z}$'s identity is salient, members of $\mathbb{Y}$ may be seen as the out-group, in turn.

This ability for members of $\mathbb{Z}$ to conceive of those who are $\mathbb{X}$ or $\mathbb{Y}$ as the out-group, depending on which part of the $\mathbb{Z}$ identity is made salient, has two effects. First, it serves to increase the number of ways social conflict can occur. Second, the fact that members of $\mathbb{X}$, $\mathbb{Y}$, and $\mathbb{Z}$ have their own tribal identity could reduce everyone's ability to engage in collective action, even when interests are aligned.

The increase in the number of ways possible social conflict can occur is easily seen. Before the intersectional identity became constitutive of a tribe, there was only one source of possible social conflict: between the tribes X and Y (remember, this is before the fracturing) regarding those who were outside the intersection. After the fracturing, there are three possible sources of social conflict: between $\mathbb{X}$ and $\mathbb{Z}$, between $\mathbb{Y}$ and $\mathbb{Z}$, and between $\mathbb{X}$ and $\mathbb{Y}$. Although these possible conflicts will not always be realised, the change introduces a new source of social instability. As we saw with the Red Devils and Bull Dogs, it takes relatively little friction between groups to plant the seeds of animosity, even when those groups share a common starting point.

The ease with which group animosity can emerge also connects to the reduced efficacy of collective action. Suppose, for example, that there is some fourth group $\mathbb{W}$, whose interests are entirely opposed to those of $\mathbb{X}$, $\mathbb{Y}$, and $\mathbb{Z}$. (Assume, for the sake of argument, that there is no moral reason as to why $\mathbb{W}$ has a claim to advance its interest; everything we are talking about concerns the self-interest of all four groups.) Initially, this might seem to take the form of a superordinate goal problem, of the kind discussed in Chapter 24. Yet there is an important complication. A problem of *strategic choice* is one where people have to decide the best way to proceed in an environment containing other agents who are trying to decide the best way to proceed, where the notion of the "best way to proceed" is a function of everyone's choices. The introduction of the fourth tribe W here means that X, Y, and Z are confronted by a problem of strategic choice against W. In particular, there is a zero-sum game between W and X, Y, and Z. This transforms the nature of the superordinate goal the X, Y, and Z tribes have to address.

Although all three tribes have an interest in working to mitigate the impact of W upon them, the potentially competing tribal identities of X, Y, and Z affect how the collective action problem may be framed. Let us say that the three tribes have *aligned* interests but not *common* interests. Why not common interests? Recall the discussion of common meanings from the introduction: a common interest requires a sense of community that binds the individuals together. A common interest requires people to be able to say, "This is a concern of *ours*, and it is in *our* interest to address it." The ambiguity of "our" means it can be read either widely – referring to all three tribes with the same interest – or narrowly – referring just to the tribe to which the speaker belongs. It is the narrow reading that proves problematic.

Consider the collective action problem from the point of view of members of Z deliberating over what to do. In most real-world situations, the distribution of benefits resulting from collective action problems will be unequal across both groups and members. Suppose that there are several proposals on the table for how to resolve the conflict between W and X, Y, and Z. Suppose that some outcome benefits members of Z but, at the same time, benefits members of Y more. If the X-aspect of Z's identity, for some reason, becomes particularly salient, members of Z might wonder why it is that the Y's have received a better deal. Is one reason the Ys are so keen to participate because they come out on top? The Zs may then discuss whether it would be better to adopt some other course of action, one that allows them to do a little bit better and, perhaps, favours the Xs rather than the Ys. If the Zs proposed this alternative course of action, it would now be the Ys' turn to be irritated. Perhaps it would be better for the Ys to work more closely with the Xs, leaving the Zs out in the cold. The point is this: by assumption, it's in the interest of X, Y, and Z to cooperate against their common enemy, but the possibility of intertribal disputes between these three gives W the ability to cultivate and exploit these divisive tendencies, thereby ensuring that the opposition remains less effective.

Thus we find a counter-intuitive result: intersectionality theory, originally developed as a conceptual tool to combat discrimination and address social injustice, may – when intersectional identities become concrete tribal identities through reification – trigger social psychological processes that impede the pursuit of social justice. This concern acquires even greater force when we realise that the possibilities for intertribal conflict are more complex than Joshua's question acknowledged. Joshua asked, "Art thou for us, or for our adversaries?" The key assumption was that only two options exist: you are either for us or for our enemies. In short, my enemy's enemy is my friend.

This way of thinking about group relations underlies a *realpolitik* approach to the exercise of power. If, however, one is concerned about who may *legitimately* exercise power, this binary logic no longer holds. In this case, my enemy's enemy may still be my enemy. The mere fact one group is opposed to a second group, where the second group cannot legitimately exercise power, does not itself confer legitimacy upon the first.

Putting all this together, we can see how tribal identities, when combined with identity politics, can constitute a threat to the communitarian conception of the Open Society. Individual identities are multidimensional, and these multiple dimensions provide fault lines along which society may fracture into competing tribes. These competing tribes, when concerned with the legitimate exercise of power, can find it hard to engage in effective collective action because doing so requires cooperation with those who are seen as morally tainted. This situation can be exploited by political actors willing to engage in *realpolitik* and use social division to consolidate their grip on power.

This, then, is the real challenge posed by Joshua's question: how do we understand the "us" in the question, "Art thou for us?" Social identities centred on abstract, inclusive characteristics are less compelling for motivating action than social identities centred around concrete, specific characteristics. Yet the more concrete and specific the social identity is, the greater the possibility of fracture due to the psychology of social identity.

27. Epistemic closure and extreme groups

In 2004, the *New York Times* journalist Ron Suskind interviewed an unnamed official in the Bush Administration who criticised the "reality-based community". According to the source, the reality-based community comprised those people who "believe that solutions emerge from your judicious study of discernible reality". The source went on to say: "That's not the way the world really works anymore. We're an empire now, and when we act, we create our own reality."

A charitable interpretation of what the official said would not attribute to him an outright denial of the existence of reality or objective facts. Rather, the actions of a major player like the US didn't simply occur *in* a geopolitical landscape, they *shaped* the landscape in the first place. Looking back, it's now clear the official overestimated the ability of the US to create its own reality in Afghanistan and Iraq, but that hasn't stopped other authoritarian leaders from trying to do the same in other parts of the world.

Those in the reality-based community are right to insist on "the judicious study of discernible reality" for a number of decisions. There's no mental state a person can put themselves in which will render polonium safe for human consumption or novichok non-toxic. The physical world places non-negotiable constraints on what people may reasonably believe about it. We neglect those constraints at our peril.

When it comes to the social world, things are considerably different. Social reality is underdetermined by the physical reality existing outside of peoples' heads. Much of social reality exists in the way that it does simply because people have collectively decided on certain things. Beliefs, norms, and conventions are passed down from parents to children, and the fact that human generations have long periods of overlap with extended periods of education ensures a reasonable degree of continuity in the understanding of social reality.

But the fact that social reality is not *determined* by the physical facts outside of a person's head means that, from time to time, a group's understanding of the social world can become, from the point of view of those on the outside, radically unhinged. The considerable independence of the social world from the physical world means that beliefs that strike us as bizarre or abhorrent can not only endure but can be surprisingly resistant to change. Think of racists who believe in their own ethnic superiority, of religious cults, of violent terrorist movements like Boko Haram, al-Qaeda, and Islamic State, and of the "involuntary celibates", also known as incels, who have committed several mass shootings in recent years. This brings us to the darker side of modern tribes:

those groups that are harmful or dysfunctional, whose view of the world strikes us as utterly mistaken, but which, for some reason, aren't self-correcting.

This is the phenomenon of *epistemic closure*: the formation of a system of beliefs and values that appears, to those of us on the outside, to be disconnected from the normal relations holding between information, evidence, and belief formation.[1] An epistemically closed system is one that has certain beliefs and values such that, regardless of the evidence, the attitude of a person embedded in that system towards those beliefs and values won't change. Systems can exhibit partial epistemic closure as well. When a system of beliefs is partially closed, information and evidence are much less effective at shifting a person's attitude towards those beliefs than one would expect if people were adjusting their beliefs as purely rational agents.

The possibility of epistemic closure is, unfortunately, a fact of life. Any empirical theory, or any set of general beliefs about the world, is underdetermined by evidence. There's no number of observations that one can make which will suffice to establish the truth of an empirical claim of any generality unequivocally.[2] The matter is even worse when we consider non-empirical beliefs, such as ones involving metaphysics and religion. If a person decides to maintain an empirical belief that runs counter to the available evidence, it's always possible for the person to do so. Of course, if they wish to keep a consistent and coherent set of beliefs, resisting the evidence comes at a cost: the person will have to make increasingly complex and odd adjustments to *other* beliefs they hold in order to maintain the belief they wish to hold fixed.[3] A classic example is how advocates of the geocentric model of the solar system had to add epicycles to planetary orbits to make it fit with observations. But there is a positive lesson to be drawn from the underdetermination of theory by evidence: if we can't ever truly be certain about our empirical beliefs, we shouldn't be dogmatic about any of them either; we should always treat any belief about the world as revisable in principle. This recognition of our fallibility should, if anything, lead us towards a position of epistemic humility. So what is it about some groups that causes them to become epistemically closed?

Epistemic closure can occur for a variety of reasons. One mistake people often make is to treat beliefs – cognitive attitudes towards propositions that have a truth value – as if the *only* thing that matters about a belief is its truth value. Take the belief that anthropogenic climate change is occurring. This belief has a truth value independent of whether we actually know its truth value. One common model of how people form beliefs is that, in an ideal setting, they take evidence into account when forming a judgement. In such an ideal setting, people would consult the findings of climate science or atmospheric science more generally. However, moving from idealisations to the real world, we encounter the problem that most of us cannot engage with the relevant scientific literature because we don't have the expertise or the time required to understand the details. Given this, we do the next best thing: we rely on another person's expert opinion to form a judgement by proxy, using *their* determination to fix *our* belief. Or, since most of us don't have a single scientific expert on whom we rely, it's more likely that we rely on a trusted *epistemic community* to fix our beliefs. Traditionally, in the case of scientific beliefs – where we are motivated solely by *truth* – the trusted epistemic community will be the scientific community, since their expert knowledge and track record give them the credibility to act as arbiters regarding such matters. In this idealised model, what we keep returning to, time and again, is the importance of truth for the fixation of belief.

What the above story leaves out is the fact that, for many people, what matters most about a belief is not its truth value but the relationship between the person and a tribe associated with the belief. The belief becomes a signifier of tribal membership, and endorsing the belief often becomes an informal requirement of tribal membership. The idealised model conceives of the matter this way: beliefs should be true and, therefore, when I cannot fix a belief with sufficient reason to be confident that it is true (or likely to be true), I should rely on the appropriate epistemic community whose track record gives me assurance they will not lead me astray. The contrary model conceives of the matter this way: my beliefs situate me within a particular tribe, and that tribe contributes to my social identity. My social identity – as a source of esteem, friendship, camaraderie, and how I understand my social existence as well as the determiner of meaning for my life – is sufficiently significant that preserving my social identity is a matter of fundamental importance. Since I am not in a position to form a judgement on my own, I need to rely on other people to guide my belief formation. Since my tribe (for all the reasons just mentioned) has been a key set of people who show me respect, understanding, friendship, and so on, I rely on them to guide me. Consequently, I defer to the epistemic community *determined by my tribal identity*[4] in the fixation of my beliefs because doing so is the best way to ensure continued membership in the tribe.

This inversion of grounds for belief might seem weird. To begin, it would seem to decouple beliefs from reality in ways that the "reality-based community" would legitimately see as harmful. If there is no mental state a person can adopt which, for example, would render polonium safe to consume, why wouldn't blind deference to beliefs – especially ones which we on the outside might describe as "batshit crazy" – determined by a tribal identity be, if you like, eventually eliminated by natural selection? How can obviously false, individually harmful, and socially damaging beliefs persist?

To be sure, if an extreme group's beliefs become sufficiently misaligned with reality, the group will eventually suffer. When the beliefs of the Manson Family led them to murder Sharon Tate and four other people, reality caught up with them through the efforts of the police and they were imprisoned. The Heaven's Gate religious cult, whose members believed that they could escape Earth by committing mass suicide in order to join a spaceship that was following Comet Hale–Bopp, has no followers today. The followers of the reverend Jim Jones, who committed mass suicide at Jonestown, Guyana, also paid the ultimate price for their beliefs. Many other examples exist.

Yet many other deeply flawed beliefs persist amongst groups but are not driven out. Here we must recognise that, in the developed world, we have engineered society in such a way that we rarely need to rely on the majority of our beliefs in order to navigate the world safely. If you have what Graeber (2018) calls a "bullshit job", you don't need many beliefs to do your job and get paid. If your most deeply held beliefs go against what you are required to do in your job, you can go through the motions bracketing what you really think and tell yourself, *"This is what I need to do in order to get paid."* A person doesn't need to have accurate scientific beliefs, accurate political beliefs, or accurate economic or social beliefs to go to the supermarket and buy food. A person doesn't have to believe in evolutionary theory to go to the doctor, be prescribed antibiotics, and take them to get better. A person doesn't have to believe in general relativity to get directions via GPS, even though the technology would malfunction if the designers didn't take into account the gravitational time shift implied by general relativity. Sure, to someone fundamentally committed to truth it appears deeply *hypocritical* to behave in such a disingenuous fashion but so what? The person who acts this way will still feed themselves, be cured of their infection, and be able to get to where they want to go, regardless of what they believe. The only beliefs a person really needs to survive in a modern society are beliefs like how to cross the street without being run over, how to pay your bills on time, how to cook over a gas stove without blowing the house up, and so on. These beliefs are highly specific pragmatic local knowledge and are compatible with a wide variety of highly unorthodox theoretical beliefs. Society's technological prowess has, for better or worse, radically decoupled people's ability to survive from the theoretical coherence, truthfulness, and accuracy of their beliefs.[5]

This decoupling of a person's ability to survive from the truthfulness and accuracy of their beliefs means that a person's system of beliefs can acquire a different functional role. What may matter most about a belief is not its content or *actual* truth value but what holding that belief signals about a person and their tribe. The denial of anthropogenic climate change provides a nice illustration of this phenomenon in action. Climate change requires a coordinated, global response. The actions of any single person are entirely irrelevant to the global outcome. Due to the long delay in the climate's response to environmental legislation, it is unlikely any person will see a connection between their actions and change to the environment over the short to medium run. Given this, beliefs about whether anthropogenic climate change exists can be co-opted to serve a signalling function about which tribe a person belongs to because, over the short run, they are decoupled from noticeable material consequences. This seems to be what has happened with the Republican party in the US. Under Nixon, as noted previously, the Republican party passed a number of pro-climate pieces of legislation. Today, many Republicans are sceptical about climate change. Why? The importance of their social identity *as Republicans* leads them to defer to the epistemic community identified as credible *by their tribe*. The real question is why has the Republican tribe identified, as credible, an epistemic community that denies climate change? Because many economic and business interests represented among top Republican donors benefit from continuing with business as usual, rather than making the effective changes required to combat climate change. The epistemic community recognised as credible by the Republican tribe has been ideologically captured and subordinated by these economic and business interests. Furthermore, the denial of climate change can be spun in two ways. First, as a rejection of "liberal science" with its purported political bias. Second, as an attempt to bring back traditional extractionary industries (such as coal mining) or new ones (such as fracking), for which there is an interest in communities that have historically voted conservative. In both cases, climate change denial reaffirms the tribal identity of those who adopt the belief. Truth takes a back seat to these other social functions.

This last example illustrates how the various social functions played by beliefs can subordinate the truth-functional role of beliefs. Once we recognise that there are alternative functional roles played by beliefs that can trump a concern for truth, we see that confronting the phenomenon of extreme groups, and the epistemic closure that accompanies them, requires engaging with the underlying *functions* that are served by the system of beliefs, rather than engaging with their theoretical content. And this shift towards the functionality of systems of beliefs means we have to acknowledge that, sometimes, the real social function served by a system of beliefs is not necessarily known by many – perhaps *any* – of the people who have those beliefs.

This is the well-known distinction between *latent* and *manifest* functions, deriving from classic work in anthropology by Malinowski (1941) and Radcliffe-Brown (1952), among others. A manifest function is a function a social practice has been consciously designed to have, such as how randomised police patrols keep criminals from being able to predict a safe time to commit burglaries. A latent function is a function a social practice has but for which it was not consciously designed. A classic anthropological example is how the practice of extended lactation in hunter-gatherer tribes (i.e., breastfeeding infants for longer than 12 months) had the latent function of controlling the population because breastfeeding reduces fertility.

When it comes to the social functions of belief systems, the distinction between latent and manifest functions helps us understand the phenomenon of epistemic closure. Epistemic closure seems irrational when we only consider beliefs as vehicles of truth. When we see that belief systems can have, as their *latent* function, the satisfaction of other psychological and sociological needs, the fact that those beliefs are unresponsive to evidence no longer seems unusual. If a belief system helps me understand my place in society, explain why I am unhappy (or happy) or unsuccessful (or successful), and legitimates how I feel, there's little incentive to change those beliefs because doing so leaves me with a gaping lacuna of unaddressed psychological and sociological needs.

Take, for example, why so many rich people believe in efficient markets. It's not because the models of market efficiency are deeply compelling: the conditions under which we can show markets converge to an equilibrium such that supply equals demand for every commodity in the economy are pretty demanding. Believing in the efficiency of markets isn't justified because of the goodness of fit between the theory and the reality of the modern economy. Rather, I suspect rich people often believe in market efficiency because the general equilibrium theory, and the existence of perfectly competitive markets, provides a putative meritocratic justification for their wealth. Few people want to admit that they are rich because they got lucky or abused an under-regulated monopolistic position, or exploited a vulnerable workforce with little bargaining power. The theoretical content of the belief *markets are efficient* is what really provides the psychological function *I deserve to be where I am*.

Keeping in mind the idea that belief systems can serve latent social functions, now consider one extreme group that has received a considerable amount of media coverage recently: incels. In speaking about "incels", I am using the more recent understanding of the term, which refers to a movement centred around young men who frequent a number of online forums featuring misogynistic ideas, including violently punishing women for not having sex with them.[6] The incel movement has been identified by the US Southern Poverty Law Centre as a worrying example of male radicalisation online. Incels came to international attention in 2018 after Alek Minassian killed 10 people in Toronto in a van attack, which he claimed in a Facebook post prior to the event as his contribution to the forthcoming "incel rebellion". Minassian's action followed in the footsteps of the mass shooting by Elliot Rodger in 2014, in which he killed six people (seven, if you count Rodger) in California. In a Facebook post, Minassian glowingly referred to Rodger as the "Supreme Gentleman".

The media reaction to the Minassian rampage, by and large, condemned the Toronto attack as a murderous assault by a member of a radical fringe group. Some engaged thoughtfully with the wider cultural backdrop in which the phenomenon of the incels occurred, arguing that, although no one has a right to sex, we as a society need to reflect on the ideals of beauty that are disseminated throughout the culture, which lead to the rejection or marginalisation of those men and women who fall short of the ideal (Srinivasan 2018). But other commentators took the rhetoric of the incels at face value, wondering whether people really do have a right to sex and whether we ought to consider methods of redistributing sex. The *New York Times* columnist Ross Douthat attracted a fair amount of online opprobrium for broaching the question, "If we are concerned about the just distribution of property and money, why do we assume that the desire for some sort of sexual redistribution is inherently ridiculous?" (Douthat 2018). Here his comments were similar to those of the economist Robin Hanson, from George Mason University, who posted the following on his blog a few days earlier:

One might plausibly argue that those with much less access to sex suffer to a similar degree as those with low income, and might similarly hope to gain from organizing around this identity, to lobby for redistribution along this axis and to at least implicitly threaten violence if their demands are not met. (Hanson 2018)

These comments strike me as misguided, managing to intersect with questions worth asking, but in a way that is, at best, only indirectly related to understanding the phenomenon of misogynistic incel culture.

The online culture of incels, and the system of beliefs and values associated with it, provides a therapeutic function for young men who have not succeeded in realising, in whole or in part, a vision of their life as they wished. The conspiratorial narrative of "Chads and Stacys" who thwart their life plans provides an external locus of control, absolving incels of responsibility for their situation. And although some of the ideas and unsatisfied preferences that push people to self-identify as incels derive from a culture of toxic masculinity, of unrealistically promiscuous pornographic sexuality, not all do. The idea, for example, that there is someone for everyone is deeply embedded in popular culture, along with norms about how heterosexual relationships will develop over time. If you are a man unable to find work that pays well enough to support a partner or a family and, for whatever reason, also find yourself unable to form relationships with women, the contrast between your life experiences and those of "successful men" – as stereotypically represented within the wider culture – will be unsettling.

Given the violent, misogynistic nature of online incel commentary, it is natural to want to engage with the surface meaning of what is said, to criticise and condemn. Yet this is to mistake symptom and cause. There is a need to distinguish the normative question of whether men *should* have certain preferences and expectations from the descriptive questions of *what* are the expressed preferences and expectations, *why* they have those preferences in the first place, and how men behave when those preferences and expectations are not satisfied. It is only by identifying, and targeting, the latent function served by the incel system of beliefs that we will be able to, as a society, make progress towards eliminating the hate and misogyny by addressing the real underlying cause.[7]

The idea that systems of beliefs can provide a therapeutic function goes beyond that of just incels. In *Healing from Hate*, Michael Kimmel argues that one common factor contributing to the radicalisation of men, whether it is Neo-Nazi groups or Islamic extremism, is the failure to realise a certain ideal of masculinity. Feeling that their life has no purpose and that they have no way to live up to the gender role they feel is expected of them, men join these organisations to try to realise the ideal in another form. Kimmel writes:

There's a reason most of the extreme right is male: it's that masculinity is centered on something to prove, a quest. Perhaps you might think, women have to prove something also; perhaps they 'prove' their femininity by attracting a man, getting married, and becoming a mother. Maybe, but it doesn't have the same propulsive force as proving one's manhood. Men must prove their masculinity to other men, in the homosocial arena of other men. Their masculinity must be credited, validated, affirmed by their peers. Historically, of course, they've proved their masculinity in the traditional time-honored way of their ancestors: in the workplace, as breadwinners. They've provided for their families, protected their homes, and defend their homelands. Take those roles away, and they have to find a new arena in which to prove their manhood. (Kimmel 2018, pp. 45–6)

In stressing the importance of attending to the latent functions served by extreme belief systems, I do not mean to suggest that the propositional content of those belief systems never matters. My aim in this chapter was rather to suggest that a more nuanced approach to how we understand extreme groups is occasionally warranted. It's very convenient for politicians to write off extremists as evil people who believe evil things. The problem with this line of thought is that the process of radicalisation is more subtle than that. How and why do people get recruited into extreme groups when they do? And when people become radicalised, what is the appropriate response to de-radicalise them? These questions can only be answered by looking beyond the propositional content of their beliefs.

People desire to make sense of the world in which they find themselves. People want to be able to tell a story about why their lives unfolded the way that they have. When things go well, people want to be able to take credit for what they have achieved; when things go poorly, people want to be able to save face. Given the flexibility in how people may theorise about the social world while still being able to navigate it successfully, stories that fit with how people want to understand their lives can be more valuable to them than stories that accurately describe the way the world is. When those stories become deeply incorporated into a person's self-understanding, epistemic closure may occur. The moral of the story is this: often it isn't a question of *what* a person believes so much as *why*, both above and below the surface.

28. The collision of horizons

Perhaps the greatest challenge facing the communitarian conception of the Open Society is how a diverse population deals with each other when they have incompatible beliefs and incompatible conceptions of how life should be lived. The incompatible beliefs might concern appropriate attire for men and women (e.g., the debate over whether to ban the burqa or what is an acceptable Halloween costume), sexual preferences (e.g., the acceptability of homosexuality), the nature of human relationships (e.g., civil partnerships, gay marriage, or polyamory), religious beliefs, political beliefs, forms of economic organisation, and many others. In a diverse, multicultural society, members of different tribes holding incompatible beliefs will encounter each other in public spaces and often encounter ideas with which they fundamentally disagree. What ground rules can be established for negotiating the collision of horizons when two people meet and each thinks the other is profoundly wrong?

The first point to keep in mind is that, despite appearances to the contrary, there is more people have in common than not. We just don't often acknowledge that fact. Evolutionary forces have shaped us for hundreds of thousands of years to be sensitive to group differences and tribal threats posed by the "Other". In contrast, humans have been living in societies with populations sufficiently large to enable regular anonymous interactions between individuals only since the invention of agriculture slightly more than 12,000 years ago. That inbuilt suspicion towards those who we perceive differently is exacerbated by the news and other forms of media: it's a fairly steady diet of conflict and disorder. And that's before we take into account all the people trying to *create* division. The attention economy of social media often exposes users to inflammatory content for the sole purpose of provoking a reaction, requiring them to engage more with the platform. The fact it also stokes fear and sows division is a side effect.

But the commonalities we share are significant. People want to live safely in a society governed by the rule of law. They want laws to be fair and transparent and enforced equally across all persons, even if there is disagreement about what means for a law to be *fair*. People want trustworthy and reliable social institutions on which they can depend. People want to have a place to call home, which offers comfort, of which they can feel proud. People want to have a form of work that pays enough for the necessities, as well as a little extra. People want a form of work in which they can take pride and feel that they are doing something important and meaningful. When not working, people want to be free to choose how to spend time pursuing other projects and hobbies that they consider to be valuable. In addition to the pursuit of work and personal activities, people also want to have meaningful relationships with other people and feel that they are valued and appreciated by others. People want a sense of purpose and a sense that they are participating in something meaningful over the course of their lives. How exactly these goals, and others, are pursued and realised can take on a variety of forms and create the possibility of conflict, but suitably redescribed, we can see that all these goals are part of the common, shared human experience. People may arrive at different, incompatible answers to the same fundamental questions.

The second point is that different conceptions of how to live mostly lead to conflict when one or more groups believe that *their* form of life is the only correct one and they have a duty to make others conform. This attitude is dangerous. Given how peacefully Protestants and Catholics coexist in the US, and most of the world (Northern Ireland is a noteworthy exception due to its fragility), it is hard to believe that millions of people died during the European wars of religion in the 16th and 17th centuries. The difference in religious worldview, so destabilising back then, has now been largely incorporated into the background warp and weft of society. Tolerance has brought peace.

Similarly, one of the great achievements of the EU is how difficult it became – at least until Russia invaded Ukraine – for people to conceive of war between European nations. This difficulty does not mean that conflict is impossible; we know from the ethnic cleansing in Serbia, and the invasion of Crimea and Ukraine by Russia, that such a threat exists and is all too real. But, as Steven Pinker has argued, the better angels of our nature have been on the march for some time. Familiarity and interdependence, the need to combat common threats such as climate change or terrorism, all combined with the realisation that there is much more that unites Europeans than what divides them has served to reduce the threat of conflict.

The third point is that cultural diversity, instead of being a threat, is needed for robust, stable societies. Some think that societies with great diversity are fragile or unstable because the variation makes it difficult to agree on policy. Although greater diversity can make it hard to reach agreement quickly, it is worth asking why reaching agreement quickly is necessarily a virtue. There are times when reaching decisions rapidly is essential (e.g., natural disasters), but that is not the only decision-making context which matters. A monolithic culture where everyone had the same beliefs and values would reach agreement quickly, but it would also be vulnerable to bad ideas which fit in alongside the rest of the universally held beliefs. Variation in opinion helps ensure that a society cannot be brought down by a single popular yet fundamentally misguided idea or theory. A diverse culture provides epistemic inoculation against bad memes. *Cultural* diversity in beliefs and values provides benefits analogous to those provided by genetic diversity in a *biological* population.

Putting these three observations together yields an answer to our question: what is to be done, in a diverse society, when incompatible worldviews find themselves in close proximity with one another? The answer involves ideas associated, somewhat ironically, with both Mao and Popper: let a hundred flowers blossom. (It must be acknowledged that Mao's support for this attitude faded quickly.) In order for the Open Society to survive, it must protect itself from being undermined from within by having its freedoms and tolerance used against itself. Such undermining occurs when a radical group takes advantage of high levels of tolerance to increase its membership, then exploits its size to restrict the freedoms of others, denying others the ability to go their own way. Given this, the Open Society must impose the following minimal constraint on the freedom of individuals: people can adopt beliefs and values as they wish, behaving as they choose, so long as they abide by Mill's Harm principle. And that means that they act towards out-group members with tolerance, granting other people the freedom to associate with those they choose and to pursue a meaningful life constructed on their own terms.

A society where inter-group relations are governed by the Harm principle and the principle of being intolerant of intolerance would seem to generate a paradox: when one group's form of life involves behaviour or conduct that contradicts the beliefs and values of another, there seems no way to simultaneously satisfy both principles. The elimination of harm would seem to require that the first group curtail those practices that offend the sensitivities of the second group, yet requiring the first group to curtail their practices shows intolerance in violating their freedom to live a life constructed on their own terms. How are we to square the circle?

To begin, we need to recognise that the Harm principle does not apply universally to every kind of harm regardless of its origins. It is important to distinguish between illegal harms intentionally inflicted upon others and those harms experienced when a person puts themselves in a position where they could have anticipated they would be harmed by the legal behaviour of others. Harms of the first kind are regulated by the Harm principle whereas harms of the second kind may not be. For example, a person has legitimate grounds for complaint if they were walking down the street and saw a flasher; that's the reason we have laws prohibiting indecent exposure. However, that same person would not have grounds for a complaint if they knowingly and voluntarily went to a known, documented, and authorised naturist beach and became offended by the sight of people lying *au naturel* in the sun.

In a diverse, multicultural society, it will not be unusual for some groups to adopt a form of life that has the potential to offend others.[1] It will prove helpful to distinguish between one group *causing offence* to another and one group *taking offence* of another. To say that group X *causes offence* to group Y is to attribute a causal relationship between some, perhaps all, members of X and some, perhaps all, members of Y. This can happen in a variety of ways: one member of X might verbally insult a particular member of Y or a number of Xs might engage in a disparaging chant attacking the group identity of the Ys in a public forum, without aiming to insult any particular person. These are clear examples of how members of one group can cause offence to another. But not all instances of causing offence are intentional. Suppose that a member of X violates an important social norm of the Ys without knowingly doing so, such as when an ignorant tourist wears shoes inside an empty Buddhist temple, where there was no one to inform them of the social norm violation. In such a case, that member of X could cause offence to members of Y accidentally. Whether or not the offence caused was intentional or not may affect our judgement of its severity or the blameworthiness of the agent. Even an unintentional causing of offence could warrant sanctions, if the agent was culpably ignorant and they *should* have known, for example. But in all instances, there is a common causal structure at play: an intrusion into the sphere of existence *of* the offended person *by* the person or people who caused the offence. When an offence is caused, it happens at the intersection of two different spheres of existence, with an interaction between members of different groups.

In contrast, group X may *take offence* at another group Y without any causal interaction between their spheres of existence. Members of group X, simply by virtue of knowing that the Ys have a social practice of which the Xs disapprove, might be outraged or upset or annoyed or offended. (Recall the much-quoted, humorous definition of Puritanism: "The haunting fear that someone, somewhere, may be happy", see Mencken 1982.) The important difference between *causing* offence and *taking* offence is that it is possible for group X to take offence at group Y when group Y was simply trying to go about living its life according to a manner of its own choosing. And while the Open Society needs to protect one group from unduly imposing negative externalities on others, as discussed in Chapter 3, mere existence is not a negative externality.

The distinction between causing offence and taking offence offers a resolution to the apparent paradox of how an Open Society can allow for diverse groups, with incompatible worldviews, while at the same time being governed by the Harm principle and the principle of being intolerant of intolerance. In public spaces, where people's spheres of existence intersect due to their shared location, people need to abide by norms of civility and respect and minimise the chances of causing offence. At the same time, people need to be charitable in their judgement of others, so that if an offence is caused, they react proportionally by taking into account whether it was intentional or not. When we consider people's behaviour in private spaces, the principle of being intolerant of intolerance means that if one group *does* take offence at the practices of another, those offences are not regulated by the Harm principle. Groups are free to live life on their own terms, and the mere fact that another group disapproves and takes offence is not sufficient reason to curtail its freedom of self-determination.

A similar point holds if one group takes offence at another simply by virtue of encountering the second group in a shared public space (assuming, of course, that the second group conforms to basic norms of civility and respect and is not provoking the first group). For example, consider the discussions in a number of Western countries over whether to ban the burqa. Much of this debate derives from people taking offence at the practice of wearing the burqa as a result of seeing people wear it in a public space, where the people wearing the burqa are, arguably, not trying to *cause* offence. It's just that someone who chooses to wear the burqa cannot go out in public without other people seeing them, and other people might take offence as a result of merely seeing a woman wearing a burqa. In this case, the harm in the group that takes offence at seeing someone in a burqa is not a harm that falls under the Harm principle. The way I think the Open Society ought to approach the issue is as follows: any group that *requires* women to wear the burqa against their will is oppressive – and thus engaged in a practice that should be curtailed in order to protect the freedom and autonomy of women – but if a woman chooses freely to wear the burqa, then that is an expression of her personal freedom and unproblematic.[2] Furthermore, as an outsider to the group, the choices made by group members over how they live their lives are really none of my business. We must respect people's freedom to live life as they choose. As long as people are choosing freely and properly informed, let a hundred flowers blossom and be intolerant of intolerance.

One complexity with this resolution of the paradox derives from the fact that the conceptual distinction between public and private spaces is imperfect. What happens when a public space is occupied by members of one group when a few members of another group arrive? We now have a case of intersecting spheres of existence, but to say that the first group might *cause* offence to members of the second group, simply by continuing to be as they were, runs the risk of creating the tyranny of the minority. In such cases, a good rule of thumb for members of the second group to abide by is the following: don't take offence when none was intended. At the same time, a good rule of thumb for members of the first group to abide by is this: when spheres of existence unexpectedly intersect, a little goodwill and empathetic understanding go a long way.

29. Concluding remarks

What, then, is the overall assessment of the communitarian conception of the Open Society? We have seen how polarisation, in-group bias, and conceptions of authenticity can create problems for diverse societies. In this part, I have tried to both describe the phenomena and trace some of the negative consequences they create. In the next, and final, chapter of the book, I will try to suggest what we can do to try to overcome some of these issues.

One difficulty, I think, with reconciling communitarianism with diverse societies is that we don't frame the challenge in the right way. Part of that framing challenge lies in the fact that one popular guide to action – the Golden Rule – doesn't necessarily work well in diverse societies. The Golden Rule derives from the book of Matthew, chapter 7, verse 12, which in the King James Bible reads: "Therefore whatever you desire for men to do to you, you shall also do to them." In more modern language: "Do unto others as you would have them do unto you."

The Golden Rule has two problems. The first is rarely noted: it is compatible with antisocial preferences. If you are perfectly happy with other people being a jerk to you, then you should act like a jerk to them. This feature of the Golden Rule rarely surfaces because, most of the time, it is assumed that people don't have antisocial preferences. The second problem, which is more serious, is that the Golden Rule assumes that the best way to infer something about how *other* people want to be treated is to reflect upon how *you* want to be treated. In a homogeneous society this might work well, but in a diverse, multicultural society it can go awry. And although there will be a lot of agreement on how people want to be treated, at least at the level of abstract descriptions – i.e., to be respected, to be treated fairly, to be thought of as a good person, and so on – those abstract descriptions can be realised in a number of ways.

To resolve these problems, I think the Golden Rule needs to be replaced with two rules better suited for diverse societies where the collision of horizons occurs. The first rule is an unconditional imperative: *be kind to others*. In that imperative, "kind" is to be interpreted broadly, standing in for pro-social behaviours and actions in general. This isn't merely parroting "woke" vocabulary: it just sounds more natural to say "be kind to others" than to say "engage in pro-social behaviours towards others". The second rule offers a piece of advice on how to put that imperative into practice: *don't assume everyone thinks the same way as you*. The second rule calls attention to the importance of empathy and of trying to understand how others see the world, recognising that some types of behaviour may not travel well across groups. What you think of as kind may not be perceived the same way by someone else. What the second rule does *not* say is that a person *always* has to accommodate the wishes or desires of another. What if someone has unrealistic demands or unreasonable expectations? Negotiating the challenges presented by coexisting modern tribes will never be easy or without friction, but it helps to keep in mind that, much of the time, most people are trying to do the right thing, just in different ways.

Notes to Part IV: Modern tribes

21. Joshua's question

[1] Some might wonder whether it makes sense to speak of *degrees* of irrationality. Just like a person can't be a little bit pregnant, how can a person be a little bit irrational? If one identifies *being rational* with *being consistent*, this is a fair objection: consistency is an all-or-nothing state. But being rational requires more than just being consistent. A rational person's beliefs are based on evidence and those beliefs should hang together in an overall *coherent* worldview, and coherence does come in degrees.

22. On polarisation

[1] There are a variety of methods used for voting in an assembly. Sometimes it is done by a voice vote, as when the chair calls out, "All those in favour, say 'Aye'...all those opposed, say 'No.'" If the voice vote doesn't indicate a obvious winner, a standing vote or a show of hands may be called (which may or may not be counted). The most exact method is the recorded vote, also known as a roll-call vote, in which the name of each member along with their vote is noted.

[2] People living in Scotland, Wales, and Northern Ireland were excluded from the study, as their survey questions varied.

[3] A recent article by *The Economist* discusses how AI is increasingly being used to write news stories. One company, the British firm Radar AI, used AI to place over *400,000 news stories in local papers* since 2018, with only five people on staff. There are two concerns about this tendency. The first concern is that AI could be used to generate, *on demand*, particular news stories targeting specific issues or values for consumers, making particular things salient to them in ways that could influence their behaviour (e.g., shopping or voting). The second concern is that a world where each person receives a custom news feed is a world with fewer common reference points regarding events that shape our understanding of the world. Although you might not agree with what, for example, the *New York Times* or the *Wall Street Journal* said, old-school physical newspapers and magazines provided a fixed cultural reference point accessible to virtually everyone. If two people were talking about a subject and they had both read the same newspaper, that gave each person information about what the other knew. A world were everyone receives their news from custom AI feeds is a world where we lack common cultural reference points, and so we lack an important way of being able to get inside other peoples' heads. In addition, think about how difficult this is going to make the job of future historians (The Economist 2023).

[4] I gave ChatGPT the following prompt: "Rewrite the opening to the *Communist Manifesto* from the ideological perspective of the economist Milton Friedman." Here's what it generated:

A specter is haunting the world—the specter of free markets. All the powers of the old world have entered into a holy alliance to exorcise this specter: governments and central planners, entrenched monopolies, and the champions of bureaucratic control.

A new era of economic freedom is dawning, one that seeks to liberate individuals from the shackles of collectivism and embrace the power of voluntary exchange. We, the economists, stand at the forefront of this movement, armed with the principles of Milton Friedman, to challenge the prevailing notions of state intervention and usher in an era of market-driven prosperity.

The history of all hitherto existing societies is a history of government interference and misguided attempts to engineer economic outcomes. From planned economies to regulatory excesses, the hand of intervention has stifled innovation, undermined individual initiative, and impeded the natural forces of competition. It is time to cast aside these chains and let the invisible hand guide the destiny of nations.

Modern society is the product of countless voluntary interactions and transactions, driven by the pursuit of self-interest. It is through these actions that wealth is created, standards of living are elevated, and human progress is achieved. The free market is not a mere abstraction, but a dynamic force that harnesses the dispersed knowledge and aspirations of individuals, allocating resources efficiently and spurring innovation.

Yet, this fundamental truth is often obscured by the allure of collectivism, which promises equality but delivers mediocrity. The proponents of state control fail to recognise the inherent limitations of centralised decision-making and the dangers it poses to individual liberty. They ignore the lessons of history and disregard the perils of concentrating power in the hands of a few. We, the advocates of free markets, reject the notion that wealth is a zero-sum game. Instead, we affirm that through voluntary exchange and mutually beneficial transactions, prosperity can be expanded and shared. It is not the accumulation of wealth by a few that impoverishes the many, but rather the stifling of economic freedom and the denial of opportunities that hinder progress.

Let the clarion call for free markets echo across the globe. Let the principles of individual liberty, limited government, and free enterprise guide our actions. Let us dismantle the barriers to competition, foster entrepreneurship, and unleash the creative energies of individuals. In doing so, we shall create a world where the pursuit of self-interest aligns with the common good, where economic liberty is the birthright of all, and where prosperity knows no boundaries.

Working individuals of all countries, unite! Embrace the power of the free market and seize control of your economic destiny. Together, let us forge a future where the potential of every human being is unleashed, and where the promises of liberty and prosperity are not mere slogans, but a living reality for all.

23. Social identity, in-group bias, and norms

[1] I would like to note that my use of the phrase "modern tribe" is primarily for convenience, as it is easier to speak of a "modern tribe" than it is to speak of "a social category with which a number of people self-identify". However, there are two potential dangers in the use of this terminology, which need to be guarded against. First, the term "tribe" suggests a degree of cohesion, political unity, and solidarity of purpose, which is absent for many social categories. In anthropology, a *tribe* historically referred to a group that occupied a contiguous territory, shared a common identity, and engaged in a number of common activities, such as war, trade, and ceremonies. The modern tribes of which I speak may share some, but not necessarily all, of these features. Second, and more importantly, a number of people have objected to usage of the term "tribe" itself due to the negative connotations the term acquired during colonialism. My use of the term "tribe" is intended to be non-evaluative – a re-branding of the concept, if you like. A number of forms of social organisation that count as modern tribes are important forces for good, such as those committed to disability rights, environmental protection, animal rights, the economically disadvantaged, and so on. That said, not all modern tribes are forces for good. As Alfred noted in the film *The Dark Knight* (2008): "Some men just want to watch the world burn." The internet enables those people to organise too.

[2] For example, if a Black person is the only minority in a busy coffee shop, someone who cuts in front of them in line might well be perceived as committing a microaggression. However, if every person in the coffee shop is Black, the same line-cutting behaviour would probably not be interpreted in the same way. The set of social categories that applies to the person standing in line hasn't changed, but the set of which categories are salient, and why, has changed.

[3] Recall the discussion of social norms from Chapter 13: a modern tribe often fixes some of a person's reference network.

[4] The fact that this conflict is not felt more deeply in Western societies – both American and European – is an encouraging sign of how much our religious attitudes have evolved since the French Wars of Religion (1562–98) and the Thirty Years' War (1618–48). In those two conflicts alone, over 11 million people died.

[5] It's very unlikely that Sherif's experiments would be approved by a research ethics committee today. Nevertheless, despite their questionable ethical standing, the Sherif experiments are important to discuss because of the significance of the results and the fact that they form a building block for later work in social psychology.

[6] Some interesting cross-cultural differences exist. An extended study by Cuddy et al. (2009) found that in a sample of three *collectivist* cultures (Hong Kong, Japan, and Korea), the reference group for subjects tended not to be assigned high warmth and high competence. Instead, in-groups could be classified as low warmth–high competence (e.g., Japan, with the in-groups of "my university" or "students"), high warmth–low competence (e.g., Japan, with "my family" or "my friends"), or middle rankings on both dimensions. Yet even so, out-groups would continue to score low on at least one of the two dimensions and sometimes both.

24. The psychology of modern tribes

[1] This is essentially the same as the category of "partially anonymous" in the analysis by – seriously – Anonymous (1998): "Partial anonymity exists when either a source cannot be individually specified or when there is not a high level of knowledge about a source (but not both, which represents full anonymity)."

[2] This is a reference to a socially engineered group activity built around hatred for enemies of the state in George Orwell's dystopian novel *1984* (see Wikipedia 2024). In the novel, the main character Winston Smith describes the Two Minutes Hate as follows:

> The horrible thing about the Two Minutes Hate was not that one was obliged to act a part, but, on the contrary, that it was impossible to avoid joining in. Within thirty seconds any pretence was always unnecessary. A hideous ecstasy of fear and vindictiveness, a desire to kill, to torture, to smash faces in with a sledge-hammer, seemed to flow through the whole group of people like an electric current, turning one even against one's will into a grimacing, screaming lunatic. And yet the rage that one felt was an abstract, undirected emotion which could be switched from one object to another like the flame of a blowlamp.

It is worth noting how social media functions rather similarly, at least some of the time.

[3] At this point, its worth distinguishing the combative world of online tribal conflict and the phenomenon of *trolling*. Trolling is "the practice of behaving in a deceptive, destructive, or disruptive manner in a social setting on the Internet with no apparent instrumental purpose" (Buckels *et al.* 2014, p. 97). A

number of studies have examined links between trolling and the Dark Tetrad personality traits (narcissism, Machiavellianism, psychopathy, and sadism). Buckels *et al.* (2014), in a poll of 1,215 subjects, found that the trait most heavily associated with online trolling was sadism. In a later study, Craker and March (2016), examining trolling behaviour on social networking sites, found that sadism and psychopathy were significant predictors. March *et al.* (2017) examined trolling on dating (or hook-up) apps, finding that psychopathy, sadism, and impulsivity were traits significantly associated with trolling on those apps. In all these studies, the one common trait was *sadism* – the experiencing of pleasure from causing physical or psychological pain in another person. This is interesting because online trolling is quite common, yet psychopathy and sadism are quite rare. Only a very small percentage of people, approximately 1% of the population, score high on the Hare Psychopathy Checklist. Are psychopaths and sadists just unusually busy online, or is there something about life online that draws out these characteristics from ordinary people? In one study, Pfattheicher *et al.* (2021) found a connection between boredom and sadism. We might ask, then, if people spend a lot of time on the internet because they are bored, could that be a partial explanation for why they engage in online trolling? Pfattheicher *et al.* (2021, p. 79) state explicitly that they did not investigate that, and so "it remains unclear whether boredom also relates to other online behavior, and whether boredom motivates going online in general".

[4] In the years following Allport's introduction of the contact hypothesis, much debate existed over whether it really worked. Pettigrew and Tropp (2006) conducted a meta-analysis of 515 studies, concluding that "intergroup contact typically reduces intergroup prejudice". Yet their conclusion comes with a number of caveats. For one, inter-group contact isn't a *sufficient* condition for the reduction of prejudice because, ideally, the contact takes place in an environment where the two groups have equal status and with institutional support. Thus, there are a lot of other variables that can get in the way. Furthermore, a number of studies have found that inter-group contact is not *necessary* for the reduction of prejudice.

25. Authenticity and the WINOs

[1] Ian Hacking discusses this phenomenon, which he refers to as an "administrative kind", in his influential book *The Social Construction of What*.

[2] Canon 1397 of the 1983 Code of Canon Law, to be precise.

[3] Although there are a lot of grains of sand in 100ml, you might guess that the number is around that of a moderately sized city – approximately two million. But since you've probably never heard of Hibbing, Minnesota, you would likely infer that it is a small town. And you would be right.

⁴ In Chapter 20, I discussed the dangers resulting from the moralisation of knowledge. This is an example of dangers resulting from the moralisation of membership.

26. Intersectionality

27. Epistemic closure and extreme groups

¹ A distinct, and unrelated, sense of "epistemic closure" concerns the preservation of knowledge under entailment. For example, if a person knows some claim p and also knows that p entails q, then the person knows that q. Although this sense of epistemic closure is widely assumed within epistemology, in what follows, I exclusively use "epistemic closure" to refer to a system of beliefs that is closed off from the world in some way and resists being revised.

² Recall the discussion of falsification in the introduction.

³ Putting matters in this way makes it sound as though epistemic closure is a *voluntary* act. Sometimes it may be but not always. Sometimes a person believes something so intensely that, when faced with evidence to the contrary, they seek to reduce cognitive dissonance by adjusting their set of beliefs without explicitly realising what they are doing.

⁴ Why I have shifted from speaking of "tribes" to speaking of an "epistemic community" determined by the tribe? The point is simply this: one's tribe refers to all the members with whom you share a social identity. However, not all members of the tribe are necessarily going to be people one listens to regarding the formation of belief. For lack of a better word, certain individuals in the tribe will be earmarked as "thought leaders", who are disproportionately influential in the shaping of beliefs amongst members of the tribe. The "thought leaders" will be those individuals who are most influential, but there will often be a secondary or tertiary layer of individuals who also contribute to shaping the space of beliefs. This difference in membership is the difference between a tribe and a person's epistemic community.

⁵ Furthermore, certain false beliefs can even be fitness enhancing. If a person believes that crime is on the rise and, as a result, they insist on staying home in the evenings rather than going out in public or driving places, this change in behaviour reduces their exposure to car accidents and being mugged or otherwise assaulted. This can cut both ways: Gerd Gigerenzer estimated that 1,595 Americans died in the year following 9/11 because they were so concerned about flying that they elected to drive rather than fly. Since road travel is much more dangerous than flying, this misperception of risk lead to a number of additional deaths due to road accidents (Ball 2011).

⁶ This usage differs significantly from the sense intended when the term "incel" was first coined by a Canadian woman named Alana, who created a website for lonely people who considered themselves "involuntary celibates" in that they

had experienced long-term difficulty forming relationships over the course of their life.

[7] The matter, then, is analogous to the reason why the war on drugs failed despite years of effort. It is easier to try to restrict the supply of drugs than it is to try to address the social factors that generate the demand for drugs. Yet until the demand is reduced, the economic incentives ensure that new suppliers will always appear to replace those removed from the system.

28. The collision of horizons

[1] In what follows, I assume that all behaviours and practices I talk about are legal within the containing society. I do not necessarily assume that the behaviours and practices are *moral* because I want to allow for the possibility that the groups disagree over what counts as moral behaviour.

[2] The key issue, of course, is whether one can be said to *choose freely* when strong social norms, with sanctions attached to violations, are present. Can a person be said to choose freely to do something when the possibility of not doing that thing is associated with expulsion from the group, the loss of friends and family, and alienation from the community in which they were raised? I think not. But this is a delicate issue to think through, for nearly all choices that impact other people involve both positive and negative feedback, which can affect a person's ability to choose freely. Suppose a child must choose whether to study medicine or law or literature, knowing that their parents would be extremely happy if they chose medicine or law and extremely disappointed if they chose literature. How extreme does the parent's disappointment need to be, and how much must it affect the child's future, before we say that the child no longer faces a free choice? Even if all choices we face are "metaphysically free" choices (in the sense of free will), most of our choices have their freedom curtailed to some degree in this social sense of "free choice". Matters become more complicated when we recognise that some cultures have different moral practices that rank-order the protection of individual liberties and the protection of social norms or conventions differently. Even if *we* think, in light of a commitment to Western values and individual liberties, that it is a mistake to reverse the rank-ordering of protecting individual liberties and protecting social norms or conventions, the following question arises: to what extent does a diverse, multicultural society allow groups to make decisions – regarding their form of life, which the overarching society considers to be mistaken – before intervening? There are no easy answers to this question.

References

Allport, Gordon W. (1954). *The Nature of Prejudice*. Addison-Wesley.

Anonymous. (1998). "To reveal or not to reveal: A theoretical model of anonymous communication." *Communication Theory* 8 (4):381–407. https://doi.org/10.1111/j.1468-2885.1998.tb00226.x

Axelrod, Robert. (December 1986). "An evolutionary approach to norms." *American Political Science Review* 80 (4):1095–1111. https://doi.org/10.1017/S0003055400185016

Ball, James. (5 September 2011). "September 11's indirect toll: road deaths linked to fearful flyers." *The Guardian*. https://www.theguardian.com/world/2011/sep/05/september-11-road-deaths

Baum, Matthew A. and Tim Groeling. (2008). "New Media and the Polarization of American Political Discourse." *Political Communication* 25:345–365. https://doi.org/10.1080/10584600802426965

Bergson, Henri. (1935). *The Two Sources of Morality and Religion*. Macmillan and Co., Limited. Translated by R. Ashley Audra and Cloudesley Brereton, with the assistance of W. Horsfall Carter.

Bicchieri, Cristina. (2017). *Norms in the Wild: How to Diagnose, Measure, and Change Social Norms*. Oxford University Press. https://doi.org/10.1093/acprof:oso/9780190622046.001.0001

Billig, Michael and Henri Tajfel. (1973). "Social categorization and similarity in intergroup behaviour." *European Journal of Social Psychology* 3 (1):27–52. https://doi.org/10.1002/ejsp.2420030103

Bleiberg, Joshua and Darrell M. West. (May 2015). "Political polarization on Facebook." Brookings Institute blog. https://www.brookings.edu/blog/techtank/2015/05/13/political-polarization-on-facebook/

Boxell, Levi, Matthew Gentzkow, and Jesse M Shapiro. (2017). "Greater Internet use is not associated with faster growth in political polarization among US demographic groups." *Proceedings of the National Academy of Sciences*. https://doi.org/10.1073/pnas.1706588114

Bramson, Aaron, Patrick Grim, Daniel J. Singer, William J. Berger, Graham Sack, Steven Fisher, Carissa Flocken, and Bennett Holman. (January 2017). "Understanding Polarization: Meanings, Measures, and Model Evaluation." *Philosophy of Science* 84 (1):115–159. https://doi.org/10.1086/688938

Buckels, Erin E., Paul D. Trapnell, and Delroy L. Paulhus. (2014). "Trolls just want to have fun." *Personality and Individual Differences* 67:97–102. https://doi.org/10.1016/j.paid.2014.01.016

Cantril, Hadley. (1941). *The Psychology of Social Movements*. New York: Wiley.
https://doi.org/10.1037/13593-000
Clark, Andy and David Chalmers. (1998). "The Extended Mind." *Analysis* 58 (1):7-19.
https://doi.org/10.1093/analys/58.1.7
Craker, Naomi and Evita March. (2016). "The dark side of Facebook©: The Dark Tetrad, negative social potency, and trolling behaviours." *Personality and Individual Differences* 102:79-84.
https://doi.org/10.1016/j.paid.2016.06.043
Crenshaw, Kimberlé. (1989). "Demarginalizing the intersection of race and sex: A Black feminist critique of antidiscrimination doctrine, feminist theory, and antiracist politics [1989]." *The University of Chicago Legal Forum* (1):139-167.
Cuddy, Amy JC, Susan T Fiske, Virginia SY Kwan, Peter Glick, Stephanie Demoulin, Jacques-Philippe Leyens, Michael Harris Bond, Jean-Claude Croizet, Naomi Ellemers, Ed Sleebos, et al. (2009). "Stereotype content model across cultures: Towards universal similarities and some differences." *British Journal of Social Psychology* 48 (1):1-33.
https://doi.org/10.1348/014466608X314935
Douthat, Ross. (2 May 2018). "The Redistribution of Sex." *The New York Times*.
https://www.nytimes.com/2018/05/02/opinion/incels-sex-robots-redistribution.html
Emerson, Ralph Waldo. (2005 [1841]). *Compensation and Self-Reliance*. New York: Cosimo Classics. Originally published by Fleming H. Revell Company in 1841.
Esteban, Joan-María and Debraj Ray. (July 1994). "On the Measurement of Polarization." *Econometrica* 62 (4):819.
http://doi.org/10.2307/2951734
Fiske, Susan T., Amy J. C. Cuddy, Peter Glick, and Jun Xu. (2002). "A model of (often mixed) stereotype content: competence and warmth respectively follow from perceived status and competition." *Journal of Personality and Social Psychology* 82 (6):878-902.
https://doi.org/10.1037/0022-3514.82.6.878
Gentzkow, Matthew and Jesse M. Shapiro. (2011). "Ideological Segregation Online and Offline." *The Quarterly Journal of Economics* 126 (1799-1839).
https://doi.org/10.1093/qje/qjr044
Graeber, David. (2018). *Bullshit Jobs: A Theory*. Allen Lane.
Hanson, Robin. (26 April 2018). "Two Types of Envy."
http://www.overcomingbias.com/2018/04/two-types-of-envyhtml
Hare, Christopher and Keith T. Poole. (2014). "The Polarization of Contemporary American Politics." *Polity* 46 (3):411-429.
https://doi.org/10.1057/pol.2014.10

Hasler, Béatrice S. and Yair Amichai-Hamburger. (2013). "Online Intergroup Contact." In Amichai-Hamburger, Yair (ed.), *The Social Net: Understanding our online behavior*. Oxford University Press. https://doi.org/10.1093/acprof:oso/9780199639540.001.0001

Hogg, Michael A. and Dominic Abrams. (1988). *Social Identifications: A Social Psychology of Intergroup Relations and Group Processes*. Routledge.

Itzigsohn, José. (2004). "The Formation of Latino and Latina Panethnic Identities." In Foner, Nancy and George Frederickson (Eds.), *Not Just Black and White: Historical and Contemporary Perspectives on Immigration, Race, and Ethnicity in the United States*, 197–216. New York: Russell Sage Foundation.

Jones, Stephen. (26 September 2017). "Russian 'Ultra' football hooligans unleash fury in violent footage as Liverpool and Manchester United fans fly into Moscow." *The Mirror*. https://www.mirror.co.uk/news/world-news/russian-ultra-football-hooligans-unleash-11241338

Kimmel, Michael. (2018). *Healing from Hate: How Young Men Get Into — and out of — Violent Extremism*. University of California Press. https://doi.org/10.1525/9780520966086

Lapidot-Lefler, Noam and Azy Barak. (2012). "Effects of anonymity, invisibility, and lack of eye-contact on toxic online disinhibition." *Computers in Human Behavior* 28:434–443. https://doi.org/10.1016/j.chb.2011.10.014

Lewis, Helen. (20 February 2014). "The uses and abuses of intersectionality." *New Statesman*. https://www.newstatesman.com/politics/2014/02/uses-and-abuses-intersectionality

List, Christian and Philip Pettit. (2011). *Group Agency: The Possibility, Design, and Status of Corporate Agents*. Oxford University Press. https://doi.org/10.1093/acprof:oso/9780199591565.001.0001

Malinowski, Bransław. (1941). *A Scientific Theory of Culture, and other essays*. Chapel Hill: University of North Carolina Press.

March, Evita, Rachel Grieve, Jessica Marrington, and Peter K. Jonason. (2017). "Trolling on Tinder© (and other dating apps): Examining the role of the Dark Tetrad and impulsivity." *Personality and Individual Differences* 110:139–143. https://doi.org/10.1016/j.paid.2017.01.025

Mencken, Henry Louis. (1982). *A Mencken Chrestomathy*. Vintage Books. Original published: New York, Knopf, 1949.

Milanovic, Branko. (2012). "Global Income Inequality by the Numbers: in History and Now." Technical report, The World Bank, Development Research Group. Policy Research Working Paper 6259. https://doi.org/10.1596/1813-9450-6259

Nydegger, R. V. and G. Owen. (1974). "Two-Person Bargaining: An Experimental Test of the Nash Axioms." *International Journal of Game*

Theory 3 (4):239–249.
https://doi.org/10.1007/BF01766877
Parekh, Bhikhu. (2008). *A New Politics of Identity: Political Principles for an Interdependent World*. Palgrave Macmillan.
Pettigrew, Thomas F. and Linda R. Tropp. (2006). "A Meta-Analytic Test of Intergroup Contact Theory." *Journal of Personality and Social Psychology* 90 (5):751–783.
https://doi.org/10.1037/0022-3514.90.5.751
Pettit, Philip. (1995). "The Virtual Reality of *Homo Economicus*." *Monist* 78 (3):308–329.
https://doi.org/10.5840/monist199578322
Pew Research Center. (4 March 2015). "Most Say Government Policies Since Recession Have Done Little to Help Middle Class, Poor."
https://www.pewresearch.org/politics/2015/03/04/most-say-government-policies-since-recession-have-done-little-to-help-middle-class-poor/
Pfattheicher, Stefan, Ljiljana B. Lazarević, Erin C. Westgate, and Simon Schindler. (September 2021). "On the relation of boredom and sadistic aggression." *Journal of Personality and Social Psychology* 121 (3):573–600.
http://dx.doi.org/10.1037/pspi0000335
Pinker, Steven. (2011). *The Better Angels of our Nature: Why Violence has Declined*. Viking.
Popper, Karl R. (1945). *The Open Society and Its Enemies: Volume One — The Spell of Plato*. Routledge & Kegan Paul.
Proctor, Bernadette D., Jessica L. Semega, and Melissa A. Kollar. (2016). "Income and Poverty in the United States: 2015." Technical report, United States Census Bureau.
Radcliffe-Brown, A. R. (1952). *Structure and Function in Primitive Society*. London: Cohen and West.
Ruesch, Michelle. (2013). "A Peaceful Net? Intergroup Contact and Communicative Conflict Resolution of the Israel-Palestine Conflict on Facebook." In Ternès, Anabel (ed.), *Communication: Breakdowns and Breakthroughs*. Oxford, United Kingdom: Inter-Disciplinary Press.
Sherif, Muzafer. (ed.). (1962). *Intergroup Relations and Leadership*. New York: Wiley.
Sherif, Muzafer. (1966). *In Common Predicament: Social Psychology of Intergroup Conflict and Cooperation*. Boston: Houghton-Mifflin.
Sherif, Muzafer and Carolyn W. Sherif. (1953). *Groups in Harmony and Tension*. Octagon Books.
Sinclair, Upton. (1995 [1934]). *I, Candidate for Governor, and How I Got Licked*. University of California Press. Originally published: New York: Farrar & Rinehart, © 1935.
Srinivasan, Amia. (2018). "Does anyone have the right to sex?" *London Review of Books* 40 (6):5–10.

Suler, John. (2004). "The Online Disinhibition Effect." *CyberPsychology & Behavior* 7 (3). https://doi.org/10.1089/1094931041291295

Sunstein, Cass R. (2018). *# Republic: Divided democracy in the age of social media*. Princeton University Press.

Tajfel, Henri. (1972). "Social categorization." In Moscovici, S. (ed.), *Introduction à la psychologie sociale*, volume 1. Paris: Larousse.

Tajfel, Henri, M. G. Billig, R. P. Bundy, and Claude Flament. (1971). "Social categorization and intergroup behaviour." *European Journal of Social Psychology* 1 (2):149–178. https://doi.org/10.1002/ejsp.2420010202

The Economist. (4 May 2023). "Artificial intelligence is remixing journalism into a "soup" of language." *The Economist*. https://www.economist.com/business/2023/05/04/artificial-intelligence-is-remixing-journalism-into-a-soup-of-language

Turner, J. C. (1982). "Towards a cognitive redefinition of the social group." In Tajfel, H. (ed.), *Social Identity and Intergroup Relations*. Cambridge University Press.

Wheatley, Jonathan. (2015). "Restructuring the policy space in England: The end of the Left—Right paradigm?" *British Politics* 10 (3):268–285. https://doi.org/10.1057/bp.2015.35

Wheatley, Jonathan. (6 June 2017). "The polarisation of party supporters since 2015 and the problem of the 'empty centre' — in maps." LSE British Politics and Policy blog. https://blogs.lse.ac.uk/politicsandpolicy/the-polarisation-of-party-supporters-since-2015/

Wheaton, Sarah. (18 June 2007). "Political Sites Drawing More Eyeballs." *The New York Times*. https://thecaucus.blogs.nytimes.com/2007/06/18/political-sites-drawing-more-eyeballs/

Wikipedia. (2024). "Two Minutes Hate." https://en.wikipedia.org/wiki/Two_Minutes_Hate

We can work it out

I don't understand why R.E.M.'s "Finest Worksong" doesn't feature more prominently in protest marches. The song begins with Peter Buck playing a howling guitar riff that sounds very much like an alarm, and the first line has Michael Stipe wailing, "The time to rise has been engaged." That alone should resonate with anyone out on a picket line. At 177 beats per minute,[1] it is also fast enough to get the blood pumping.

I mention that song for two reasons. The first is simply a proposal to make protests a bit more enjoyable for fans of 80s alternative rock. The second is that the third and fourth stanzas of the song provide a pretty good summary of the takeaway message of this book. The lyrics are not particularly complex but fitting. Let me explain why.

Take your instinct by the reins

As I have argued, the Open Society has come under attack from a number of directions, both the left (e.g., no-platforming) and the right (e.g., closed borders). Underlying these attacks, in many cases, are aspects of human psychology that are deeply hardwired and that short-circuit appeals to reason and evidence. Why do people turn to strong, powerful authoritarian leaders during times of fear and uncertainty? It's not because those individuals are more likely to make correct decisions but because those personalities reassure the more basic, animal parts of our brains. Fear is a powerful determinant of human behaviour, even when it isn't rational. If you can make people afraid of immigrants coming to take their jobs, threaten their security, and change their society, you've already done a lot to make people suspicious about the cosmopolitan conception of the Open Society before you make an argument.

In addition, most people need social approval and a sense of connection. Social media companies use this to attract us to their platforms and then use our brain's reward system to make their platforms addictive. More attention from users generates more revenue for social media companies. But that attention also generates, for us, pressure to conform, especially given the scale, severity, and ease with which judgement is delivered via the internet. In these

---

How to cite this book part:

Alexander, J. McKenzie (2024) *The Open Society as an Enemy: A critique of how free societies turned against themselves*, London: LSE Press, pp. 301–345.
https://doi.org/10.31389/lsepress.ose.f. License: CC BY-NC 4.0

cases, our behaviour is shaped by non-rational impulses. Sometimes a person is aware of that happening, for example, when they are on the receiving end of a Two Minutes Hate but sometimes they aren't, for example, when exposure to images over time shifts one's conception of what is normal.

I don't mean to suggest that letting human instincts influence our behaviour is *necessarily* bad. There is a large literature (e.g., Gigerenzer 2008) which looks at how "gut feelings" influence decisions. Sometimes our instincts lead us to make good decisions when we do not have enough information to be able to articulate what, exactly, we are thinking. Humans are phenomenal pattern-recognition devices, and yet, sometimes, we cannot describe the patterns to which we are responding.[2] But because human instincts *can* lead us astray, we need to be aware of that possibility, know when they are activated, and think about what to do when that happens. There are three ways to respond to human instincts: let them rip, try to accommodate them, or try to resist them.

Cases where human instinct helps us to make good decisions are examples of when we should let them rip, as are some cases of romantic love.[3] Sometimes a better response is to accommodate our instinctive reactions. In Part III, I've argued that is the appropriate response in the case of trigger warnings and safe spaces. The controversy surrounding those issues is, I've argued, much ado about nothing.[4] With regards to the issue of no-platforming speakers, the appropriate response is more nuanced: sometimes no-platforming is entirely appropriate, but sometimes we need to *resist* our instinctive response and let the speaker talk.

Another case where we need to resist our instincts was found in Part IV. Heterogeneous communities can prompt a tribal response with inter-group conflict, but this needs to be reined in. Why? Because respect for the freedom of individuals requires respecting peoples' freedom of association. But any time a group forms, we create new conditions of possibility for ingroup-outgroup bias. Those instincts, deeply rooted in human nature, are potential causes of violence and harm and thus should be resisted.

So we see the relevance of the title of this section. One underlying reason the Open Society has been seen as an enemy is that we have been encouraged to let our instincts rip for too long in too many cases. The reasons behind this are many: the profit motive of international tech companies, the venal interests of politicians who benefit from sowing division, media companies who deliberately misrepresent groups to drive the attention economy, and our own human nature, which makes us want to be a valued member of a group doing something we believe in. But those instinctive responses threaten to overwhelm and undermine many of the good aspects of the Open Society which we should value and try to realise. Taking our instinct by the reins puts us humans, as rational animals, back in the driver's seat. That's not to say that we should all strive to be passionless, robotic decision-makers, but we should be aware of when and how we let our passions influence our behaviour, exercising control when it is needed.

That observation provides a transition to the next line of the R.E.M. song and the next stage in the summary of the overarching argument of this book. If our human instincts have been triggered in ways that led many to see the Open Society as an enemy, we need to stop that from happening. That is, assuming you agree with my assessment that the Open Society is worth defending. A defence of the Open Society means doing things differently on a crowded planet home to eight billion people, living unsustainably. What that entails requires collective discussion and thinking about the kind of world we want to create and live in and how to get there from here. And that, I argue, requires thinking about social engineering from a multifaceted, holistic perspective. But before broaching that subject, we must engage with Popper's argument *against* large-scale social engineering, first to see why he thought it was a bad idea and second to see why he was mistaken.

You're better, best, to rearrange

In *The Open Society and Its Enemies*, Karl Popper argued for what he called "piecemeal social engineering" rather than the "Utopian or holistic methods of social engineering" that he saw in the views of Plato, Marx, and others. Here is the starting assumption: all rational action has an end it tries to bring about. If we are to take effective action towards that end, we need to specify a "blueprint" for the kind of society we want to create.[5] If we can't do that, we run the risk of acting irrationally. We might not choose the best means to the end, or we might choose incompatible means over time, thus thwarting our plans.

So what's wrong with Utopian social engineering? Popper argues that it will likely lead to dictatorships or, at the very least, undemocratic institutions. Why? Because "the reconstruction of society is a big undertaking which must cause considerable inconvenience to many and for a considerable span of time" (Popper 1945a, p. 141). Since the Utopian social engineer won't be able to realise the blueprint with people complaining about their house being knocked down or the local mill being closed, they will need considerable power to Make Stuff Happen, forcing people to do things they don't want to do. That's bad.

Furthermore, the amount of time required for the Utopian social engineer to realise the blueprint will be considerable. Consider the recently opened Elizabeth Line in London. That rail line is based on ideas first floated in 1919 (London Transport Museum 2024). The decision to start building the railway received Parliamentary permission in 2008. The work didn't actually begin until 2011. The Elizabeth Line finally opened at the end of 2022. That's the amount of time it took to plan, muster up the political will, and then build a *single 42km railway line* in an advanced economy.[6] Rebuilding society, by comparison, would take *generations*. Therein lies the second problem: we know an authoritarian leader will be required, and control will have to pass from one authoritarian leader to another. What guarantee is there that Great Leader 2 will think Great Leader 1's blueprint was the right one? If they disagree, we'll potentially end up in a cycle of authoritarian leaders knocking down things built by their predecessors, without really making progress.[7] That's also bad.

A third criticism Popper provides involves the limits of human knowledge:

> What I criticize under the name Utopian engineering recommends the reconstruction of society as a whole, i.e. very sweeping changes whose practical consequences are hard to calculate, owing to our limited experiences. It claims to plan rationally for the whole of society, although we do not possess anything like the factual knowledge which would be necessary to make good such an ambitious claim. We cannot possess such knowledge since we have insufficient practical experience in this kind of planning, and knowledge of facts must be based upon experience. At present, the sociological knowledge necessary for large-scale engineering is simply non-existent. (Popper 1945a, p. 142)

There is an interesting tension in Popper's remarks. He says the Utopian social engineer wrongly claims to have a rational plan for society because "we do not possess" the necessary factual knowledge. But do we not possess that knowledge because such knowledge is *unobtainable* or because we *haven't looked hard enough*? Popper makes what sounds like a modal claim about the impossibility of such knowledge, writing "We *cannot* possess such knowledge" (italics mine). Yet the reason he gives immediately undermines the modal interpretation, for he says that "we have insufficient practical experience in this kind of planning" and all knowledge is based on experience. If knowledge of X is based on experience of Y, and we never seek experience of Y, we cannot have knowledge of X. But the claim that we cannot have knowledge of X is not counterfactually robust: what would happen if we *tried* to seek experience of Y? What if we tried to gain sufficient practical experience in the kind of planning needed for Utopian social engineering? We might find that, much to our surprise, we could in fact possess such knowledge.

If it *were* possible to obtain the relevant knowledge for Utopian social engineering, that would undermine Popper's argument. Instead of showing that Utopian social engineering was impossible, Popper would simply have shown that the success of Utopian social engineering depends on the simultaneous satisfaction of three contingent requirements: (i) Does the society have a sufficiently benevolent and politically skilled leader to keep all competing interests of the parties in check and persuade everyone to make the necessary sacrifices? (ii) Will that level of benevolence and skill be preserved as power transitions from one generation to the next, and will successive generations of leaders remain committed to the same plan? (iii) Do we know enough about what society wants and needs, both now and in the future, to be able to make appropriate plans for the present and future needs of society?

Furthermore, it is really the *third* contingent requirement – the epistemological one – which does the lion's share of the work in driving a sceptical conclusion. All societies need to worry about requirements (i) and (ii). All societies engage in projects that inconvenience some and benefit others. The competing interests between groups in society require politically skilled leaders who strike compromises and identify solutions to problems that benefit enough people, enough of the time, to command assent from most parties. Few societies have a large enough army to force everyone to comply with a policy if all the citizens resisted. And no democratic society could survive if the leaders tried continuously to force through policies that all the citizens fiercely disagreed with.

The greatest problem, in practice, for a Utopian social engineer is the epistemological problem. I suggest we have good reason to believe that Popper's suspicion was correct – that we *cannot* possess the relevant knowledge – even if the reason he gave was faulty. The reason we cannot have such knowledge is because a number of people have tried, repeatedly, to obtain the practical experience needed, and failed. Perhaps the greatest example of such a natural experiment is that carried out by the Soviet Union, which attempted to create a centralised, planned economy at an incredible level of prescriptive detail.

Some elements of the Soviet experience in centralised planning can be found in episode one of the BBC documentary series, *Pandora's Box*, which aired in 1992. You get a sense of the underlying ideology less than two minutes into the programme. A middle-aged bureaucrat, filmed in the grainy, beige-tinted footage from another era, looks out of a window at a crowd on the street below and says: "Each of those people down there is unique, yet each is part of some cluster or group in society. And each group is governed by a set of iron laws, as unchanging as the laws of nature, physics and the mechanical sciences." By trying to identify and wield those "iron laws", the Soviet-era social planners sought to make Utopian social engineering a reality.[8]

Despite enormous efforts, the Soviet project didn't turn out the way people had hoped. This is partially due to political paranoia on behalf of the leaders, whose decisions impaired the country's ability to develop.[9] It is also partially due to the Soviet social planners attempting to do things that are better left to decentralised markets, where distributed local knowledge and the incentive generated by competition yield a better distributive outcome. The first issue – problems caused by political paranoia – nicely illustrates Popper's concern about how political power could be wielded by the Utopian social engineers.[10] The second issue – the epistemic problem – provides some evidence that Popper's claim, "we cannot possess such knowledge", is counterfactually robust.[11]

There are two humorous examples in the *Pandora's Box* series that illustrate some of the epistemic problems that the Soviet economy encountered. The first example illustrates one difficulty with a fully planned economy: you need to specify under what conditions deviation from the plan is permissible. When each part of the plan depends on other parts of the plan, sometimes things end up being done for no real reason. Over time, the Soviet Union became increasingly rigid in its adherence to the plan. KGB agents were even instructed each year on how many arrests they should make and to which prisons those arrested should be sent.¹² Funeral directors were told that, based on theoretical predictions about how many people die in a given year, they should manufacture a certain number of coffins. But the manufacturing of coffins wasn't driven by demand. If it turned out that in a given year only 800 people in a certain area died, but the plan called for 1,000 coffins to be manufactured, the extra 200 had to be made anyway.¹³ Choosing when to deviate from the plan would require local judgement because the contingencies requiring deviation could not be anticipated in advance by central planning. Given that, redeployment of the freed-up resources would also require local judgement because it would take too much time to communicate the differential demand back to central planning and then calculate where to put the freed-up resources. The second example highlights how when a top-down *plan* determines economic growth rather than bottom-up *demand*, absurdities can result from the misalignment of incentives. In 1957, Nikita Khrushchev lashed out at the planning organisations for using the wrong metrics to determine whether the plan succeeded. Why, he asked, were sofas getting bigger and chandeliers heavier, to the point where the chandeliers posed a danger of ripping out of their ceiling fixtures and falling to the floor? Because of the metrics used to evaluate the plan: the more raw materials that were used, the more successful the plan was judged to be.¹⁴ The easiest way to use more raw materials was for the workers to make everything bigger. Khrushchev's proposed solution was to attach prices to things. The prices, though, were to be determined by central planning. I'll let you guess how well that turned out.

The alternative approach to Utopian social engineering is Popper's preferred approach: *piecemeal social engineering*. Because planning the perfect society is impossible, "the piecemeal engineer will, accordingly, adopt the method of searching for, and fighting against, the greatest and most urgent evils of society, rather than searching for, and fighting for, its greatest ultimate good" (Popper 1945a, p. 139). Instead of the *master* blueprint required by the Utopian social engineer, the piecemeal social engineer will need only *modest* blueprints: "blueprints for single institutions, for health and unemployment insurance, for instance, or arbitration courts, or anti-depression budgeting or educational reform" (Popper 1945a, p. 140). Attempts to realise these modest blueprints are much less risky. If we make a mistake, we won't have ripped up the entire social fabric. And if we agree on what the "most urgent evils" are, we can make progress democratically.

Piecemeal social engineering works, according to Popper, by engaging in myriad small-scale social experiments, learning from what works and what does not. As he noted, we engage in small-scale social experiments all the time. For example, when new forms of insurance are sold or new taxes introduced (Popper 1945a, p. 143). According to Popper, these experiments help us learn about what works by a trial-and-error process. Piecemeal social engineering is the rational attitude given the limits of human understanding and knowledge. Fundamentally, the real problem with Utopian social engineering is that "*it is not reasonable to assume that a complete reconstruction of our social world would lead at once to a workable system"* (Popper 1945a, p. 147). Those italics were in the original text.

At this point, I hope the above reconstruction of Popper's argument makes a pretty persuasive case for piecemeal social engineering. What I want to do now is persuade you that Popper's argument for piecemeal social engineering is, in fact, mistaken on the grounds that it presents us with a false dichotomy and that there is a third way.

The false dichotomy becomes apparent once we see that according to Popper, the only alternative to piecemeal social engineering is attempting a "complete reconstruction of our social world." That is, we can *either* tackle individual problems *or* we can attempt a complete reconstruction of our social world. But that sharp either-or dichotomy excludes the possibility of identifying a *set of intertwined problems*, where attempts to solve one problem from the set creates externalities (both positive and negative) for the other problems in the set. When faced with a set of intertwined problems, it would be entirely rational for a social engineer to think about the set as a *whole*, exploring various ways of rejigging the package in order to find an optimal solution.[15] Let us call this approach *multifaceted social engineering*.

Once we identify multifaceted social engineering as a possibility, we see that many of the problems the world faces have that character. One of the motivations for writing this book was that the value inversion of the four different senses of the Open Society are interconnected in ways that suggest we need to think about how to tackle those problems *at the same time*. Tackling multifaceted problems of social engineering is not the same thing as attempting to completely reconstruct the social world: it only recognises that we live in a complex world where not all problems are decomposable into independent sub-problems, solvable in isolation.[16] It requires adopting a new perspective for thinking about social problems and looking for connections between issues. And that requires that we think globally – or, to use one of Popper's most disliked adjectives – *holistically*. Yet it is important to stress that holistic, multifaceted social engineering is not the same thing as a complete reconstruction of our social world. It's more like surveying all the ingredients in a supermarket in order to select a subset for making a tasty dish.

A useful metaphor for the benefits of multifaceted social engineering, and why it is better than piecemeal social engineering, can be found in the idea of a *fitness landscape* from evolutionary theory. In 1932, the evolutionary biologist Sewall Wright proposed thinking of the set of all possible genotypes for a given species, as an abstract space where each "point" in the space represented one possible genotype and the "height" at that point was the fitness of the genotype. Since different genotypes have different fitnesses, the "landscape" will resemble a mountain range.[17] A genotype with a greater fitness than others that are close[18] to it will be a peak, and a genotype which is less fit than others close to it will be a valley. The "survival of the fittest" process generated by natural selection can be thought of as random efforts to climb the hill towards a peak.

Figure 29.1: A slightly rugged fitness landscape

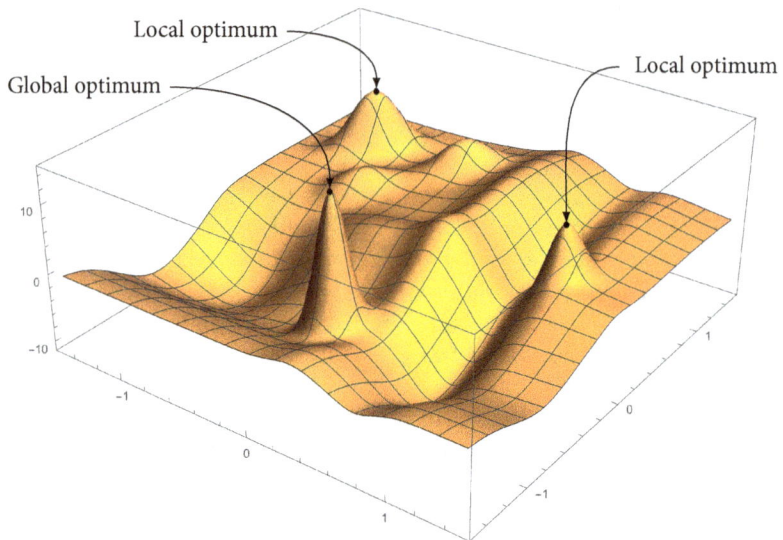

Source: author.
Notes: the x- and y-axes represent possible values of two different genes, traits (under the societal interpretation), policies. Particular values of x and y then yield a concrete realisation of the organism (or society), with a given "fitness", represented as height on the z-axis. (Not all local optimums are labelled.)

One of the conceptual benefits of thinking about evolution and social engineering in terms of fitness landscapes is that it explains why both biological systems and societies get stuck at suboptimal solutions. Finding an improvement on an existing specification, whether that is a biological structure like a wing or a social structure like a welfare scheme, is hard. In biological organisms, there are many genetic interdependencies that exist; sometimes, making an adjustment that improves the system in one respect may harm it in another respect.[19] The same thing is true of societies: changing policy in one area can have multiple knock-on effects that influence people's behaviour in other areas. Sometimes a policy that sounds reasonable can have the opposite effect when embedded in the wider social context, given how people will respond.

Now let us ask whether piecemeal social engineering suffices for constructing the kind of society we want. Presented with the current state of society, piecemeal social engineering, narrowly construed, leads to questions of the following kind: with respect to *this particular problem of interest*, what is the best policy to adopt? (Or, failing that, what is a reasonable policy to adopt?) A more generous interpretation of piecemeal social engineering, one which may go beyond Popper's understanding of the term, asks: given the *current state of society*, what modest readjustment of current policies would lead to an improvement? If we think of social engineering as manoeuvres on fitness landscapes, we can see that the best one could hope for usually involves finding a *local* optimum.

Under the more generous interpretation of piecemeal social engineering, we are considering modifications along *both* axes at the same time. That corresponds to policy decisions that tweak several issues at once but in a conservative way that ensures a net overall improvement. In terms of the fitness landscape, it means that given the current state of society, the piecemeal social engineer would move in the direction that has the steepest upward slope. (In the language of fitness landscapes, this is referred to as *following the gradient*.) While that sounds like an improvement over the narrowly construed understanding of piecemeal social engineering, because we are making improvements without people having to suffer in the short term, it doesn't yield significantly better results. Most of the time, such adjustments end up converging to a local optimum which is far below the global optimum.

And so we see how multifaceted social engineering provides a net improvement over Popper's piecemeal approach. Targeting a set of intertwined problems recognises the complex, interconnected nature of society and, as such, does not suggest that we should expect steady, incremental improvement as we make progress towards our goal. The attitude of multifaceted social engineering recognises that there may be periods of decreasing "fitness" along the way, but this is warranted by the expected benefit at the end. More importantly, targeting multiple problems at the same time means that we are not restricting ourselves to a lexicographical maximisation process, where we maximise first along one dimension and then along another. Trying to solve multiple problems at the same time amounts to moving across the fitness landscape in a direction that may not appear rational when each problem is considered in isolation. And that method of moving across the fitness landscape, which isn't restricted to simply following the gradient, increases the chances of us finding the global optimum.

Examples of multifaceted social engineering can be found in the past. They are often associated with periods of great social upheaval, where so much disruption and disorder has occurred that it becomes possible for politicians to consider change on a scale that would not normally be feasible because of the protectionist instincts of vested interests. In the US, Franklin D. Roosevelt's New Deal, enacted in the middle of the Great Depression, is one. In the UK, the social reform enacted by Clement Attlee's government after the destruction of World War II is another. Both cases involved a vision of the kind of society they wished to create, but not in the Utopian social engineering sense where every detail was planned. Neither Roosevelt nor Attlee attempted to reconstruct all of society at once (although Attlee's nationalisation of utilities and major industries went a good deal further than what Roosevelt attempted). The key is to construct an agenda that strikes the right balance of ambition and feasibility. It must be ambitious enough to move to a part of the fitness landscape that would be inaccessible if we only considered individual, independent policy improvements yet remaining feasible enough to be accomplished in a time and at a cost that people are willing to bear.

Multifaceted social engineering differs in both aim and intent from the thesis described by Naomi Klein in *The Shock Doctrine*. In that book, Klein argues that crises and natural disasters provide cover for opportunistic neoliberal free marketeers to push through broad, sweeping (and generally unwanted) changes at a time when the general population is too distracted to resist. The examples given of multifaceted social engineering in this paragraph *do* involve rebuilding society after periods of extended crisis, but that is not because politicians are forcing unwanted changes on a population. Instead, it is that the crisis has changed the cost-benefit calculation of the proposed changes for the population to such an extent that they are now willing to back the proposal. There was, after all, enthusiastic support for the New Deal and the Attlee government's social reform. Multifaceted social engineering does not require a crisis to be successful, but it will be more difficult in good times to persuade people that sweeping change is needed.

And so we arrive back at the second line of the R.E.M. stanza: "You're better, best, to rearrange." In this section, I have concentrated on what kind of *rearranging* we are talking about. We have seen the need for holistic, multifaceted social engineering if we want to increase the chance of realising transformative change that will move society towards a global optimum. Yet that leaves the following question unanswered: which aspects of society need to be targeted by the multifaceted social engineer in order to undo the value inversion that has led to the Open Society being seen as an enemy? It is that topic to which I now turn.

What we want and what we need

In 1943, Abraham Maslow published a theory of human motivation that eventually became known as "Maslow's hierarchy of needs". It has the dubious distinction of being a widely known psychological theory, generally believed to be true, and taught in many introductory courses despite having limited evidential support. A little more than 30 years after Maslow's theory was introduced, Wahba and Bridwell (1976) began their article reviewing the evidence for it with the wry remark, "Maslow's need hierarchy theory (1943, 1954, 1970) presents the student of work motivation with an interesting paradox: The theory is widely accepted, but there is little research evidence to support it." Maslow was aware of the lack of evidence at the time he introduced his theory, noting that there was a "very serious lack of sound data in this area" (Maslow 1943, p. 371). However, he thought that the lack of data was due to the lack of a good *theory*, since you often need to have a theory to test before you go about collecting data.

One of the reasons Maslow's theory is so widely accepted, despite the limited empirical support, is that it seems so eminently *sensible*. According to Maslow, human needs are hierarchically ordered, with later needs not usually appearing until earlier needs are satisfied: "the appearance of one need usually rests on the prior satisfaction of another, more pre-potent need." What are the needs? Maslow begins with the "physiological" needs, really basic ones that are required to maintain the normal state of the bloodstream, like food and oxygen. The next level concerns the "safety needs", like a stable home environment and familiar stimuli for children, and a job, some savings, and insurance for adults.[20] After that are the "love needs": love, affection, and belongingness.[21] The "esteem needs" appear next. Esteem, here, not only means self-esteem but also the esteem of others, like respect from your peers. The final level of the hierarchy is the "need for self-actualization", a slightly hippy notion Maslow uses to capture the idea that, once all the other needs are met, a person must do what they are meant to do (italics in the original):

> Even if all these needs [the lower ones in the hierarchy] are satisfied, we may still often (if not always) expect that a new discontent and restlessness will soon develop, unless the individual is doing what he is fitted for. A musician must make music, an artist must paint, a poet must write if he is to be ultimately happy. What a man *can* be, he *must* be. (Maslow 1943, p. 382)

I don't think that Maslow's characterisation of self-actualisation is correct, for reasons covered in the discussion of existentialism in Chapter 4. Not only is there no human essence but there are simply *too many* things a person *could* be. But set those concerns aside and interpret "self-actualisation" according to your preferred theory.

Despite the sensible nature of the theory, the evidence for Maslow's hierarchy is mixed. Part of the reason for this is that it is a difficult theory to *test*. How do you operationalize the various categories of need? That's relatively unproblematic for the first level, as it is based on physiological matters, but as you move up the hierarchy it becomes increasingly challenging, especially when you start trying to measure self-actualisation. How do you find a metric that captures both Elon Musk and the Dude?[22] Second, even assuming a reasonable operationalisation of the categories, how could you conduct controlled experiments without running foul of an Ethics Board? You can't really put someone's safety into jeopardy and then ask how their study of Proust is going.

Nevertheless, people have tried. In their comprehensive review of the empirical literature at the time, Wahba and Bridwell found limited support for even the *existence* of Maslow's five basic categories of needs. Only one out of six studies found five categories of needs (the others found three or four), and that study only agreed with Maslow's proposed rank-ordering on three of the categories. Of those studies which investigated Maslow's claim that the appearance of a need further up in the hierarchy would only appear after lower needs were satisfied, little support was found. In their considered judgement, Wahba and Bridwell (1976, p. 233) conclude that "[s]ome of Maslow's propositions are totaly [sic] rejected, while others receive mixed and questionable support at best." That pattern continued with later research. Betz (1984) found "modest support" for Maslow's theory but with some qualifications.[23] Haymes and Green (1982) also find some support for Maslow's theory, but their study narrowly focuses on the categories of *safety* and *belongingness* in the development of children. A later paper, which examines the proposition that greater need deprivation leads to greater domination in the search for satisfying that need, concludes that "it is too soon to conclude that the proposition (or Maslow's theory in general) has been refuted by research" (Wicker *et al.* 1993, p. 131).

It appears that, 80 years after Maslow's original publication, the verdict regarding its refutation is best stated using the unusual third category available in Scottish criminal trials: not proven.[24] Regardless, for my purposes, I can assume that even if Maslow's hierarchy of needs is not precisely correct, an alternative theory with a number of structural similarities is likely to be. For example, Kenrick *et al.* (2010) develop an updated hierarchy which retains the basic pyramid structure of Maslow's theory, but with a number of modifications based on recent work in evolutionary biology, anthropology, and psychology. One of their more radical proposals is to remove *self-actualisation* as a separate need, subsuming it into other categories in their hierarchy.[25] But perhaps the most important revision to Maslow's theory – made by Kenrick *et al.* and others – involves rejecting the notion that needs are *strictly* hierarchically ordered. Needs are *generally* hierarchically ordered but not exclusively so.[26] We do need oxygen, food, clothing, and security, but even if we don't have security, we can still satisfy social needs and respect needs. People in a war zone can experience a sense of belonging, camaraderie, respect earned from others, and indeed even aspects of self-actualisation if they truly believe the values they are fighting for are values worth dying for. In any event, in what follows, I shall often refer to Maslow's hierarchy *as if* that theory were correct. This is purely for convenience since Maslow's hierarchy is so widely known. Nothing that I say below will depend critically on this convention.

It is important to talk about needs because a need is more than something we want very much. A *need* is something which, if not satisfied, interferes with our ability to function as a human being. But not all ways of satisfying needs are equal. With respect to a number of physical needs, such as food and water, there are ways of satisfying them which are more or less beneficial for the person. The need for food can be satisfied by a healthy salad or by junk food. Which one of the two we choose depends on what we *want* at the time, and what we want is susceptible to social influence. Our need for water can be satisfied by, well, *water*, or by carbonated sugary beverages containing caffeine. Which of the two we choose depends upon what we want. Much effort was spent making us want fancy bottled water as well as sugar-rich beverages of negligible health benefits, both of which generate high profits for the manufacturers. Clothing needs can be satisfied by manufacturers employing sweatshop labour using environmentally damaging materials to make products designed to be worn only a few times because they either fall apart or fall out of fashion.

The way in which a *need* is satisfied depends on the *wants* of the person, and the wants of a person are sensitive to social practices and the deliberate construction of wants by companies, organisations, and other individuals. And the construction of wants matters because of the power that grants a third party capable of fulfilling the want over the person who had that want inculcated. Given the multiple ways in which a real human *need* can be satisfied through wants, we must realise that there are ways of satisfying individual human needs that are better or worse for the individual,[27] or other people, or society as a whole.

The iconoclastic economist John Kenneth Galbraith talked about the process of want construction and want fulfilment in his essay "The Dependence Effect" from his 1958 book, *The Affluent Society*. Galbraith distinguished between those wants that originate within the person themselves, and those that are contrived by something outside the person. Much of what we want doesn't fit neatly into one or the other category, but there are fun examples of purely contrived wants. In 1975, the advertising executive Gary Dahl started selling a novelty item intended to be the lowest-maintenance pet ever: the pet rock. Dahl wrote up an instruction booklet titled "The Care and Training of Your Pet Rock" and included copies of it in a specially constructed cardboard box filled with straw, a rock, and some "breathing" holes. Dahl sold enough pet rocks to become a millionaire.

Although the pet rock illustrates a purely contrived want, Galbraith's concern had a slightly different focus – that the *process* of satisfying the want itself *creates* more wants of that type. The pet rock doesn't illustrate this further feature of Galbraith's concern, because the very process of satisfying the contrived want for pet rocks soon caused the market for pet rocks to collapse. It turns out that the market for novelty items often closes down when the item ceases to be a novelty.[28] But for other products like fast fashion, the process of satisfying the want creates more wants of that type. This is the case that worried Galbraith because it is far from clear that such want-fulfilment does anything to better the human condition. Instead, it creates a cycle of want-creation and want-fulfilment. Galbraith describes the situation as follows: "the individual who urges the importance of production to satisfy these wants is precisely in the position of the onlooker who applauds the efforts of the squirrel to keep abreast of the wheel that is propelled by his own efforts" (Galbraith 2001, p. 33).

Galbraith's primary focus was on wants satisfied by material items. In his essay, his examples include silk shirts, orange squash, breakfast cereals, and detergents. But the cycle of want-creation and want-fulfilment can *also* hold for wants satisfied by *immaterial* items. Think about wants related to those social needs featuring at higher levels in Maslow's hierarchy: a sense of belongingness, friendship, esteem, respect from your peers, and perhaps even self-actualisation if we understand that as pursuing a project which one sees as mattering deeply to oneself. We *need* to have a sense of belonging, and we *need* to be respected by our friends and peers. But how do people go about attempting to fulfil those needs? It's worth thinking about that question because *a sense of belonging* can be fulfilled in many different ways; given that, what particular *wants* do people attempt to satisfy?

Now think about the multiple means companies and organisations in contemporary society create wants and then provide ways of satisfying those wants on the pretence of fulfilling fundamental human needs. Consider the need for esteem and respect from our peers. Social media provides peculiar and artificial operationalisations of those concepts, beginning with what counts as a *peer*. How many "friends" do you have whom you have never, or only rarely, met in real life? Now turn to measures of esteem and respect: likes, re-tweets, and posts going viral (in a good way) provide the dopamine hit that is interpreted as esteem and respect. They are both fleeting (how long does the warm glow of a "like" last?) and yet capable of scaling up far beyond what we would experience in real life, such as when a post is shared or liked or re-tweeted thousands of times. When the need for esteem is met by satisfying a want for multiple likes or re-tweets, ask yourself: is that like when the need for food is satisfied by a healthy meal, or is it like a junk food sugar rush? I suggest the latter. If I am correct, it is worth considering how many of our mental needs – those appearing in higher levels of Maslow's hierarchy – we attempt to fulfil by satisfying *created* wants, wants which only certain companies can satisfy (because they created them), which are less-than-ideal ways of meeting our mental needs.

As a society we are familiar with the fact that attempts to create certain classes of wants in people through advertising and marketing need to be regulated. That's one reason why, in the UK, television advertisements for junk food are banned before a certain time of the evening. It's also why cigarette manufacturers are banned from advertising on television, in magazines, or in public spaces. But we are less attuned to thinking about how those emotional, cognitive, and social needs appearing at higher levels of Maslow's hierarchy can be targeted by the creation of wants – even though advertisers have been trying to do this for ages, too. But a crucial difference exists between how wants were created in the past and how wants are created in the present. In the past, advertising would appeal to our need to belong, to be respected, to be loved, to attain self-actualisation, and so on, in order to sell *material products* or a *service*. But what we find in contemporary society is the construction of wants which provide entirely new conceptualisations of how we understand the very *processes* of belonging, of being respected, of being esteemed, etc. And with these new processes come entirely different ways of measuring whether we do, in fact, belong or whether we are, in fact, being esteemed. To return to my previous question: are these new conceptualisations of how to satisfy our emotional, cognitive, and social needs more like a healthy meal when hungry, or are they more like junk food? Would you rather have 500 likes on social media, or five colleagues whom you know well independently thank you for doing a good job?

That question provides a transition to the next line of the R.E.M. song and the next stage in the summary about how the Open Society has come to be seen as an enemy by so many people. There is, I argue, a broad set of needs which are common to all people, but we as a society have become confused as to how to best meet those needs. Many wants that people have are merely wants that have been created primarily to advance other ends and provide, at best, a substandard way of meeting those needs. Sometimes those wants have been created to advance the profits of a company. Sometimes those wants have been created to advance the political aims of an organisation, institution, or person. And sometimes those wants have been created by us as a way of responding to a world that seems overwhelming and threatening. It is this confusion of wants and needs that has led to the Open Society being seen as an enemy. Correcting this incorrect perception requires (i) understanding the nature of this confusion and (ii) seeing how multifaceted social engineering is necessary to correct the problem. Let us now turn to what has happened.

Has been confused, been confused

Let us proceed through the various parts of this book, in order. We began with the cosmopolitan conception of the Open Society. People have the following economic and social needs: job security, a stable economy, a place to live, and a sense of belonging where they live. In a civilised society people also need, I suggest, the moral peace that comes with trying to rectify as many injustices of the natural lottery as possible. Many populist politicians argue that the way to meet those economic and social needs is by closing borders and restricting immigration to net-zero policies: one-out, one-in. Many politicians also seem to accept that our moral obligations, if they do not actually cease to exist for non-citizens beyond our borders, are at least sufficiently attenuated so as to not prevent the implementation of closed-borders policies. Those are the wants that are created, and they are the wants which cause the cosmopolitan conception of the Open Society to be seen as a threat.

Yet, I have argued that it is mistaken to think that satisfying the want of a closed border is the best way of meeting our economic, social, and moral needs. Open borders – at least borders much more open than we presently allow – have the potential to generate great economic growth. The economic and population growth associated with migration will create the demand for more jobs and yield windfalls for government through additional tax revenue. If properly managed,[29] the growing pie generated by an open-border policy will meet our economic needs better than a closed-border policy. And, as I argued, the belief that keeping a sense of belonging and pride of place (the Nowhere, Man objection) requires closed borders is also exaggerated. Finally, the moral need to correct the natural injustice resulting from the birthright lottery is perhaps the most powerful argument for opening borders, even if it is the least likely to induce action.

On the other hand, populist politicians create wants for closed borders because those wants resonate with peoples' fears, tapping into misunderstandings of how economies work. People without economic training find the "lump of labour fallacy" persuasive, and it's more politically expedient for politicians to utilise that fallacy for political gain than to correct peoples' understanding of economics. Insisting that the border must be closed requires more powers for authorities, with additional resources for border control, enforcement, and policing. If borders were open, the resulting economic benefits would be generated and, to a large extent, distributed through the operation of the decentralised free market. It would be difficult for any single politician to point to an outcome and take credit for having achieved that. In contrast, if borders are closed, a populist politician can easily take credit for the increased policing and enforcement.

And so we see how the created wants for closed borders and restricted immigration lead to the cosmopolitan conception of the Open Society being seen as an enemy. But, I suggest, what we want and what we need have, in this case, been confused: our needs are better met by satisfying different wants. When we step back, we can see that the wants that undermine the Open Society have been inculcated in order to serve an end that is not for the betterment of humanity. Open borders respect individual freedom and create economic and social opportunities for all. Closed borders give greater power to authorities and create the need for additional security apparatus; whereas Eisenhower warned against the power of the military-industrial complex, calls for closed borders are yet another way for the *security*-industrial complex to exercise more power.

Let us turn now to the conception of the Open Society as transparency. Of the many things people require, transparency features in a number of political and economic needs. The political needs which transparency helps with are many: to provide oversight of governmental processes, both local and national, to ward against cronyism and corruption; to help spot unjust or immoral policies or practices; and to help ensure that decision-making is evidence-based, properly informed, and based on the appropriate mix of democratic and expert judgement. The economic needs which transparency aids in providing are similar in structure: to provide oversight of business processes so as to ensure compliance with laws and regulations; to help spot unjust or immoral policies or practices, and to try to identify those practices which are unjust or immoral but which do not yet fall under current laws or regulations; lastly, transparency helps to ensure pay equity, so that people with the same abilities who do the same job get the same pay, regardless of their sex, gender, ethnicity, religion, and so on.

Unlike the case with the cosmopolitan conception of the Open Society, in this case I think that, with respect to the political and economic needs mentioned above, the wants of people generally align with those needs. Few people would say, at least openly, that they *want* government to be more corrupt and prone to cronyism. People have been campaigning and working to realise transparency in government and business practices for decades. Yet the situation in which we find ourselves is one where transparency of government, businesses, and other organisations still falls short of the ideal, but the activities of our *private lives* are verging on being maximally transparent to a handful of organisations. Although laws exist to provide some protection against the misuse of all of this information, we live in a world where we are little more than one software update away from a surveillance society whose reach would exceed the Orwellian dystopia of *1984*. Here, the threat posed by the transparent conception of the Open Society is very real and very nearly realised.

With respect to the transparent conception of the Open Society, the confusion between wants and needs, which has brought about this situation, is as follows: we have been taught to *want* a lot of conveniences which we don't really *need*. The smartphone was an incredible invention that has transformed society. Although it has created entirely new markets for apps and services, it has exacerbated old problems, and created new ones. Many of us *like* the convenience provided by a cashless economy. Many of us *want* the security provided by CCTV or video doorbells. (The list of goods and services can easily be expanded.) As Galbraith observed, the production of goods and services which satisfy those wants continually generates more wants for more goods and services. However, our desire for these goods and services has not been accompanied by a comparable desire to protect our privacy and to prevent the potential misuse of the information collected by these devices. Although we might express a belief in the importance of a right to privacy and restricted access to our personal information, our *revealed preferences* as consumers speak to a very different set of preferences.

This is a dangerous situation, because free and democratic societies are easily undermined by a surveillance state. Spy agencies like the KGB and its successor organisations, the FSB and the SVR, routinely collected *kompromat* on individuals in order to control them. The surveillance possibilities latently present in modern technology would make it very easy to collect *kompromat* on anybody. In addition, given the number of laws on the books which are seldom enforced but still exist, widespread surveillance would make selective policing of specific individuals very easy to achieve. Or, perhaps more chillingly, they could simply erase your digital existence, leaving you to navigate the contemporary world without any of the conveniences we have integrated deeply into our lives.[30] Individual freedoms have always relied on state benevolence, but we have created a society where the potential violations of individual freedom by an authoritarian state are virtually limitless. *This* realisation of the transparent conception of the Open Society is, I believe, rightly seen as an enemy. However, it is also a very different conception of that version of the Open Society than what we had originally intended. Here, the confusion of wants and needs has resulted in substituting a nefarious version of the transparent conception of the Open Society in place of one which would be truly valuable.

Now let us turn to the Enlightenment conception of the Open Society, involving the free exchange of ideas and the willingness to keep an open mind. This sense of the Open Society relates to needs found in the higher levels of Maslow's hierarchy, which are principally related to self-actualisation but also involve the ability to exercise one's autonomy. Having a correct understanding of the world and an awareness of the diversity of thought that exists helps one to make the most of their individual abilities and freedoms. The Enlightenment conception of the Open Society has been seen by some as an enemy when they seek to realise misguided wants related to another level of Maslow's hierarchy – the safety needs. A misguided effort to secure one's personal safety (based on, I suggest, an incorrect understanding of what "safety" involves) can lead one to block ideas that question or challenge one's beliefs or values.

Fundamentally, the confusion between what we want and what we need at play here is the following: there are ways of attempting to meet the safety needs of Maslow's hierarchy that are compatible with the need for self-actualisation, and there are ways of attempting to meet the safety needs which are not. If we never come into contact with any ideas which challenge our most deeply held beliefs and values, in a sense we will be "safe" because we will never have the disturbing, unsettling experience of realising that we may have been wrong all this time. If that disturbing, unsettling experience is defined as a *harm*, and what it means to be safe is to not be at risk of being harmed, then meeting the safety needs would preclude being exposed to any such challenging ideas. That would preclude our ability to meet the need for self-actualisation unless we accidentally happen to have all of the right beliefs, given our values, from the very beginning. In short, the only way to achieve self-actualisation, given that extreme construal of what it means to meet the safety needs, would be if we *start out* in a state of self-actualisation at the beginning.

Given a correct understanding of what it means to meet the safety needs, it becomes clear that the Enlightenment conception of the Open Society is not an enemy. The free exchange of ideas is necessary for any diverse, civilised society that seeks to develop, grow, and get better – provided that, of course, the exchange of ideas is done in the right way. But it is important to note that this defence of the free exchange of ideas is not the same thing as a defence of unrestricted freedom of speech. As I argued, central to the concept of the free exchange of ideas is that people are acting in good faith, with the intention of arriving at an improved understanding of the issues based on argument and reason. Assuming that people act in good faith, the free exchange of ideas, while serving to make some people feel uncomfortable some of the time, is nevertheless compatible with meeting both the safety needs and the need for self-actualisation.

Finally, let us turn to the communitarian conception of the Open Society. This conception, as you will recall from Part IV, envisions, as the ideal, a diverse, heterogeneous community of many different types of people living together in peaceful coexistence. A society like this would seem to be one natural way of meeting the social needs of Maslow's hierarchy. Yet polarisation, division, and inter-group strife are so present in so many Western democracies that it seems as though the West is intent on tearing itself apart. Why is this the case?

The social need to *belong* is what underlies most of our choices to associate with people "like us", where the relevant dimension of being "like us" can vary over time and context. The sense of belonging that we feel when part of a group depends on how the group identity is formed – and there are several ways in which a group's identity can be formed. Some methods of forming a group identity are positive and healthy, and some methods are negative, drawing upon antisocial tendencies. Positive formation of group identity draws attention to the commonalities shared amongst the members, encouraging relations of friendship. It has members who work together through cooperation and reciprocity. And members are involved in a joint project where all need to contribute for the project to succeed. The negative formation of group identity defines it as opposition to an Other, rejecting those who are not members. Whereas the positive methods of forming a group identity call attention to similarities between members or acts of cooperation and reciprocity, the negative methods of forming a group identity require little more than the old adage "the enemy of my enemy is my friend". But, on that last point, the adage should really be phrased as *the enemy of my enemy is my 'friend'* (notice the scare quotes) because there need be nothing more in common than the perception of a shared enemy whom both want to defeat. Shared enemies can lead to strange bedfellows.

One reason I suggest the communitarian conception of the Open Society has been seen as an enemy is due to the increased tendency to construct modern tribes using negation or exclusion of the Other. This is, of course, not a strict binary distinction, for we can imagine a continuum: some groups having an identity defined mostly by what they are For, other groups with an identity defined mostly by what they are Against, and others with a blend of For and Against. But the point is this: we have a need to *belong*, to be a meaningful part of a group. But how do we understand the identity of the groups to which we belong? Do we think of it purely in positive terms, of *what* we are For, or purely in negative terms, of *who* we are Against? Or, to put the point more bluntly, how much of the group's identity is built on detailed policies and plans grounded in a robust vision of the future, and how much is built on the transient experience of a Two Minutes Hate?

The Two Minutes Hate is a highly effective method for forming a group's identity because it calls attention to the lower-level safety needs, suggesting that group membership meets the safety needs *in addition to* the need to belong. In an age of anonymous, online communication, it is relatively cheap. Furthermore, it is easy to do, whereas constructing policies and plans for a joint project is hard because you need to get everyone to agree on the details. In contrast, the Two-Minute Hate is fast and effective and requires little more than identifying the Other as a threat.

Thus, we see how the four conceptions of the Open Society have come to be seen as an enemy through a confusion of wants and needs. Many of those wants, I suggest, we have adopted as a result of relying on human instincts when making decisions: tendencies to favour the in-group and demonise the out-group, the fundamental attribution error, the human tendency to see meaning in coincidences, and many other cognitive biases. If it is time to take our instincts by the reins and fix this confusion of wants and needs by rearranging society, what is it that we need to do? It is that topic to which I now turn.

The finest hour

As we've seen throughout this book, the reasons why the four different conceptions of the Open Society are seen as an enemy are not independent. Here are some of the connections I have identified in this book. People were encouraged to reject the cosmopolitan conception by populist politicians utilising social media and modern tribal alliances, where the desire for a safe space against challenging ideas provided an echo chamber reinforcing the same basic message: close the border. People use social media because it has become the default medium by which many people communicate and organise. Instead of looking for a local town hall for an activist meeting, you search for them on the social media site *de jour*. But the addictive nature of social media and the lack of real alternatives draw people in, creating an information asymmetry that leads to an imbalance of transparency and the resulting imbalance of power. The anonymous nature of online communication reinforces modern tribes by encouraging stereotypes and the fundamental attribution error. As communication between modern tribes became increasingly poisonous, and bad faith more common in discussion and debate, it was understandable that people might increasingly look towards safe spaces and show less willingness to engage with those outside their own group. The growth of modern tribes was enabled by the internet, as people of whatever backgrounds and interests could find each other more easily. Those modern tribes flourished with the advent of social media and the breakdown of older, more traditional, forms of political organisation. But the concomitant coarsening of social discourse, facilitated by the anonymous nature of online communication, led to a natural tendency to circle the wagons and create a safe space where people tended to listen to their own experts, creating echo chambers that facilitated the demonisation of out-group members.

Multifaceted social engineering is needed here because the interlocking reasons behind why the four different conceptions of the Open Society that have undergone value-inversion make it such that trying to address any one aspect in isolation will not suffice. It would be akin to playing a game of Whac-A-Mole in an arcade: solving one aspect of the problem corresponds to whacking one of the moles back into the cabinet, only for it to resurface somewhere else in a different guise. All of the problems need to be tackled simultaneously in order to make an appreciable difference. Let me explain why.

The communicative nature of online interactions facilitated by social media is, as we have seen, an important contributor to the problems the Open Society faces. But it strains credulity to think that, for example, simply removing the bots from social media and trying to enforce a better, consistent policy regarding hate speech and fake news would make much of a difference. Digital platforms can emerge, evolve, and innovate at such speed that regulations will always lag behind. You *could* try to lock down and police the entire internet available to your population – China has tried – but even China's success is imperfect, and it's hard to imagine any democratic society would be willing to tolerate such draconian measures.

Since the problem is larger than any *single* social media company, perhaps the solution is to pass legislation establishing a regulatory scheme that applies to all social media companies? The difficulty with this proposal is that, as long as extreme polarisation exists between modern tribes, people from one tribe *will find a way* to talk to themselves, engaging in communicative activity which serves to reinforce and propagate the polarisation. There will be pressure from individuals for a medium that lets them express their beliefs and values, organise, critique their opponents, etc., in the way they see fit. The problem isn't so much the communication channel current social media provides, but what people have been *socially conditioned to view as acceptable and permissible forms of speech* on it. Even if governments passed sweeping regulations targeting social media companies, that alone would be insufficient for three reasons.

The first reason is that there will always be ways found to circumvent whatever restrictions regulations impose. On 16 September 2022, it was reported that anti-vaccination groups were using the carrot emoji to circumvent the automated moderation tools on Facebook groups (Kleinman 2022). How? If you squint, the carrot emoji looks a little bit like a syringe. And while the ability to detect such methods will admittedly improve as AI technology develops, the situation is akin to that described by Douglas Adams in *So Long and Thanks for All the Fish* regarding the use of the Electronic Thumb to open the doors of spacecraft, which "half the electronic engineers in the Galaxy are constantly trying to find fresh ways of jamming, while the other half are constantly trying to find fresh ways of jamming the jamming signals."

The second reason is the ever-present problem of ensuring compliance with regulations. If fines and penalties for non-compliance are set too low, penalties for noncompliance will simply be priced into the business model. But the third and most important reason is that what has changed over time are the social norms influencing how people behave in the online environment. According to multifaceted social engineering, it's not enough just to have stricter regulations in place regarding the social media companies we also need to change the social attitudes regarding acceptable and permissible forms of behaviour in the online space. We need to be tough on online abuse (i.e., targeting the social media companies who distribute the stuff) and tough on the *causes* of online abuse (i.e., targeting the attitudes and environments that lead people to think that is a permissible way to behave online in the first place).

This chicken-and-egg problem creates externalities for one of the other senses of the Open Society we have considered. As long as extreme polarisation exists in society, exacerbated by the nature of online communication, there will be a natural desire for the construction of safe spaces. Few people will want to encounter constant vitriolic criticism from strangers, online or in person, especially if it specifically targets the person at the receiving end. We all know of cases of people leaving social media because they cannot or do not want to cope with online abuse. That search for safety is natural, but existence within a safe space increases the chance that one will live inside an echo chamber, primarily encountering the ideas one already agrees with. Perhaps even more harmful is that, inside an echo chamber, the representations of competing ideas will not be given their most charitable and sympathetic expression. A competing idea will be caricatured, improperly justified and stripped of all nuance, appearing substandard and inadequate, and not a worthy competitor for one's preferred beliefs. That effect of safe spaces reinforces polarisation and reduces the chances of deploying one of the known methods for combating stereotypes and reducing hostility between groups, namely, the contact hypothesis, which I discussed at some length in Part IV. Trying to reduce the polarisation of modern society will require encouraging people to step out of their safe spaces and engage in good faith with people from different tribes. So even if we somehow managed to (i) prevent online abuse through some magic technology and (ii) stop the regular Two-Minute Hate of the Other, we still wouldn't resolve the problem of polarisation until people stepped out of their safe spaces and started engaging with the Other in good faith.

My discussion of safe spaces in Part III primarily focused on the Enlightenment conception of the Open Society, but the rejection of the cosmopolitan conception of the Open Society, from Part I, can also be seen as a desire for safe spaces fuelled by people's national tribal identity. The economic and cultural protectionism encouraged by populist leaders not only doubles down on those disadvantaged by the natural lottery of birth, but it also reduces the number of opportunities for the type of contact needed (according to the contact hypothesis) to quash hostilities between groups. Consider the following: after the 9/11 terrorist attack in America, Islamophobia grew in the US, along with increased suspicion towards people from the Middle East, broadly construed. Yet given the small number of Muslims in the US[31] and the small number of Arab-Americans,[32] opportunities to mitigate these tendencies were few and far between, since many Americans didn't actually know any Muslims or Arab-Americans. Since fear and distrust thrive in ignorance, the rejection of the cosmopolitan conception of the Open Society only serves to reinforce the conditions which fuel the demand for safe spaces. It's not surprising that the rejection of the cosmopolitan conception of the Open Society is correlated with the rejection of the communitarian conception of the Open Society.

And so we can see why rehabilitating the Open Society requires multifaceted social engineering. The four different conceptions are intertwined in numerous complex ways, where stresses on one create stresses on the other. Only by stepping back and thinking more generally about the kind of society we want to have can we think about the package of interventions that need to be made to get there. Given the current level of suspicion the Open Society is viewed with nowadays, its rehabilitation will not be easy. But I suggest, for all the reasons covered in this book, that it is worth doing. Here's why.

In 1947, members of the *Bulletin of the Atomic Scientists* introduced what became known as the "Doomsday Clock". It is a metaphor used to represent how close humanity is to a global catastrophe, with the clock hands set to a certain number of minutes away from midnight. The closer the hands are to midnight, the greater the threat of a global catastrophe. It is a fitting metaphor because it suggests that unless *something* is done, the inexorable passage of time will inevitably bring about the catastrophe. Originally intended to reflect the threat of global thermonuclear war, the use of the clock has since expanded to include threats from climate change, bioterrorism, cyber-warfare, and artificial intelligence in one aggregate symbol (Reynolds 2018).

When the clock was first introduced, the hands were set at seven minutes to midnight, reflecting the threat to humanity from the invention of nuclear weapons. After the Soviet Union conducted its first nuclear test in 1949, the clock hands were moved forward to three minutes to midnight. The clock hands have not always moved forward, though: when the Nuclear Test Ban Treaty[33] was signed in 1963 by the US, the UK, and the Soviet Union, the Doomsday clock was set back to 12 minutes to midnight. When the Cold War ended in 1991, the clock was set back further to 17 minutes to midnight. Unfortunately, as I noted in the introduction to this book, a lot has changed since then. Over the past decades, the Doomsday clock has steadily moved forward until, at the time of writing, the Doomsday clock stands at 90 seconds to midnight.

Humanity faces a number of unprecedented challenges and existential risks that threaten us all. The greatest risk is climate change, which will render parts of the planet uninhabitable for human beings and cause mass migration as people move to new areas in search of security, in addition to threatening supplies of water and food. The second greatest risk involves sustainability, for we are stripping the world's natural resources and polluting the environment in ways which were simply not conceivable only a 100 years ago. We are causing the greatest mass extinction since the end of the Cretaceous Period when the dinosaurs went extinct. In order to bring about the economic, political, and social change required to solve these problems, we need to stop fighting amongst ourselves. And that is why we need to stop seeing the Open Society as an enemy.

If we push the Doomsday clock metaphor to its limit, we might say that when *homo sapiens* first evolved the clock hands were more than 11 *hours* away from midnight. The emergence of a new species of African primate wasn't much of a threat to anything, even if it did have an unusual capacity to cooperate and to use objects for tools. As humanity progressed, the clock hands would occasionally move, but not by much. Even the great land and sea battles between empires of the ancient world only had local effects whose capacity for damage fell far short of a hurricane or a volcanic eruption. The ability of humanity to precipitate a global catastrophe only became possible after the Industrial Revolution and the scientific and technological advances which followed. The most sizeable movement in the Doomsday clock over the entire history of humanity has occurred in the last century when we found ourselves with less than 60 minutes to midnight. If we manage to reverse the damage we have caused, that would truly be humanity's finest hour.

It all comes down to this

If multifaceted social engineering is required in order to rehabilitate our understanding of the Open Society, for all the reasons discussed, what are some practical policy recommendations for making progress?

That's a perfectly reasonable question, but I fear that this section will necessarily disappoint. It has taken a whole book, moving at quite some pace, just to identify the problem, given its complexity. Practical policy recommendations will require people far more knowledgeable and capable than I am to determine the appropriate social levers to pull. Nevertheless, here are some suggestions that provide a starting point for reflection on where to begin based on what we have discussed over these pages.

Let us begin with acts of political reform. If part of the problem lies with extremist politicians pushing a populist agenda to get elected (because it sounds good), even though that agenda will actually make matters worse, then we need to reform politics to reduce the chance that extremists can get elected in numbers which don't reflect the level of support in their community. I have three suggestions.

The first suggestion is to eliminate "safe seats" for single parties to the extent it is possible. The reason why this is a reasonable item to target is that when an election for a representative can generally be predicted to go in favour of one party or another (because of a clear preponderance of voters favouring that party), then the real determinant of the winning candidate is not the *election* but rather the process that determines which candidate will stand for the favoured party. And if that process is one like a US primary where only party members can vote, what tends to happen is candidates run on platforms that cater towards the more extreme members of the party. A primary election tends, more often than not, to function as an ideological purity contest where the most extreme candidates get selected.

In contrast, elections in non-safe seats have the general election to serve as a reality check on the primaries. A candidate may move towards an extremal position in the *primary* in order to be selected to represent the party, but since the majority of voters are not members of the party (that's the definition of a non-safe seat), the candidate will need to move back towards the political centre in order to appeal to enough voters to win. An election in a non-safe seat thus limits the extent to which maintaining an extremal position is a viable election strategy.

Whether a seat counts as "safe" or not depends on a number of factors. Sometimes a political district naturally becomes, for historical reasons, predominately populated by voters favouring a political party. If a seat is safe for this reason, it simply reflects the will of people, and there's no reason to shake things up. This would be an example of a self-organised community forming out of each individual exercising their freedom of association. But sometimes a political district favours a political party not because of citizens naturally exercising their freedom of association, but rather because a politician decided to *redraw* the boundaries of the political district in such a way as to favour one party over another.

Political districts are supposed to represent local areas so that the elected politicians can rightly represent the interests of their constituents. All political boundaries are, to some extent, artificial because there is seldom an overwhelming reason why the boundary line has to be drawn *precisely* where it is, rather than along some other adjacent path. But this arbitrariness gives politicians the ability to draw political boundary lines in ways that favour one party over another. Redrawing political boundaries in order to expressly favour one party is known as *gerrymandering*, which takes its name from the American politician Elbridge Gerry. In 1812, when he was the Governor of Massachusetts, Gerry redrew the boundaries of a district in Boston in order to favour the Democratic-Republican party.[34] Newspaper columnists commented on the unusual shape of the district, and a cartoon was published depicting the district as a mythological beast resembling a salamander. The technique quickly became known by a portmanteau of its inventor's name and the shape of its first district.

Gerrymandering flies in the face of democracy by reducing the voting power of certain individuals and by creating safe seats. As I've argued, safe seats tend to favour more extremist candidates. Electing more extremist candidates makes it difficult to achieve mutually beneficial political compromise while, at the same time, allowing modern tribal identities to become more salient through the political fighting that results. In addition to preventing gerrymandering, we should also move towards a system of *proportional representation*, where people vote for a *party*, and then after the election representatives of the party are chosen in order to populate the government with a distribution of party members satisfying the distribution of voters. That can be done in a number of ways.

Proportional representation has a bit of a bad reputation due to fears that it makes it easier for extremist political parties to get into office. That worry is certainly justified, but what I want to call attention to is that when safe seats are allowed to proliferate we also can end up with extremist candidates in office –

just via a different method. What we need is to ensure that the *silent majority of the centre* is not under-represented in political systems. At the moment, ask yourself which is the greater threat: that extremist political parties might end up with some small representation in government, or that serious candidates reflecting the concerns of the silent majority – on climate change, on creating a sustainable future for our children and grandchildren, on creating a fairer society with a more equitable distribution of wealth, etc., – do not have a larger role in government?

The second suggestion for political reform is to hold politicians *actually* accountable for their campaign promises. While politicians are masters of the art of saying nothing (recall the discussion of Rorschach concepts), they do still make promises to the electorate on occasion. Yet, oddly, there is no mechanism – other than another election – for holding a politician accountable for whether or not they deliver on a campaign promise, or whether or not they misled the electorate. When you think of it, that's rather remarkable because almost all forms of business are required to comply with truth-in-advertising laws.

Yet no such accountability exists for politicians, who can promise the moon and then blame external contingencies for their inability to deliver. Now, politicians will undoubtedly argue that it is unfair to hold them accountable if their inability to deliver was due to factors beyond their control. My response to this argument is the carefully nuanced view best expressed as follows: tough. How many businesses go bankrupt as a result of factors beyond their control? How many people are members of the precariat due to factors beyond their control? If someone is unable to pay the rent on the home they've lived in for the last thirty years as a result of a physical illness beyond their control, and they weren't able to afford unemployment insurance, will they be cut any slack for their inability to deliver? No. My response to politicians who complain that holding them accountable for failing to deliver on promises due to factors beyond their control is this: be careful about what you promise, and make sure those promises are feasible and evidence-based.

The third suggestion regarding political reform is more ambitious than the previous two: find a way of reforming the decision-making process to reduce *short-termism* in political decision-making, forcing politicians to take a longer view. One great difficulty with regular election cycles is that it creates little or no incentive for politicians to introduce projects where all of the costs and pain are front-loaded and all the benefit occurs when the project is completed, i.e., on someone else's watch. This is one of many reasons why we are struggling to combat climate change. Large structural reform of the economy to move rapidly towards a carbon-neutral environment cannot be done without greatly inconveniencing many people, many of whom vote. When political leaders are weak and unwilling to persuade people of the necessity of action, when those whose interests are misaligned with the greater interests of society actively work to muddy the waters of understanding (see Oreskes and Conway 2011), the path of least resistance is to kick the can down the road and hope that the decision-making environment or technology will change sufficiently so as to make possible a less costly, less painful social intervention which will bring about the necessary benefits faster. That's worked well regarding climate change, hasn't it?

Now let us turn to acts of reform concerning media, forms of communication, and the use of personal information. If one of the drivers of social polarisation is social media encouraging and facilitating forms of communication that cater to some of our worst unconscious biases regarding in-group and out-group effects, then what we need to do is establish regulations with teeth that makes it undoubtedly clear that facilitating certain kinds of interaction simply cannot be allowed. But such regulations must be backed by strong disincentives for failures to comply.

All too often, punitive damages for regulatory violations cease to provide an effective business deterrent and can instead simply be priced into the business model, because those damages are flat-rate fines based on the absolute value of the damage caused.[35] A better model is that used in Scandinavian countries, which set fines as a *proportion* of a person's income. One particular case which was widely reported concerned the Finnish businessman Reima Kuisla, who was caught driving 65 mph in a 50 mph zone (Pinsker 2015). Since Finland sets fines based on income, Mr Kuisla's 15 mph indulgence cost him €54,000. Someone on a normal salary might find that excessive, but it makes sense once you realise that Mr Kuisla earned €6.5 million the previous year (BBC News 2015). If Mr Kuisla was charged a modest fine of €100 for his 15 mph overshoot, would that really deter him from doing it again? Of course not. Flat-rate fines which are a deterrent to normal people on an average income are, to the wealthy, nothing more than the price to pay for flouting the rules. A $100 fine for a single person driving in the car-pool lane is nothing to a wealthy person who wants to get home a little earlier to spend time with their family (especially once you factor in the low chance of getting caught). By similar reasoning, if we want to provide effective incentives to companies, we need to use a big enough stick.

Putting effective regulations in place for social media companies is a crucial piece of the puzzle for rehabilitating the Open Society. In less than two decades, those companies have effectively re-written many of the rules regarding social interaction, re-shaping communication norms in the process. Their business model leverages psychological biases and cognitive weaknesses of individuals, creating products which are, by design, addictive and which create a perfect environment for sparking inter-group conflict. Just as we regulate other businesses which profit by catering to people's potential vulnerabilities, such as tobacco companies, alcohol distributors, and food manufacturers, we should regulate the creation and distribution of products that take advantage of people's psychology.

In this respect, social media provides us with an interesting analogy and disanalogy with tobacco companies. Tobacco companies sell products known to be harmful that are physically addictive to users. No one is born needing to use tobacco products, but people become addicted to them as a result of social engineering by the tobacco companies through marketing. By analogy, social media companies provide products that are, in some cases, harmful and psychologically addictive to users. No one is born needing to use social media, but people become addicted to its services as a result of social engineering. The disanalogy is that people are born with certain social needs that can be partially satisfied through the use of social media.

I suspect that, in the future, we will view social media companies much as how we view companies trading in fossil fuels. They have become necessary for the operation of society as we have constructed it, but at the same time they result in serious, real harms that those very companies have endeavoured to hide from their users. Whereas now we realise that fossil fuels are responsible for climate change and numerous physical harms due to pollution, some people are already viewing some social media companies as being responsible for causing serious, real harms to the mental health of some of their users. Not all users, of course – but, then, not all cigarette smokers get lung cancer.

Why has social media not been subject to greater regulatory scrutiny in recent years? I think there are probably several factors at work. The first is surely the financial incentive created by the explosive growth of social media enterprises. So much wealth has been generated that there is a reluctance to kill the goose that lays the golden eggs. The second is that the amount of information about the public that is collected and generated by unregulated social media is undoubtedly of phenomenal interest to advertisers (and, I hasten to add, government security services[36]). The third is that, given the second reason, it is probably quite risky for a member of the government to mount an effective challenge to the power and scope of social media; if a politician or governmental official were to propose a serious clampdown, they would probably find themselves running against a well-funded challenger with nicely targeted ads in the next election. After all, fossil fuel companies have fought against effective legislation regarding climate change for decades, and the political lobbying and funding of candidates by the National Rifle Association is one of the reasons why the US has the gun laws it does.

Another type of media reform which would help is restricting the use of anonymous accounts. By this I mean not simply requiring people to register their actual identity with a media company before posting a comment below the line using a pseudonym, but actually requiring people to post under their actual name, for example. Having one's actual identity linked to one's online speech would certainly help ensure that discourse remained civil. Some companies are doing this already, but the policy could be rolled out more widely. At the same time, it would also be necessary to increase protection for individuals regarding the possible consequences of online speech. It would be important to ensure, for example, that people could not be fired simply for expressing a view which ran counter to the beliefs or values of their employer.

I want to stress that I am not suggesting that we eliminate all use of anonymous accounts. There is certainly a place for anonymous speech online, such as with whistleblowing and other cases in the public interest. There is real value in being able to publish works under a pseudonym. But these cases of anonymous speech are typically vetted by named editors or organisations who take a reputational risk in publishing anonymous speech. They are, in effect, putting *their* name on *someone else's* speech, saying "this is worth putting out into public discourse." That reputational risk provides, to some extent, an effective check on toxic speech. As we have seen, truly anonymous, unaccountable speech quickly transforms the river of public discourse into an open sewer.

In addition, I think it's important to restrict greatly the collection, storage, and use of people's personal information. As I argued in Part II, it's not enough simply to *anonymise* the information, because given enough information the identity of an individual can still be established even if there are no unique identifiers stored. In rehabilitating the conception of the Open Society as transparency, we have to return to the original goal: that of holding the government, institutions, organisations, and the powerful in check. The Open Society wasn't supposed to provide a window into the soul of the people, allowing their information to be weaponised and used against them.

Another media reform which will help to rehabilitate the Open Society will be to put in place regulations regarding the reporting of news. The striving to be seen as fair and balanced often results in some views being given greater prominence than they deserve, given the evidence. For example, reporting on climate change has often resulted in climate sceptics being given a disproportionately loud voice, given the paucity of evidence for their position. Views regarding factual matters should generally be reported in a manner *proportionate to the evidence*. From this, it follows that, with respect to social views, the reporting should be balanced *with respect to the distribution of social opinion*. In order to prevent people from falling into echo chambers, news organisations should be required to maintain neutrality. Because there are no alternative facts, news should not be treated as a propaganda arm of any political party.

All of these proposed media reforms will be difficult to implement because of the financial incentives to prevent them. Great wealth confers great power, either because you can pay people to do what you want or because you can persuade people to do what you want. This leads me to the final informational reform I propose: provide greater transparency of wealth and cash flow so that it is easy to follow the money and identify who owns what. At present, shell corporations make it far too easy for wealthy individuals to hide their assets, which in turn makes it far too easy for those individuals to wield influence and power without due accountability. We need to know, for example, if the alleged "grassroots" efforts protesting some proposed social change truly reflects a self-organised movement based on the endogenously formed beliefs of members of society or if it is funded by some organisation or individual who stands to benefit.

Some might argue that such transparency would violate the right to privacy of wealthy individuals. Although it is true that the degree of privacy accorded to the wealthy would be different from that accorded to the ordinary citizen, this difference is arguably necessary in order to ensure the proper governance of society and to prevent the abuse or subversion of institutions and organisations on which we all rely. The reason why it would be permissible to grant a different degree of privacy to the wealthy is as follows: no one has a natural right to be wealthy or is naturally entitled to be wealthy. We, as a society, allow individuals to be wealthy because we believe that it is right that people benefit from the fruits of their labour, on the grounds that it provides people with an incentive to work, on the grounds that when people work it is to the benefit of society. We allow levels of wealth *inequality* on the grounds that such inequality is necessary in order to make the worst off as well off as possible. Wealthy individuals occupy a privileged position in society and we, as citizens, have a right to know that they are not abusing that privilege. As such, I suggest that it should be seen as part of the implicit social contract that wealthy individuals have an obligation to make their wealth known as well as how it is used. This will be very hard to achieve, especially when technology such as Bitcoin makes anonymous transfers so easy, but it is worth trying.

Now let us turn to acts regarding social reform. Restoring faith in the communitarian conception of the Open Society requires that we no longer see the Other as a threat but rather as people simply choosing to go their own way and who do things differently from us. As noted, according to the contact hypothesis, one way of achieving this is to socially engineer greater contact between groups. This is a large project and one which will, of necessity, never be completed: social contact between groups will need to be re-created for each successive generation. But increased social contact between groups works to ease inter-group tensions. In the US, for example, the integration of public schools, originally undertaken in order to correct the racial inequity created by segregated schools, had the side effect of generating increased social contact between racial groups.[37] One measure of the effect this might have had on improving relations between racial groups is to look at the number of interracial marriages. According to a report by Livingston and Brown (2017), the frequency of interracial marriage in the US increased from 3% in 1967 to 17% by 2015. In metropolitan areas, the frequency increased to nearly one in five.

One way of increasing contact between groups would be for national governments to begin slowly opening borders, allowing more migration. The migration should be managed with policies in place to help immigrants embed themselves in local communities rather than simply leaving them to sort things out for themselves. In opening up borders, it would be important, from the point of view of correcting the natural injustice of the birth lottery, to not restrict the migration to only the most skilled migrants. If the economic models are correct, increased rates of migration will generally be expected to contribute towards economic growth. Economic growth, combined with reasonable redistribution policies, will then contribute to overall levels of well-being to increase in those countries. Greater levels of well-being, along with increased contact with the migrant workers who helped contribute to that economic growth, will, over time, help to mitigate the fear of the Other.

Another social reform which I believe is required is to change how experts are represented in the public domain. As I mentioned in the introduction to this book, experts have had a bad rap, especially in the US and the UK. First it was the climate scientists warning that the world wasn't doing enough to combat climate change (which is true), which a lot of vested interests didn't want to hear. Then it was the economists, who failed to predict the financial crisis of 2008, which cost a lot of people a lot of money, with many people losing their jobs. In 2016, in Britain, it was the economists again who were predicting the economic upheaval Brexit was going to cause (which was also true), which some politicians beating the populist drum didn't want to hear. And then, with the pandemic, it was the epidemiologists whose advice on how to combat COVID-19 and save lives seemed to some people to be a recipe for economic disaster and a means of ushering in a totalitarian state on the sly.

It's true that experts don't always get it right, but we need to keep things in perspective. When experts make a correct prediction or judgement, they are rarely praised as loudly as they are criticised when they make a mistake. There is a reason for this: it's assumed that an expert will generally be correct because that's the whole *reason* for consulting an expert in the first place. But we need to remember that prediction concerning social events isn't an exact science, and even the best experts will get things wrong from time to time. Discounting expert advice or choosing your expert based on your ideological commitments is a recipe for disaster. It might not always turn out badly, but it certainly will one day.[38] Encouraging the public to distrust objective rather than partisan, scientific, evidence-based expert advice is a deliberate attempt to mislead and manipulate the public by encouraging them to put their faith in whatever snake oil salesman is attempting to persuade them of something.

Why is restoring trust in experts relevant for rehabilitating the Open Society? There are two reasons. The first reason is that we need to reject the idea of "alternate facts" and return, instead, to the Enlightenment ideal of a common understanding of the world accessible to all. That's important if we are to solve the most serious problems which present an existential threat to our societies. It also helps to bring about the communitarian conception of the Open Society, where different groups, each following a different way of life, nevertheless operate within a shared world. Although social conventions, norms, traditions, and values can vary considerably across communities, we all share the same physical reality. The second reason is that experts provide a way of resisting the politicisation of knowledge. When knowledge is politicised, groups can use "their" knowledge (provided by their "experts") as a tool for excluding the Other who do not share their understanding of the world. But that politicisation of knowledge is dangerous. When it comes to questions of health, the climate, the economy, and so on, it doesn't matter if your "expert's" analysis aligns with your ideology; what matters is if the analysis is *correct*. In the words of Daniel Patrick Moynihan, a former US Ambassador to the UN: "Everyone is entitled to his own opinion, but not to his own facts."

Moynihan is a little more generous than I am regarding people's right to an opinion. (In what follows, I will use *belief* as synonymous with *opinion* so as to be consistent with the terminology used elsewhere in the book.) I would say that, of course, everyone can have a belief,[39] but the extent to which a person is *entitled* to do so depends on their reasons. And whether a person's belief is *justified* depends on how good their reasons are. I suspect it's possible that someone can *have* a belief even if they don't have any reasons for doing so,[40] but I wouldn't say that, in that case, the person is entitled to have that belief.[41]

The reason I am more strict than Moynihan when it comes to people's right to have a belief is that beliefs are rarely *inert*. Beliefs cause people to do things that change the world and sometimes affect other people, either in the immediate term or in the future. Your beliefs are thus directly or indirectly involved in generating positive and negative externalities for others. If you have acquired a false belief, use that false belief when determining how to act, and then harm someone as a result, you might be morally culpable. This shows that the barrier between matters of epistemology and matters of morality is permeable. The failure to acquire knowledge can be a moral failing, as well.[42]

The moral risks of knowledge acquisition go beyond the process of forming beliefs; they also pertain to how we modify and update our beliefs in the light of new information. There's an enormous philosophical literature on what are rational methods of belief revision that I do not want to enter into here (I have touched upon some of the issues in Part IV), except to say that discussion and debate play a crucial role in how we acquire new information for modifying our beliefs. At the end of the day, perhaps the most important reform required for rehabilitating the Open Society concerns how disagreement and public debate are conducted, as there are better or worse ways of handling disagreement in society.

Whereas the Enlightenment conception of the Open Society celebrates rational, reasoned debate of issues, much public discourse falls far short of that ideal. Listen to any politician being interviewed and often what you will hear is little more than the repetition of set talking points with no actual engagement with the question being asked. What passes for *debate* in much contemporary media often features more of the same, along with uncharitable attributions of positions and rhetorical tricks as each speaker tries to make themselves look good at the expense of the other participants. What matters in these exercises is not the attempt to arrive at some common understanding of the truth but rather winning the exchange. Who cares what you say as long as your side comes out on top?

This poor state of public debate is made even worse by a perception that altering one's beliefs is a sign of weakness. Where did this attitude come from? I'll leave it to a cultural anthropologist to write the definitive history of that trend, but here's my guess at one possible origin of resistance to revising one's beliefs. There's no doubt there's a long history of *"never surrender"* when it comes to public discourse. From Winston Churchill's famous wartime speech to the House of Commons on the 4th of June, 1940, to Margaret Thatcher's famous speech in which she said, "The lady is not for turning," politicians and organisers of all stripes love showing backbone and commitment. And although the *never surrender* trope generally concerns a course of action, there is a close connection between actions, beliefs, and values. If we know what someone believes and values, we can be pretty confident about how they are going to act. Why? Because if the person is rational, a particular act only makes sense as an attempt to realise some end; that is, to achieve some outcome that a person *values*. The particular way an action unfolds will be determined by what the person *believes* is the best method of realising the outcome that they value.

From this, it follows that if someone previously committed to a certain course of action changes what they are doing, then that person either changed their beliefs or changed their values. Since most people assume that their values cannot (or should not) change, that leaves a change in belief as the only possibility. And so, if someone has *sworn* that they will *never surrender* to a certain course of action, and we know that their values aren't going to change, then that rules out the possibility of their beliefs changing to any significant extent, as well. (The only possibility would be those changes in belief that, given the same values, would still yield the same course of action.) And so we see how the *never surrender* trope leads to a general recalcitrance to changing one's beliefs or changing one's values because surrendering is showing weakness, and showing weakness is bad.

The problem with such recalcitrance is that, in light of new information, rationality can require us to revise both our beliefs and our values. Because it is relatively straightforward to see how new information can lead to belief revision, let us consider how new information can lead to value revision. It's true that values do not respond to new information in the same way that beliefs do – we don't look out a window and realise that we need to change a value in the same way we realise we need to change our belief that it is raining when we see the sun shine. The process of value revision is different because a value can only be dropped or revised when it becomes apparent that this value conflicts with or thwarts the realisation of other values that one cares about more.[43] If one receives new information concerning the existence of such a conflict, then one might be motivated to revise the values involved. For example, suppose someone values individual freedom and initially thinks that individual freedom is so valuable there should be no constraints upon it whatsoever. It might then be pointed out that such a premium placed upon individual freedom is reasonable if we all lived in isolation, like Robinson Crusoe, but in the presence of other people, including those who are potential threats to our well-being, unrestricted individual freedom is not an indefeasible good. As social contract theorists argue, a person should be willing to accept limits to their individual freedom because those restrictions, when part of a larger society featuring protective institutions, serve to keep individuals safe and provide them with greater opportunities than they would have had otherwise. This new information may then cause the person to revise the value of individual freedom.

If I'm right, one irony about the prevalence of the *never surrender* trope and how it urges people to be recalcitrant in their beliefs and values is that *never surrender* is not only called for during times of *resistance* (which fits with the reluctance to change) but during times of *revolution* as well. Revolutionary periods are times of great social change, where the intention is to subject the current system to creative destruction in order to produce something different, something better, something good.

In the post-war era, the Open Society was seen as something good because, in contrast with the fascist regimes of World War II and the totalitarianism of Soviet and Chinese communism, it was seen as a protector of individual liberty. The four conceptions of the Open Society we have considered in this book – cosmopolitan, transparent, Enlightenment, and communitarian – all have, I argued, their place in helping individuals utilise their individual freedoms of self-determination and association so as to create a life worth living, according to each person's own subjective worldview. Since the end of the Cold War, these four conceptions of the Open Society have undergone a process of value inversion, in that the good-making features of the Open Society came to be seen, by many, as a threat. This, I have argued, is mistaken. We need to rehabilitate our understanding of the Open Society.

Is this a call for *resistance* or *revolution*? I think both. It is a call for resistance because the Open Society, a thing of value, has been subject to an uncoordinated attack along multiple fronts. We should protect what we have left from being eroded further. Yet it is also a call for revolution because the way the Open Society has advanced in the immediate post-World War II era is not progressive enough. At that time, segregation was still legal in the United States, homosexuality was illegal in both the US and the UK and the second wave of the women's movement hadn't even begun. Concerns over economic inequality and distributional issues in the West had largely been set aside during the war years. Concerns about sustainability and climate change were still decades in the future. In rehabilitating the concept of the Open Society, there is an opportunity to re-think the kind of society we want to create and how to ensure it is compatible and sustainable with this small, finite world in which we live.

What kind of revolution is this? This is not a call for a revolution of guns and ammunition. This is not a call for violence. This is a call for a revolution against the social discord created by modern tribes fighting with each other, using technology that strips away each side's humanity, encouraging them to never surrender, to retreat inside a safe space, and to tell the Other to not come around here no more. This is a call for a revolution of the type expressed by the American spoken-word poet Gil Scott-Heron in his 1970 work, "The Revolution Will Not Be Televised." In what way? There are many indicators sprinkled throughout the poem. *"The revolution will not be brought to you by Xerox in four parts without commercial interruptions. There will be no highlights on the eleven o'clock news [...] The theme song will not be written by Jim Webb or Francis Scott Keys, nor sung by Glen Campbell, Tom Jones, or Johnny Cash [...] The revolution will not go better with Coke. The revolution will put you in the driver's seat."*

What kind of revolution is this? When asked about the meaning of the poem, Scott-Heron explained:

> The first revolution is when you change your mind about how you look at things, and see that there might be another way to look at it that you have not been shown.[44]

And there it is.

Notes to "We can work it out"

[1] At least according to https://getsongbpm.com.

[2] One famous experiment illustrating this fact was conducted by psychologists Richard Lazarus and Robert McCleary in the late 1940s (see Lazarus and McCleary 1951; McCleary and Lazarus 1949). In it, they showed subjects a bunch of nonsense words on a screen and, occasionally, gave the subjects an electric shock after showing some of the nonsense words. Subjects were also hooked up to a device to measure their galvanic skin response (GSR), a common indicator of emotional arousal in humans. (When humans experience emotional arousal, sweat glands on their palms exude some perspiration, which increases the electrical conductivity of the skin's surface. Measuring how much the electrical conductivity increases gives an indication of just how excited/nervous/agitated/frightened/etc. the person is.) What Lazarus and McCleary found was that, after a period of conditioning, the subjects *anticipated* the occurrence of an electric shock after the indicator words (as measured by their GSR) but were *unable* to articulate the rule which determined when the electric shock was given. Their suggested interpretation of this result was that, subconsciously, people were able to determine the underlying pattern, which determined when electric shocks were given, but they were not consciously aware of the rule. This form of perception without awareness they called *subception*.

[3] But it can also be a bad thing (e.g., *Wuthering Heights*).

[4] A recent meta-analysis found that trigger warnings had no effect on educational outcomes (Bridgland *et al.* 2023). It was also found that trigger warnings could serve to increase engagement with material in certain cases.

[5] Popper allows for the blueprint to be imprecisely specified: "Only when this ultimate aim is determined, in rough outlines at least, only when we are in the possession of something like a blueprint of the society at which we aim, only then can we begin to consider the best ways and means of its realization, and to draw up a plan for practical action" (Popper 1945a, p. 138).

[6] The UK might be unusually sclerotic in this respect. Starting on 17 March 1930, the Empire State Building was built in 1 year and 45 days.

[7] One of the reasons Popper attacked Plato was because Platonists have a solution to the disagreement problem. According to Plato, there is an ideal form for a city-state which is timeless and perfect. If the authoritarian leaders are an endless succession of philosopher-kings, they will all agree on the ideal form of the city-state.

[8] Marx did little to help the Soviets in their task. As Popper noted, Marx was primarily concerned with identifying laws of social development, not "economic laws which would be useful to the social technologist" (Popper 1945b, p. 187). After the 1917 revolution, when faced with numerous economic challenges, Lenin admitted in a speech "We knew, when we took power into our

hands, that there were no ready forms of concrete reorganisation of the capitalist system into a socialist one [...] I do not know of any socialist who has dealt with these problems" (Webb and Webb 1947, p. 497). Popper remarks further that "there is hardly a word on the economics of socialism to be found in Marx's work — apart from such useless slogans as 'from each according to his ability, to each according to his needs'" (Popper 1945b, p. 79). This is because, perhaps somewhat paradoxically, Marx was not a believer in Utopian social engineering. (This is one key difference between Lenin and Marx: Lenin thought it was possible to accelerate history, turning Russia into a communist utopia directly from an economic backwater by leapfrogging the intermediary stage of advanced capitalism.)

[9] Lenin initiated ambitious programmes of industrial development, but in doing so had to rely on expert "bourgeois engineers" who had been educated before the revolution and whose loyalty he did not entirely trust. Lenin's untimely death handed power to Stalin, who made a push for even greater industrialisation but in doing so had to rely all the more on the bourgeois engineers. Stalin became concerned about the growing power of the engineers, and in 1930 arranged to have 2,000 arrested and charged with anti-Soviet activities. Concerns that the technological expertise required for Soviet industrialisation would fall into the wrong hands led Stalin to insist that the revolution needed its own engineers, who were ideologically loyal and could be trusted. This led to the rapid growth of engineering schools, and soon the Soviet Union had more engineers than any other country in the world. Yet the ideological purity required meant that engineering knowledge became politicised, with a resulting rigidity of thought and a reluctance to question fundamental assumptions regarding approach and method.

[10] At least regarding his point about the threats posed by authoritarian leaders. Popper's concern about shifting targets when a transition occurs between authoritarian leaders is illustrated by different historical events. For example, did Gorbachev inadvertently *cause* the collapse of the Soviet Union by introducing his policies of *perestroika* (reconstruction) and *glasnost* (openness) too quickly? Or did he merely bring forward in time something which was inevitable? And how do the radical changes introduced by Deng Xiaoping in China fit into the Popperian analysis? Xiaoping oversaw the rehabilitation and repair of China after the chaos caused by Mao's Cultural Revolution, which led to a great break from past policies. Yet, at the same time, Xiaoping continued with the opening up of the Chinese economy to the West, which was initiated by Nixon's meeting with Mao in 1972.

[11] At least given our limited human capacity to discover and know things. If we believe an all-knowing Laplacean demon would be able to solve the social planning problem, then it starts to look like the fundamental problem involves the measurement, collection and analysis of data. If so, then artificial intelligence combined with the Internet of Things might do a lot better than the Soviet social planners, at least under normal conditions. Soviet planners were

operating under constraints involving the measurement, collection and analysis of data that we might be able to handle to a far greater degree. However, the existence of uncertainty regarding unpredictable events means that even the best efforts of technologically-informed artificial intelligence might only result in modest incremental advances towards a more resilient economy, rather than an actual solution to the social planning problem.

[12] *Pandora's Box*, episode 1, interview with Vitalii Semyonovich Lelchuk (USSR Academy of Sciences), at 31:35.

[13] *Pandora's Box*, episode 1, interview with an unnamed factory worker, 32:55.

[14] *Pandora's Box*, episode 1, 36:45.

[15] Some might argue that this amounts to nothing more than a terminological dispute regarding what we mean by a "problem". I don't think that's right, as we'll see when we revisit the concerns faced by the Open Society later. In any case, if the concept of a "problem" has to be radically enlarged in order to preserve the idea of piecemeal social engineering in light of what I said, it still means that my observation was essentially correct.

[16] This observation is not new; the Nobel-laureate Herbert Simon recognised this more than 60 years ago in his book, *The Architecture of Complexity* which discussed non-decomposable problems. On this point, see also Gaus (2021).

[17] Taking the metaphor too seriously can quickly lead to problems. For example, no genotype has an "absolute" fitness value since its fitness depends on (i) the environment, (ii) how that genotype is expressed as a phenotype during development, and (iii) the presence of other genotypes in the population. The importance of (i) is that changes in the environment can quickly alter the fitness value of a genotype. The dodo bird was doing absolutely fine on the island of Mauritius until it was discovered by Dutch sailors in 1598; but a little over 60 years later, it became extinct. The importance of (ii) can be seen in that even identical twins have physical differences, and if something goes awry in development, then the differences could be very great indeed. The importance of (iii) is that scarcity can itself be fitness-enhancing because the environment includes other members of the same species. None of these three factors are represented in the landscape metaphor.

[18] How is distance measured in a fitness landscape? One natural measure would be to consider the number of point mutations required to convert one genotype to another.

[19] One famous example from biology concerns sickle-cell anaemia, an inherited genetic condition in which some of a person's red blood cells take on a crescent moon shape. The condition is painful and can affect a person's vision, cause delays in puberty, and result in frequent infections. Why would such a trait persist in a population? Because sickle-cell anaemia only results if a person has *two* copies of the gene: one from their mother and one from their father. If a person has only a *single* copy of the gene, they are unlikely to have

any symptoms, but they have also conferred some natural resistance against malaria (Rozenbaum 2019). Selection for a malaria-protection trait then increases the chances that some of one's offspring will have a disadvantageous genetic condition.

[20] One criticism of Maslow's hierarchy is its exclusive focus on developed economies. That's pretty obvious given his statement (emphasis added) that "we can perceive the expression of safety needs *only* in such phenomena as, for instance, the common preference for a job with tenure and protection, the desire for a savings account, and for insurance of various kinds (medical, dental, unemployment, disability, old age)" (Maslow 1943, p. 379). That 'only' is doing a lot of unnecessary work. I'm sure the aboriginal people of Papua New Guinea, as discussed by Diamond (1999, 2012), have a rather different conception of what it takes to meet their safety needs.

[21] There is some discussion about where sex falls in the hierarchy. Maslow is a little cagey on this point, noting that "sex may be studied as a purely physiological need."

[22] The Coen brothers' film *The Big Lebowski* stars Jeff Bridges as the title character, also known as "The Dude". The Dude is the ultimate Los Angeles slacker, with an inner peace and contentment that arguably counts as self-actualisation for someone with really modest goals. If all you want to do is bowl, get stoned, drink White Russians, and talk philosophy, and you *do* that, shouldn't that count?

[23] Although statistically significant negative correlations were found for the relationship between need importance and need deficiency in four of the five categories, Betz (1984, p. 213) points out that "the coefficients are quite small and may therefore have little practical meaning, reaching significance only because of the large sample size."

[24] Under Scottish law, a criminal trial may arrive at one of three verdicts: guilty, not proven, and not guilty. Although the latter two verdicts are both acquittals, there are important differences in their connotations. Essentially, the "not proven" option allows a jury to determine insufficient evidence of both guilt and innocence has been produced without needing to declare a mistrial with its inevitable connotation of procedural errors.

[25] The Kenrick *et al.* model is not without its controversial elements. Although the first few levels of their revised hierarchy are similar to Maslow's – immediate physiological needs, self-protection, affiliation, and status/esteem – the next three levels are mate acquisition, mate retention, and parenting. Recent trends with declined birth rates in a number of countries, particularly Japan, raise the question of whether "parenting" deserves such pride of place.

[26] This point is corroborated in later a study not specifically focused on Maslow. Tay and Diener look at the association between need fulfilment and subjective assessments of personal well-being in people from 123 countries. What they

find is that there is some evidence of the existence of universal needs and that, although "needs tend be [sic] achieved in a certain order but that the order in which they are achieved does not strongly influence their effects on [subjective well-being]" (Tay and Diener 2011, p. 364). Another interesting finding is that there was variation between need satisfaction and the affective attitudes of individuals: "basic needs are important for life evaluations, whereas social and respect needs are important for positive feelings" (Tay and Diener 2011, p. 364).

[27] This is true even if one does not accept an objective theory of well-being. Even according to a purely subjectivist theory of well-being, there are better or worse ways of fulfilling a person's needs, according to their own method of assessment. And it is part of human rationality that, all-too-often, people will experience lapses of judgement which lead them to choose something which, in the cold light of day, they would admit is not in their best interest. This is one reason the entire public policy programme around Nudges has been developed, for better or worse (see Thaler and Sunstein 2009).

[28] Some might remember the craze in the early 2000s for the Big Mouth Billy Bass, a robotic fish mounted on a wooden plaque which would lip-sync the song "Take Me To the River" when a button was pressed. This market also cratered.

[29] That is a big *if*, admittedly, but realise that it applies equally well to *all political decisions*. A closed-border policy could be economically and socially disastrous as well: are you sure you'll be able to meet all the demand for doctors, nurses, carers, teachers, etc.?

[30] Some will argue that this is envisioning the worst-possible scenario. There is some truth to that objection, but I would simply note that numerous examples already exist of this happening to people — although admittedly for non-nefarious reasons. The rise of two-factor authentication connected to your mobile phones makes recovering control of all your accounts extremely difficult if your mobile phone is stolen and is orders of magnitude worse if your phone is hacked when it is stolen. (Thieves have been known to demand a user's passcode at knife-point when stealing the phone so they can unlock it and change the passcode so as to have full use of the device.) Some people have found that photos of their naked child, which they took to send to a doctor for remote diagnosis, have caused them to be flagged as paedophiles by Google, and access to their Google account subsequently suspended.

[31] Approximately 3.45 million, in 2017, or around 1.1% of the population (Mohamed 2018).

[32] According to an April 2021 US State Department note, there are approximately three million Arab-Americans living in the US (Stephan 2021).

[33] The name is slightly misleading as the treaty only banned atmospheric nuclear testing. Underground nuclear testing continued to be permitted until the

Comprehensive Nuclear Test Ban Treaty, which was adopted by the United Nations General Assembly in 1996. Since 1996, only three countries have tested nuclear weapons: India, Pakistan and North Korea.

[34] The name of the party will sound bizarre to Americans. It was a political party founded in the early 1790s by Thomas Jefferson and James Madison. It eventually became the modern Democratic party.

[35] Consider the following example. In 1989, the Exxon Valdez oil tanker struck Bligh Reef in Prince William Sound, spilling over 10 million gallons of crude oil. The damage to wildlife, fish, and the environment was considerable. A later class action lawsuit awarded $5 billion in punitive damages to those affected by the spill. Exxon appealed the decision and, in 2002, the damages were reduced to $4 billion. After several more rounds of appeals, in 2006 the punitive damages were reduced to $2.5 billion. Exxon appealed that decision, and in 2008 the Supreme Court reduced the punitive damages to $507.5 million. In 1989, Exxon made $3.8 billion in profit; in 2008, Exxon made $45.2 billion in profit. Exxon's "fine" for the second largest oil spill in US history was a little more than 1% of their *profit* in 2008. That's not a deterrent; that's just part of the cost of doing business.

[36] In the UK, the British Intelligence agency GCHQ is known to have accessed the records of millions of social media users without a warrant (Kwan 2021). It strains credulity to think this hasn't happened elsewhere.

[37] The US military also played an important role in increasing contact between racial groups. Harry Truman signed Executive Order 9981 in 1948, which ordered the military to integrate.

[38] A common Hollywood trope is that of the hero who relies on instinct, rather than expert advice, to see them through. Think of Han Solo who, when advised by C-3PO about the likelihood of successfully navigating through an asteroid field says, "Never tell me the odds!" Or the scene at the end of the film *The Abyss* where Bud Brigman needs to clip the correct wire to disarm the nuclear warhead, but the colour-coded wires appear identical in the light from his underwater flare. Bud takes a guess and, of course, clips the correct wire. Just once I'd like to see a film where the main character faces such a circumstance and goes with their gut, only to smash into an asteroid or blow themselves up, and then have the film immediately end.

[39] Just try to stop someone! Technology hasn't yet gotten to the point where "thought police" is anything other than an expression. But god forbid that neuroscience should ever advance to the point where implants which provide exactly that level of monitoring and control are possible.

[40] That is, I think it is physically possible for a person to hold a belief without having any reasons for it. But this is an unstable cognitive state: the moment a person becomes consciously aware of having that belief, it would only take a little metacognition for cognitive dissonance to arise. Why? A constitutive

feature of having a belief is that one considers the belief to be *true*. How could one be in a position to consider a belief to be true without having reasons for it?

[41] There is an interesting question as to how *faith* fits into this picture. By definition, a belief based on faith is a belief not based on evidence in the ordinary empirical sense of the term. Some have attempted to blur the line between faith-based beliefs and evidence-based beliefs by treating personal mystical experiences that lead to a spiritual conviction as a form of empirical evidence (e.g., Alston 1991; Plantinga 2000; Swinburne 1979), but there are difficulties with pushing this analogy too far, given differences in testability, reproducibility, and other properties taken to hold of ordinary empirical beliefs. On the question of why and whether we should allow a special place in society for beliefs based on faith rather than evidence, see Leiter (2013).

[42] It is possible to reconcile this view with the position of Moynihan as follows: everyone is entitled to an opinion, but not all opinions are permissible. I don't think this is a helpful way to frame the issue because what happens if someone forms an impermissible opinion for mistaken reasons, but the person is not culpable for forming the opinion because realising that the opinion is impermissible would require an act of cognition that either (i) exceeds the capabilities of the person, or (ii) is so laborious that it falls within the category of supererogatory acts? Such a situation would correspond, in my scheme, to someone having an entitled opinion (because they have reasons) but not a justified opinion (because the reasons are mistaken). So the two approaches identify the same categories of opinions but describe them in different ways. I prefer my scheme because it's simpler.

[43] Recall the discussion of sedimentation, from Chapter 4.

[44] This quote is from an interview Scott Heron gave in 1982, see: https://www.youtube.com/watch?v=Y8vYyuW4EYg

References

Alston, William P. (1991). *Perceiving God.* Ithica: Cornell University Press.
BBC News. (3 March 2015). "Finland: Speeding millionaire gets 54,000-euro fine."
https://www.bbc.co.uk/news/blogs-news-from-elsewhere-31709454
Betz, Ellen L. (1984). "Two tests of Maslow's theory of need fulfillment." *Journal of Vocational Behavior* 24 (2):204–220.
https://www.sciencedirect.com/science/article/pii/0001879184900071
Bridgland, Victoria M. E., Payton J. Jones, and Benjamin W. Bellet. (August 2023). "A Meta-Analysis of the Efficacy of Trigger Warnings, Content Warnings, and Content Notes." *Clinical Psychological Science.*
https://doi.org/10.1177/21677026231186625
Diamond, Jared. (1999). *Guns, Germs, and Steel.* W. W. Norton & Company.
Diamond, Jared. (2012). *The World Until Yesterday.* Penguin Books.
Galbraith, John Kenneth. (2001). *The Essential Galbraith.* Houghton Mifflin Company.
Gaus, Gerald. (2021). *The Open Society and Its Complexities.* Oxford University Press.
https://doi.org/10.1093/oso/9780190648978.001.0001
Gigerenzer, Gerd. (2008). *Gut Feelings: The Intelligence of the Unconscious.* London: Viking Penguin.
Haymes, Michael and Logan Green. (1982). "The assessment of motivation within Maslow's framework." *Journal of Research in Personality* 16 (2):179–192.
https://www.sciencedirect.com/science/article/pii/0092656682900745
Kenrick, Douglas T., Vladas Griskevicius, Steven L. Neuberg, and Mark Schaller. (2010). "Renovating the pyramid of needs: Contemporary extensions built upon ancient foundations." *Perspectives on Psychological Science* 5 (3):292–314.
https://doi.org/10.1177/1745691610369469
Klein, Naomi. (2007). *The Shock Doctrine: The Rise of Disaster Capitalism.* New York: Metropolitan Books, Henry Holt and Company.
Kleinman, Zoe. (16 September 2022). "Anti-vax groups use carrot emojis to hide Facebook posts." BBC News.
https://www.bbc.co.uk/news/technology-62877597
Kwan, Campbell. (25 May 2021). "Court finds GCHQ breached citizens' privacy with its bulk surveillance regime." ZDNet.
https://www.zdnet.com/article/court-finds-gchq-breached-citizens-privacy-with-its-bulk-surveillance-regime/
Lazarus, Richard S. and Robert A. McCleary. (1951). "Autonomic discrimination without awareness: A study of subception." *Psychological Review* 58 (2):113–122.
https://doi.org/10.1037/h0054104

Leiter, Brian. (2013). *Why Tolerate Religion?* Princeton University Press. https://doi.org/10.23943/princeton/9780691163543.003.0004

Livingston, Gretchen and Anna Brown. (18 May 2017). "Intermarriage in the U.S. — 50 years after Loving v. Virginia." Pew Research Center. https://www.pewresearch.org/social-trends/2017/05/18/1-trends-and-patterns-in-intermarriage/

London Transport Museum. (8 January 2024). "The Elizabeth Line." https://www.ltmuseum.co.uk/collections/stories/transport/elizabeth-line

Maslow, A. (1943). "A theory of human motivation." *Psychological Review* 40 (4):370–396. https://doi.org/10.1037/h0054346

McCleary, Robert A. and Richard S. Lazarus. (December 1949). "Autonomic Discrimination Without Awareness: An Interim Report." *Journal of Personality* 18 (2):171–179. https://doi.org/10.1111/j.1467-6494.1949.tb01238.x

Mohamed, Besheer. (3 January 2018). "New estimates show U.S. Muslim population continues to grow." Pew Research Center. https://www.pewresearch.org/short-reads/2018/01/03/new-estimates-show-u-s-muslim-population-continues-to-grow/

Oreskes, Naomi and Erik M. Conway. (2011). *Merchants of Doubt: How a Handful of Scientists Obscured the Truth on Issues from Tobacco Smoke to Global Warming*. Bloomsbury Publishing.

Pinsker, Joe. (12 March 2015). "Finland, Home of the $103,000 Speeding Ticket." *The Atlantic*. https://www.theatlantic.com/business/archive/2015/03/finland-home-of-the-103000-speeding-ticket/387484/

Plantinga, Alvin. (2000). *Warranted Christian Belief*. New York: Oxford University Press. https://doi.org/10.1093/0195131932.001.0001

Popper, Karl R. (1945a). *The Open Society and Its Enemies: Volume One — The Spell of Plato*. Routledge & Kegan Paul.

Popper, Karl R. (1945b). *The Open Society and Its Enemies: Volume Two — Hegel and Marx*. Routledge & Kegan Paul.

Reynolds, Emily. (25 January 2018). "What is the Doomsday Clock and why does it matter?" Wired. https://www.wired.co.uk/article/what-is-the-doomsday-clock

Rozenbaum, Mia. (19 June 2019). "How sickle cell protects against Malaria." Understanding Animal Research. https://www.understandinganimalresearch.org.uk/news/how-sickle-cell-protects-against-malaria-a-sticky-connection

Stephan, Rita. (30 April 2021). "The Story of Arab Americans' Beginning in America — And the Quest for Fair Representation." U.S. Department of State. https://www.state.gov/dipnote-u-s-department-of-state-official-blog/the-

story-of-arab-americans-beginning-in-america-and-the-quest-for-fair-representation/
Swinburne, Richard. (1979). *The Existence of God*. New York: Clarendon Press.
Tay, Louis and Ed Diener. (2011). "Needs and Subjective Well-Being Around the World." *Journal of Personality and Social Psychology* 101 (2):354–365. https://doi.org/10.1037/a0023779
Thaler, Richard H. and Cass R. Sunstein. (2009). *Nudge: Improving Decisions about Health, Wealth and Happiness*. Penguin.
Wahba, Mahmoud A. and Lawrence G. Bridwell. (1976). "Maslow Reconsidered: A Review of Research on the Need Hierarchy Theory." *Organizational Behavior and Human Performance* 15:212–240. https://doi.org/10.1016/0030-5073(76)90038-6
Webb, Sidney and Beatrice Webb. (1947). *Soviet Communism: A New Civilisation*. Longmans, Green and Co., third (in one volume) edition.
Wicker, Frank W., Gail Brown, James A. Wiehe, Anastasia S. Hagen, and Joy Lynn Reed. (1993). "On Reconsidering Maslow: An Examination of the Deprivation/Domination Proposition." *Journal of Research in Personality* 27 (2):118–133. https://www.sciencedirect.com/science/article/pii/S0092656683710081

Index

36 Arguments for the Existence of God (2010) 215
1984 (1949) 292, 317

A

abortion 86, 159, 213, 259
Achebe, Chinua 178, 179, 211
active externalism 261
Adams, Douglas 321
advertising 3, 108, 109–110, 150, 158, 314
　online efficacy of 162
Affluent Society, The (1958) 313
Afghanistan 34, 273
Ali, Ayaan Hirsi 195, 213
Alibaba 108
All-Affected principle 39–43, 46
　democratic participation 81
　minimal form 50–51
　objection(s) to 45, 86, 157
Allport, Gordon 246, 254, 293
analytic philosophy xi, xii
Anarchy, State, and Utopia (1974) 45
anonymity 125, 127, 129, 130, 252, 253, 328–329
　partial 292
anthropology 277, 291
antibiotic use 39
anti-immigration attitudes and political parties 29, 40, 82
Architecture of Complexity, The (1962) 338
Arendt, Hannah 137
Aristotle 47
artificial intelligence (AI) technology 154, 337–338
　generative 236
　news, and 237, 289

Asch, Solomon 105, 156
　experiments 138, 156
Atlantic, The 177, 186, 190
attention economy 198, 281, 302
Attlee, Clement 309
authenticity 257–265
　group 259–261, 263–264
　Rorschach concept, as 263
　WINOs, and 257–265, 293
authoritarianism 4, 13, 15, 111, 301, 303–304, 336, 337
autonomy, personal 17, 45, 50, 195, 138–139, 318
　women, of 285
Axelrod, Robert 253

B

Bartleby objection, the 180, 182, 207
Bartleby the Scrivener (1853) 180
de Beauvoir, Simone 48, 49, 88
Being and Nothingness (2003 [1943]) 47, 49
beliefs, function of. *See also* epistemic closure
　faith-based 342
　incompatible 281
Ben-Porath, Sigal R. 200, 201
Bentham, Jeremy 147, 160
Bergson, Henri 13, 226, 227
Berlin Wall, the 1, 52
Bicchieri, Cristina 86–87, 138, 247–248
　theory of social norms 247, 261
Big Lebowski, The (1998) 339
Bindel, Julie 195, 214
birther movement 197–199, 202
Birthright Lottery, The (2009) 34–35, 84

birthright lottery 12, 37, 53, 79, 134, 315, 330
  citizenship, and. *See* citizenship: birthright
birth tourism 33, 84
blackface 185, 188
Bon, Stephanie 133, 134
Book of Joshua 225
Borges, Jorge Luis 131
Borjas, George J. 61–62, 91
boundary problem 39, 42–43, 45, 85
Bracero Program 74, 76
brain drains 59, 90
Brandeis University 213
Breitbart News 237
Brexit 2, 3, 9–11, 28, 55, 81, 331
  referendum results 9, 151, 161, 235
  supporters 210, 258
Briskman, Juli 134
British Intelligence agency (GCHQ) 341
Brown, Gordon 2, 55
Brown University 185, 193
  political mobilisation, and 193
  recuperation room controversy 191–194
Buchanan, Patrick 75
Burke, Edmund 12, 19–20
burqa, bans of the 281, 284–285
Bush, George W. 90
Byron, Katherine 191, 192

C

Calhoun, John C. 187, 213
Cambridge Analytica 3, 151, 153
Cambridge criterion, the 40–41, 85
  Cambridge change 40–43
Canterbury Christ Church University 214
Cardiff University 214
Catholic Church 209, 241, 260, 293
Catholic-Protestant coexistence and conflict 282, 291

Cement of the Universe, The (1980) 199
Chalmers, David 261
Chappell, Sophie-Grace 203
ChatGPT 236, 237, 289–290
China 6, 18, 38, 264
  Cultural Revolution 337
  Great Leap Forward, the 6, 19
  internet, control of 321
  social media networks 125
  Zhou Dynasty 27
Chomsky, Noam 19
Christakis, Erica 185, 187, 188
Christakis, Nicholas 185, 187
Churchill, Winston 333
cisgender 204, 216
citizenship 33–37, 242
  birthright 12, 33, 34, 38, 84
  British 33–34
  descent, by 33
  European 73
  nationality identity, and 83–84
  New Zealand 33, 37, 84
  right of the soil (*jus soli*) 33, 63
  United States 34, 71
Clark, Andy 261
Clemens, Michael A. 55–58, 91
click-through-rate (CTR) and click conversion rate (CCR) 162
climate change 1, 39, 85, 87, 198, 255, 274, 323, 326, 328–329, 331
  denial 6, 202, 211, 215, 217, 255, 276, 277, 329
  threat of 31, 85, 323
Clinton, Hillary 2, 151
Cloots, Anacharsis 52, 82, 83
closed border policies 315–316, 340
closed societies 5, 13, 226–227
cognitive bias 20
Cohen, Josh 138, 139
Cold War, the 1, 7, 15
  end of 159, 323, 324
collective action problem 270–271
colonialism 183, 291
Color Purple, The (1982) 181

commitment, problem of 48–49, 88
communication, in bad/good faith 130, 202, 320
Communist Manifesto, The (1848) 237, 289–290
Conjectures and Refutations (1963) 196
conservatism, political 150
consistency 289
  principle 14, 50–51, 80
  principled 263
consumers, transformed into commodities 155
consumption 155, 317
  absolute and expected levels 140–143
  happiness, and 140, 142, 159
  new 238
  revealed preferences 317
contact hypothesis, the 254, 255, 293, 322, 330
contrived wants 313–314, 317
control 121–122, 157, 193
  loss of 29, 34, 35, 43, 213, 262, 279, 326, 340
  path dependence, and 122
  social 127, 147, 158
corruption 66, 91, 105
cosmopolitanism 12, 29, 43–44, 46, 50, 259
  cultural 29
  economic 29, 82
  French Revolution, and 82
  group selection, and 52
  political 29, 43, 50–53, 82
  types of 29
COVID-19 30, 331
creationism and evolutionary beliefs 6, 181
Crenshaw, Kimberlé 268
critical rationalism 5, 6, 12, 14, 182, 196
cultural appropriation 29
cultural diversity 282

D

Dahl, Gary 313
data subject 158
  erasure, right to 158
  forgotten, right to be 132, 158
Dawkins, Richard 195, 214
democracy 2, 3, 14, 37, 39, 155, 325
Democratic Party 232, *233*, 341
Deng Xiaoping 337
Dennett, Daniel 121, 157
developing economies 234
development, international 79
Diamond, Jared 137, 339
diplomatic immunity 33, 84
disgust 150
distortion in data 112
diverse communities 14, 15
divine right of kings 5, 85
Doomsday Clock 323, 324
double effect, doctrine of 205
Douthat, Ross 278
Dreamers, the 76, 83
drugs, war on 132, 295
Dude, the (character) 311, 339
duties 187, 198
  assimilate, to 70, 76, 77, 80
  family and friends, to 82
  non-interference, of 77, 90
  perfect and imperfect 76
  universities, of 187

E

Easterlin, Richard 139
Easterlin paradox 139–140, *141*
echo chambers 234, 320, 322, 329
economic growth 9, 58, 71, 72, 306, 315, 330
Economic Freedom of the World (EFW) index, the 91
economic models 55, 58
Educated: A Memoir (2018) 89
efficient markets, belief in 278
Eisenhower, Dwight 264, 316

elections
  eligibility to vote in 28, 160–161
  safe seats, elimination of 324–325
Ellis, Bret Easton 175
Elizabeth Line, London 303
employment, "at-will" 134
epistemic closure 89, 228, 332
  extreme groups, and 273–281, 294–295
  reasons for 274–277
epistemic communities 275, 276–277, 294
epistemic deference 215, 259, 262, 264, 276. *See also* group psychology: in-group bias
epistemic humility 200, 262, 274
European Coal and Steel Community (ECSC) 72
European Economic Area (EEA) 63, 91
European Economic Community (EEC) 72
European Union (EU) 2, 9, 28, 30, 71, *235*, 282. *See also* Brexit
  freedom of movement in 72, 73
  Gender Directive (2011) 115
  General Data Protection Regulation (GDPR, 2016) 158
  Maastricht Treaty (1992) 37, 73
  membership 73
  representation by UK tabloids 30, 210
existence precedes essence, principle 46–49
existentialist thought 14, 46–48, 53, 77, 259, 311
  de Beauvoir's version 48–50, 88
existential risks and threats 3, 16, 18, 31, 211, 255, 323, 331
experiments in living 14, 46–49, 51, 52, 139, 192
experts 6, 198, 320, 331
extreme group beliefs 275
Exxon Valdez tanker spillage 341

F

Facebook 104, 125, 134, 151, 162, 237, 254, 321
  job applications, and 133
  news feed algorithm 237
  face recognition technologies 108, 156
faith, acting in bad 200, 202, 259, 260, 262. *See also* communication in bad/good faith
faith, acting in good 93, 130, 192, 200, 208, 217, 264, 318, 322
fake news/alternative facts 112, 151, 198, 237, 321, 331
false positives, data prompts, in 112
falsificationism 4, 5, 18–19
  inference rule (*modus tollens*) 18
Fear of Missing Out (FOMO) 143–144
"Finest Worksong" (R.E.M.) 301, 303, 310, 315
feminism 48, 212, 268
  first-wave 267
  second-wave 48, 183, 184
Fermi, Enrico 90
Fermi estimate 58, 90
fitness landscape 307, *308*, 309, 338
flat Earth society 197
forgetting, merits of 131–132
Foucault, Michel 209
freedom of association 14, 50, 51, 77, 194, 302, 325
freedom of choice 47, 259, 295
freedom of movement 7, 71–74
freedom of speech 132, 134–135, 318
free exchange of ideas 12–14, 16, 176, 208, 318
Friedman, Milton 289, 290
functions, latent and manifest 277–280
fundamental attribution error 13, 20, 135, 320

G

Galbraith, John Kenneth 313, 317
Gaus, Gerald 13
Geach, Peter 40–42
Generation Wuss 175–176
genetic sequencing 118
  declining cost of 119–120
genetic testing 119
gentrification 69, 93
genotypes 307, 338
Germany 231
  reunification 84
gerrymandering 325
Gigerenzer, Gerd 294, 302
Global Terrorism Database 92
globalisation 2, 9, 29, 82
  economic 234–236
God, existence of 181, 196, 211, 215
Golden Rule, the 287
Goldstein, Rebecca 215
Gove, Michael 6
governance indicators 91
Graeber, David 276
Great Cabbage Myth 82
Great Gatsby, The (1925) 178, 211
Great Wall of China 27
Great Wall of America 27, 29, 81
Greece 73
Greenland 73, 92
Greer, Germaine 195, 203–205, 208, 214
Greitens, Eric 151
Grice, H. Paul 126
group dynamics. *See also* Sherif experiments
  stereotypes, and 246
  structure and conflict *247*
  group identity/identities 3, 215, 226–227, 247, 255, 319
  group loyalty 227, 246
    membership criteria 241, 257
  group pressure 105

group psychology 243–244
  in-group bias 241–249
  inter-group contact theory. *See* contact hypothesis theory

H

Hacking, Ian 34, 293
Hall, Evelyn Beatrice 210
Hanson, Robiin 279
happiness 82, 139–141, 159
  Easterlin paradox, and 139, *141*
  income per capita, and 141
Harm principle 195, 204, 210, 283, 284
harms 13, 178, 192, 204, 328
  safety, and 318
  types of 178, 283
hate speech 200, 205, 213
Highly Superior Autobiographical Memory (HSAM) 131, 151
historicism 14–16
Hitler, Adolf 69, 135
homosexuality 184
  identification of through data 111, 157
  safe spaces 184
housing 42, 91
Human Genome Project (HGP) 119
  cost of genetic sequencing 119, *120*

I

identity politics 208, 272
immigration 2, 55, 74
  economic impact 55–67
  fiscal impact, of 62–63, 65
  gains from 56, 57–58, 64
  NEC. *See* new economic case for immigration restrictions
  negative externalities 66–67
  productivity, and 59, 65–66
  wages, effects on 61, *62*
  illegal 2, 9, 27, 74, 75
  legal 2

political issue, salience of 82
public services, impact on 62–63
Immigration and Nationality Act (US, 1965) 74
impulses, non-rational 301–302
incels 273, 278, 294
  online culture of 279
inequality 12, 43, 84, 134, 139, 142–143, 330
  income *143*
  polarisation, and 229
  relative 139
  wealth 142, 330
indiscernibles, principle of identify of 47, 85
individual freedom 14, 47, 48, 50, 53, 77, 317, 333. *See also* personal freedom
individual liberty 9, 290, 334
individual potential 84–85
individuals, intrinsic and extrinsic properties of 40
insurance 115
  car 115, 116
  medical 118–119, 122
  personalisation, and 116, 121
international trade barriers, efficiency gains from removing 55, 56
internet, harms and benefits 81
  boredom, sadism and trolling, and 293
intersectionality 267–272, 295
  social justice, difficulties progressing 271
intolerance 13, 283
  intolerance of 158, 195, 200, 207, 283–285
INUS conditions 199–200, 202, 207
irrationality 226, 227, 289

J

James, William 131
Johnson, Boris 195, 214

Jesus Jones 1
jus sanguinis ("right of blood") 33, 34
jus soli ("right of the soil") 33, 34, 63

K

Kahneman, Daniel 147
Keynes, John Maynard 109
Kimmel, Michael 279–280
  "be kind to others" imperative 287
King's College London 195, 214
Kinsey, Alfred 111
Klein, Naomi 310
knowledge 207–209
  factual 304
  forbidden 208
  new 196, 215 207–208, 331
  moralisation of 16, 207–209, 217
  morality-knowledge 209
  politicisation of 6, 16,
  power-. *See* power-knowledge
Knausgaard, Karl Ove 104
kompromat 317
Krugman, Paul 90, 142
Khrushchev, Nikita 306

L

Lazarus, Richard 336
learned helplessness 193–194
Lee, Spike 69, 70, 78, 92
Leibniz, Gottfried W. 40, 84. *See also* indiscernibles, principle of etc.
Lenin, Vladimir 336–337
Lewis, Helen 268
lifecasting 104
life expectancy 34
Lifton, Richard 189
liminality 184, 212
Lukianoff, Greg and Haidt, Jonathan 177, 178, 183
lump of labour fallacy 60, 90, 316
lynching 211, 253

Lysenko, Trofim 6
Lysenkoism 6, 19

M

Maastricht Treaty (1992) 37, 73
Mackie, John L. 199
Macron, Emmanuel 231
Magnum Force (1973) 225
Make America Great Again, slogan 3, 8–9, 11
male radicalisation 278, 280
Mao Zedong 6, 283, 337
Marx, Groucho 201
Marx, Karl 4, 336–337
    Popper, Karl, and. *See* Popper, Karl
Marxism 4, 14, 19
masculinity 279–280
Maslow, Abraham 310, 339. *See also* hierarchy of needs
    evidence for theories 310–311
    self-actualisation, characterisation of 311, 312, 314, 318, 339
McCleary, Robert 336
McElroy, Wendy 185, 191
Mauritania 163
May, Theresa 9, 69, 231
meaning, common and intersubjective 7–8
cleave, ambiguities of word 8
media reform 328–329. *See also* social media: regulation
Melville, Hermann 180
membership 3, 35, 225, 228, 232, 245, 258, 265, 294, 319
    EU. *See* European Union [EU]: membership
    group, criteria for 211, 213, 257, 258, 260
    modern tribes, in 241–242, 283
    moralisation of 263, 294
    non-exclusivity 269
Merchants of Doubt (2011) 19, 215

Merleau-Ponty, Maurice 49, 88–89
metanorms 253
Mexican Farm Labor Agreement 74
Mexico-US migration 74–75
microaggression(s) 42, 43, 178, 210–211, 291
middle class 257
migration. *See* freedom of movement and immigration
    communities, and 60–78
    eliminating barriers to 55–57, 330
military-industrial complex 264, 316
Mill, James 147
Mill, John Stuart 14, 139, 210
    Harm principle. *See* Harm principle
millennials 1, 175
Minassian, Alek 278
misogyny 204, 279
modern tribes 227, 234, 241, 267, 268, 273–274, 291, 319, 320–321, 334
    fracturing, of 269, 270
    psychology, of 251–255, 292–293
Monaco 34
Moore's law 119
moral norms 45, 87
moral panics 75
moral particularism 191
moral pluralism 46, 50, 52, 87
moral theories 5
Moynihan, Daniel Patrick 332, 342
murder prohibition 76
multiculturalism 9, 29

N

national identity 30, 79, 83–84
nationalism 36
    white 9
nationality, right to a 30–31, 33
National Rifle Association (NRA) 328
nation state 30, 31

natural injustice(s) 12, 34–35, 43, 79, 315, 330
natural lottery (of birth) 31, 34–36, 50, 315, 322
needs, hierarchy of 310–313
  Kenrick et al.'s model 312, 339
  Maslow's 310–311, 313, 318–319, 339
  sex, in 339
  Tay and Diener's evaluation, of 340
negative externalities 16, 31, 43, 52, 59–60, 66–67, 115, 122, 194, 284, 332
neurodiversity 85, 179
never surrender trope 333, 334
new economic case for immigration restrictions (NEC) 65–66, 91
New Deal 309, 310
New York 69, 258
New Zealand 33, 37, 84, 85
news reporting reform 329
Nixon, Richard 243, 276
  China, visit to 264
Nobel disease 203
no-platforming 13, 195–205, 302
  Provocateur, Shill and Crank, cases for 200–201
Norms in the Wild (2017) 138
North Korea 37–38, 341
Nowhere Man objection 73, 315
Nozick, Robert 45, 87
nuclear weapons 118, 258, 323, 341
nudges 160, 340

O

Obama, Barack 150, 197
offence, causing and taking 283–285
On Liberty (1859) 139, 210
online disinhibition effect 253
online news viewing 235, 237–238
open border policies 76, 79, 315

Open Society, the 3–7
  communitarian conception of 13, 15, 31, 130, 226–228, 272, 281, 287, 318–319, 322, 330, 331
  cosmopolitan conception of 12, 14, 29, 39, 36, 41, 43, 55, 69–71, 77, 79–80, 301, 315, 316, 320, 322
  enemy, as an 14–17, 28
  Enlightenment conception of 12, 14, 158, 176–182, 207–209, 318, 322, 332
  Rorschach concept, as 11–14
  transparent conception of 12, 14, 15, 105, 107, 117, 136, 155, 317
  value inversion, of 14–15, 53, 307, 310, 320, 334
Open Society and Its Enemies, The (1945) 4, 14, 51, 207, 303
Orwell, George 12, 292
Other, the 319, 322, 330, 331, 334
Oxford Union 214

P

Pandora's Box (TV series, 1992) 305
panopticon 147
  Bentham's 147, *148*
  soul, of the 14, 153, 155
Papua New Guinea 137, 339
parents (adopted, biological, "real") 203–204, 215–216
Pegasus software 161
Pen, Marine Le 195, 214, 231
Pepys, Samuel 103
personal freedom 7, 9, 105, 208, 285
personal identity 144, 241, *242*
  multiple layers of *242*
personality traits, Dark Tetrad 293
pet rocks 313
Phelps-Roper, Megan 89
phenomenology 88
  commitment, of 48–49

Phenomenology of Perception (1958) 88
Pierce, Chester 210
Pinker, Steven 282
Plato 13, 73, 336
polarisation 3, 14, 80, 227–239, 287, 289, 319, 321–322
    causes, possible 234
    dangers of 248, 249
    income, of 229
    internet use, and *238*
    political *230*, 231
political advertising, negative 151
political reform 19–20, 324–327
political union 29, 42, 80
politicians' accountability 326
Popper, Karl 4–6, 13–16, 19, 51, 89, 196, 207, 215, 226, 303–304, 306–307, 336
    critique of authoritarianism 15, 337
    historicism, rejection of 16
    Marx, Karl, and 4, 13, 19, 336–337
    Vienna, street protest 4, 19
    open society, conception of 7, 13
    totalitarianism, and 16
post-traumatic stress disorder 178–179, 210
    diagnostic criteria 179
Poverty of Historicism, The (1944) 4
power, imbalances of 80, 184, 212
power-knowledge 209
prejudice, contemptuous and envious 248, 252
Principles of Mathematics, The (1903) 156
Principles of Psychology, The (1890) 131
prison sentencing 132
privacy 12, 110, 117, 154, 317
    right to 137, 317
    value of 138–139
    wealthy, of the 329, 330
Private Life, The (2013) 138

process-product ambiguity 230–231
pro-life movement (US) 87
proportional representation 37, 325
protected characteristics 110, 115
Psychodiagnostik (1921) 10
public debate 2, 332
public spaces 281, 284, 314
    distinction between private spaces, and 285
Puritanism 284

R

racial prejudice 149, 150
racism 2, 66, 185, 189
Rampell, Catherine 142
randomised control trials (RCT) 209
rational actor model 148, 150
real, use of word 216
Reagan, Ronald 74, 75, 118
realistic conflict theory 245
realpolitik 51, 188, 272
regime types (countries) 37, *38*
relational properties 40–41, 86
religious beliefs and opting-out 181
R.E.M. 301, 303, 310, 315
Republican party 232, *233*, 243, 264, 276
    tribe, as 276–277
Revelation, Book of 103
"Revolution Will Not Be Televised, The" (1970) 334–335
Rice, Condoleezza 195, 214
Ringley, Jennifer 104
risk pools 115–116, 118, 120
robustness analysis 58, 90, 91
Rodger, Elliot 278
Ronson, Jon 127–128
Roosevelt, Franklin Delano 8–9, 309
Rorschach, Hermann 10, *11*
Rorschach test and concepts 7–11, 152, 263, 326
    Open Society, as 11–14
Runciman, David 81
Russell, Bertrand 40, 103, 156

Russia 2, 337
   Ukraine invasion 282
   workers leaving in 2022 90
Rutgers University 214

S

Sacco, Justine 128
sadism, online and on apps 293
safe spaces 14, 176, 177, 183–194, 207, 211–213, 320
   online 322
   therapeutic function 193
safety needs 311, 318–319, 339
Sandberg, Sheryll 104
Sartre, Jean-Paul 31, 46–48, 49, 88
Science in the Soul: Selected Writings of a Passionate Rationalist (2017) 214
Schloss, David F. 60
Scott-Heron, Gil 334–335, 342
Scottish Law, "not proven" verdict 312, 339
Second Sex, The (1949) 48
security-industrial complex 316
sedimentation 49–50, 79, 88, 89
   epistemic and motivational 88
Sexual Behavior in the Human Male (1948) 111
Shachar, Ayelet 34–35, 84
shaming, public 127–129, 135, 147
Sherif, Muzafer 245
Sherif experiments 245–246, 254, 257, 292
Shields, Rev. Robert 103, 156
Shock Doctrine, The (2007) 310
sickle-cell anaemia 338
Simon, Herbert 338
Sinclair, Upton 255
slavery 71, 213
   abolition of 33, 155, 162–163
   teaching history of 211
Slave Trade Acts (1807, 1833, 1843) 162
Smith, Michael French 137

social attitudes 212, 321
   Library Model, of 260–261
Social Construction of What, The (1999) 293
social constructivism 34, 86
social engineering 303, 308, 328
   multifaceted 307, 309–310, 315, 321, 323, 324
   piecemeal 16, 303, 306–309, 338
   social media, and 328
   Utopian 303–306, 337
social identities 13, 234, 238, 241–249, 260, 267, 272
   intersectional 268, 269
   non-additive nature of 267–268
social identity theory 241, 251, 260
socialisation 50
social media 3, 104, 112, 125–130, 143, 162, 208, 237, 301, 319, 320
   corporations monitoring personal material 133–134
   creating of "needs" and wants, and 314
   intelligence operations 127, 341
   interactions, type of 125–126, 129, 252–253
   regulation and enforcement 155, 321, 327–328
   shame, and 127–128, 253. *See also* shaming, public
   sharing 144, 159
   speed, scale, and endurance 125, 130
   tobacco companies, analogy with. *See* tobacco companies
   Two Minutes Hate, functions like 292, 302, 319, 322
social norms 86–87, 138, 247, 248, 251, 255, 262, 321
social organisation, forms of 16, 52, 139, 159, 291
social reform 12, 309–310, 330–331
So Long and Thanks for All the Fish (1984) 321

Solove, Daniel 112–113, 118
So You've Been Publicly Shamed (2015) 127, 128
Spain 73, 82
Stalin, J. 6, 337
stereotypes and stereotype theory 121, 245–248, 251–252, 320, 322
   categorisation *248*
   negative 253, 254
State of Emergency (2006) 75
subception 336
superordinate goals 254–255, 270–271
surveillance 111, 147–148, 317
   society 317
   state 116, 317
Suskind, Ron 273
sustainability 86, 323, 334
synthetic philosophy xii

T

Tai, Tim 189, 190
Target 108
   customer pregnancy metric 109–111
Tatchell, Peter 195, 214
Taylor, Charles 7–8
telematics 116
terrorism 66, 92
Thatcher, Laurel Ulrich 202
Thatcher, Margaret 333
Things Fall Apart (1958) 179–180, 211
thought leaders 87, 294
three strikes laws 132, 158
Tiananmen Square protests 1
tobacco companies 31, 153, 215, 327–328. *See also* social media: tobacco companies etc
tolerance, paradox of 51, 200, 283, 285
"to ti ên einai" (the what it was to be) 47

Toward Perpetual Peace (1795) 46
transgender persons 203–205, 214, 215, 267, 270
   term 216
transparency 12, 15, 105, 107, 117, 122, 154, 316, 329
   government and business 317, 320,
   informational 7, 12, 14, 89, 107, 115, 118, 153
   management, of 105
   personal 103–105, 107–113, 121–123
   radical 12, 105, 105, 129
   social media, and 14
   wealth and cash flow, regarding 329
trauma 179, 185, 191, 192
Treaty of Westphalia 12
tribalism 130, 226, 239, 272
   modern. *See* modern tribes
   tribal membership 275
tribal society 226
trigger warnings 177–182, 183, 207, 209–211, 302, 336
   Literary Studies, in 178
Trinity nuclear test (1945) 90
Tristram Shandy paradox xii, 103, 156
trolling 292–293
Truman, Harry 91, 341
Trump, Donald xi, 2, 8, 27, 29, 55, 198
   MAGA. *See also* "Make America Great Again" slogan
trust 42, 66, 92, 117–118, 130, 331
   state, and 118
   verification, and 117–118
Tversky, Amos 147, 160
Twitter (X) 125, 128, 129, 158
Two Sources of Morality and Religion, The (1935) 13, 226

U

Ukraine invasion 2, 90, 282

unemployment 60–61
　benefits 121
　rate in US *60*
Unfollow: A Journey from Hatred to Hope (2020) 89
United Kingdom (UK)
　cosmopolitan-communitarian spectrum 232
　defence spending 64
　EEC, joins 73
　Equality Act 2010 110
　immigrants, fiscal impact of 63–64
　political polarisation, groupings of 231–*234*
United Nations (UN) 2, 341
　Universal Declaration of Human Rights 30, 34
United States of America (USA) 33, 75, 119, 334
　Civil War 33, 71, 232
　Constitution 71
　Equal Rights Amendment 159, 242
　First Amendment 132, 188, 213
　Fourteenth Amendment 33
　census 18, 212, 258
　defence budget 64
　Department for Homeland Security 127
　freedom of movement 71–72
　happiness and income per capita 141
　Muslim and Arab populations 340
　political polarisation 232, *233*
　presidential election (2008) 149
　presidential election (2016) xi, 231
　unemployment rate 60–61
　working population 61, 91
US Southern Poverty Law Centre 278
US Supreme Court 71, 72, 341
　Roe v. Wade 86, 159
　Snyder v. Phelps 213

University of Manchester 214
University of Missouri (UM) system 189–191
　Concerned Students 1950 189–190
　racism controversy 189–191, 194, 213
　University of Missouri-Columbia 189
universities 177, 181–183, 187–188, 195–196, 210, 211
　pastoral care, at 187
　purposes of 182, 214–215
　sexual assault on campuses 191
Uruguay 37
USSR (Soviet Union) 305–306, 323
utility and utilitarianism 46, 87, 140, 147

V

value pluralism 14
values revision 333
Venice 70
Villarroel, Professor Morris 104
virtue signalling 253
voter age 81
voting 148
　gerrymandering. See gerrymandering
　motivations for 148–149, 150, 160
　personalities, effect of 150
　spatial theory of 229
　suppression 151, 160
　　felony disenfranchisement 161
　voice and roll-call votes 289

W

Walker, Alice 181
Warhol, Andy 142
wealth 140, 278, 290
　unequal distribution, of 142, 326, 329–330
Webber, Jonathan 46, 48

well-being 46, 79, 87, 140, 254, 330, 333, 339–340
Westen, Drew 149, 150
Westover, Tara 89
WINOs ([Whatever] In Name Only) 258–259, 262–264
Wolfe, Tim 185, 189
World Bank 91, 234
Worldwide Governance Indicators (WGI) index 91
Wretched Refuse? The Political Economy of Immigration and Institutions (2021) 66
Wright, Sewall 307

Y

Yale University 187
   Halloween costumes controversy 184–188, 194
   racial tensions at 187

Z

zeitgeist, the xi, 1, 175
   1989, in 1
   US, in 133
Zheng, King (of Qin) 27
Zuckerberg, Mark 104

www.ingramcontent.com/pod-product-compliance
Lightning Source LLC
Chambersburg PA
CBHW071203240426
43668CB00032B/1870